A Fireside Book

Published by Simon & Schuster

New York

London

Toronto

Sydney

Tokyo

Singapore

THE
CONCERNED CITIZEN'S GUIDE
TO THE LEADING ADVOCACY
ORGANIZATIONS IN AMERICA

DAVID WALLS

FIRESIDE
Simon & Schuster Building
Rockefeller Center
1230 Avenue of the Americas
New York, New York 10020

FIRESIDE and colophon are registered trademarks
of Simon & Schuster Inc.
Designed by Liney Li
Manufactured in the United States of America
1   3   5   7   9   10   8   6   4   2
Library of Congress Cataloging in Publication Data
Walls, David.
The activist's almanac : the concerned citizen's guide to the leading advocacy
organizations in America / David Walls.
p.   cm.
"A Fireside Book"—
Includes bibliographical references and index.
1. Social action—United States—Handbooks, manuals, etc.   2. Social action—United
States—Directories.   3. Social reformers—United States—Handbooks, manuals,
etc.   4. Social reformers—United States—Directories.   5. Lobbying—United States
—Handbooks, manuals, etc.   6. Lobbyists—United States—Directories.   I. Title.
HN55.W35   1993
361.2—dc20   92-38161
                                                                    CIP

ISBN: 0-671-74634-0

CONTENTS

HUMAN RIGHTS ORGANIZATIONS

MULTIISSUE ORGANIZATIONS

Contents

ALPHABETICAL LIST OF

ORGANIZATIONS PROFILED

PREFACE

Will the 1990s see an upsurge of activism corresponding to the turbulence of the 1930s and 1960s? Trend-spotters, political pundits, and social scientists who trace an apparent thirty-year social movement cycle have been waiting patiently for a new wave of social idealism to replace the presumed self-interested materialism of the 1980s. The news is: It's here. It's already happening.

At least eight to ten million people (members of organizations profiled in *The Activist's Almanac*) are actively supporting movements to protect the environment, preserve the peace, and defend human rights—more people than at any other time since the 1960s. Organizations as varied as the Sierra Club, the National Audubon Society, Greenpeace, the Natural Resources Defense Council, the Environmental Defense Fund, The Nature Conservancy, the World Wildlife Fund, the Union of Concerned Scientists, Amnesty International, and the American Civil Liberties Union find their membership and financial support at record or near-record levels. It's likely that activity for social change is more widespread—if moderate in tone—now than at any time during the 1960s or 1970s. But why don't we see this clearly?

Part of the answer may be that we've been expecting a rerun

of previous activist cycles. Social movements revive and recur, but never in quite the same way. In the 1960s the most visible indicators of social movements were mass demonstrations and acts of nonviolent civil disobedience. Although these remain legitimate and valuable tactics for any movement for change, by and large current movements operate in other, less visible, modes—neighborhood organizing, grassroots lobby networks, electoral campaigns, public interest law, professionalized advocacy groups, think tanks, urgent action letter-writing, checkbook activism.

Instead of full-time movement cadres with lives totally dedicated to the cause, we have citizen activists with spare-time commitments in the midst of normal daily life. Highly visible groups are the least characteristic of contemporary citizen organizations—AIDS activists in ACT-UP, abortion opponents in Operation Rescue, and disability rights protesters in ADAPT are the fringe on a coat of many colors, the tip of an iceberg of social activism beneath the viewfinders of media cameras.

Social myopia is nothing new, of course. No one in 1928, with the possible exception of coal miner chieftain John L. Lewis, could foresee the vast upsurge in industrial union organizing that would begin in the mid-1930s. And in 1950 no experts in race relations predicted that within five years the Supreme Court would toss out the "separate but equal" doctrine and that in a decade and a half a black freedom movement would sweep away the legal structure of segregation in the American South. And in 1967, in the midst of an antiwar movement of unprecedented size, no student leaders imagined the imminent rebirth of feminism and a new women's liberation movement, much less the emergence of an openly militant movement for gay and lesbian rights. The new feminists of 1971 could not imagine that in 1973 the Supreme Court would suddenly legalize abortion before it had become a widespread public issue—and thereby provoke a pro-life countermovement. Nor did the conservationists of 1968 anticipate the emergence of an energetic environmental movement on Earth Day 1970. And in the 1970s environmentalists did not foresee the birth of the animal rights movement in the 1980s, in part a revival of nineteenth-century antivivisectionism. And yet all of these events came to pass—because, we argue, dedicated and persistent people built organizations that helped carry the movements from one cycle of activism to the next.

Our present determined but undramatic activism represents something fresh and largely unanticipated—an emergent practical idealism, concerned with ethics and social responsibility in all areas of civic and daily life. What is novel today is not new issues or constituencies, but new methods of attacking political, social, economic, and ecological injustices—direct-mail, door-to-door, and telephone canvassing, personal computer networks, activist alert systems, satellite space-bridge conferences and concerts.

From the 1960s through the 1980s a new breed of public interest entrepreneurs provided leadership to revitalize old organizations or establish new organizations to meet emerging challenges. David Brower drew the Sierra Club into an era of conservation activism, and went on to found three new environmental organizations—Friends of the Earth, League of Conservation Voters, and Earth Island Institute. Ralph Nader inspired and spun off a galaxy of consumer advocacy and public interest organizations, Public Citizen and the Public Interest Research Groups foremost among them. Eleanor Smeal led the National Organization for Women to a new militancy, and launched her Fund for the Feminist Majority. Marian Wright Edelman created the Children's Defense Fund as an independent advocate for poor children. John Gardner created Common Cause as a good government watchdog. Faye Wattleton reinvigorated Planned Parenthood, reviving its original mission as advocate for reproductive rights as well as provider of family planning services. Saul Alinsky, Wade Rathke, Heather Booth, and Gail Cincotta reinvented neighborhood and community organizing, and set up enduring training centers and networks to pass on the varied successful models they developed. And Michael Harrington gave intellectual and organizational leadership to the remnants of the Old and New Lefts, maintaining an alliance with progressive forces in organized labor and the Democratic party through the Democratic Socialists of America.

Conservatives mounted countermovements to challenge the liberal and radical ascendance over social movements. William F. Buckley, Jr., and his associates at the *National Review* forged a Cold War fusion of traditional conservatives and libertarians into a new conservative movement, and helped inspire and catalyze the Young Americans for Freedom and the American Conservative Union. Phyllis Schlafly rallied her Eagle Forum to block ratification of the Equal Rights Amendment. Beverly LaHaye created a national network of Concerned Women for America to oppose abortion, the ERA, pornography, gay rights, and secular humanism in the schools —in the name of traditional family and religious values. Paul Weyrich helped build two major multiissue institutions of the New Right: The Heritage Foundation and the Free Congress Foundation.

Our theme also contains a story of political generations: During the 1990s the leading edge of the baby boomers, the cohort who came of age in the 1960s and 1970s, will move into midlife and consolidate its hold on organizations and institutions throughout American society—including the public interest groups. George Bush will, in all likelihood, be the last president of the World War II generation. His successor, Bill Clinton, born in 1946, is a representative of the baby boomers. We tend to think of the 1960s in a liberal or progressive light: the civil rights movement, the election of John Kennedy, the New Left and opposition to the Vietnam War, the emergence at the end of the decade of the women's and environmental movements. Yet the 1960s also marked the organization of a conservative movement that turned the ashes of Barry Goldwater's defeat in 1964 into the triumph of Ronald Reagan's election in 1980. During the 1990s the progressive and conservative components of the sixties generation will battle, through their organizations, to define the vision that guides the United States into the twenty-first century.

Our contemporary social movements are the first to operate in a post–Cold War, post-Marxist, and "postmodern" world. Activists of the 1990s are unlikely to be guided by utopian schemes or to contemplate revolutionary breaks from the deadweight of the past. If there is a strategic guide for movement organizations, it may well be Michael Harrington's notion of "visionary gradualism" (a thesis as useful for conservatives as it is for progressives, by the way), which acknowledges the complexity of the modern world, and the extended time it takes to win a majority of citizens to significant structural change, and that persevering through the compromising marshes of practical politics is the only democratic alternative to authoritarian elitism.

ABOUT THIS BOOK

Chicago's former mayor Richard Daley liked to say, "In the final analysis, all politics is local," and we agree that local activity is the foundation of political power. But to influence events on a national and an international scale in a federal polity like the United States, local power must be consolidated and coordinated on the state and national levels. *The Activist's Almanac* looks at organizations that, by and large, meet the following criteria: (1) They are national in scope or impact; (2) they have a membership structure that promotes individual involvement, or substantial support by individual contributions (rather than grants from foundations, corporations, or government); (3) membership or support is open to the general public, not restricted by ethnicity, occupation or industry (such as labor unions and professional or trade associations), or denominational religious affiliation; (4) they are nonprofit organizations, classified as 501(c)(3), (c)(4), or PAC, not political parties; (5) their orientation is toward changing public policy, not primarily providing services; (6) their prospects are for continuing activity for the next five years; and (7) they influence public policy or promote innovative ideas with significant potential for policy impact.

We have no desire to add to what writer Richard Saul Wurman calls "information anxiety," the overload of data that swamps meaning. *The Activist's Almanac* tries to move beyond an avalanche of facts toward useful knowledge—insight and understanding that provide the reader with a feel for the historical context of the organizations discussed in this book, the current issues, and the personalities who give vitality to social change activity in the early 1990s. We have tried to walk the tightwire of sympathetic detachment—not to let our own affinities overcome a fair assessment of a group's achievements, shortcomings, and dilemmas. In each section we usually place organizations in the order of their founding, so reading through the profiles provides a sense of a movement's historical development. We'll be pleased if you, the reader, get a better sense of what specific organizations are really up to, how you might fit in, and how you can best go about changing the world for present and future generations.

I acknowledge with gratitude the hundred-plus organization leaders who granted personal interviews over the last several years, and hundreds more who responded to letters and telephone calls. Thanks also to two writers who helped with research and profile drafts: Laurie Rubin, who contributed to certain profiles on peace, women, human rights, and food, shelter, and sustainable development; and Deborah Macintosh, who contributed to profiles on animal rights. The final versions are my own responsibility. I offer special thanks to Milton Moskowitz, Robert Levering, and Michael Katz, who not only inspired this book with their guide *Everybody's Business* (Harper & Row, 1980; Doubleday, 1990) but also offered valuable advice and encouragement. The files on nongovernmental organizations at the Data Center in Oakland, California, proved helpful in the early stages of research. My appreciation extends particularly to three people who helped move my proposal to a reality: my literary agent, Sandra Dijkstra; Malaika Adero, who bought the book for Simon & Schuster; and my editor, Kara Leverte, at Fireside Books, who saw it through to the final version. Without talented and hardworking colleagues at Sonoma State University I would not have been able to complete this project—my thanks especially to Carol Tremmel, John Hayes, Katie Pierce, and Marilyn Sisler. Support from my wife, Lucia Gattone, and our son, Jesse, has been invaluable.

The Activist's Almanac is a continuing project that will improve with your help. Give us your feedback on what is useful and what is not, your experience with specific organizations, your perspectives on movements, and your suggestions for additions and corrections. Write The Activist's Almanac, P.O. Box 111, Sebastopol, CA 95473; or send E-mail on EcoNet/PeaceNet to dwalls.

INTRODUCTION:
MAKING CHANGE

"How can I make a difference?" An activist is anyone who asks that question about a public issue, has the courage to act on the basis of a tentative answer, and revises action in response to experience. *The Activist's Almanac* argues that organizations are the key to social change, and that activists trying to make a difference need to connect with groups with programs to address issues of change. No organization is without its problems and shortcomings. The search for the perfect organization is like looking for the perfect lover—chances are you'll wait a long time and end up disappointed. It's better to make a commitment to a relationship with all its imperfections and be willing to struggle, to accommodate, to compromise—for the sake of what you can accomplish together over the long run.

Activists often begin with a sense of anger at injustice, at discrimination, at the needless destruction of nature, at the triumph of greed over generosity. But anger or outrage alone can produce frustration and insensitivity to other activists—followed by exhaustion and burnout. A passionate intensity, to be effective, has to be channeled into a long-term commitment. Anyone serious about social change has to be determined and patient. In his autobiography, *The Long Haul,*

Myles Horton (the radical founder of the Highlander Folk School) describes how during the 1930s he learned to harness his anger:

I had to learn that my anger didn't communicate to people what I wanted to communicate. . . . I had to turn my anger into a slow burning fire, instead of a consuming fire. You don't want the fire to go out—you never let it go out—and if it gets weak, you stoke it, but you don't want it to burn you up. It keeps you going, but you subdue it, because you don't want to be destroyed by it. . . . I started saying, "Horton, get yourself together, get ready for the long haul and try to determine how you can live out this thing and make your life useful."

Horton's work at Highlander made vital contributions to the civil rights movement in the 1950s and 1960s: Septima Clarke developed her adult literacy and voter education schools with Highlander's support, and Rosa Parks attended a workshop at Highlander not long before her famous arrest in 1955 for not giving up her bus seat—launching the Montgomery bus boycott and the civil rights movement that followed. And Highlander's work continues as Myles Horton's legacy.

The vital lesson of social movements is: Develop the perspective of a long-distance runner. Activists have to cope with setbacks, discouragement, partial victories, and defeats. The fruits of victory come only with persistence and perseverance. Here's where organizations come in: They develop long-range strategies, sustain personal networks, mobilize movements, test tactics, win victories, consolidate gains, defend advances against the inevitable backlash, sum up experiences, pass on lessons, and hold a movement together through the doldrums so it can advance during the next historic window of political opportunity.

SECULAR TRENDS AND SOCIAL REFORM

Citizen action and public interest organizations are surf riders on the great waves of social movements; as with our current environmental movement, a good number of organizations can be riding different sections of the same wave—it can get crowded out there. But they'd be motionless in the water without the wave of the underlying movement. The waves themselves are generated and shaped by the profound economic, social, political, and demographic undercurrents of our time. A few examples follow:

• Over the last century we moved from an agricultural to an industrial to a post-industrial or information economy—and our occupational and class structure has grown with corresponding complexity. The conditions of work changed with industrialization; the eight-hour working day and five-day work week produced "the weekend" and leisure time. We've become an urban people who've developed a new appreciation and enjoyment of the outdoors and nature.

• The invention of air-conditioning led to the growth of the Sunbelt, allowing cities in the South and Southwest like Atlanta, Houston, Phoenix, and Los Angeles to become great industrial and commercial centers. As population shifted westward, political cultures were transplanted: The civic culture of New England was carried into Michigan, Wisconsin, and Minnesota and on to Washington and Oregon, and the distinctive subculture of the Southeast was carried into the Ozarks, the Texas and Oklahoma plains, and on to the great valley of central California. Between 1910 and 1960 nearly five million African Americans from the rural South moved to the cities of the North and West.

• Since the end of World War II an international market economy has developed, along with international political institutions, and superpower status for the United States. The Cold War between the NATO allies and the Warsaw Pact dominated international politics and shaped the U.S. response to the anticolonial revolutions in the developing world.

• Other powerful trends include the growing proportion of women in the labor force; increased immigration from Mexico, Latin America, and Asia; and the maturing baby boom generation. These great undercurrents generate structures of political opportunity for social movements.

CYCLES AND GENERATIONS

Beyond the increasing complexity of modern life, the fortunes of public interest organizations are influenced by cyclical patterns. Historian Arthur Schlesinger, Jr., describes a thirty-year cycle from public purpose to private interest and back again. The social movements of the post–World War II era—civil rights, women's rights, human rights, environmentalism, consumerism, peace, animal rights—have antecedents in the nineteenth and early twentieth centuries—abolition, woman suffrage, trade unionism, conservation, the agrarian revolt, antivivisection and the humane treatment of animals.

Elaborating Schlesinger's analysis, William Strauss and Neil Howe's *Generations* (Morrow, 1991) posits a four-type cycle of idealist, reactive, civic, and adaptive generational cohorts—with each generation marked by its "coming-of-age" phase of about twenty-two years—so the full cycle is repeated every eighty-eight years or so. The defining events for generations are secular crises (which mark the "coming-of-age" of the civic generations) and spiritual awakenings (for the idealist generations)—one of each to an eighty-eight-year cycle. In this framework the GIs marked by the secular crisis of World War II are a civic generation who have provided presidents from Kennedy to Bush; the Silent Generation who came of age in the 1950s are an adaptive generation; and the baby boomers who came of age in the 1960s and 1970s are an idealist generation marked by the spiritual awakening of the 1960s. Strauss and Howe's framework may be suggestive for political and cultural elites, but it appears to be out of phase for nonelite groups, classes, and subcultures. Leadership for the black freedom movement came from dissenting members of the Silent Generation—Martin Luther King, Jr., Malcolm X, Jesse Jackson—as did the Beat poets and writers, and socialist Michael Harrington. Whatever its specific merit, the Strauss and Howe framework contains the valuable idea of the "generational diagonal," that a single generation moves in time through the life stages of youth (learning), rising adults (activity), mid-life adults (leadership), and elders (stewardship)—retaining a distinctive orientation from its "coming-of-age" or rising adult period. The "sixties" generation is a case in point.

Baby boomers, the idealist generation that contributed to the social movements of the 1960s and 1970s, will come into mid-life adult leadership from the 1990s through 2020. They will move into top leadership in corporations, government, and the nonprofit sector. They will also inherit the money of their parents from the GI generation—$8 trillion by one estimate—the wealthiest cohort to date, who benefited most from the sharp rise in stocks and real estate values over the last thirty years. Although most of this money will pass between generations in the wealthiest 20 percent of the population, more activists will be able to endow their favorite causes than ever before.

The 1960s gave birth to two opposing political currents: the New Left, which provided the early activists of the civil rights, antiwar, women's liberation, environmentalist, and gay liberation movements; and the New Right, which developed from the Goldwater campaign of 1964. In the 1990s these two broad factions of baby boomers face the challenge of organizing a post–Cold War world. Both will need to rethink their ideologies and seek out fresh ideas that go beyond old polarizations. Right now, baby boomers are striving to find effective ways to be activists while in the middle of building careers and raising families. Organizations are exploring new techniques for "quick and easy activism"—including legislative alert networks, telegram services, and letter-writing programs.

Within social movements themselves there are cycles that activists need to understand. Bill Moyer of the Social Movement Empowerment Project notes that a successful social movement goes through stages, from normalcy to ripening conditions to take-off to majority support and success. As movements attain partial success, leaders frequently experience an identity crisis, fail to recognize achievements, and fall into a sense of failure and powerlessness—just as they are on the verge of widespread acceptance of a substantial portion of the movement's practical agenda, if not its utopian component. Not all movement activists have the long-range perspective to persevere toward visionary objectives in the next—and possibly distant—cycle of resurgence. Moyer also identifies four roles of activists: rebel, change agent, reformer, and citizen, noting that each role can be enacted either in a positive and effective manner or a negative and ineffective way. The different roles may fit best at different points in a movement's cycle: "rebels" to rally an activist core in the early stages, "change agents" to organize wider networks of the concerned public, "reformers" to consolidate victories through legislation and regulations after the movement achieves widespread acceptance and success, and then "citizens" to carry on in normal times.

MAKING SENSE OF THE NEW SOCIAL MOVEMENTS

The study of social movements ebbs and flows along with movements themselves, and it should be no surprise that the social movements of the 1960s and 1970s inspired a younger generation of sympathetic scholars to new insights about movement dynamics. So what's new about the new social movements and how they operate? The "old" social movement was the movement of the working class, as embodied in unions and in labor and socialist parties, in its conflict with capital. By the mid-twentieth century the Western industrial societies had largely tamed the old conflict between labor and capital by institutionalizing collective bargaining within a framework of parliamentary democracy and a more or less regulated market economy. Social conflict became fragmented along lines not of class but of race, gender, and ethnicity. Movement participants sought not only economic interests but often the construction of new identities. People asserted rights against corporations and the state less as workers than as citizens, consumers, members of disadvantaged groups, and inhabitants of a common environment.

Students of social change viewed these "new social movements" with post-Marxist eyes. Sympathetic analysts now describe social movements as rational efforts by individuals banding together to pursue their collective interests through the political process. Political scientists see a movement's constituency as one more interest group, with its various "public interest organizations." The "resource mobilization" school of sociologists take the existence of grievances as a constant, and ask how "movement entrepreneurs" marshal financial and political support both from external elite sponsors and from internal members. Social scientists go on to ask what in the "political opportunity structure" enabled, for example, the civil rights movement to succeed in eliminating segregation in the early 1960s when it had been unable to attain that goal for the previous century? What accounted for the victories of the conservation movement in the 1960s, and its expansion to a wider and even more successful environmental movement in the 1970s? Why did a feminist movement reawaken in the 1960s and make notable advances after seeming to be dormant since winning the Nineteenth Amendment in 1920? Explanations come from a focus on organizations, social and economic trends, and the political process.

THE SMALL-TIME PHILANTHROPIST AND CHECKBOOK ACTIVISM

Labor unions, the prototypical social movement organizations, built their strength and independence on dues and volunteered services from their membership. Successful public interest organizations and movements similarly have built upon a membership base, supplemented by gifts from individual major donors and grants from foundations, corporations, and public agencies. Only a small minority of most organizations' members are actively involved in local groups or national structures at any given time. Yet the dues and modest contributions from numerous members remain the bedrock foundation of any durable organization, freeing it from the vicissitudes of interest, fashion, and politics inevitably influencing institutional funders. The Reagan administration, responding to the Right's call to "defund the Left," gave some groups little choice but to cultivate internal support. The "small-time philanthropist," who can contribute money more easily than time, through "checkbook activism" has become the most important supporter of contemporary public interest organizations.

Several new ways to contribute have been devised: The affinity credit card is one favorite, through which the nonprofit organization typically gets one-half of 1 percent of the retail sales charged to the card. The National Audubon Society receives over $100,000 from its members' use of affinity cards. Working Assets Funding Service pioneered the use of credit cards, long-distance telephone service, and travel services to divert a portion of revenues to a fund that supports social action organizations. The member organizations of the Funding Exchange network have built regional progressive public foundations through which donors and community activists share responsibility for channeling contributions to local organizations.

Donors able to make large contributions at crucial moments have also made a difference: Mrs. Frank Leslie's bequest of $2 million to Carrie Catt of the National American Woman Suffrage Association supported field organizers throughout the country who pushed Congress to pass the Nineteenth Amendment in 1920. And Charles Garland, who inherited a million dollars in 1919, established the American Fund for Public Service—better known as the Garland Fund—which in the 1920s agreed to support a litigation program for the National Association for the Advancement of Colored People (NAACP). Even though the Fund went bankrupt in the Depression and never paid its full commitment, the NAACP had launched the legal work that would culminate in the *Brown* v. *Board of Education* decision in 1954, overturning the "separate but equal" justification for segregation in the American South. The Tax Reform Act of 1969 contains incentives even for individuals of moderate means to benefit from setting up charitable remainder trusts that can provide important support to activist organizations over the long run. Anyone can make public interest organizations contingent beneficiaries in their will, and anyone of moderate to substantial means should explore the creative variety of planned giving arrangements that can benefit both the donor and the nonprofit organization.

NONPROFIT STRUCTURES

Elsewhere in the world, they are known as "nongovernmental" organizations (or NGOs). In the United States, they are "nonprofit" organizations. All nonprofit organizations are "tax exempt"; that is, they do not pay income tax on revenue related to their exempt purposes (they do have to pay tax on any "unrelated business income"). But not all nonprofit organizations qualify for "charitable contributions" for income tax deduction purposes. To clarify how advocacy is organized, and which contributions qualify for charitable deductions and which don't, it's important to understand the legal framework of activist nonprofit organizations. The Internal Revenue Service has set up rules by which it classifies nonprofit organizations into a host of 501(c) categories. Charitable and educational organizations—the ones that qualify for charitable contributions if you itemize deductions on your income tax return—are 501(c)(3)s. Lobbying organizations, officially called social welfare organizations, are 501(c)(4)s, and money you give them does not qualify as a charitable contribution. Political action committees (PACs) support candidates for public office, and contributions to them are not deductible either. In other words, federal tax policy will give you a break for supporting charitable and education activities, but Congress is not willing to subsidize efforts to influence legislation or elections to public office.

Many large (and some small) public interest organizations have set up at least two and sometimes three (or more) legally distinct corporations and committees for separate functions. The Sierra Club provides a good example: The Sierra Club itself is a (c)(4)—it lobbies for environmental legislation, so it collects basic dues (nondeductible) through this structure. For larger gifts or major contributions many people want tax deductibility, so there is a 501(c)(3) organization, the Sierra Club Foundation, for this purpose. The Club wants to support strong environmental candidates for Congress, so there is a Sierra Club Political Committee, technically known as a "separate, segregated fund" of the Sierra Club, to which only members can contribute.

501(c)(3)	501(c)(4)	PAC
SIERRA CLUB FOUNDATION	SIERRA CLUB	SIERRA CLUB POLITICAL COMMITTEE

You'll discover many variations on this theme. The National Organization for Women (NOW) has two PACs—one for congressional races and one for state legislature races. The National Rifle Association (NRA) has two (c)(4)s, four (c)(3)s, and one PAC. Some organizations like Common Cause basically lobby, so they are set up as (c)(4)s. Other large organizations like the National Wildlife Federation have large educational programs (four magazines, in this case), so they set up as (c)(3)s and "elect" (through a special IRS procedure) to spend no more than 20 percent of their budgets lobbying, which they can then do to influence Congress without having to set up a (c)(4).

To keep individual electoral campaigns from setting up tax-exempt fronts for voter registration, in 1969 the Congress amended the tax code to provide a special status, 4945(f), for organizations receiving foundation support for voter registration. Such groups must operate in five or more states, hold registration drives in more than one election period, and receive no more than 25 percent of their income from any one source. A few groups have used this designation, notably the Voter Education Project in Atlanta, Southwest Voter Registration and Education Project in San Antonio, Project Vote, HumanSERVE, and the Midwest Voter Registration and Education Project.

WHY THIRD PARTIES DON'T WORK, WHY ADVOCACY ORGANIZATIONS DO

Our dominant political parties seldom take distinctive policy positions until pushed by social movements. Frustrated with what can appear as minor differences between the Democratic and Republican parties, activists on both the left and right have attempted to build "third" parties—or, more precisely, *minor* parties. The role once played by minor parties of interjecting new political ideas and programs into the public arena, however, has been largely superseded by the rise of nonprofit advocacy organizations and think tanks—at least since the New Deal.

The American constitutional system is stacked against minor parties. We don't have a parliamentary system with proportional representation and a prime minister chosen by the parliament—which is what it takes for a true multiparty system to flourish, as it does in Germany, Italy, and Israel, to take some interesting if not always encouraging examples. Our single-member district, winner-takes-all elections, with chief executive elected at-large (a system duplicated at the national and state levels), contains a logic of winning that leads to a two-party system, in which each party seeks to build a broad, majority coalition.

As a result, the Republican and Democratic parties are loose electoral alliances, not the disciplined, ideological parties of Europe. American parties are permeable; they're open to anyone who registers with the party—and most primaries are open to any registered member who files, and choices are made through open primary elections. With parliamentary parties, you join only if you agree with a given ideology and program, candidates for public office are chosen only by party conventions, and party discipline is imposed on elected officials. The open American system presents space for issue-oriented organizations and movements, along with a variety of special interest groups, to influence public policy both from within and from outside official party structures.

Since the Goldwater presidential campaign in 1964, conservatives have captured much of the Republican party organization at the grassroots, often controlling the nominating process. In 1980 they finally nominated their candidate for president—Ronald Reagan. Their success meant that conservatives who start "third" parties quickly get marginalized—look at the experience of the Libertarian party or the American Independent party. Similarly, most progressive social movements are found in the Democratic party—labor unions, African Americans, Hispanics, feminists, gays and lesbians, environmentalists. The Congressional Black Caucus, for example, is the most consistently progressive force in the Congress. When insurgent social movements have succeeded in the United States, it has been through one of the two major parties—the farmers' Non-Partisan League in North Dakota in the 1910s (largely as Republicans), the labor movement in the 1930s, and the civil rights movement in the 1960s (the latter two largely as Democrats). Left efforts at "third" parties have been symbolic gestures at best—the People's party of the 1960s and the Citizens' Party of the 1970s—and disasters at worst, as with the Progressive party of 1948. Our only example of a minor party becoming a major party is the emergence of the Republican party after the collapse of the Whigs—and that was once, in the 1850s, over 140 years ago.

SOCIALLY RESPONSIBLE INVESTING
AND CONSUMING

Socially responsible investing is no small potatoes: *Money* magazine estimates that some $625 billion, 5 percent of all investments in the United States, is invested using "social screens" reflecting ethical principles—primarily by public agencies and pension funds, insurance companies, colleges and universities, and religious institutions. Not bad for a movement barely twenty years old. Although some church groups avoided investing in "sin stocks"—liquor, tobacco, and gambling—as early as the 1920s, the ethical investing movement began to have a significant impact during only the 1960s with shareholder resolutions and proxy fights at corporate annual meetings. Saul Alinsky's FIGHT organization in Rochester, New York, used Eastman Kodak's annual meeting in 1966 to push the company to hire more minority workers. That same year civil rights leaders campaigned against Chase Manhattan and Citibank for supporting the South African government in the wake of the Sharpeville massacre, urging church groups to withdraw their funds from the banks. Antiwar leaders used shareholder resolutions and boycotts in 1969 and 1970 to target Dow Chemical for its production of napalm and Honeywell and Whirlpool for their manufacture of antipersonnel fragmentation bombs. And in 1970 Ralph Nader's Project on Corporate Responsibility began "Campaign GM" to introduce shareholder resolutions on corporate governance at General Motors' annual meeting. In 1971 Protestant denominations established groups that became the Interfaith Center on Corporate Responsibility (ICCR) to monitor shareholder resolutions. Although shareholder resolutions could generate publicity, they seldom received even the 3 percent (later raised to 5 percent) needed for reintroduction the next year, under Security and Exchange Commission regulations. Other approaches were needed.

Direct investment looked like a promising alternative. Boston securities analyst Alice Tepper Marlin founded the Council on Economic Priorities (CEP) in 1969, after she had been asked by a local synagogue to design a "peace portfolio." Two Methodist ministers, J. Elliott Corbett and Luther Tyson, formed Pax World Fund in 1971, appealing to church groups with a portfolio that avoided weapon makers, sin stocks, and companies doing business in South Africa. Howard Stein established Dreyfus Third Century Fund in 1972 to invest in companies with good records in consumer and environmental protection, occupational safety and health, and equal opportunity employment. Social investing developed slowly during the 1970s, but began to thrive in the 1980s with the formation of several new funds: Calvert Social Investment Fund in 1981, New Alternatives Fund in 1982, Working Assets Money Fund in 1983, Parnassus Fund in 1985, and Muir Investment Trust and Domini Social Index Fund in 1991. Working Assets Common Holdings introduced stock and bond mutual funds in 1992. Ethical investing is no longer the exclusive province of the wealthy or the institutional investor. Now the small investor can use these socially responsible mutual funds for IRAs, SEP-IRAs for individual proprietorships or small businesses, or for general saving and investing—and "do well by doing good."

During the 1980s several organizations developed innovative approaches to social responsibility in consumption. Alice Tepper Marlin and the CEP developed guides to socially responsible shopping. Consumers Union, the stalwart publisher of *Consumer Reports*, traditionally concerned with product safety and value for the dollar, began to pay attention to the environmental impact of products. Co-op America developed health and other insurance plans for small companies and independent proprietors, distributes a mail-order marketing catalog, and regularly publicizes boycotts in its quarterly magazine. The "greening" of investment and consumption is proving to be a significant set of tools for exercising personal and collective responsibility for social change.

WORKING FOR CHANGE

According to data compiled by Independent Sector, the U.S. nonprofit sector in 1990 included nearly 1 million organizations, employing 8.7 million people (6.3 percent of total U.S. employment) and utilizing the services of 5.8 million volunteers. Roughly half of the revenue and jobs were in health-related organizations, including hospitals and clinics.

Organizations working on environmental, animal, peace, civil rights, and other advocacy activity composed a small proportion of the total nonprofit sector. Yet a job or a second career with a public interest organization is not that hard to find. There are some 9,500 people employed by the organizations profiled in *The Activist's Almanac* alone (3,650 of them with the environmental organizations). Most nonprofit jobs are advertised through local newspapers and newsletters, but national job opportunities can be found in such progressive publications as *The Nation* and *In These Times*, and through the Boston organization ACCESS and its monthly newspaper, *Community Jobs*.

COMPUTER NETWORKS

If the world is becoming a global village, it needs what EcoNet pioneer Rocky Rohwedder calls a global "village green," a place where notices can be posted, soapbox speeches made, and conversations held—both casual and intense. Computer networks have opened the prospect of inexpensive worldwide communication among activists with access to a microcomputer, telecommunications software, modem, and telephone line. Most bulletin board services (FidoNet) and commercial services (CompuServe) have conferences discussing environmental and human rights topics. Several environmental organizations have private networks through commercial services, although Greenpeace set up its EnviroNet with public access. The Institute for Global Communications has advanced furthest toward an inexpensive system open to environmental, peace, and human rights activists around the world. IGC systems include EcoNet, PeaceNet, ConflictNet, and LaborNet in the United States. IGC links up with related networks in the Association for Progressive Communications including GreenNet in Britain, The Web in Canada, Pegasus in Australia, Alternex in Brazil, NordNet/PeaceNet in Sweden, and GlasNet in Russia. Other domestic networks include HandsNet for food, housing, and legal services activists, and SeniorNet for elders. Conservatives have developed AIM NET for conferences and legislative alerts.

THE CITIZEN ACTIVIST

Becoming a citizen activist is as simple as picking up a pen, or sitting down at a word processor. Writing letters to legislators or the local newspaper is a useful place to begin. Notices of current key bills are available to anyone who joins a legislative alert network. You can lobby legislators by telephone to their Washington or home offices, or make an appointment to visit when they are back in the district. Join or help organize a local group of a national organization. Learn how to raise money, put out a newsletter, take part in direct action. Have fun, and learn from experience. Keep in mind what David Cohen, dean of public interest lobbyists, concludes: "The challenge is to blend the visionary with the mundane."

ENVIRONMENTAL ORGANIZATIONS

1.

FROM CONSERVATION
TO ENVIRONMENTALISM

Environmentalism is the most popular social movement in the
United States today. Five million American households contribute to national environmental organizations, which together
receive over $350 million in contributions from all sources. On
the local level some 6,000 environmental groups are active.
Seventy-five percent of Americans in 1989 identified themselves as environmentalists—all the more remarkable given
that twenty-five years before there were no "environmentalists" and ecology was an obscure branch of biological science.
In 1965 there were no more than a half-dozen national conservation organizations with citizen members and some degree of
influence, and most were on a shaky financial footing. Although conservationists were beginning to win important victories preserving wilderness and protecting air and water from
pollution, no one anticipated the explosion of activism that was
about to take place.

The roots of the American environmental movement are
nourished by New England transcendentalism. When Henry
David Thoreau left Concord in 1845 to write and study nature
for two years at Waldon Pond, he became the harbinger of
twentieth-century conservationists who would preserve the
natural world for its beauty and potential for spiritual en-

lightenment, not merely for its practical value. In an era when vast portions of the country remained unsettled, few of Thoreau's fellow citizens embraced his vision. Only well after the Civil War, perhaps not until the figurative closing of the frontier in 1890, would any significant number of Americans share a sense that the bounty of the nation is not limitless, that progress threatens the very survival of native forests and wildlife, and that nature and wilderness contain an antidote to the ills of industrial civilization.

TWO TRADITIONS IN AMERICAN CONSERVATION

The traditional conservation movement took form in the 1890s, marked by the founding of the Sierra Club in California in 1892 and the first state Audubon Societies in Massachusetts and New York in 1896. In its origins more an elite activity than a mass movement, conservation nevertheless drew support from a broad segment of the public who enjoyed hunting, fishing, and camping. Two distinct tendencies emerged among the early conservationists: a pragmatic "utilitarian" wing, typified by Gifford Pinchot (1865–1946), the first director of the U.S. Forest Service; and an idealistic "preservationist" wing, represented by naturalist John Muir (1838–1914).

Gifford Pinchot, a Connecticut Yankee and Yale graduate from a wealthy family, studied forestry in France and Germany and returned to the United States to preach the gospel of scientific management of natural resources. He defined conservation with the utilitarian outlook of "the greatest good of the greatest number in the long run." In the spirit of the Progressive political movement of his time, Pinchot defended natural resources against shortsighted exploitation by irresponsible businessmen, opposing "the interests," not timbering and mining in themselves. He sought to bring forest and mineral resources under rational, long-term management, overseen by professionals employed by government.

The utilitarian resource-management advocates retained a predominant influence on public conservation policy through the 1940s. Professional forestry, soil and water conservation, flood control and watershed development, scientific game management, and the development of state departments of natural resources are among their significant and lasting accomplishments. Organizations in this tradition include the Izaak Walton League (founded in 1922) and the National Wildlife Federation (1935). By the end of the New Deal the innovative impulse of this tradition was exhausted. Its most notable institutional achievements—the Forest Service, the Tennessee Valley Authority, the Bureau of Reclamation—would become targets of the environmental movement in later decades.

In contrast, the preservationist wing of the conservation movement saw the natural world not as a factor of production but as something to be enjoyed and valued in its own right. John Muir, born to a zealous Christian family in Scotland, was transplanted as a boy to a farm in Wisconsin. Inventor, botanist, geologist, wanderer—Muir arrived in California at age thirty in 1868 and began several years of roaming the Sierras. Drawn by friends into writing about his experiences, Muir was soon publishing essays in such major eastern magazines of the day as *Harper's, Scribner's,* and *Century.* An eloquent spokesman for the redemptive character of nature and the value of preserving wilderness, Muir joined the political battles to save the Yosemite, Sequoia, and Kings Canyon areas as national parks. The Sierra Club, which Muir helped organize in 1892, and the National Audubon Society (founded in 1905) are early reflections of this tradition; the National Parks Association (1919), an ancestor of Defenders of Wildlife (1925), and The Wilderness Society (1935) followed.

Preservationists drew on a widespread "back to nature" spirit, a romantic reaction to the rapid urbanization and industrialization of the early decades of the twentieth century. The evils of city life could be countered, it was believed, by city parks, Boy and Girl Scouting, summer camps, nature study in schools and museums, and suburban green belts. With the introduction of the eight-hour working day and the two-day weekend, more city people had time to enjoy hunting, fishing, and the out-of-doors. Early achievements of this tradition include the national park system, wildlife sanctuaries, and the protection of birds threatened with extinction. More recently, preservationists have spearheaded the protection of endangered species, vast areas of wilderness, and wild and scenic rivers. By the 1960s, John Muir had displaced Gifford Pinchot as the popular embodiment of the American conservation movement.

The contemporary environmental movement's strength is rooted in the transformation of American society brought about by the long period of prosperity following World War II. Increased real income and a higher standard of living, accompanied by the spread of paid vacations to a wide range of occupations, meant many more people had both the financial means and the leisure time to enjoy outdoor recreation. Advancing levels of education also helped produce a shift in social values favoring protection of natural areas. With the widespread ownership of automobiles and the development of freeways, the number of visits to the expanding national park system jumped from 12 million in 1946 to 282 million by 1979. Access to natural environments became an essential aspect of the quality of life to millions of Americans.

The first major wave of national environmental legislation came in the mid-1960s as long-sought victories from the preservationists' agenda: the Wilderness Act of 1964, the Land and Water Conservation Fund of 1964, and the Wild and Scenic Rivers and National Scenic Trails acts of 1968. Stewart Udall's *Quiet Crisis*, published in 1963, had helped focus attention on the threats to our wilderness heritage. Preservationist victories continued in the midst of new concerns, with such landmarks as the Eastern Wilderness Act of 1974 and the Alaska National Interest Lands Conservation Act of 1980. Organizations in the traditional conservation movement share credit for this impressive string of legislative victories.

1963: Clean Air Act. Encouraged cooperative programs by state and local governments to prevent and control air pollution; established federal grants for air pollution control agencies.

1964: Wilderness Act. Preserved nine million acres of wilderness in the western states.

1965: Water Quality Act. Required states to establish and enforce water quality standards.

1968: Wild and Scenic Rivers Act; National Scenic Trails Act. WSRA designated eight rivers for immediate inclusion and twenty-seven others to be evaluated. NSTA designated the Pacific Crest and Appalachian trails as the first two national scenic trails.

1970: National Environmental Policy Act. Required federal agencies to prepare "environmental impact statements" of projects; established the Council on Environmental Quality.

1970: Resource Conservation and Recovery Act. Authorized Environmental Protection Agency (EPA) to promote the recovery and recycling of solid wastes.

1972: Federal Environmental Pesticide Control Act. Required manufacturers to register pesticides with the EPA and disclose contents and test results; authorized the EPA to ban sales and seize products.

1973: Endangered Species Act. Authorized the secretary of the interior to list endangered or threatened species.

1976: Toxic Substances Control Act. Required manufacturers to test products for risk to human health or the environment before marketing them.

1980: Comprehensive Environmental Response, Compensation, and Liability Act (Superfund). Set up a fund to clean up abandoned hazardous waste dumps and toxic spills; made dumpers and owners responsible for cleanup costs.

1980: Alaska National Interest Lands Conservation Act. Preserved 104 million acres of wilderness in Alaska.

1990: Clean Air Act. Reauthorized and strengthened the regulation of air pollution by the EPA.

Sources: David Bollier and Joan Claybrook, *Freedom from Harm* (1986), pp. 275–292; The Wilderness Society.

CONSERVATIONISTS REVITALIZED

Federal support for environmental protection, in one form or another, had stretched from the clean water legislation of the Eisenhower administration to the Alaska lands act of the final Carter years. When Ronald Reagan won the Presidential election of 1980, he swept the western states on the winds of the "Sagebrush Rebellion," a revolt against federal regulation of land and its use by ranchers, miners, and other businesses. Reagan appointed as secretary of the interior the former legal counsel for the free-market Mountain States Legal Foundation, James Watt. As a political strategy, Watt attempted to divide the "daisy sniffers" from the "hook and bullet boys," the preservationists from the hunting and angling constituency, which he mistakenly imagined did not share substantial portions of the conservation vision. The two traditions of American conservation stood together, united in defense of the legislative victories of the 1960s and 1970s.

As Reagan and Watt threatened to undo the gains of the 1970s, membership skyrocketed in the Sierra Club and other activist environmental organizations. Scandals were uncovered at the Environmental Protection Agency. The popular consensus on environmental protection was apparent in the united front of all the major conservation groups. Watt resigned rather than become an issue in Reagan's campaign for reelection in 1984. The following year the Group of Ten, leaders of organizations ranging from Friends of the Earth to the National Wildlife Federation, issued a common action agenda for the environment. The defeat of the Sagebrush Rebellion and the rout of James Watt left the counterenvironmentalists regrouping as the Wise Use Movement on the populist right. Only the libertarians with their free-market environmentalism mounted a serious intellectual challenge to regulatory environmentalism.

By 1988 Democratic and Republican presidential candidates alike were hailing themselves as champions of the environment. Ocean dumping off Atlantic beaches and pollution in Boston Harbor became issues in the campaign. George Bush proclaimed his intention to become "the environmental President," in the tradition of Teddy Roosevelt. As the twentieth anniversary of Earth Day was celebrated in April 1990, protection of the environment was one of the most popular political priorities in the United States, as it had been throughout the 1980s. Whether the commitment to global ecological protection is deep or shallow remains to be tested by competition in the world economy among advanced nations and pressure for economic growth from developing nations. This tension was apparent during the 1992 presidential campaign as the Bush administration debated its stance toward the U.N. Conference on Environment and Development (UNCED), the "Earth Summit" held in Rio de Janeiro in June, which pushed to limit greenhouse gases and achieve environmentally sustainable development. Environmental sociologist Riley Dunlap reports that surveys on public support for enviromental protection show a "clear consensus" in favor, but an "ambiguous commitment" when it comes to voting on environmental referenda, paying the cost, or modifying life-styles.

Despite widespread public support, the environmental movement harbors its own fractures and vocal critics. Tension between the "ecoactivists" at the grassroots and the "envirocrats" at the headquarters of the large conservation organizations centers on the priorities given to local action versus Washington lobbying on national legislation. The "ecophilosophers" of deep ecology, bioregionalism, and Green politics bring new debates and divisions to the preservationist camp. Environmental organizations are also being challenged by the

Southwest Organizing Project and others to reach past their overwhelmingly white, professional, college-educated membership to form alliances with minorities and labor unions, and institute affirmative action programs to diversify their staff.

The laundry list of environmental problems facing the planet —depletion of the ozone layer, global warming, destruction of tropical rain forests, extinction of species, toxic and radioactive wastes—can appear overwhelming and insurmountable. Yet reviewing the successes of the last thirty years—millions of acres of wilderness saved; air, water, and pesticide pollution reduced; nuclear power development halted; public consciousness raised; and powerful organizations built—should give all environmentalists a second wind. As Harold Gilliam, the veteran San Francisco environmentalist, wrote on Earth Day 1990, "When you've been climbing a mountain for a long time and the summit seems to be as far away as ever, it can give you new heart for the ascent to look back and see how far you've come."

SIERRA CLUB

SIERRA CLUB

730 POLK STREET

SAN FRANCISCO, CA 94109

(415) 776-2211

FOUNDED: 1892   MEMBERS: 580,000
LOCAL GROUPS: 382   BUDGET: $40 million
STAFF: 250   TAX STATUS: 501(c)(4): Sierra Club; 501(c)(3): Sierra Club Foundation; PAC: Sierra Club Political Committee

PURPOSE: "To explore, enjoy and protect the wild places of the Earth."

The Sierra Club is the foremost membership organization of environmental activists working on a broad range of conservation programs. In addition to

mustering troops for national campaigns, Club chapters exercise considerable clout on state and local issues— in many areas they are the only group around. Although it only moved to the forefront of the conservation movement in the 1960s, the Club carries an early tradition of activism. Founded by the prophet of environmental preservation, John Muir, the triumphs and defeats of the Sierra Club have instructed the conservation movement as a whole. After initial victories in preserving Yosemite and Sequoia parks, and a loss over Hetch Hetchy Dam, the Club operated through the 1930s primarily as a recreation society, but revived its crusading spirit in the late 1950s and the 1960s under the leadership of David Brower to aid in a vast expansion of designated wilderness and national parks. In the early 1980s it led the opposition to James Watt, President Reagan's conservative secretary of the interior.

BACKGROUND: In 1892 two professors at the University of California at Berkeley helped John Muir launch a club modeled after the eastern Appalachian Mountain Club. With 182 charter members, the Sierra Club's officers elected Muir president, an office he held until his death in 1914. Among the Club's first goals were establishing national parks, including Glacier and Mount Rainier, convincing the California legislature to give Yosemite Valley to the federal government, and saving California's coastal redwoods. Muir escorted President Teddy Roosevelt through Yosemite in 1903. Two years later the California legislature ceded Yosemite Valley and Mariposa Grove to the federal government, marking the Sierra Club's first lobbying victory and the establishment of the country's second national park, after Yellowstone in 1872.

At the turn of the century, the Sierra Club became embroiled in the famous Hetch Hetchy controversy that divided the preservationists from the utilitarian "resource management" conservationists. The city of San Francisco had been having problems for years with a privately owned water company that offered poor service at high rates and failed to provide adequate water to fight the fires that destroyed much of the city following the great earthquake of 1906. A reform administration under Mayor James D. Phelan wished to establish a municipally owned water utility and revived an earlier proposal to dam the Hetch Hetchy Valley, a twin sister to Yosemite, located within the boundaries of the park as first laid out in 1890.

Gifford Pinchot, a progressive supporter of public utilities and head of the Forest Service, which then had jurisdiction over the national parks, backed the Hetch Hetchy Dam. Muir appealed to his friend President Roosevelt, who would not commit himself against the dam, noting its popularity with the people of San Francisco (a referendum in 1908 confirmed a seven-to-one majority in favor of the dam and municipal water). Muir and attorney William Colby began a national campaign against the dam, attracting the support of many eastern conservationists. With the 1912 election of Woodrow Wilson, who carried San Francisco, the supporters of the dam had a friendly administration in the White House. The bill to dam the Hetch Hetchy passed Congress in 1913, and the Sierra Club had lost its first major battle. In retaliation, the Club supported the creation of the National Park Service in 1916, to remove the parks from the oversight of the Forest Service. Stephen Mather, a Club member from Chicago and an opponent of Hetch Hetchy Dam, became the first Park Service director.

During the 1920s and 1930s, the Sierra Club served its members as a social and recreational society, conducting numerous outings, improving trails, and building huts and lodges in the Sierras. Preservation campaigns included a several-year effort to enlarge Sequoia National Park (achieved in 1926) and over three decades of work to protect and then preserve Kings Canyon National Park (established in 1940). The leaders of the Club appear as conservation moderates—certainly not zealots—from today's perspective. Historian Stephen Fox notes, "In the 1930s most of the three thousand members were middle-aged Republicans."

But the New Deal was to bring many conservationists to the Democrats, and many Democrats into the ranks of conservationists. Leading the generation of Young Turks who took control and revitalized the Sierra Club after World War II were attorney Richard Leonard, nature photographer Ansel Adams, and the man who would become the most important figure in the Club since Muir, David Brower. Brower was twenty-one when he met Ansel Adams on a trail in the Sierras in 1933. Adams sponsored Brower for membership in the Club later that year, and he was appointed to the editorial board of the *Sierra Club Bulletin*. Brower moved to Yosemite in 1935 and lived there for three years, working on the park staff and making the first ascents of thirty-three mountain peaks. He returned home to Berkeley in 1941 and began working with the University of California Press. During the war he served in Europe and trained troops in the mountaineering techniques pioneered by Sierra Club members. Returning to his job with the university press after the war, Brower began editing the *Sierra Club Bulletin* in 1946.

In 1950 the Sierra Club showed little promise of becoming an environmental powerhouse. Some 7,000 members, mostly on the West Coast, were bound together in social networks around local chapters. That year the Atlantic chapter became the first formed outside California. An active volunteer board of directors ran the organization, assisted by a small clerical staff. Brower was appointed the first executive director in 1952, and the Club began to catch up

with those major conservation organizations—the National Audubon Society, the National Wildlife Federation, The Wilderness Society, the Izaak Walton League—which had long had a professional staff.

The Sierra Club made its reputation in the battle against the Echo Park Dam in Dinosaur National Monument in Utah, first announced by the Bureau of Reclamation in 1950. Brower led the fight, marshaling support from the full range of conservation groups. Brower's background in publishing proved decisive—with the help of publisher Alfred Knopf, *This Is Dinosaur* was rushed into press. Invoking the specter of Hetch Hetchy, conservationists effectively lobbied Congress, which deleted the Echo Park Dam from the Colorado River project as approved in 1955. Recognition of the Sierra Club's role in the Echo Park Dam victory boosted membership from 10,000 in 1956 to 15,000 in 1960.

The Sierra Club was now on the map, and preservationists moved to the offensive with wilderness proposals. The Club's Biennial Wilderness Conferences, launched in 1949 in concert with The Wilderness Society, became an important force in the campaign that secured passage of the Wilderness Act in 1964. Building on a photography exhibit the Club assembled in the mid-1950s, Brower launched the Exhibit Format book series with *This Is the American Earth* in 1960, followed two years later by *In Wildness Is the Preservation of the World*, with spectacular color photographs by Eliot Porter. These elegant coffee-table books introduced the Sierra Club to a wide audience. Fifty thousand copies were sold in the first four years, and by 1960 sales exceeded $10 million. Soon Brower was publishing two new titles a year in the Exhibit Format series, but not all did as well as *In Wildness*. However successful the books were introducing the public to wilderness preservation and the Sierra Club, they lost money for the organization, some $60,000 a year after 1964. Financial management became a subject of contention between Brower and his board of directors.

The Sierra Club's most publicized crusade of the 1960s was the effort to stop the Bureau of Reclamation from building two dams that would flood portions of the Grand Canyon. "Should we also flood the Sistine Chapel so tourists can get nearer the ceiling?" asked full-page ads the Club placed in the *New York Times* and the *Washington Post* in June 1966. "This time it's the Grand Canyon they want to flood." The ads generated a storm of protest to the Congress, prompting the Internal Revenue Service to announce it was suspending the Sierra Club's 501(c)(3) status pending an investigation. The board had taken the precaution of setting up the Sierra Club Foundation as a (c)(3) organization in 1960 for endowments and contributions for educational and other nonlobbying activities. Even so, contributions to the Club dropped off, aggravating its annual operating deficits. Membership, however, climbed sharply in response to the attack by the IRS from 30,000 in 1965 to 57,000 in 1967 and 75,000 in 1969.

Despite the Club's success in blocking plans for the Grand Canyon dams and weathering the transition from 501(c)(3) to 501(c)(4) status, tension was growing over finances between Brower

and the board of directors. The Club's annual deficits rose from $100,000 in 1967 and 1968 to some $200,000 in 1969. Another conflict occurred over the Club's policy toward the nuclear power plant to be constructed by Pacific Gas and Electric (PG&E) at Diablo Canyon near San Luis Obispo, California. Although the Club had played the leading role blocking PG&E's nuclear power plant proposed for Bodega Bay in the early 1960s, that case had been built around the local environmental impact and earthquake danger from the nearby San Andreas Fault, not from opposition to nuclear power itself. In exchange for moving the new proposed site from the environmentally sensitive Nipomo Dunes to Diablo Canyon, the board of directors voted to support PG&E's plan for the power plant. A membership referendum in 1967 upheld the board's decision. Brower, however, came to the conclusion that nuclear power at any location was a mistake, and he voiced his opposition to the plant—contrary to the Club's official policy.

As pro- and anti-Brower factions polarized, the annual election of new directors took on special urgency. Brower's supporters won a majority in 1968, but in the April 1969 election the anti-Brower candidates won all five open positions. Two of his closest friends on the board, Ansel Adams and president Richard Leonard, led the opposition to Brower, charging him with financial recklessness and insubordination and calling for his ouster as executive director. The board voted ten to five to accept Brower's resignation. Brower went on to found Friends of the Earth in 1969 and the Earth Island Institute in 1981. Eventually reconciled with the Sierra Club, Brower was elected to the board of directors in 1983 and served until 1988.

Mike McCloskey, hired by Brower in 1961 as the Club's first northwest field representative, became the Club's second executive director in 1969. An administrator attentive to detail, McCloskey had set up the Club's conservation department in 1965 and guided the campaigns to save the Grand Canyon and establish the Redwood and North Cascades national parks. During the 1970s McCloskey led the Club's legislative activity—preserving Alaskan lands and eastern wilderness areas, and supporting the new environmental agenda: the Toxic Substances Control Act of 1976, the Clean Air Act amendments, and the Surface Mining Control and Reclamation Act of 1977, passed during the administration of President Jimmy Carter. The Sierra Club made its first presidential endorsement in 1984 in support of Walter Mondale's unsuccessful campaign to unseat Ronald Reagan. McCloskey resigned as executive director in 1985 after sixteen and a half years and assumed the title of chairman, becoming the Club's senior strategist, devoting his time to conservation policy rather than budget planning and administration. After a two-year interlude with Douglas Wheeler, whose Republican credentials were disconcerting to liberal members, the Club hired Michael Fisher, former head of the California Coastal Commission, who served from 1987 to 1992. Carl Pope, on staff since 1973, was named in October 1992.

As the Sierra Club attempted to negotiate logging plans for the Northwest timber harvest, some rank-and-file members became angry about the deals being made. David Orr (P.O. Box 1591, Davis, CA 95617) has started the Association of Sierra Club Members for Environmental Ethics (ASCMEE) to push a harder line, "not blind opposition to compromise, but opposition to blind compromise."

CURRENT PRIORITIES: Every two years the Club's board of directors consults with chapter leaders and agrees on a list of conservation campaign goals for staff and volunteers. The current program priorities are (1) the protection of the coastal plain in the Arctic National Wildlife Refuge; (2) the protection of the ancient forests of Washington, Oregon, and California; (3) the expansion of wilderness areas in national forests, parks, and Bureau of Land Management jurisdictions; (4) the reauthorization and improvement of the Resource Conservation and Recovery Act, to include stricter regulation of toxics and hazardous waste disposal; (5) the support of policies to halt global warming, emphasizing auto fuel efficiency; (6) the reform of environmentally destructive international development lending practices, with emphasis on protecting tropical rain forests; (7) the limitation of global population growth, by full funding for international family planning programs; (8) the revision of state clean air plans to meet the goals of the Clean Air Act of 1990, emphasizing auto emission standards, cleaner fuels, and alternative transportation plans; (9) the establishment of state biodiversity programs and passage of a federal biodiversity act; and (10) the establishment of good municipal waste programs in ten new states. The Sierra Club also supports, as lower priorities, campaigns including defense and energy facilities cleanup, Great Lakes water quality, reform of the 1872 mining law, replacing the Highway Trust Fund with a program emphasizing mass transit, and wetlands protection.

MEMBERS: The Sierra Club was in a strong position to benefit from the birth of the new environmental movement that followed Earth Day in 1970. Expanding its chapter structure to cover all fifty states, Club membership doubled to 154,000 by 1975, finally helping to erase its debts and annual deficits. With the election of President Ronald Reagan another dramatic expansion began. Direct mail brought over 140,000 new members in 1981 and 1982, as the organization led a campaign that gathered one million signatures calling for the resignation of Reagan's secretary of the interior, James Watt—who quit in 1983 to avoid becoming a central issue in Reagan's reelection campaign. The membership of the Club continued to grow, reaching 363,000 in 1985 and 600,000 in 1990. Total membership declined slightly to 580,000 by early 1992. The membership of the Sierra Club is still concentrated on the West Coast, with more than a third of the members residing in California. An activist network of 84,000 members writes letters and telephones Capitol Hill to support environmental legislation.

STRUCTURE: The Sierra Club is among the most democratic of the large public interest organizations. An elaborate chapter and group structure encour-

ages members to participate in Club activities and policy formulation. There are fifty-seven chapters (fifty-five in the United States and two in Canada), each usually covering a state (although California includes thirteen chapters, and New England and the Dakotas are each covered by a single chapter). Within the chapters are some 350 groups, typically covering a local area, county, or cluster of counties. All chapters and groups have executive, conservation, and outing committees, staffed by volunteers. In addition to the new San Francisco headquarters acquired in 1985, the Sierra Club maintains a Washington, D.C., office and fourteen regional field offices with paid staff. The membership elects the executive committees of the chapters and groups, and the national board of directors. There is no periodic national membership convention.

The Sierra Club Foundation (established in 1960), governed by a fourteen-member, self-recruiting board of directors, accepts tax-deductible gifts and manages the endowment. The Sierra Club Legal Defense Fund (established as an independent organization in 1971) handles litigation for the Club and other environmental organizations. The Sierra Club Political Committee (established in 1976) supports candidates for public office.

RESOURCES: In 1990 the Club received $40.7 million in revenue, with 40 percent from membership dues, 31 percent from contributions and grants, and the remainder from outings, book sales, royalties, advertising, and investments. Expenses totaled $39.7 million with 61 percent spent for program services— influencing public policy, information and education (including *Sierra* and Sierra Club Books), outdoor activities, and allocations to chapters. Support for management, membership development, and fund-raising took 39 percent. The Club has a fund balance (net worth) of $9.2 million. Response to direct mail was down for 1991, however, and the Club was forced to cut some twenty-five positions, laying off twenty employees, including cutbacks at Sierra Club Books. The Foundation received $4.4 million in revenue in 1990, spending $2.3 million in grants and $1.8 million for administrative and fund-raising expenses. Assets of the Foundation include $1.1 million in land and property, $1.6 million in endowment funds, and $1 million in charitable remainder interest funds. The Sierra Club Political Committee raised $532,000 in the 1988 campaign cycle, and $235,000 in the 1990 cycle.

PUBLICATIONS AND SERVICES: Membership starts at $35 and includes subscriptions to *Sierra* magazine (circulation 518,000), published six times a year, the chapter newspaper, and the local group newsletter. The "Outings Catalog," printed annually in the January/February *Sierra*, lists hundreds of Club-planned trips to national and international destinations. "Sierra Singles" meetings are a new form for an old Club tradition (photographer Ansel Adams met his wife on a Club outing). The *Sierra Club National News Report*, issued twenty-six times a year and available by subscription, is the best single source on national environmental legislation (the *Report* is also available on EcoNet). Legislative bulletins are recorded on a twenty-four-hour Washing-

ton hotline, (202) 547-5550. Sierra Club Books publishes an extensive series of wilderness books and hiking guides, available at a discount to members through catalog mail order. A new member's handbook, *The Sierra Club: A Guide* (1989), contains a history, year-by-year chronology, historic photographs, organizational bylaws, a guide to the workings of the Club, and lists of chapters and directors. For the official history, with a focus on the board of directors, see Michael P. Cohen, *The History of the Sierra Club: 1892–1970* (1988). To mark its centennial, the Club issued an illustrated coffee-table book, *Sierra Club: 100 Years of Protecting Nature*, by Tom Turner (1991). David Brower's autobiographical notes and edited writings are available in two volumes, *For Earth's Sake: The Life and Times of David Brower* (Peregrine Smith, 1990) and *Work in Progress* (Peregrine Smith, 1991). An annual financial report is published in the March/April issue of *Sierra*. Separate annual reports are published by the Legal Defense Fund and the Foundation. A Sierra Club affinity VISA card, "the plastic that's actually good for the environment," is available. □

NATIONAL AUDUBON SOCIETY

700 BROADWAY

New York, NY 10003

(212) 979-3000

FOUNDED: 1905   MEMBERS: 560,000
CHAPTERS: 519   BUDGET: $41.9 million
STAFF: 370   TAX STATUS: 501(c)(3)

PURPOSE: "The preservation and wise use of our natural heritage."

It's not just for bird-watchers anymore. The National Audubon Society has become the leading membership organization advocating preservation of wildlife and habitat. Audubon maintains wildlife sanctuaries, environmental education centers, and ecology camps. Intent on gaining a contemporary image for the organization, president Peter Berle has presented hard-hitting TV wildlife specials that have provoked controversy and lost a few corporate sponsors. A new Audubon Activist network mobilizes members on local, national, and global environmental issues.

BACKGROUND: Songbirds hunted as game, no bag limits on ducks, the passenger pigeon extinguished, egrets shot for feathers for ladies' hats—there was little protection for birds in late-nineteenth-century America. George Bird Grinnell, a big-game hunter who had been raised in wildlife painter John James Audubon's former home and estate in upper Manhattan, opposed this indiscriminate slaughter while he was editor of *Forest and Stream*, the major sportsmen's magazine of his day. When Grinnell proposed an Audubon Society as the country's first bird protection association in 1886, he attracted some 50,000 members within two years. The administrative chores of maintaining the group soon overwhelmed him, and he dropped the idea. Ten years later in 1896, Mrs. Augustus Hemenway helped

found the Massachusetts Audubon Society. Over the next two years the movement spread throughout New England and the Atlantic coast; there were sixteen state chapters by 1898. These state societies banded together to pass the first federal bird protection law in 1900, the Lacy Act, which forbids the interstate shipment of birds killed in violation of state laws. One of Audubon's most venerable traditions, the Christmas Bird Count, was begun in 1900 as an alternative to bird-shoots over the holidays.

Insurance agent William Dutcher, leader of the New York Audubon Society, took on the job of coordinating a national committee of the state Audubon groups in 1901. The mounting debts of Dutcher's committee were paid off in 1904 by Albert Wilcox of New York, who offered to leave the organization a substantial sum in his will if the groups would incorporate and expand their concerns to protecting wild animals as well as birds. The National Association of Audubon Societies was incorporated in 1905. Wilcox died in 1906, leaving the Societies over $300,000. Assured an income from the bequest, Dutcher proceeded with a vigorous campaign to enforce the new state laws protecting birds. Less than adept at raising money, he overreached the resources of the association, and ran up an $8,000 deficit in 1907. When Dutcher was disabled by a stroke in 1910, the Audubon board of directors replaced him with T. Gilbert Pearson, who remained president of the Association for two decades. Conservative and frugal, Pearson courted hunters and gun companies, turning down their financial support for the Audubon

Society only after a storm of criticism.

Unable to control a campaign to protect game birds through the Audubon Society, the gun and ammunition companies organized the American Game Protective Association (AGPA). Audubon and the AGPA worked together in 1913 to secure passage by Congress of a law to protect migratory birds, giving the federal Biological Survey the power to set hunting seasons, limit the daily bag of birds, and protect endangered species. The Migratory Bird Act served as the basis of a treaty signed in 1916 by the United States and Canada.

During the 1920s some Audubon members grew uneasy with Pearson's alliance with the gun companies and his lack of apparent zeal for the conservation cause. In 1929 naturalist Willard Van Name teamed up with Rosalie Edge, a wealthy New Yorker, veteran of woman suffrage campaigns, and a life member of the Audubon Association. Charging that Audubon was characterized by "inertia, incompetency and procrastination," Edge and Van Name formed the Emergency Conservation Committee (ECC), with the intention of reforming the Audubon. For the next three years Edge continued her attack on Pearson's leadership and his connections with hunters and trappers. Receiving national publicity, her criticism resulted in a loss of membership in the Audubon Association from 8,400 to 3,400. In 1934 Wall Street broker John Baker became chairman of the Audubon board of directors and soon forced Pearson's resignation. Edge sustained the ECC for some thirty years, becoming what historian Stephen Fox terms "the first woman to have a considerable impact on the conservation movement." Her ECC represented, Fox writes, "in its purest form the Muir tradition of the radical amateur in conservation."

Under the leadership of Baker the organization changed its name in 1940 to the National Audubon Society, and initiated a new structure through which payment of annual dues provided membership in both the national organization and local Audubon affiliates. The Society slowly regained membership, reaching 8,400 in 1947, 12,000 in 1951, and over 20,000 by 1954. Although an improvement in comparison to Pearson's administration, Baker's twenty-five years at the head of the Audubon Society left much to be desired. He was secretive, refusing to publish budget reports or accurate membership figures, and, most importantly, kept the Society from any lobbying on conservation legislation, fearing to endanger the Society's nonprofit status and thereby its growing endowment.

Following Baker's retirement in 1959, the board named Carl Buchheister president; he had been vice president at the Society for fifteen years. Buchheister enlivened the organization by moving the annual meeting from New York to various cities around the country and making the affairs of the Society more open. Membership began to climb, reaching 41,000 by 1962 and 52,000 by 1967, the year Buchheister retired. Elvis Stahr followed as president, opening a Washington office in 1969 and presiding over a period of robust expansion. In the wake of Earth Day, membership leaped from 81,500 in 1970 to 148,000 in 1971 and continued to grow to 321,500 by 1975. Russell W.

Peterson, former Republican governor of Delaware and head of the Council on Environmental Quality under Presidents Richard Nixon and Gerald Ford, became president in 1979. He initiated an era of greater public visibility for the organization, highlighted by the "World of Audubon" television specials, and increased the lobbying and legal staff, running up a substantial budget deficit in the process.

Peter Berle was named president in 1985. Despite its increased membership, Audubon had begun to experience a financial pinch. Membership growth flattened, and plateaued at 500,000 to 550,000 in the mid-1980s. Berle was forced to retrench, trimming staff and closing one regional office in 1988. Determined to expand Audubon's membership and clout, Berle began updating the organization's image in 1991 to embody a wider environmental purpose than birds, replacing *Audubon* magazine's twenty-five-year editor Les Line (who had a prohunting stance) with Michael Robbins, former editor of *Oceans*. Audubon's airborne egret logo was briefly swapped for a rectangular blue flag, but the popular egret was soon restored to its place of glory. Audubon is positioned to use its chapter strength and national programs to protect wildlife and habitat through education and political action at all levels from the local to the global.

CURRENT PRIORITIES: Audubon's action agenda derives from "The Audubon Cause," a broad statement of goals including (1) conserving native plants and animals and their habitats; (2) protecting life from pollution, radiation, and toxic substances; (3) furthering the wise use of land and water; (4) seeking solutions for global problems involving the interaction of population, resources, and the environment; and (5) promoting rational strategies for energy development and use, stressing conservation and renewable energy sources. In 1991 Audubon set out a five-year action campaign to preserve wetlands by involving activist networks, through lobbying and lawsuits, through congressional legislation, by expanding its sanctuary system, and through a media campaign.

MEMBERS: Before the founding of the Izaak Walton League in the Midwest in 1922, Audubon was the largest wildlife protection group in the country, with over 5,000 members in 1920, nearly three-quarters residing in New England, New York, New Jersey, and Pennsylvania. Membership has been relatively steady around 550,000 for several years, settling at 560,000 in 1991. Presently over 60 percent of the members live east of the Mississippi River. Over 40,000 members participate each year in the traditional Christmas Bird Count. Some 100,000 members have joined Audubon's activist network by pledging to take action on behalf of the environment.

STRUCTURE: Membership in the National Audubon Society also includes membership in one of the 512 local chapters, which provide many opportunities to get involved with outings, educational programs, and conservation activities. The national board of directors has thirty-six members, who serve three-year terms; each year twelve directors come up for election. A bylaw change in 1987 provided for nine of each year's group of directors to be nominated by region, for a total of twenty-seven directors representing regions and nine at-large. All members vote annually on the directors. There is a national convention open to all members every two years, with a West Coast meeting on alternate years. There are nine regional and five state offices, and a Washington, D.C., office to coordinate lobbying on federal environmental policy. Following the example of the Natural Resources Defense Council, Audubon is renovating a new headquarters building at 700 Broadway in New York City, at a cost of $24 million, with the latest in engineering and design innovations for energy savings, nontoxic work environments, and recycling.

RESOURCES: The Society received income of $41.9 million in fiscal year 1991, 27 percent derived from membership dues, 31 percent from contributions and grants, 21 percent from earned income, 8 percent from investment income, 7 percent from bequests, and 6 percent from other sources. Expenditures totaling $41.9 million were divided 71 percent for program services (conservation, research, publishing, education, and chapter support), and 29 percent for support services (management, membership development, and fund-raising). Audubon has an endowment of $34.2 million. Audubon maintains a system of eighty-eight wildlife sanctuaries, ranging from the 12 acres surrounding Theodore Roosevelt's grave in New York to the 26,000-acre Paul J. Rainey sanctuary in Louisiana, acquired in 1924, which provides $1 million a year in natural gas royalties for the organization.

PUBLICATIONS AND SERVICES: Membership is $35 and includes a subscription to *Audubon* magazine (circulation 470,000), published six times a year. *American Birds* (circulation 10,000), published five times a year, is an ornithological journal for serious birders, available by subscription; one issue each year is devoted to the Christmas Bird Count. A youth education program, featuring the bimonthly *Audubon Adventures*, reaches some 320,000 children in 10,000 clubs. The 100,000 members of Audubon's activist network receive the monthly *Audubon Action* and occasional action alerts in exchange for a pledge to write two letters and make two telephone calls. A telephone "Actionline" offers a recorded update on current national environmental legislation at (202) 547-9017. An annual report is available from the national office. Frank Graham, longtime editor of *Audubon* magazine, has written *The Audubon Ark: A History of the National Audubon Society* (Knopf, 1990). An affinity VISA card is available.

Audubon operates six wildlife education centers in Connecticut, California, Ohio, New Mexico, and Wisconsin, where outdoor classes and teacher-training workshops are held. Three summer ecology camps in Connecticut, Maine, and Wyoming provide classes for adults; the Maine camp also has sessions for children ages ten through fifteen. An expedition institute provides travel-study programs for high-school and college students. Several tours and cruises to international destinations are also offered. □

NATIONAL PARKS AND CONSERVATION ASSOCIATION

1776 MASSACHUSETTS AVENUE, NW

WASHINGTON, DC 20036

(202) 223-6722

FOUNDED: 1919   MEMBERS: 285,000
BUDGET: $9.6 million   STAFF: 48
TAX STATUS: 501(c)(3)

PURPOSE: "Defending, promoting, and improving our country's National Park System."

The National Parks and Conservation Association (NPCA) is the only environmental organization devoted solely to education and action in support of the national parks. Emerging during the 1980s from relative obscurity, NPCA has helped promote and defend an increasingly beleaguered national park system.

BACKGROUND: The National Parks Association was started in 1919 by Robert Sterling Yard, a journalist whose publicity helped build support for the creation of the National Park Service in 1916. With personal financial backing from his friend Stephen Mather, the first director of the Park Service, Yard set out to build a citizens' group that could be an advocate and watchdog for the national parks. Yard campaigned to restrict commercialization of the national parks, objecting to the jazz bands and bear shows he saw at Yosemite Park—leading to a break with Mather.

During the 1920s the Association fought to protect the parks against the dams of the Bureau of Reclamation and from encroachment by the automobile. With protection of wilderness areas in the parks a growing concern in the 1930s, Yard became a founder and first president of The Wilderness Society in 1935.

The Association continued to resist pressures for mining, logging, and hunting in the national parks, championing protection of the Everglades and establishment of the North Cascades National Park and the Cape Cod and Assateague national seashores in the 1960s. Recognizing that many environmental issues affect the parks—air and water pollution, population growth, patterns of development—the organization changed its name in 1970 to the National Parks and Conservation Association (NPCA) to acknowledge its wider interests.

CURRENT PRIORITIES: In the 1980s the NPCA was part of the coalition opposing the Reagan administration's environmental policies, and has continued to advocate a larger share of resources for the national parks. NPCA supports adding new parks to the federal system and expanding the boundaries of several existing parks and also emphasizes the preservation of cultural and historic resources and the development of urban parks. NPCA led a lawsuit against the National Rifle Association's effort to hunt and trap in the parks. NPCA also administers a million-dollar trust fund that buys privately owned land within the national parks and holds it for the National Park Service to purchase when federal funds are available.

MEMBERS: By 1992 the Association grew to 285,000 members, a number that increased rapidly from 25,000 in 1979, 60,000 in 1988, 100,000 in 1989, and 200,000 in 1990. A network of volunteer activists in the National Park Activist Program monitors conditions in specific parks and submits reports to the Washington office. "Contact" program volunteers write letters to Washington officials on issues as needed.

STRUCTURE: NPCA is governed by a thirty-three-member self-recruiting board of trustees, composed of business, academic, and conservation figures. An annual meeting is open to all members. NPCA maintains two regional offices, in Salt Lake City, Utah, and Cottonwood, Arizona.

RESOURCES: Revenue for 1991 of $9.6 million was derived from dues (49 percent), contributions (26 percent), grants (5 percent), bequests (11 percent), and other sources (9 percent). Expenditures of $8.6 million were divided 76 percent for program services and 24 percent for administration and fund-raising.

PUBLICATIONS AND SERVICES: Membership is $25 and includes *National Parks* magazine (circulation 300,000), published six times a year. Action Program participants receive a monthly newsletter, *Exchange*. For information on the national parks, see NPCA's catalog of books and guides that can be purchased by mail order. In 1986 NPCA published a ten-volume program for the national parks, *Investing in Park Futures*; a single-volume executive summary provides a handy synopsis. Information on travel to national parks, an affinity Gold MasterCard, and a photo-processing

service are available to members. NPCA has a toll-free hotline for information and for reporting poaching in the national parks: (800) NAT-PARK. ☐

THE IZAAK WALTON LEAGUE OF AMERICA
Defenders of soil, air, woods, waters and wildlife

IZAAK WALTON LEAGUE OF AMERICA

1701 N. FORT MYER DRIVE, SUITE 1100

ARLINGTON, VA 22209

(703) 528-1818

FOUNDED: 1922   MEMBERS: 53,000
CHAPTERS: 400   BUDGET: $1.8 million
STAFF: 27   TAX STATUS: 501(c)(3)

SLOGAN: "Defenders of soil, air, woods, waters and wildlife."

The Izaak Walton League of America (IWLA), whose members are fondly known as "Ikes," is centered on fishing and outdoor recreation, and has an impressive record promoting clean water in our nation's streams, rivers, and lakes.

BACKGROUND: IWLA, named after the patron saint of sport fishermen, was founded in 1922 by fifty-four sportsmen meeting in Chicago. Will Dilg, an advertising executive, became its energetic promoter. Dilg launched the League's magazine, *Outdoor America*, and turned it into the key journal of the conservation movement. Quickly gathering chapters in the Midwest, the League became the first conservation organization with a mass membership. At a time when neither the Sierra Club nor the National Audubon Society had more than 7,000 members, IWLA had attracted over 100,000 participants by the end of 1924. Conservation historian Stephen Fox characterized a typical League chapter as "a Rotary Club that liked to go fishing." Dilg and the League won an early legislative victory by getting Congress to establish the Upper Mississippi Wildlife and Fish Refuge, but the expense of the campaign and Dilg's erratic management left the League deeply in debt. The directors removed Dilg, who was dying from cancer, from the editorship of *Outdoor America* in 1925, and the annual convention ousted him as president in 1926.

IWLA took the lead in combating water pollution, preserving wetlands, and establishing wildlife refuges, spearheading unsuccessful efforts for clean water legislation throughout the 1930s. Initial victories were achieved with the weak federal water pollution acts in 1948 and 1956. The League's long campaign for strong federal legislation finally reached fruition with passage of the Clean Water Act of 1972. The League has been a significant participant in coalitions supporting federal legislation preserving wilderness and forests, and protecting such recreation areas as the New River in North Carolina and the Boundary Waters Canoe Area in Minnesota. Concerned with poaching by hunters in the central and Mississippi flyways, the League raised $600,000 to buy a helicopter and two airboats for the U.S. Fish and Wildlife Service. Jack Lorenz has been executive director of the League since 1974.

CURRENT PRIORITIES: Attempting to strike a balance among the varied interests of its members, the League has supported national parks as well as hunting preserves, and has worked to protect wilderness as well as areas for a variety of outdoor recreations. Presently the League is concentrating on four program areas within its tradition of interest and expertise: clean water and wetlands, including waterfowl management; clean air, acid rain, and related issues of energy efficiency; land and soil conservation; and outdoor ethics. The Save Our Streams (SOS) program is a long-running water quality–monitoring program involving activists in all fifty states. Since 1984 the League has emphasized its Chesapeake Bay regional program, which covers a watershed within which 25 percent of its members live. The League's Public Lands Restoration Task Force promotes rangeland restoration in the western states.

MEMBERS: Membership in IWLA declined from its peak of 100,000 in the 1920s to a stable level of some 50,000 members throughout the 1960s and 1970s. Never expanding much beyond its base in the Midwest and the Tidewater, the League did not share in the influx of members into such major environmental groups as the Sierra Club, the National Audubon Society, and The Wilderness Society in recent years.

STRUCTURE: IWLA is justly proud of being "an organization run by its members." At the annual convention delegates from the chapters elect the ninety-member board of directors and vote on the League's conservation poli-

cies. Implementation of policy is overseen by a thirteen-member executive
board that meets quarterly. Recently
the League has begun a program to
develop leadership at the grassroots.
There are 400 chapters and twenty-one
state divisions; most state divisions also
have an annual meeting. IWLA maintains a Midwest office in Minneapolis.
The League plans to build a new headquarters and national conservation center in its park outside Gaithersburg,
Maryland.

RESOURCES: IWLA's 1990 income of
$1.8 million consisted of membership
dues (39 percent), contributions and
grants (57 percent), and interest earnings and bequests (4 percent). Expenditures of $1.8 million were split 69
percent for conservation and education
programs, 11 percent for membership
services, 16 percent for administration,
and 4 percent for leadership development.

PUBLICATIONS AND SERVICES: Membership is $20 and includes *Outdoor
America* magazine (circulation 55,000),
published quarterly. *League Leader*
provides information to 2,000 chapter
and state officers. *Splash!* is a quarterly
newsletter for activists in the Save Our
Streams program. *Outdoor Ethics* (circulation 7,500) is a quarterly newsletter
for natural resource managers, outdoor
writers, hunter safety instructors, and
recreational groups. The League also
distributes a guide to citizen enforcement of the Clean Water Act. League
staff post legislative alerts on Compu-
Serve's Outdoors Forum. □

THE WILDERNESS SOCIETY

900 17TH STREET, NW

WASHINGTON, DC 20006

(202) 833-2300

FOUNDED: 1935   MEMBERS: 400,000
BUDGET: $18.1 million   STAFF: 128
TAX STATUS: 501(c)(3)

PURPOSE: "Preserving wilderness and
wildlife, protecting America's prime
forests, parks, rivers, and shorelands,
and fostering an American land ethic."

The vision, leadership, and persistence
of the Society were central to the passage of The Wilderness Act of 1964,
which preserved some 9 million acres
of federal lands as wilderness. The Society also played a major role in securing the Eastern Wilderness Act of 1971
as well as the Federal Land Policy and
Management Act (the charter for the
Bureau of Land Management) and the
National Forest Management Act, both
passed in 1976. Broke and on the ropes
by 1976, the Society recovered in time
to push the Alaska National Interest
Lands Conservation Act of 1980, which
preserved 104 million acres of wilderness. The Society works to protect the
federal public land systems, including
the national parks, national forests, national wildlife refuges, national wild
and scenic rivers, and federal land
overseen by the Bureau of Land Management—a territory that altogether to-
tals nearly one million square miles,
better than one-quarter of the nation's

land base. The Society's staff, whom an observer once likened to a band of wilderness guides, are now polished experts at legislative and administrative advocacy, backed by economic and ecological research and analysis, and combined with public outreach and education. In the Washington image of The Wilderness Society, the business suit has replaced the Pendleton shirt.

BACKGROUND: The Wilderness Society was organized in 1935, under the leadership of militant conservationist Robert Marshall. An anomaly in the WASP, Republican conservationist milieu, Marshall came from a Jewish family and was an active socialist. Although raised on the Upper West Side of Manhattan, Marshall spent summers with his family in the Adirondacks and decided to study forestry. After receiving a doctorate, he worked for the Bureau of Indian Affairs and the Forest Service. Joining Marshall in organizing the Society were Appalachian Trail advocate Benton McKaye; naturalist Aldo Leopold from the University of Wisconsin (author of *A Sand County Almanac* in 1949 and inspiration of the Society's "land ethic" philosophy); Robert Sterling Yard, former director of the National Parks Association; and Harold Anderson, an organizer of the Potomac Appalachian Trail Club.

Yard served as the Society's first secretary and editor of its new magazine, *The Living Wilderness*. Much of the budget of the Society was provided by gifts from Marshall, and after his sudden death in 1939 at age thirty-eight, the Society received income from a trust provided by Marshall's estate. After Yard's death in 1945, the direc-

tor's job was assumed by naturalist Olaus Murie, assisted by his wife, Margaret, from their home in Jackson Hole, Wyoming, while Howard Zahniser became editor of *The Living Wilderness* from Washington, D.C. Beginning in the late 1940s the Society began working more closely with the Sierra Club, particularly in the fight to save Echo Park in the Dinosaur National Monument from a Bureau of Reclamation dam. The eventual victory in 1955 resulted from increased cooperation among conservation groups, and inspired Zahniser to draft legislation giving permanent statutory protection to federal wilderness areas. Originally proposing some fifty million acres of wilderness, the wilderness bill went through eight years of hearings and redraftings in the Congress and was eventually reduced to nine million acres.

The Wilderness Act was passed by Congress in the summer of 1964 and signed by President Lyndon Johnson in September. Zahniser did not live to savor the victory; he died three months before passage of the act. As Olaus Murie had died in 1963, leadership of the Society's efforts to influence the implementation of the Wilderness Act fell to its new director, Stewart Brandborg. With federal agencies dragging their feet, the wilderness protection process went slowly, taking four years before the first units of land were designated. As a series of hearings were held, Brandborg and the Society alerted activists and organizations about the dates and places and the issues involved. The Wilderness Society grew with the new environmental movement, increasing in membership from 20,000 in 1960 to 87,000 by 1975.

Despite new members, financial problems arose. The cost of the legislative campaigns, expanded staff, and an expensive and unsuccessful lawsuit against the Alaskan oil pipeline led to several years of deficits. The lack of sound financial management, compounded by disputes with the staff, led the governing council to fire Brandborg in January 1976. The Society went through three difficult years, with membership dropping to 39,000 before a new long-term executive director was found. The last of the principal in Bob Marshall's endowment went to meet a payroll.

When William A. Turnage took over as executive director in November 1978, the survival of The Wilderness Society was in doubt. Within two years he had recruited a highly professional and talented new staff, enlarged the governing council by seeking out new members with backgrounds in philanthropy and politics, and begun to obtain major grants from foundations for the first time. Many of the old staff left or were pushed out—including Dave Foreman, who went on to form Earth First! The Republican electoral victories of 1980 removed from office former Democratic governor and three-term senator Gaylord Nelson of Wisconsin and Cecil Andrus, secretary of the interior under Jimmy Carter. Nelson joined the Society's staff in the new position of chairman, and Andrus serves as corporate consultant.

Even during the turmoil of reorganization, the Society continued its pressure for wilderness legislation, helping win passage of the Alaska National Interest Lands Conservation Act of 1980, which preserved 103 million acres as parks, refuges, and wilderness. In 1984, despite the hostility of the Reagan administration, the Society and the environmental movement won further victories with the passage of legislation that preserved an additional 8.6 million acres of wilderness. Turnage resigned as executive director of the Society at the end of 1985, leaving the organization with a membership of 125,000, a staff of 85, and an annual budget of $6.3 million. Attorney George Frampton was hired as executive director and has presided over a period of continued rapid growth.

The Wilderness Society has a strategic advantage in its mission, the protection and preservation of wilderness on federal lands, which is both vast in scope and limited in focus. By directing its attention only at a single level of government, the Society has developed a Washington staff skilled in lobbying at the center of federal legislative and administrative authority, and a field staff who can concentrate on a limited number of congressional representatives and senators. Frampton estimates that the Society can mobilize as many staff to lobby on wilderness issues as all other conservation organizations together, drawing on its management, conservation and research department, and field staff. The Wilderness Society also continues to develop the idea of a "land ethic," as proposed by its visionary cofounder, conservationist-author Aldo Leopold. Environmental historian Stephen Fox concludes, "Now The Society is one of the old-line, established conservation groups—but professionalized, its advocacy honed and polished. It has long since shed any trace of undirected and uninformed zeal. Yet . . . the organization is still far more than just another Washington interest group." It is what it set out to be, the foremost advocate of wilderness preservation.

CURRENT PRIORITIES: In a special series of seven issues of *Wilderness* from spring 1983 through fall 1984, the Society outlined its agenda for the rest of the century in seven key areas of concern for public lands: national parks, national forests, wildlife refuges, Bureau of Land Management lands, Alaska, the wilderness system, and the wild and scenic river system. The board of directors developed a four-year plan of action covering 1988–91 that identified major goals for the Society; included are (1) advocacy for wilderness in the fifty-year plans being developed by the Forest Service for the national forests, (2) protecting the great natural ecosystems surrounding the national parks, (3) obtaining wilderness designation for appropriate portions of Bureau of Land Management lands, and (4) defense of the Arctic coastal plain and the Tongass National Forest in Alaska. In 1991 the Society made protection of the ancient forests of California and the Pacific Northwest a top priority.

MEMBERS: Membership continued to grow rapidly during the second half of the 1980s, from 125,000 in 1985 to 360,000 by 1990. Members who sign up with the activist network receive Action Alerts on wilderness issues.

STRUCTURE: The Society's founders designed a self-recruiting governing council in hopes of perpetuating their steadfast commitment to wilderness.

Presently chairing the twenty-six-member council is Alice Rivlin, Brookings Institution economist and former director of the Congressional Budget Office. There is no chapter structure or direct election of representatives, but all members may participate in an activist network for lobbying activity. The Society maintains fourteen regional offices, which work to coordinate grassroots groups, Sierra Club and Audubon chapters, and regional organizations for legislative campaigns on wilderness and wildlife issues.

RESOURCES: Revenue in 1991 totaled $17 million, 49 percent derived from membership dues, 16 percent from contributions, 13 percent from telemarketing, 10 percent from grants, 5 percent from bequests, and 7 percent from other sources. Expenditures totaled $18.1 million, divided 74 percent for program services, 10 percent for administration, and 16 percent for fundraising and recruitment. In 1989 the Society launched a campaign to establish The Wilderness Fund, a $25 million permanent endowment.

PUBLICATIONS AND SERVICES: Membership is $30 and includes the quarterly magazine *Wilderness* (circulation 330,000). An excellent article by conservation historian Stephen Fox, " 'We Want No Straddlers' " (quoting founder Bob Marshall), in the Winter 1984 *Wilderness* traces the fifty-year history of the Society. On the twenty-fifth anniversary of the Wilderness Act, the Society reviewed its vision for the future of the nation's wildlands in the Spring 1989 *Wilderness*. Annual financial reports are published in the spring issue.

An affinity VISA card is available. For a biography of the central figure in the creation of the Society, see James Glover, *A Wilderness Original: The Life of Bob Marshall* (The Mountaineers, 1986). Seth Zuckerman's *Saving Our Ancient Forests* (Living Planet Press, 1991) is a handy brief guide developed by the Society. □

NATIONAL WILDLIFE FEDERATION

1412 16TH STREET, NW

WASHINGTON, DC 20036

(202) 797-6800

FOUNDED: 1936   MEMBERS: 1 million members of state affiliates, 970,000 associate members, and an additional 3.3 million subscribers to children's magazines and purchasers of materials   BUDGET: $90 million   STAFF: 630   TAX STATUS: 501(c)(3)

PURPOSE: "The wise use, conservation, aesthetic appreciation, and restoration of wildlife and other natural resources."

The largest of the conservation organizations, the National Wildlife Federation (NWF) is built upon a network of state affiliates, originally sportsmen's clubs. Concerned with conservation education for most of its history, NWF moved into environmental lobbying and litigation after 1976. Its wildlife publications have attracted an audience of adults and children that numbers in the millions.

BACKGROUND: J. N. "Ding" Darling was a celebrated editorial cartoonist for the Des Moines *Register*, a Republican, and an ardent duck hunter when his old friend agriculture secretary Henry Wallace offered to put him in charge of the Biological Survey in 1934. Although an unlikely bureaucrat for the New Deal administration of President Franklin Roosevelt, Darling in a year and a half established the Migratory Waterfowl Division within the Bureau, obtained several million dollars from Congress to establish wildlife refuges primarily for duck breeding grounds, and pushed Congress to pass the Duck Stamp Act. When he left the federal service in 1935, Darling was convinced that sportsmen needed a strong national organization to influence a sympathetic Roosevelt administration, which was under great pressure from commercial and business interests seeking to exploit natural resources. Darling and supporters called a national wildlife conference in Washington in 1936, at which a new organization, the General Wildlife Federation (GWF), was formed.

Rather than compete for individual members with the Audubon Societies and the Izaak Walton League, the new organization was structured as a federation of local and state sportsmen and conservation clubs. GWF held its first annual meeting in 1937 (the name was changed to National Wildlife Federation in 1938). The meeting set plans for what would become National Wildlife Week, an enduring tradition of the Federation. Its first lobbying victory came in 1937 with the passage of the Pittman-Robertson Wildlife Restoration Act, which established a federal excise tax on guns and ammunition to fund state wildlife conservation agencies.

Despite support from gun companies —its first cash contribution was $750 from the Remington Arms Company— the Federation remained in financial difficulty for several years. State affiliates were not obliged to send any dues revenue to the national Federation, and Darling started the NWF wildlife stamp program—even designing the first stamps himself—as a major fund-raising activity. As revenues did not meet expenses, NWF was forced to depend on loans to survive. Angered at the lack of support from the state groups and what he described as the "damned incompetent bunch of chowderheads" running the national organization, Darling resigned as honorary president in 1954, becoming reconciled with the Federation only a few months before his death at age eighty-five in 1962.

NWF was not able to hire its first full-time executive director until 1949. But by 1956 the Federation had over a million members in its state affiliates, and with sales of its Christmas wildlife stamps its gross income exceeded $1 million for the first time. A substantial bequest allowed the Federation to construct a headquarters several blocks north of the White House on 16th Street in Washington; the building was dedicated by President John Kennedy in 1961. The full potential of the Federation began to be realized under the leadership of Tom Kimball, a former director of the Colorado Fish and Game Department and organizer of the Colorado Wildlife Federation, who headed NWF from 1960 to 1981, a period in which the organization's annual budget increased from $500,000 to $31 million.

In 1961 Kimball introduced the concept of individual nonvoting associate membership, which would come along with a subscription to a new magazine, *National Wildlife*. The board of directors were skeptical—conservation magazines were already being published by the National Audubon Society, the Sierra Club, and The Wilderness Society. Modeled after the use of color nature photography by the successful *Arizona Highways* and promoted through the Federation's extensive mailing lists of affiliate members and buyers of wildlife stamps, *National Wildlife* at $5 a subscription was an immediate success, bringing in 67,000 associate members with its first issue in 1962. *International Wildlife* was added in 1969, alternating months with *National Wildlife*.

Board members representing sportsmen's clubs worried about losing influence to preservationists as the organization evolved in contradictory directions: Policy is made by the state sportsmen representatives in the annual meeting; the funding base is provided by the increasingly urban associate members, few of whom hunt or fish; and the organization's activities are carried out by a growing professional staff with a broad environmental vision. One controversy that challenged the sportsmen constituency was a request from the U.S. Fish and Wildlife Service that the 1976 NWF annual meeting endorse a ban on lead shot in hunting ammunition, which was accumulating in lakes and poisoning ducks. The National Rifle Association (NRA) opposed the requirement of steel shot loads, saying they would damage modern shotguns. NWF held firm in opposing lead shot, going to court to fight NRA, which filed suit to void the ban order. In the late 1970s NWF supported the Alaska National Interest Lands Conservation Act, opposed by NRA, various mining, oil, and timber interests—and by its own Alaska sportsmen's club. In the course of the dispute NWF dropped its Alaskan affiliate and organized a new Wildlife Federation of Alaska from its associate members in the state.

NWF had been shy of lobbying since its early dispute with the U.S. Treasury Department over tax-exempt status; it was unable to get the equivalent of today's charitable and educational designation (making contributions tax-deductible) until 1943, because of its support for the Pittman-Robertson Act in 1937. Once its (c)(3) status was confirmed, the NWF board was unwilling to rock the boat. Only when the Tax Reform Act of 1976 gave charitable and educational organizations greater latitude for legislative advocacy did NWF resume lobbying. Also in the 1970s NWF began to develop a staff of lawyers to challenge the government in court on wildlife issues. By 1989 there were eighteen litigating attorneys on the staff, with a docket of some ninety lawsuits; important victories were won to make states enforce surface mining reclamation laws and to limit mining on federal lands.

Following Kimball's retirement, Jay D. Hair, a former professor of zoology at North Carolina State University, was hired as chief executive in 1981. Optimistic and energetic, Hair moved quickly to establish his vigorous leadership and a more aggressive profile on environmental issues for the organiza-tion. He pushed NWF toward an uncharacteristic confrontation with the Reagan administration, calling for the resignation of James Watt as secretary of the interior and opposing the naming of Anne Burford, who had resigned under intense criticism as administrator of the Environmental Protection Agency, to chair the National Advisory Board on Oceans and Atmosphere. Hair was criticized by more radical environmentalists for inviting Dean Buntrock, chairman of Waste Management—who had been active with NWF's advisory corporate Conservation Council—to join the NWF board of directors. Replying in an interview "We're not selling out, we're buying in," Hair intends to position NWF as the most influential organization in the environmental policy arena.

CURRENT PRIORITIES: Conservation education remains NWF's primary activity through its magazines, special materials for teachers (including its NatureScope publication series), and its sponsorship of National Wildlife Week. The delegates to the NWF annual meeting each March adopt conservation policy resolutions to guide the staff; current priorities include (1) global environmental quality; (2) effective implementation of the federal "no net loss" policy for wetlands, and the wildlife habitat provisions of the 1990 Farm Bill; (3) continuing required use of excluder devises to protect sea turtles from shrimp nets; (4) increased emphasis on protecting forest ecosystems and biological diversity; (5) a national energy policy emphasizing efficiency and alternative technologies; (6) protection of wildlife habitat on Bureau of

Land Management lands from oil and gas exploration and drilling; and (7) opposition to building polluting facilities in economically disadvantaged and minority communities.

MEMBERS: NWF claims 5.3 million "members and supporters," a number that calls for examination. An impressive 1 million of these are members of the state wildlife federation affiliates, clearly establishing NWF as the largest of the conservation organizations. Another 970,000 people are "associate members," subscribers to *National Wildlife* and *International Wildlife*. The number of affiliate members peaked at 1.5 million in 1971 and has been declining since, as the associate ranks have grown. The 1.1 million children who receive *Ranger Rick* and *Your Big Backyard* magazines are also counted as supporters, as are the 1.9 million people who buy such NWF educational materials as wildlife conservation stamps and make catalog orders.

STRUCTURE: NWF is a federation of state affiliates, autonomous organizations in each of the fifty states, Puerto Rico, and the Virgin Islands, each with its own budget and membership, which may include local clubs as well as individuals. In 1991 the affiliates had budgets totaling nearly $16 million. Each affiliate organization selects a representative to the NWF annual meeting in March, which sets the policies that guide the national staff and provide a focus for the state organizations. The affiliate representatives also elect the NWF officers (including three regional vice presidents) and thirteen regional

directors, who constitute a majority of the twenty-seven-member board of directors; the board also elects several at-large directors. Criteria for affiliation are set by the board; occasional controversies have led to disaffiliation of state sportsmen groups and the formation of new state wildlife federations. NWF recently completed a $40 million expansion of its headquarters building in Washington, D.C. There are eight regional offices: Anchorage; Ann Arbor; Atlanta; Bismarck, North Dakota; Boulder; Missoula, Montana; Portland, Oregon; and Montpelier, Vermont.

RESOURCES: Revenue for 1991 totaled $87 million, derived from sale of nature materials (37 percent), associate memberships (19 percent), donations and bequests (16 percent), Ranger Rick memberships (14 percent), Your Big Backyard memberships (6 percent), and investment income and other revenue (8 percent). Expenditures totaled $85.9 million, divided among conservation education programs, including the cost of publications (69 percent), and support services, including membership and sales development (21 percent) and administration and fund-raising (10 percent). The NWF Endowment, Inc., a closely related 501(c)(3) corporation with an eleven-member board of trustees, increased its fund balance by $4 million to $40.9 million, the largest of any environmental group.

PUBLICATIONS AND SERVICES: Associate membership at $16 brings a subscription to *National Wildlife* (circulation 886,000) or *International Wildlife* (circulation 520,000), each published six times a year. "World members" at $22 receive both magazines, on alternate months. *Ranger Rick* (started in 1966, current circulation 890,000) is a monthly for children ages six to twelve available for a $15 subscription; and *Your Big Backyard* (launched in 1980, circulation 500,000) is a monthly for preschoolers ages three to five, available for a $12 subscription. A monthly newsletter with a focus on federal legislation, *EnviroAction* (circulation 30,000), is available free to members who sign up for NWF's activist network, the Resource Conservation Alliance. NWF's annual *Conservation Directory* contains an extensive listing of private organizations and government agencies at both national and state levels. Thomas B. Allen wrote the official fiftieth anniversary history, *Guardian of the Wild: The Story of the National Wildlife Federation, 1936–1986* (Indiana University Press, 1987). An annual report is available from the national office. NWF has a catalog of conservation education materials, and distributes a catalog of nature guides, wildlife books, and gifts along with its trademark conservation stamps. NWF also sponsors summer vacation programs for educators and conservationists, and camps for children and teenagers. The NWF Legislative Hotline offers a recorded message of current news: (202) 797-6655. An NWF affinity VISA card is available. □

DEFENDERS OF WILDLIFE

1244 19TH STREET, NW

WASHINGTON, DC 20036

(202) 659-9510

FOUNDED: 1947   MEMBERS: 80,000
BUDGET: $4.3 million   STAFF: 31
TAX STATUS: 501(c)(3)

PURPOSE: "The protection of all native wild animals and plants in their natural communities."

Defenders of Wildlife is the leading organization advocating protection of predator animals and their habitat and seeking the strengthening and enforcement of the Endangered Species Act and related legislation.

BACKGROUND: Founded as Defenders of Furbearers in 1947, Defenders of Wildlife changed its name in 1959 to reflect a broader interest in all threatened and endangered species. Mary Hazell Harris led the organization for many years, serving both as executive director and editor of *Defenders* magazine. Defenders was established to carry on work begun by the Anti-Steel-Trap League, founded in 1925 by Edward Breck, a navy intelligence officer, writer, adventurer, sportsman, and naturalist. Although most members personally oppose hunting and trapping, to preserve a broad alliance on wildlife issues Defenders has taken no official position in opposition to hunting—a perennial source of conflict within the organization. Defenders works comfortably in coalition with such groups as the Sierra Club and The Wilderness Society, and cooperates less easily on environmental education materials with the National Wildlife Federation and its sportsmen constituency.

Among its accomplishments, Defenders has had substantial success in emphasizing the positive role of predators in natural systems—particularly wolves, coyotes, bears, mountains lions, lynxes, and bobcats. Defenders encourages ranchers to rely on guard dogs to protect sheep, rather than use such dangerous poisons as strychnine. In recent years the organization has shifted its emphasis from single species to animal habitat and biological diversity, promoting habitat corridors between protected lands, thus allowing predators to move longer distances.

In the mid-1980s, Defenders experienced management problems, running through four chief executives in five years. Rupert Cutler, an experienced wildlife manager and assistant secretary of agriculture in the Carter administration, brought greater administrative stability to the organization in his term as president from 1988 through 1990. In 1991 Roger Schlickeisen was named president. He came to Defenders from four years as chief of staff to Senator Max Baucus (D-Montana), and from 1982 to 1986 he had been chief executive of Craver, Mathews, Smith and Co., a fund-raising and organizational development consulting firm that works with public interest groups and political campaigns.

CURRENT PRIORITIES: Defenders lobbies to strengthen and support the provisions and administration of such environmental laws as the Endangered Species Act, the Marine Mammal Protection Act, the Coastal Zone Management Act, the National Wildlife Refuge Administration Act, and the Convention on International Trade in Endangered Species (CITES). Current priorities include protecting the Arctic National Wildlife Refuge, banning wild bird imports, and reintroducing the wolf to the Yellowstone area. Continuing program concerns are the identification and protection of endangered species, the protection of natural wildlife ecosystems on public lands, and ecosystem management that enhances wildlife generally. Defenders champions nonlethal predator control—particularly protection of the wolf and bobcat—and limiting livestock grazing on public lands. Defenders also promotes wildlife education and appreciation, developing wildlife viewing guides in cooperation with state wildlife agencies, following a model publication for Oregon.

MEMBERS: Membership in Defenders has been at about 80,000 for several years. Among environmentalists, they are probably closest in sympathy with the humane and animal rights movements. An activist network of 8,500 members write letters and lobby on wolf reintroduction, dolphin protection, wild bird trade, wildlife refuge reform, and related issues.

STRUCTURE: Defenders is governed by a twenty-two-member board of directors elected by the membership at-large; directors serve three-year terms.

RESOURCES: Revenue for 1991 of $5.2 million was derived from membership dues (25 percent), contributions (39 percent), bequests (26 percent), investment income (5 percent), and other sources (5 percent). Expenditures of $4.4 million were divided 61 percent for program services (wildlife action, education, membership communication) and 39 percent for support services (management, membership development, and fund-raising). Defenders' endowment funds increased in 1991 to $3.6 million. A gift of some $9.2 million received in the late 1970s from the estate of eccentric millionaires George and Elia Whittel allowed Defenders to establish a wildlife sanctuary. In 1975 Defenders moved its Washington headquarters to a Victorian townhouse near DuPont Circle occupied for many years by *The New Republic* magazine.

PUBLICATIONS AND SERVICES: Membership dues are $25 and include *Defenders* magazine (circulation 65,000), published six times a year. Activist alerts go to members who sign up to write and lobby. Defenders affinity VISA and MasterCard are available. An annual program and financial report is published in the July/August issue of *Defenders*. □

THE NEW ENVIRONMENTALISTS

On Earth Day in April 1970 our contemporary environmental consciousness seemed to burst on the scene full-grown, in the midst of a turbulent era of civil rights, women's rights, and antiwar agitation. Standing back for perspective, we can see environmentalism as the confluence of the older conservation tradition and more recent efforts to apply ecological perspectives to quality of life and public health concerns—water and air pollution, toxic wastes, pesticides, and nuclear radiation.

Rachel Carson's surprise best-seller *Silent Spring* in 1962 popularized the idea that nature has a delicate balance and we humans are disrupting it to our own eventual grief. By the late 1960s a second wave of environmental legislation responded to the growing public concern with the impact of industrial society on the quality of life: the Water Pollution acts of 1967, 1970, and 1972; the Clean Air acts of 1965, 1970, and 1972; and the Pesticides Act of 1972, which finally banned the DDT denounced by Carson a decade before. The National Environmental Policy Act of 1970 consolidated responsibility for many regulative and enforcement jobs in the new Environmental Protection Agency. In 1963 Harry Caudill published *Night*

Comes to the Cumberlands, which described the devastation of eastern Kentucky by the coal industry as a human and an environmental catastrophe; the book helped spark not only a concern for regional poverty but also the long struggle leading to the Surface Mining Control and Reclamation Act of 1977.

Increased attention to personal development, physical fitness, and wellness contributed to a growing concern for the environment as a public health issue. As air and water pollution, pesticides, and toxic wastes came to public attention and debate, the protection of human beings became an important focus of the new environmental issues, much as animals and the natural world had been the center of the earlier conservation movement. The Santa Barbara oil spill of 1969; the energy crisis in the winter of 1973–74, precipitated by the oil cartel price hike; the Three Mile Island nuclear plant accident of 1979; the discovery of the greenhouse effect (first discussed by the Council on Environmental Quality in 1979 but only fastened in the public mind by the summer 1988 drought); the *Exxon Valdez* Alaska oil spill of 1989; the oil spills and wellhead fires of the Persian Gulf War in 1990—all focused attention on the ways industrial society damages the global environment to the detriment of human beings as well as wildlife.

Earth Day 1970 highlighted the emergence of a new environmental activism, which drew upon the youthful energy and demographic clout of the baby boom generation and gave rise to such organizations as Friends of the Earth (founded in 1969), Environmental Action (1970), Greenpeace (1970), and Clean Water Action (1971). Over the following decade they were joined by such groups as Earth First! (1980), Citizen's Clearinghouse for Hazardous Wastes (1981), Earth Island Institute (1982), and the National Toxics Campaign Fund (1984). The Student Environmental Action Coalition (1988) established a network of activists on college campuses, the largest national organization of student activists since the 1960s.

FRIENDS OF THE EARTH

FRIENDS OF THE EARTH

218 D STREET, SE

WASHINGTON, DC 20003

(202) 544-2600

FOUNDED: 1969   MEMBERS: 39,000
BUDGET: $3.1 million   STAFF: 50
TAX STATUS: 501 (c)(3): Friends of the Earth;
501(c)(4): Friends of the Earth (Action);
PAC: FOEPAC

PURPOSE: "Committed to the preservation, restoration, and rational use of the earth."

Friends of the Earth (FOE), the second organization founded by David Brower, barely survived his departure in 1986 in an acrimonious dispute that echoed his rift with the Sierra Club. Revitalized in 1989 through a merger with the Environmental Protection Institute (EPI) and the Oceanic Society (OS), FOE provides technical assistance to grassroots groups and leads the largest international network of autonomous environmental organizations.

BACKGROUND: Shortly after being forced to resign as executive director of the Sierra Club in 1969, David Brower founded Friends of the Earth, just in time to ride the wave of environmental enthusiasm generated by Earth Day 1970. Membership increased rapidly from the 1,000 charter members to 7,000 by 1971. FOE got an additional boost that year by a series of articles in *The New Yorker* by John McPhee, later published as *Encounters with the Arch-druid* (Farrar, Straus & Giroux, 1971), which sketched Brower's meetings with three antagonists—a geologist/mining engineer, a resort developer, and the head of the Bureau of Reclamation. Brower predictably began a publishing program, which achieved its major success with *The Environmental Handbook* on the heels of Earth Day. FOE established its headquarters in San Francisco, and quickly moved to set up an office in Washington, D.C. Two new organizations soon separated from the FOE Washington staff, the League of Conservation Voters in 1970 and in 1971 the Environmental Policy Center (which later refocused its activities as the Environmental Policy Institute).

FOE stationed itself at the cutting edge of the environmental movement. Although Brower's roots were in wilderness preservation, FOE took on many of the new issues raised by environmentalists. In addition to campaigns to preserve wild and endangered animals, FOE campaigned against the Alaska pipeline, the supersonic transport airplane (SST), and nuclear power—and in conjunction with board member Amory Lovins, promoted "soft energy paths." FOE played a major role in the statewide initiative against nuclear power in California in 1976 (although the initiative was defeated, it had the effect of stopping the development of new nuclear power plants in the state). In 1970 FOE entered an arena of controversy avoided by the rest of the conservation movement by opposing the Vietnam War and calling attention to the danger of the defoliant 2,4-D, better known as Agent Orange. With the election of President Reagan in 1980, FOE took out full-page newspaper ads soliciting membership while denouncing Interior secretary James Watt's plans to sell public lands in the West, expand leasing of federal lands for oil, gas, coal, timber, and grazing, and develop land along the edges of the national parks. In 1983 FOE again led the environmental movement by opposing the MX missile, arguing that nuclear war is the ultimate environmental issue.

Brower's international contacts had led to the formation in 1971 of FOE International, a loose federation of sister organizations. By good fortune, "Friends of the Earth" adapts favorably in most languages and countries, unlike such specifically American names as "Sierra Club." A small international office was established to assist cooperation among the affiliates. Groups in forty-four countries work together on acid rain, pesticides and agriculture, whaling, saving Antarctica from exploitation, preservation of tropical rain forests, ocean dumping of nuclear wastes, and nuclear disarmament.

FOE under Brower was a loosely structured organization, in which individual programs and projects maintained considerable autonomy. When Brower retired as executive director on the tenth anniversary of the organization in 1979 (continuing as chairman of the board of directors), FOE had substantial debt and a growing tension between Washington lobbying and grassroots activity. The succession to Brower was never clearly resolved, and several executive directors came and went. The publishing program had lost money and was suspended in 1982. In the face of a $700,000 deficit, serious staff cuts appeared inevitable early in 1984. With a majority of the board supporting cuts to reduce the debt, Brower on his own appealed to the members for emergency contributions. Brower was removed from the board for insubordination, threatened a lawsuit, and was reinstated. By the end of 1985, the board voted to close the San Francisco office and move its headquarters to Washington, D.C. A membership referendum sustained the board majority and the move, and Brower left FOE in 1986 to work through his Earth Island Institute.

Cynthia Wilson, former head of the National Audubon Society's Washington office, was hired as executive director in 1986 and struggled to sustain the organization while reducing its mountain of debt. FOE worked as the Washington lobby for grassroots campaigns on ozone depletion, pesticides, water resources, and energy conservation, and helped sustain the flourishing network of FOE International affiliates. FOE also strengthened its ties with the leading conservation organizations as a participant in the Group of Ten (Wilson was the only female executive director in the bunch). But FOE's future looked precarious—membership was down around 10,000, and weighed down with debt the organization had no working capital for a direct-mail campaign for new members. Discussions of a merger with Environmental Action were not successful. When a merger was arranged in 1989, there were two partners: the Environmental Policy Institute (the think tank that split from FOE in 1971) and the Oceanic Society, founded in 1972.

CURRENT PRIORITIES: The merged FOE brings together expertise on groundwater, coast, and ocean issues; nuclear policy; radioactive and toxic wastes; coal strip-mining; atmosphere and ozone; agriculture and biotechnology; and the ecological impact of international development. EPI's influence on Capitol Hill will be continued in the educational sphere by FOE and through direct and grassroots lobbying by FOE (Action).

MEMBERS: The new organization combines the 9,000 remaining members of FOE with the 30,000 of the Oceanic Society (EPI was not a membership group). Musician Paul McCartney promoted FOE International on his world tour in 1989–90, boosting efforts to reach a new generation of potential environmental activists.

STRUCTURE: FOE's merged board of directors has twenty-seven members, initially including eighteen from EPI, five from FOE, and four from OS. FOE (Action) has a five-member board of directors. An annual membership meeting in Washington fills vacancies on the FOE board. Philanthropist Herman Warsh, who chaired the board of EPI, chaired both FOE boards through the merger process; Washington attorney Linda Heller Kamm succeeded Warsh as chair in 1991. Mike Clark moved from president of EPI to direct the merged FOE, and stepped down in 1991. Jane Perkins, a founder of the New Populist Forum and former AFL-CIO staffer, was named president in 1992. FOE International, headquartered in Amsterdam, coordinates sister organizations in forty-four countries.

RESOURCES: FOE received revenue of $3.1 million in 1990, about one-third from member contributions and two-thirds from foundation grants. Expenses of $3 million were allocated 84 percent for program activities and 16 percent for management and fund-raising. FOE reduced its inherited deficit by $161,000 in 1990, leaving a debt of $258,000.

PUBLICATIONS AND SERVICES: Membership is $25 and includes the newsletter *Friends of the Earth* (circulation 15,000), published ten times a year. Oceanic Society Expeditions continues as the environmental travel arm of FOE, organizing ecotours worldwide from its San Francisco office: (415) 441-1106. An FOE affinity VISA card is available. For a view of FOE that communicates the excitement of the environmental movement during the 1970s, see the brief organizational history by Brower associate and former *Not Man Apart* editor Tom Turner, *Friends of the Earth: The First Sixteen Years*, available from Earth Island Institute. □

ENVIRONMENTAL ACTION

6930 CARROLL AVENUE, 6TH FLOOR

TAKOMA PARK, MD 20912

(202) 745-4870

FOUNDED: 1970   MEMBERS: 20,000
BUDGET: $1.25 million   STAFF: 29
TAX STATUS: 501(c)(4): Environmental Action;

501(c)(3): Environmental Action Foundation;
PAC: EnAct PAC

PURPOSE: "EA concentrates on the human environment and the dangerous impact of short-sighted corporate practices on environmental quality and public health. We believe in empowering citizens to work through the political process to win effective environmental protection with full citizen and corporate responsibility."

Best known for its "Dirty Dozen" campaigns, Environmental Action (EA) was the first major environmental group to avoid wilderness and wildlife issues and focus on the human environment and support to grassroots groups. EA has been the clearest embodiment of the new concern for the human environment as a matter of public health and welfare.

BACKGROUND: Environmental Action grew out of Earth Day, a nationwide day of rallies, demonstrations, and teach-ins on April 22, 1970. Denis Hayes, the organizer of the first Earth Day as well as the twentieth-anniversary event, served for a year as the first EA coordinator. EA jumped into public attention in 1970 with its annual Dirty Dozen campaign, a list of the twelve members of the House of Representatives who have the worst voting records on the environmental legislation before the Congress during the previous year (the campaign functions through EA's political action committee). In 1982 EA also announced a Filthy Five list of corporations whose political contributions were directed at candidates who opposed environmental legislation.

Always a relatively small organiza-tion, EA has developed its niche with expertise on three key issues: (1) electric utilities, including nuclear power generation and alternative renewable energy sources; (2) hazardous wastes and toxic substances; and (3) recycling and materials conservation. Staff attorney Scott Hempling has fought numerous cases with electrical utilities on behalf of grassroots ratepayer groups and environmental coalitions. EA staffs the Energy Conservation Coalition, targeting auto efficiency, least-cost electrical energy plans on the state level, and federal Department of Energy policy. EA has tackled plastic waste, calling for its reduction in packaging and for use only of truly recyclable plastics. Ruth Caplan, one of the few women to lead a national environmental organization, joined EA as a lobbyist in 1982 and has been executive director since 1985. Caplan uses a nautical analogy to describe EA's advantage as a small organization in responding rapidly to change: "Once the steamships—the Sierra Club, National Wildlife Federation, NRDC—set their course, they are very effective; but it takes them longer to make a mid-course correction. That's both their strength and their weakness. We like to play tugboat and help move larger organizations in new directions."

CURRENT PRIORITIES: EA's current legislative priorities include (1) a stronger Resource Conservation and Recovery Act to go beyond Superfund and develop tougher standards for toxic wastes and promote new markets for recycled materials; (2) the cleanup of radioactive wastes at nuclear weapons facilities; and (3) the reduction of global warming through increased energy efficiency and the reduced use of fossil fuels. EA's Toxics Education, Action and Mobilization (TEAM) campaign helps enforce the Community Right-To-Know law, winning a settlement from a citizen suit in Virginia and preparing cases in Maryland and Pennsylvania.

MEMBERS: EA's membership has been around 20,000 for several years. Three activist networks connect local efforts to national programs: the Solid Waste Alternative Project (SWAP), the Toxics Education, Action, and Mobilization (TEAM) campaign, (covering Maryland, Pennsylvania, and Virginia), and the Utility Action Network (emphasizing Ohio, Michigan, Indiana, and California).

STRUCTURE: EA's staff works as a collective and determines policy. In an unusual organizational innovation, all full-time staff are members of the board of directors. The EA Foundation has a seven-member board. In 1988 EA absorbed the Environmental Task Force (ETF), incorporating its newsletter *Re:Sources* as part of *Environmental Action* magazine, and adopting ETF's logo.

RESOURCES: EA refuses contributions from corporations, relying on membership dues, contributions from individuals, and foundation grants to the EA Foundation. The annual budget of EA and its foundation totaled $1.25 million in 1991. EA had income of $433,000, 61 percent from membership dues and contributions; and expenses of $509,000, including 76 percent for programs and the remainder for adminis-

tration and fund-raising. The EA Foundation had income of $818,000, 32 percent from contributions and 61 percent from grants; and expenses of $825,000, 85 percent for programs and the remainder for administration and fund-raising. EnAct/PAC spends modest amounts to publicize its Dirty Dozen and Filthy Five campaigns—$30,000 in 1986.

PUBLICATIONS AND SERVICES: Membership is $25 and includes *Environmental Action* magazine (circulation 16,000), published six times a year. *Wastelines*, a newsletter reporting on solid waste issues, and *Power Line*, covering citizen action on energy and electric utility issues, are available by subscription. For the twentieth anniversary of Earth Day, Ruth Caplan and the EA staff produced a useful guide to protecting the environment, *Our Earth, Ourselves* (Bantam Books, 1990). □

GREENPEACE

GREENPEACE USA

1436 U STREET, NW

WASHINGTON, DC 20009

(202) 462-1177

FOUNDED: 1971
CONTRIBUTORS: 1.8 million
BUDGET: $66.6 million   STAFF: 220
TAX STATUS: 501(c)(3): Greenpeace USA;
501(c)(4): Greenpeace Action

PURPOSE: "Preserving the Earth and all the life it supports."

From improvised protests to stop nuclear weapons testing in the Pacific and haphazard campaigns to save the whales, Greenpeace has grown into a powerful international structure of environmental activists. With principled agreement on nonviolent direct action, nonpartisanship, and internationalism, the pragmatic idealists of Greenpeace have mastered the vivid confrontational image to publicize their causes, score victories on issues from whales to toxic discharges, and mobilize a worldwide network of supporters.

BACKGROUND: Greenpeace began with a brief blockade of the border between the United States and Canada near Vancouver in October 1969, protesting U.S. underground nuclear testing at Amchitka in Alaska's Aleutian Islands. Two American pacifists and environmentalists, Jim Bohlen and Irving Stowe, had helped organize a chapter of the Sierra Club in British Columbia. Together with Paul Cote, a young Canadian lawyer, they set up the Don't Make a Wave Committee—consisting mostly of B.C. Sierra Clubbers—to continue protesting the nuclear weapons tests. Marie Bohlen suggested sailing a ship into the Amchitka test zone (the ships *Golden Rule* and *Phoenix* had attempted to sail into a nuclear test zone in 1958). During a planning meeting, Bill Darnell, a young Canadian, suggested combining peace and conservation concerns with the name "Greenpeace." Bohlen agreed their boat, if they could find one, would be called *Greenpeace*.

After searching for an appropriate and affordable vessel for several months, Bohlen met Captain John Cormack and learned of his old halibut seiner, the *Phyllis Cormack*. Deep in debt, Cormack was willing to lease his ship for the voyage to Amchitka. The Committee assembled a crew of twelve (three Americans and nine Canadians), dubbed the ship the *Greenpeace*, and set sail in September 1971. Five days from the test site, the ship was stopped by the U.S. Coast Guard in Alaska. Meanwhile a second ship, a fast former minesweeper named *Edgewater Fortune ("Greenpeace II")*, had secretly been leased by Bohlen and Stowe and was racing toward Amchitka—but was still 700 miles away when the blast was detonated. What might have been a failure was turned into a victory when the United States announced it would abandon nuclear testing on Amchitka and turn the site into a wildlife sanctuary.

Following the Amchitka campaign, the Don't Make a Wave Committee reorganized as the Greenpeace Foundation and decided its next project would be opposing French atmospheric nuclear testing at Moruroa in the South Pacific. Greenpeace recruited David McTaggart, a Canadian formerly from Vancouver, who was in New Zealand with his thirty-eight-foot ketch, *Vega*. McTaggart was a minor celebrity in Canada, known as a world-class badminton champion in the 1950s and the construction industry figure who built a ski lodge at Bear Valley in California, which he publicized with the famous "Ski Bear" poster, featuring his third wife skiing nude. The *Vega*, designated *Greenpeace III*, sailed for Moruroa in April 1972 with a crew of three including McTaggart. In July the *Vega* was rammed at sea by a French frigate and limped back to Rarotonga while the French nuclear tests went on as scheduled. The next summer McTaggart and the *Vega* returned to Moruroa with considerable attention from the international press. This time French commandos using a swift inflatable boat boarded the *Vega* and brutally beat McTaggart, permanently injuring his right eye, and threw cameras and film overboard. Fortunately a crew member had hidden a camera with one roll of film, providing wire services with pictures demolishing the French story that McTaggart had injured himself in a fall. In September 1973 McTaggart was in a Paris court suing the French government for ramming the *Vega* the previous year. On the first of November, France announced it was suspending all atmospheric nuclear tests in favor of underground testing.

After this victory, the Greenpeace activists were uncertain what to do next. The newly elected chairman of the Vancouver group, attorney Hamish Bruce—described as "an amazing blend of legalistic practicality and unfettered mysticism"—promoted a campaign to save the whales. Having learned from the French the tactical uses of motorized inflatable rafts called zodiacs, Greenpeace decided to sail the *Phyllis Cormack* out to challenge the Soviet whaling fleet in 1975. The voyage captured the world's attention with its dramatic film image of the Soviet ship *Vlastny* firing a harpoon within a few feet of a Greenpeace zodiac attempting to protect a pod of whales. The following year Greenpeace sent a team led by Paul Watson (who later split from the group to found the Sea Shepherd Soci-

ety) to protest the annual slaughter of baby harp seals on the ice off Newfoundland, producing another set of shocking images.

Greenpeace kept up its confrontations with the whaling fleets of the Soviet Union, Spain, Peru, Iceland, and Japan from the late 1970s through the 1980s. The campaigns produced results: The sperm whale was protected after 1979 and the International Whaling Commission declared a moratorium in the commercial harvest of whales—reducing the kill from over 25,000 in 1975 to 1,000 for "scientific research" after 1986—and the European Economic Community banned the import of seal fur. Successful in drawing attention to nuclear testing and the threat to marine mammals, Greenpeace initiated a third campaign—against ocean pollution—in 1977, intercepting a British ship transporting nuclear waste to an ocean dump site, blocking waste dumping ships in the Netherlands in 1980 and 1982, and confronting ocean incinerator ships burning hazardous wastes in the North Sea in 1984. In the United States the toxics fight was brought to inland waterways with the Great Lakes campaign in 1985, when Greenpeace activists blocked a Dow Chemical toxic discharge pipe on the shore of Lake Huron.

Greenpeace's continuing campaign against French nuclear testing in the Pacific drew a violent response in 1985 when French secret agents planted bombs that sank the *Rainbow Warrior* while docked in Auckland, New Zealand. Crew member Fernando Pereira, a journalist and photographer from Portugal, was killed by the explosions. After an initial cover-up, scandal, and special investigation, the French socialist government admitted responsibility and eventually provided Greenpeace with $8 million in settlement of damages. The bombing of the *Rainbow Warrior* drew attention and sympathy, and in the following years Greenpeace vastly expanded its donor base and contributions with fund-raising techniques ranging from a door-to-door canvass to "World Alert" video commercials on cable music channel VH-1. The "Rainbow Warriors" record album—featuring such groups as U2, Sting, R.E.M., and The Grateful Dead—sold four million copies in the Soviet Union, launching a new Greenpeace office in Moscow. The mutual affinity between rock musicians and Greenpeace may relate to the youth of the Greenpeace staff—a majority are in their twenties and thirties, including Greenpeace USA executive director Peter Bahouth and Greenpeace International executive director Stephen Sawyer.

CURRENT PRIORITIES: Charged in the past with a disorganized and scattergun approach to publicizing environmental problems, the board of directors of Greenpeace now conducts an annual review of activities and identifies the campaign targets for the coming year. Presently Greenpeace focuses on six primary campaigns: (1) *Ocean Ecology:* Continuing its famous efforts to protect whales, dolphins, and sea turtles, the organization has added the Antarctica campaign, spearheaded by Greenpeace's World Park Base, the only nongovernmental installation on the continent. (2) *Nuclear Disarmament:* In addition to ongoing work to end nuclear weapons testing, in 1987 Greenpeace initiated a campaign for nuclear-free seas, with the goal of eliminating all naval nuclear weapons (this effort has been criticized by some peace groups that view submarine-based weapons as a nearly invulnerable, and therefore stabilizing, deterrent force while nuclear disarmament is being negotiated). (3) *Toxics:* Greenpeace opposes hazardous waste incineration and waste dumping in Third World countries, emphasizing prevention through safe technologies at the industrial source and comprehensive recycling programs. (4) *Atmosphere and Energy:* In this new campaign initiated in 1989, Greenpeace supports the immediate substitution of safe alternatives to all ozone-destroying chemicals, the sharp reduction of pollution from automobiles and fossil fuel energy plants, and the development of energy-efficient homes and businesses as well as renewable energy sources. (5) *Pacific:* Following Greenpeace's tradition in defense of the Pacific Ocean, the new flagship *Rainbow Warrior* will oppose ocean incineration, nuclear weapons testing and transport, hazardous waste trade, pesticide abuse, and destructive fishing methods. (6) *Tropical Forests:* Greenpeace opposes the destruction of rain forests by commercial logging, cattle ranching, and industrial development.

Greenpeace has been spared ideological controversy by not developing a full-blown world view (although a "vision statement" has been under discussion), retaining instead a pragmatic idealism that concentrates on attainable objectives. McTaggart has developed a consensus around three principles: nonviolent direct action, avoiding alliances with political parties, and international approaches to global issues.

CONTRIBUTORS: Greenpeace does not accept contributions from governments or private corporations. The number of individual contributors in the United States expanded rapidly, from 450,000 in 1985 to 600,000 in 1988 and leaped to 1.38 million in 1989 and 2.1 million in 1990, as a result of an effective door-to-door canvass, direct mail, and publicity through rock concerts and videos. Contributors fell back to 1.8 million in the 1991 recession. A 1985 survey suggests the typical Greenpeace USA contributor is younger (46 percent between ages eighteen and thirty-four) and more likely to be female (72 percent) than supporters of other environmental groups. By 1990 Greenpeace International had over 4 million contributors worldwide and a total income of over $100 million.

STRUCTURE: For several years Greenpeace operated with a very loose structure—regional offices in the United States incorporated as separate organizations. Greenpeace functioned as a staff-directed organization, emphasizing such dramatic and often dangerous activities as scaling polluting smokestacks, hanging banners from bridges, and rappelling down cliffs, leading many participants to burn out after periods of intense activity. Rapid turnover often resulted in chaotic administration. Conflicts came to a head when the Vancouver office charged the San Francisco office with trademark violations for using the Greenpeace name. McTaggart intervened and fashioned a new Greenpeace International structure and a unified organization in the United States, where six independent regional groups were merged into a single 501(c)(3) organization, Greenpeace USA, in 1987. Greenpeace Action was incorporated as a 501(c)(4) organization to emphasize grassroots lobbying on legislation. Greenpeace USA has a minimal three-member board of directors, elected by staff with six or more years of service. Greenpeace has regional offices in Boston; Chicago; Denver; Honolulu; Jacksonville Beach, Florida; San Francisco; and Seattle.

During the 1970s Greenpeace groups spread across Canada, Western Europe, Australia, and New Zealand. Greenpeace International was incorporated in the Netherlands in 1979, with David McTaggart serving as chairman, promoting closer cooperation among the often feisty national organizations. Finnish lawyer Matti Wuori was appointed chairman in 1991. Headquartered in Amsterdam, Greenpeace International coordinates a network of affiliates in twenty-three countries, now including Japan, Costa Rica, and Russia. All affiliates that contribute 24 percent of income to the International organization are represented on the International's board of directors. Greenpeace International is taking a significant initiative to support new affiliates in the former USSR and in Latin America, its first important push outside the developed countries. Greenpeace USA is one of twelve voting members of the Stichting Greenpeace Council, the body of Greenpeace affiliates around the world that develops campaign policies.

RESOURCES: For 1990, Greenpeace USA received $47.6 million in revenues, 76 percent from contributions and donations, 7 percent from grants from affiliates, 7 percent from merchandise sales, and 10 percent from other sources. Expenses totaled $48.2 million, allocated 38 percent for program campaigns, 40 percent for other program services (including grants to Greenpeace International), 19 percent for fund-raising, and 3 percent for management. Although it ran a $587,000 deficit, Greenpeace USA retained reserves of $12.6 million. In 1990 Greenpeace Action received $16.5 million in revenue, almost entirely from contributions, and spent $18.4 million, 64 percent on program campaigns, 6 percent on publications, 22 percent on fund-raising, and 8 percent on management. Fund-raising in 1991 was down over 20 percent, a result of the recession, requiring a reduction in staff. Greenpeace International estimates the total income of its affiliates at $160 million in 1991, from some five million contributors worldwide. The International organization operates with a $32 million budget. Title to the "Greenpeace navy" of seven ships and the "Greenpeace air force" of two helicopters and one hot-air balloon is held by the International organization.

PUBLICATIONS AND SERVICES: Contributors of $30 or more receive *Greenpeace* (circulation 1.5 million), published quarterly—reduced from a magazine to a newsletter in 1992 as an economy measure. You can pay your bills with Greenpeace "message checks." Clothing and other merchandise are available via catalog mail order. Greenpeace's computer network, EnviroNet, has E-mail and conferences open to the public without charge, but there is only one general access telephone number: (415) 861-6503 (a toll-free 800 number is available to nonprofit organizations upon approval). Greenpeace press releases are posted on EcoNet.

The first years of Greenpeace are recounted in Robert Hunter, *Warriors of the Rainbow: A Chronicle of the Greenpeace Movement* (Holt, Rinehart and Winston, 1979). The initial challenge to French nuclear testing in the Pacific is covered in *Greenpeace III: Journey into the Bomb*, by David McTaggart with Robert Hunter (London: William Collins Sons, 1978). David Robie's *Eyes of Fire: The Last Voyage of the Rainbow Warrior* (New Society Publishers, 1986) tells the story behind the sinking of the Greenpeace flagship in New Zealand by agents of the French secret service. Michael Brown and John May's *The Greenpeace Story* (1989; New York: Dorling Kindersley, 1991) is a recent illustrated history updated for Greenpeace's twentieth anniversary. □

CLEAN WATER ACTION

1320 18TH STREET, NW

WASHINGTON, DC 20036

(202) 457-1286

FOUNDED: 1971   MEMBERS: 400,000
BUDGET: $6 million   STAFF: 90
TAX STATUS: 501(c)(4): Clean Water Action;

501(c)(3): Clean Water Fund; PAC: CWA Vote Environment

PURPOSE: "Working for clean and safe water at an affordable cost, control of toxic chemicals, and protection of our natural resources."

Clean Water Action (CWA) emerged from Ralph Nader's task force on water pollution to become a powerful lobby for the major clean water legislation of the early 1970s. After developing a grassroots canvass program in the mid-1970s, CWA has linked up citizens groups in several key states to fight for safe drinking water, combat toxic hazards, and battle to protect lakes, bays, and ocean coasts.

BACKGROUND: David Zwick, a Harvard law student working with Ralph Nader's Center for Study of Responsive Law, coauthored *Water Wasteland: The Ralph Nader Report on Water Pollution* (Grossman, 1971)—which led him to create an advocacy organization to lobby for passage of the Clean Water Act of 1972 and the Safe Drinking Water Act of 1974. Between 1975 and 1978 Zwick worked for the Illinois Public Action Council, where he learned how to run a door-to-door canvass. Returning to Washington, Zwick revitalized CWA as a canvass-based organization devoted to clean water issues. CWA moved into toxic hazards issues working to pass the Superfund Act in 1986.

CURRENT PRIORITIES: CWA's agenda includes (1) enforcement of the Clean Water Act and the Safe Drinking Water Act; (2) toxic hazard campaigns emphasizing solid waste, moving away from incineration and landfills toward source reduction and recycling; (3) a program on coastal and inland waterways emphasizing Chesapeake Bay, the Atlantic shore and the New England coast, and the Great Lakes (CWA has a joint program with Friends of the Earth on coastal policy, emphasizing sewage treatment and ocean dumping); and (4) an environmental shopping campaign emphasizing safer products.

STRUCTURE: CWA has a ten-member, self-recruiting board of directors.

RESOURCES: CWA raises virtually all of its $5 million revenue through its canvass operation. The Clean Water Fund raises $1 million through foundation grants, corporate matching gifts, and special events. During the 1990 campaign cycle, CWA Vote Environment raised $100,000 for electioneering. CWA is strongest in the New England, Mid-Atlantic, and Midwest regions, with twenty-four field offices in fourteen states: Maryland, Virginia, Pennsylvania, New Jersey, Massachusetts, Rhode Island, Minnesota, Michigan, Iowa, North Dakota, Wisconsin, Texas, Colorado, and California.

PUBLICATIONS AND SERVICES: "Subscribing members" (who contribute $24 or more) receive the quarterly *Clean Water Action News* (circulation 200,000). □

EARTH FIRST!

P.O. BOX 5176

MISSOULA, MT 59806

(406) 728-8114

FOUNDED: 1980   SUBSCRIBERS: 15,000
BUDGET: $84,000   STAFF: 4
TAX STATUS: 501(c)(4): Earth First! Journal;
501(c)(3): Fund for Wild Nature

SLOGAN: "No compromise in defense of Mother Earth!"

Demonstrators in grizzly bear suits confront rangers at Yellowstone National Park. A 300-foot zigzag strip of black plastic, simulating a crack, is unfurled down the face of the Glen Canyon Dam in Arizona—dramatizing a demand that the dam be torn down. Tree-sitters in California stop a logging operation in old-growth redwoods. It could only be Earth First!, a network of loosely affiliated groups and individuals, the militant direct-action, no-compromise wing of the environmental movement.

BACKGROUND: Dave Foreman helped start the Earth First! network in 1980 after leaving the staff of The Wilderness Society. As the southwest regional representative and a Washington, D.C., lobbyist for the Society, Foreman grew critical of the compromises of environmental politics in Washington and of the professionalization of environmental organizations. He was joined by like-minded friends, including Howie Wolke, Bart Koehler, Ron Kezar, Mike

Roselle, and Susan Morgan, most of whom were also former staffers of environmental groups, to rally direct action in defense of wilderness and wildlife. Although it adopts—even defines—the style of the new enviroactivists, Earth First!'s concerns remain largely within the domain of the traditional conservation movement.

Much of the early Earth First! activity was directed toward the Roadless Area Review and Evaluation Act (RARE II) studies of wilderness land by the Forest Service. Earth First! has conducted non-violent civil disobedience in blockades of logging operations in western and southwestern Oregon, occupied the Missoula office of Montana Senator John Melcher to protest the exclusion of a critical grizzly bear habitat from the Montana Wilderness Bill, and opposed the proposed nuclear waste dump near Canyonlands National Park in Utah.

Although its usual tactics are guerrilla theater or nonviolent civil disobedience, Earth First! introduced the specter of environmental sabotage or "ecotage" into the movement. Some adherents take tactical inspiration from Edward Abbey's novel, *The Monkey Wrench Gang* (Lippincott, 1975). "Monkeywrenching," which its advocates defend as nonviolent, includes spiking trees, disabling heavy equipment, cutting fences, disrupting traplines, and cutting down billboards. In a 1985 interview with the *Wall Street Journal*, a Louisiana-Pacific Company spokesman denounced Earth First!'s monkeywrenching tactics, tree spiking in particular, as "environmental terrorism." Many environmentalists committed to nonviolent action concur. Writer Edward Abbey, the Earth First! guru who died in 1989, offered the most influential defense of ecotage. In a "Plowboy Interview" in *The Mother Earth News*, May/June 1984, Abbey—a self-described "half-time crusader and part-time fanatic"—distinguished between terrorism as violence against human beings and sabotage as "violence against inanimate objects: machinery and property." Sabotage, he argued, may be morally justified when legal resistance to the destruction of the environment has failed.

Although hundreds of Earth First!ers have chosen to be arrested in nonviolent direct actions, few have ever been charged with surreptitious ecotage. In 1986 Earth First! cofounder Howie Wolke was sentenced to six months in jail in Pinedale, Wyoming, for pulling up survey stakes on a road being built by Chevron Oil Company in the Bridger-Teton National Forest. Wolke's action remained the leading case until overshadowed by the FBI's dramatic arrest in May 1989 of three people—Mark Davis, Marc Baker, and Peg Millett—surprised in the desert ninety miles northwest of Phoenix while cutting the base of a power line tower. The next day the FBI charged Dave Foreman and the three others with conspiracy to destroy nuclear facilities in Arizona, California, and Colorado. In December a grand jury indicted a fifth activist, Ilse Asplund. Of the three at the tower, only Millett had been active with Earth First! The Arizona Earth First! groups had been infiltrated by an FBI agent. Foreman denied any connection with the plot, but as his trial began he entered a guilty plea to one count of conspiracy and received a sus-

pended sentence. Davis, Baker, Asplund, and Millett pleaded guilty to charges of sabotaging ski lift pylons at Snowbowl near Flagstaff in 1987 and received jail sentences.

Meanwhile, other controversies—some practical, some philosophical—were creating fissures in the Earth First! network. Foreman saw Earth First! grounded in "deep ecology," a term coined by Norwegian philosopher Arne Naess in a 1973 essay, a vision of the world that is nature-centered rather than human-centered. Deep ecology's notion of biocentric equality argues that all life forms have equal value. As articulated by "Miss Ann Thropy" in a discussion of overpopulation in the May 1987 *Earth First! Journal*, AIDS and the Ethiopian famine are nature's way of responding to human pollution. Although such pen names as "Australopithecus" and bumper stickers as "Back to the Pleistocene" are tongue-in-cheek humor, to critics they also reflect the romantic primitivism and heedless antihumanism of some Earth First! proponents. The argument over deep ecology within Earth First! coincided with a similar debate in the growing Green political movement. Social ecologist Murray Bookchin led the attack on deep ecology and Foreman, calling his approach "eco-brutalism." Foreman responded to criticism from other Earth First!ers by withdrawing from editing the *Journal* and retreating to work on his autobiography.

A related debate over monkeywrenching came to a head during the Redwood Summer demonstrations in 1990. Proposed by northern California Earth First! activists on the model of the Mississippi Summer Project of

1964, Redwood Summer appealed to young people to come to Mendocino and Humboldt counties to stop clear-cutting of remaining old-growth forests. Judy Bari, a leader of the protests, had worked as a union organizer and saw the importance of reaching out to workers whose jobs were being threatened by timber company overcutting as well as by pending initiative legislation and the Earth First! demonstrations. Redwood Summer planners decided the protest would be guided by the principles and tactics of nonviolent direct action. Two years before, a sawmill worker had been injured in adjacent Sonoma County when a blade shattered on a spiked tree; Bari explicitly denounced tree spiking and affirmed the nonviolent character of Redwood Summer. Earth First! cofounder and northern California action team leader Mike Roselle, who had defended monkey-wrenching for several years, supported Bari, and seventeen Earth First! activists in the Pacific Northwest signed a letter renouncing tree spiking. Foreman reacted with anger, seeing the statement as a betrayal of biocentrism in favor of humanism. The issue was temporarily displaced by a sudden tragedy.

Just as Redwood Summer was getting under way in late May, a pipe bomb exploded in Judy Bari's car in Oakland, severely injuring her and causing lesser injuries to Darryl Cherney. To the astonishment of many supporters, Bari and Cherney were themselves arrested by Oakland police as suspects. An anonymous letter claiming responsibility for the bombing, signed "The Lord's Avenger," was received by a Sonoma County newspaper. No charges were brought against Bari and Cherney, how-ever, and the police investigation continues at the time of this writing. A coalition of environmental and civil liberties groups—including Greenpeace, Friends of the Earth, the Sierra Club, the National Audubon Society, the National Wildlife Federation, and the American Civil Liberties Union—criticized the conduct of local officials and the FBI and requested a full and impartial congressional investigation of the bombing.

As the Redwood Summer protests were winding up, Dave Foreman announced his resignation from Earth First!, saying he was no longer comfortable with the northern California activists, whom he denounced as advocating class struggle rather than wilderness preservation, and as being leftist in political orientation and overtly counter-culture and anti-establishment in style. Mike Roselle, a leading target of Foreman's criticism, responded, "We don't need Foreman in Earth First! if he's going to be an unrepentant right-wing thug. He's a retired old man out on the lecture circuit." Critics charge Foreman as a college student supported Barry Goldwater's 1964 campaign for president, is still a registered Republican, and underneath his radical rhetoric is really a misanthropic conservative who supports wilderness preservation.

CURRENT PRIORITIES: Local Earth First! groups around the country continue to monitor Forest Service proposals and devise alternative wilderness plans. In the eastern United States, Earth First!ers have drawn up detailed surveys of remaining old-growth forests. Across the West, Earth First! groups fight timber-harvest plans for national forests, fight the use of motor vehicles in the desert (inspiring the creation of the Sahara Club, a self-styled "direct reaction" group of off-road motorcyclists), and oppose livestock grazing on public lands.

Without a formal organizational structure, Earth First! has no democratic means of resolving or compromising conflicts that threaten to tear it apart. Lacking a clear principled commitment to nonviolence in direct action, Earth First! is especially vulnerable to agents provocateurs. A contrasting comparison can be made with Greenpeace, which adopted nonviolent direct action in the Quaker spirit and enhanced its organizational accountability through a strengthened formal structure. Former *Journal* editor John Davis noted three aspects to Earth First!— movement, philosophy, tribe—and analyzed their evolution. Although the movement for direct action in defense of wilderness and wildlife has expanded rapidly and found many supporters, not all share Foreman's embrace of monkeywrenching. The philosophy of biocentrism is challenged by many with sympathies closer to social ecology. Finally, the "tribal" friendship of the founding group who gathered in the first few years for the Round River Rendezvous has been overwhelmed by newcomers as well as by the tactical and philosophic controversies that threaten to split the non-organization.

STRUCTURE: Earth First! defines itself as a movement, not an organization. Each issue of the *Journal* contains a directory that lists groups identified with the Earth First! movement: In 1992 there were twelve offices with specific projects, international groups in five countries (Australia, Germany, India, Poland, and United Kingdom), and over 110 local groups and contacts in the United States and Canada.

With no central organization, there are no formal members, just "Earth First!ers," as Foreman described in the May 1985 *Journal,* including a diversity "from animal rights vegetarians to wilderness hunting guides, from monkeywrenchers to careful followers of Gandhi, from rowdy backwoods buckaroos to thoughtful philosophers, from bitter misanthropes to true humanitarians." An annual summer Round River Rendezvous, traditionally held in a national forest, serves as the "tribal gathering of stronghearts," an occasion for discussing issues and planning actions around the campfire.

RESOURCES: The Earth First! Foundation was incorporated as a 501(c)(3) organization in 1982, and in 1991 changed its name to Fund for Wild Nature (P.O. Box 1683, Corvallis, OR 97339). The Fund, governed by a volunteer board of nine directors including Bill Devall, Linda Wells, Richard Grossman, and Randy Hayes, accepts contributions to provide technical assistance to local groups and to make small grants for research and legal action on wilderness issues and related educational programs. From 1989 to 1991, the Fund distributed $188,000 in grants to Earth First!ers and other conservationists. A nondeductible Direct Action Fund (P.O. Box 210, Canyon, CA 94516; 510-376-7329), coordinated by Karen Pickett, raised $27,000 and spent $20,000 in 1991.

PUBLICATIONS AND SERVICES: *Earth First! Journal,* subscription $20, is published eight times a year in newspaper tabloid format. In 1991 publication of the *Journal* was transferred from associates of Dave Foreman to a new collective in Missoula, Montana; Foreman views the current *Journal* as an entirely new publication. Memorable articles from the first decade are collected in *The Earth First! Reader: Ten Years of Radical Environmentalism*, edited by Foreman associate John Davis (Peregrine Smith, 1991).

Dave Foreman sells books by mail order from Ned Ludd Books, P.O. Box 5141, Tucson, AZ 85703. Included are *Ecodefense: A Field Guide to Monkeywrenching*, edited by Dave Foreman and Bill Haywood, 2nd ed. (Ned Ludd Books, 1989); *The Big Outside: A Descriptive Inventory of the Big Wilderness Areas of the USA*, by Dave Foreman and Howie Wolke (Ned Ludd Books, 1990), updating Bill Marshall's classic 1936 roadless area inventory; and Foreman's autobiography, *Confessions of an Eco-Warrior* (Harmony Books, 1991). Foreman is executive editor of the new journal, *Wild Earth* (circulation 3,600), P.O. Box 492, Canton, NY 13617, available for a $20 subscription. □

CITIZEN'S CLEARINGHOUSE FOR HAZARDOUS WASTES

P.O. BOX 6806

FALLS CHURCH, VA 22040

(703) 237-2249

FOUNDED: 1981   MEMBERS: 7,000
BUDGET: $806,000   STAFF: 14
TAX STATUS: 501(c)(3)

SLOGAN: "People united for environmental justice."

Citizen's Clearinghouse for Hazardous Wastes (CCHW), founded by Love Canal activist Lois Gibbs, is the hub for a network of local organizations battling polluters. CCHW provides training and technical assistance for the "grassroots movement for environmental justice," local groups fighting for clean and healthy places to live and work.

BACKGROUND: Lois Gibbs was a homemaker who became president of the Love Canal Homeowners Association in Niagara Falls, New York, representing 900 families who fought for relocation benefits between 1978 and 1980 after learning their neighborhood was built next to 21,000 tons of toxic wastes left behind by Hooker Chemical and Plastics. As women had miscarriages and kids got sick, people began to ask questions. Gibbs's Homeowners Association helped get the national attention that in 1980 resulted in the Superfund legislation to clean up toxic chemical dumps.

Gibbs founded CCHW in 1981 to assist local groups in organizing and fighting polluters, emphasizing low-income, rural, and minority communities. CCHW has a flair for the dramatic, sponsoring the "McToxics Campaign" in 1989, sending Styrofoam back to McDonald's—protesting a token recycling program. McDonald's agreed to commit $100 million toward source reduction and recycling (but the Environmental Defense Fund claimed credit for negotiating the agreement). By linking groups together across the nation, CCHW hopes to change people's attitudes from NIMBY (not in my backyard!) to NIABY (not in *anybody's* backyard!). Gibbs received the Goldman Environmental Prize in 1990 as a "grassroots environmental hero."

CURRENT PRIORITIES: CCHW continues to assist local groups opposing incinerators, solid waste dumps, and military waste hazards. CCHW provides grassroots groups with organizing training, technical assistance, and information services. The organization has been considering changing its name to Center for Environmental Justice.

MEMBERS: CCHW's network includes 1,700 grassroots toxics groups, 400 multi-issue neighborhood groups, 300 labor and religious leaders, and 1,300 local chapters of national environmental organizations.

STRUCTURE: CCHW has a ten-member, self-recruiting board of directors; five are grassroots leaders, four are professionals, and one works for a national labor union. Emphasizing services to Appalachia, the South, the Midwest, and the Southwest, there are five regional offices in Riverside, California; Atlanta, Georgia; Spencerville, Ohio; Wendel, Pennsylvania; and Floyd, Virginia. Gibbs serves as executive director.

RESOURCES: With a low-income constituency, CCHW's revenue of $806,000 in 1991 relied on foundations for 70 percent of its support, contributors and members for 22 percent and other sources for 8 percent. Expenditures of $752,000 went for program services (84 percent), and administration and fundraising (16 percent).

PUBLICATIONS AND SERVICES: The newsletter *Everyone's Backyard*, published six times a year, is available for a $25 subscription. An annual report is available. CCHW's publications catalog lists four dozen guides and handbooks. □

Earth Island Institute

EARTH ISLAND INSTITUTE

300 BROADWAY, SUITE 28

SAN FRANCISCO, CA 94133-3312

(415) 788-3666

FOUNDED: 1982   MEMBERS: 35,000
BUDGET: $1 million   STAFF: 30
TAX STATUS: 501(c)(3): Earth Island Institute;
501(c)(4): Earth Island Action Group

PURPOSE: "To foster environmental awareness and action on the local, regional, national and international levels."

Earth Island Institute is archdruid David Brower's incubator of environmental projects with a global reach. Like a public interest venture fund, Earth Island nurtures visionary ecological start-ups, spinning off some autonomous projects and maintaining others.

BACKGROUND: Earth Island Institute is the third major organization (after Friends of the Earth and League of Conservation Voters) Brower founded after leaving the Sierra Club in 1969. When he lost a fight for control of the FOE board in 1985 and the group moved to Washington, Brower activated the structure he had incorporated in 1982 and kept on the shelf. Remaining in the San Francisco Bay area, Brower set up a loosely structured home for innovative environmental projects.

Earth Island won its most publicized victory in the campaign to stop tuna fleets from setting drift nets on dolphins. Industry denials of dolphin slaughter ceased when Sam LaBudde, working undercover on a tuna seiner, videotaped dolphin kills in purse-seine nets. Following a consumer boycott led by Earth Island, in 1990 StarKist owner H. J. Heinz became the first company to refuse to purchase tuna caught by techniques endangering dolphins.

CURRENT PRIORITIES: As an "early warning system for environmentalists," Earth Island provides a start-up home for projects often combining ecology, peace, minority rights, and Third World development issues: Randy Hayes's Rainforest Action Network started under Brower's umbrella; the Environmental Project on Central America (EPOCA) addresses ecology and social justice. After the dolphin victory, Earth Island began a campaign to pressure the Mexican government to protect the giant olive ridley sea turtle, which lays its eggs at a few beaches along the Pacific coast.

STRUCTURE: Earth Island has a nineteen-member, self-recruiting board of directors (the staff elects one member), chaired by David Brower, who stays in the background as codirectors David

Philips and John Knox coordinate day-to-day activities. Brower continues a tradition from the Sierra Club and FOE with his Biennial Congress on the Fate and Hope of the Earth (the 1989 conference was held in Managua). Sympathetic organizations around the country are loosely affiliated as Earth Island Centers.

RESOURCES: Over half of Earth Island's budget of $1 million comes from foundation grants for projects; the remainder is primarily individual contributions.

PUBLICATIONS AND SERVICES: Contributors of $25 or more receive the quarterly magazine *Earth Island Journal* (circulation 35,000). □

NATIONAL TOXICS CAMPAIGN FUND

1168 COMMONWEALTH AVENUE

BOSTON, MA 02134

(617) 232-0327

FOUNDED: 1984   AFFILIATES: 1,400 labor, environmental, and citizens groups
BUDGET: $1 million   STAFF: 35
TAX STATUS: 501(c)(3): National Toxics Campaign Fund

PURPOSE: "Protecting the health and environment of communities by preventing pollution at the source."

The National Toxics Campaign Fund (NTCF) coordinates a nationwide network of grassroots groups fighting toxic wastes, incineration projects, pesticides, and ozone layer destruction.

BACKGROUND: John O'Connor, who had worked for Massachusetts Fair Share and coauthored the Massachusetts Right-to-Know law, founded the National Toxics Campaign (NTC) in 1984 together with a group of friends from Clark University. NTC coordinated a major campaign around the Superfund authorization fights in the mid-1980s.

From Boston Harbor to Yellow Creek in the mountains of eastern Kentucky, NTC joined with grassroots community groups to build its national network. One of the largest affiliates was the 70,000-member Texans United, which got Governor Ann Richards to call for a two-year moratorium on toxic incineration and injection wells. Pioneering an environmentalist-labor alliance, in Louisiana NTCF has joined hands with the Oil, Chemical and Atomic Workers union against the German chemical manufacturer BASF, to save jobs and protect workers and their communities. The NTCF Consumer Pesticides Project worked with five major supermarket chains to hammer out an agreement to stop selling fruits and vegetables treated with cancer-causing pesticides by 1995.

Major lobbying and community victories include reauthorization of the Resource Conservation and Recovery Act (RCRA); joining Greenpeace Action and Clean Water Action in the "War on Waste" campaign; lobbying Congress to limit incineration of waste, reduce toxic chemicals, expand citizens' right-to-know about toxic facilities, and end siting of unwanted facilities in low-income and minority neighborhoods.

CURRENT PRIORITIES: Current programs include the Military Toxics Network, which monitors the nation's largest polluter, the Department of Defense. NTCF has set up its own facility for chemical analysis, the Citizens' Environmental Laboratory (certified by the EPA), to serve members and affiliated groups at reduced rates. NTCF is making a major effort against "environmental racism," the placement of toxic dumps and hazardous facilities in communities of color.

STRUCTURE: NTC was set up as a (c)(4) lobbying organization; after running up a substantial deficit, NTC was shut down in 1992. Emphasis shifted to the (c)(3) NTCF, which can be supported by foundation grants. NTCF has a twenty-eight-member, self-recruiting board, selected to represent the geographic, gender, race, and age diversity of its grassroots constituency. John O'Connor is the NTCF chair, and Gary Cohen is the executive director. There are eight field offices in six states—Maine, Oklahoma, North Carolina, California, Vermont, and Louisiana.

RESOURCES: NTCF's budget of $1 million is supported by foundation grants (70 percent) and contributions (30 percent) raised primarily through a door-to-door canvass.

PUBLICATIONS AND SERVICES: Contributors of $15 or more receive the quarterly newsletter *Toxic Times*. NTCF publishes a variety of manuals and reports for organizers and activists. For a useful citizen's guide by NTCF leaders see *Fighting Toxics: A Manual for Protecting Your Family, Community and Workplace*, edited by Gary Cohen and John O'Conner (Island Press, 1990). □

STUDENT ENVIRONMENTAL ACTION COALITION

P.O. BOX 1168

CHAPEL HILL, NC 27514-1168

(919) 967-4600

FOUNDED: 1988   MEMBERS: 3,000

CHAPTERS: 1,000   BUDGET: $250,000

STAFF: 8   TAX STATUS: 501(c)(3)

PURPOSE: "A grassroots democratic network working to build a strong student movement to save the planet."

Student Environmental Action Coalition (SEAC—pronounced "seek") is the first national student environmental organization, and the largest national student group since Students for a Democratic Society in the 1960s.

BACKGROUND: During 1988 students in an environmental group at the University of North Carolina (UNC) at Chapel Hill began working with students from neighboring Duke University to help preserve the Arctic National Wildlife Refuge. Realizing that a national network would give students greater impact, UNC students placed a note in *Greenpeace* magazine and were surprised to get responses from 200 campus groups. Over the summer of 1989, the UNC SEAC group planned the first national student environmental conference, "Threshold." Held in October 1989 at the University of North Carolina at Chapel Hill, Threshold drew 1,700 students. In spring 1990 students held state rallies supporting a federal Native Forest Protection Act, and brought 500 students to Washington to lobby for a strong Clean Air Act renewal. The second national conference, "Catalyst," in October 1990, was planned for 3,000 and drew 7,600 to the University of Illinois. A democratic structure was developed. The third national conference, "Common Ground," was held in October 1991 at the University of Colorado.

CURRENT PRIORITIES: The ASEED program (Action for Solidarity and Equality in Environment and Development) developed an international youth platform on environmental and social justice issues for the 1992 United Nations Conference on Environmental Development in Brazil. The 1992 Toxic Summer project provided a dozen student internships with community environmental groups fighting toxic pollution in Louisiana. The annual conference is a major activity for the national office and the host campus.

MEMBERS: Although SEAC has built an impressive network of campus groups, it has not done as well getting students to pay national membership dues; only some 3,000 individuals were paid members in 1992.

STRUCTURE: SEAC is organized into seventeen regions, each with an elected regional coordinating group (RCG), which organizes state and regional conferences. Over 1,000 colleges and high schools have groups or contacts. The SEAC national council is composed of representatives from the seventeen RCGs, three at-large members from the people of color caucus, the national office representative, and the five-member accountability board. Regional councils and state and local groups retain complete autonomy. The national office remains in Chapel Hill, North Carolina. SEAC functions as a sponsored project of the Partnership for Democracy (formerly The Youth Project).

RESOURCES: With a limited group of individual dues-paying members, most of SEAC's funding comes from foundations, including W. Alton Jones, New World, and Rockefeller Family Fund.

PUBLICATIONS AND SERVICES: Student membership is $15 and includes the newsletter *Threshold* monthly during the school year. The *SEAC Organizing Guide* and *High School Organizing Guide* are manuals for setting up active chapters, and *Campus Environmental Audit* is a guide to researching the environmental condition of a college campus. SEAC wrote *The Student Environmental Action Guide* (Earthworks Press, 1991). □

LEGAL EAGLES AND PACS

A "third wave" of organizations developed sophisticated legal, technical, and lobbying strategies, including the Environmental Defense Fund (1967), the Natural Resources Defense Council (1970), and the Sierra Club Legal Defense Fund (1971). The Sierra Club,

Friends of the Earth, Environmental Action, and Clean Water Action developed affiliated PACs to communicate with and solicit contributions from their members. The League of Conservation Voters (1970) was set up as a single major independent environmental PAC, free to solicit from the general public. In reaction to the success of environmentalists, conservatives formed their own groups to pursue legal strategies and develop market-oriented energy, environmental, and land-use approaches; examples include Pacific Legal Foundation (1973)—profiled in Chapter 10, Conservatives—and Mountain States Legal Foundation (1977).

ENVIRONMENTAL DEFENSE FUND

ENVIRONMENTAL DEFENSE FUND
257 PARK AVENUE SOUTH
NEW YORK, NY 10010
(212) 505-2100

FOUNDED: 1967 MEMBERS: 200,000
BUDGET: $18.5 million STAFF: 130
TAX STATUS: 501(c)(3)

SLOGAN: "The power of positive solutions."

The Environmental Defense Fund (EDF) combines law, science, and economics—and a particular talent for comparing the price tags of policy alternatives and making the market work for the environment. From a modest start dealing with DDT on New York's Long

Island, EDF now fields a nationwide staff widely acknowledged as experts in endangered species, utility rates, water conservation, and recycling. EDF staff have changed the framework for electrical energy planning in California, developed the pollution control approach adopted in the 1990 Clean Air Act amendments, and established a task force with McDonald's to reduce trash generated by its 11,000 restaurants worldwide.

BACKGROUND: Concerned that the pesticide DDT had harmed the local osprey population, a group of scientists and naturalists on Long Island teamed with an attorney in 1966 to present courtroom testimony that succeeded in eliminating the use of DDT in local mosquito control. Encouraged by this success, they organized the Environmental Defense Fund in 1967, housing its office first in the attic over the Stony Brook Post Office and then from 1970 to 1977 in a farmhouse in Setauket. Taking their case to other states, EDF staff finally convinced the Environmental Protection Agency to ban the use of DDT nationwide in 1972. Wildlife protection and toxic chemicals, concerns central to the DDT campaign, continue to be two important areas of environmental expertise at EDF. The model of teamwork established between attorneys and scientists has been expanded to include economists and computer experts. EDF has developed a special niche applying economic analysis to energy alternatives, water allocation, and pollution control.

EDF has assisted many important wildlife conservation victories since the DDT ban. Representing a group of con-

servation organizations, EDF won a federal court ruling under the Marine Mammal Protection Act of 1972 that reduced the porpoise kill by the tuna fishing industry from 300,000 to 15,000 by 1979. EDF supported the strengthening of the Convention on International Trade in Endangered Species (CITES), and worked for reauthorization of a strengthened Endangered Species Act in 1985. EDF has made the protection of rare wild plants a special concern, helping states develop programs to qualify for federal assistance under the act. As many developed countries begin to assess the commercial potential of Antarctica's natural resources, EDF has taken the lead to protect this wilderness continent.

EDF's energy program produced the classic example of harnessing economics and computer technology to the environmental cause. Economist Zach Willey was convinced conservation and alternative energy sources would prove cheaper than building new nuclear and coal electrical generating plants. When the complex mathematics of investment costs outran his hand calculator, Willey hired programmer Daniel Kirshner to develop a computer model, now widely known as ELFIN. The California Public Utilities Commission uses ELFIN, and after several years of opposition the program was adopted by Pacific Gas and Electric Company, which proceeded to develop model programs of conservation and alternative energy sources (the story is related by EDF attorney David Roe in *Dynamos and Virgins*, Random House, 1984). Willey has gone on to work on California's heavily subsidized, underpriced, and wasteful water programs. He is setting up mechanisms for owners of agricultural water rights to sell surplus water at market rates to cities and other consumers. Staff senior scientist Michael Oppenheimer has become a nationally recognized authority on acid rain and global climate change (his book *Dead Heat: The Race Against the Greenhouse Effect*, coauthored by Robert H. Boyle, was published by Basic Books in 1990), and EDF developed the market incentive approach to acid rain reduction included in the 1990 Clean Air Act. Executive directors have included Janet Welsh Brown (1978–1983) and Frederick Krupp, from 1984 to date.

CURRENT PRIORITIES: EDF's list of nine critical environmental problems and program priorities for the 1990s includes (1) the greenhouse effect, (2) wildlife and habitat, (3) ozone depletion, (4) saving the rain forests, (5) acid rain, (6) clean water, (7) toxic wastes, (8) preserving Antarctica, and (9) recycling.

MEMBERS: Membership has increased rapidly, from 50,000 in 1985 to 200,000 in 1990.

STRUCTURE: EDF has a forty-member, self-recruiting board of trustees, chaired by George Montgomery, Jr., managing director of investment banker Hambrecht and Quist. Field offices are located in Austin, Texas; Boulder, Colorado; Oakland, California; Raleigh, North Carolina; and Washington, D.C.

RESOURCES: EDF received $18.5 million in revenue in 1991, 67 percent from its 200,000 individual contributors, another 24 percent from foundations, and the remainder from investments, attor-

neys' fees, and other sources. Expenditures of $17.8 million were divided 80 percent for program services and 20 percent for support services (management, membership development, and fund-raising). EDF launched a capital campaign in 1987 with a goal of $7.5 million; by 1992, $9 million in gifts and pledges had been raised and fifteen endowed funds established. Included among the professional staff are twenty-five attorneys and thirty-nine scientists and economists.

PUBLICATIONS AND SERVICES: Membership is $20 and includes the *EDF Letter*, published six times a year, and an annual report. Retired staffer Marion Rogers has written an organizational history, *Acorn Days: The Environmental Defense Fund and How It Grew* (1990), available from the New York office. Affinity VISA and MasterCard are available. □

NATURAL RESOURCES DEFENSE COUNCIL

40 W. 20TH STREET

NEW YORK, NY 10011

(212) 727-2700

FOUNDED: 1970   MEMBERS: 170,000
BUDGET: $17.5 million   STAFF: 150
TAX STATUS: 501(c)(3)

SLOGAN: "The power of law, science and people in defense of the environment."

The Natural Resources Defense Council (NRDC) is often called a "shadow EPA." It combines the clout of the New York liberal legal establishment with the savvy of Washington beltway insiders. With a staff of dedicated scientists and lawyers, NRDC has earned its reputation as the most influential environmental legal advocate, and has undertaken a dramatic initiative to end nuclear weapons testing.

BACKGROUND: NRDC was organized in 1970 with the help of a Ford Foundation grant by a group that included recent Yale Law School graduates, led by Gus Speth, and established New York lawyers, including Whitney North Seymour, Jr., and Stephen P. Duggan. Duggan had been involved with the famous Storm King case, which blocked a power plant on the Hudson River and established vital precedents for environmental law. An initial emphasis on enforcing and expanding the Clean Air Act has led to a highly regarded record of environmental litigation and advocacy. A survey of Washington environmental policy professionals, reported in the April 1985 issue of *The Environmental Forum*, ranked NRDC as the most effective group attempting to influence federal policy-making on pollution control issues.

NRDC has a substantial record of achievement making clean air, clean water, and toxic substances into public health issues. In 1973 NRDC pushed the Environmental Protection Agency to restrict lead additives in gasoline; it continued to campaign for the elimination of lead and other dangerous additives and for emission standards for gasoline and diesel engines. Attorneys from NRDC have led court battles over sulfur dioxide emissions from coal-burning electrical power plants—the leading cause of acid rain. They have also sued steel companies over air and water pollution. The effort to ban fluorocarbons in aerosol products was led and won by NRDC in 1976. NRDC has also pushed federal and state agencies for strict enforcement of laws regulating strip-mining for coal.

In 1986 NRDC established a partnership with the Soviet Academy of Sciences to demonstrate that underground nuclear tests can be detected, the central issue of verification essential for a nuclear testing moratorium or test ban treaty. A research team established three seismic monitoring sites around the primary Soviet nuclear weapons test site to gather data on how shock waves travel through the earth in that region. Subsequently a Soviet team was invited to the United States under NRDC sponsorship for similar monitoring. The exchange angered conservatives, who saw it as an unprecedented private intrusion into arms control negotiations.

The all-American apple is unsafe? NRDC's campaign against the use of Alar in its 1989 report, "Intolerable Risks: Pesticides in Our Children's Food," brought widespread attention to NRDC's long-standing battle against dangerous agricultural chemicals. CBS's "60 Minutes" featured the story, and actress Meryl Streep led a public education campaign that quickly led to the abandonment of Alar by apple growers. Industry leaders, government officials, and conservatives maintained the risk was greatly exaggerated.

John Adams, a former assistant U.S. attorney, has been executive director of NRDC since its founding in 1970. Many of the NRDC senior staff have been on board for several years, providing more stability and continuity than most public interest groups achieve.

CURRENT PRIORITIES: NRDC uses four tools of environmental advocacy—litigation, lobbying, public education, and negotiation—in six program areas: (1) The *Water and Coastal* program aids citizen enforcement of clean water laws, conserving western water supplies, and protecting coastal resources, including the Arctic National Wildlife Refuge; (2) the *Land* program works to protect national forests, endangered species, desert and prairie lands, agricultural resources, and tropical rain forests; (3) the *Public Health* program exposes the dangers of toxic wastes and pesticides; (4) the *Urban* program concentrates on challenges faced by New York City and Los Angeles with recycling and waste reduction, clean air standards, waste water treatment, energy conservation, and environmental justice for people of color; (5) the *Air and Energy* program includes enforcing the Clean Air Act, limiting acid rain, and seeking low-cost alternatives to power plant construction, including energy efficiency and renewable energy resources; (6) the *International and Nuclear* program includes promoting environmentally sound assistance to developing countries by the World Bank and the U.S. Agency for International Development, methods of eliminating nuclear weapons, and cleaning up the environmental damage from nuclear weapons production.

MEMBERS: Membership has increased substantially from 29,000 in 1980 to 55,000 in 1985 to 170,000 in 1990.

STRUCTURE: NRDC has a forty-two-member board of trustees, chaired by Adrian W. DeWind, elected by the membership (most voting by proxy) from a nominated slate at the annual meeting. Stephen P. Duggan was the founding board chairman, serving from 1970 to 1980. The board includes philanthropist Laurance Rockefeller and actor Robert Redford. Field offices are located in Honolulu, Los Angeles, San Francisco, and Washington, D.C.

RESOURCES: In 1991 NRDC received revenues of $17.5 million, with 59 percent contributed by individuals and 27 percent by foundations; and 14 percent received from fees, investment income, special events, and contracts. Expenses of $17.7 million were divided 78 percent for program services, 11 percent for management, and 11 percent for membership development and fundraising. NRDC's new $6 million headquarters in New York is "the most energy-efficient remodeled office space in the United States." NRDC lists twenty-nine attorneys, nine scientists, and eighteen resource specialists among its employees. A Rockefeller and two third-generation Kennedys work on the legal staff.

PUBLICATIONS AND SERVICES: Membership is $20 and includes the quarterly magazine *The Amicus Journal* (circulation 170,000), a highly respected forum for discussion of national and international environmental affairs, founded in 1979 and edited by Peter Borelli through 1990 and subsequently by Francesca Lyman. A summary annual report is published. NRDC's *Nuclear Weapons Databook* series is an important reference. *The Rainforest Book*, by Scott Lewis with NRDC (Living Planet Press, 1990), is a convenient popular guide. Mary Nichols and Stanley Young coauthored *The Amazing L.A. Environment: A Handbook for Change* (1991) to help southern Californians restore their environment. □

SIERRA CLUB LEGAL DEFENSE FUND

180 MONTGOMERY STREET, SUITE 1400

SAN FRANCISCO, CA 94104

(415) 627-6700

FOUNDED: 1971 CONTRIBUTORS: 120,000
BUDGET: $9.8 million STAFF: 87
TAX STATUS: 501(c)(3)

SLOGAN: "The law firm for the environmental movement."

The Sierra Club Legal Defense Fund (SCLDF) has represented not only the Sierra Club but over 175 environmental organizations in numerous significant cases. It provides legal services without charge to environmental groups ranging from national organizations to neighborhood associations. A network of cooperating attorneys extends SCLDF's reach throughout the country.

BACKGROUND: The field of environmental law began to emerge in the mid-1960s following victory in the *Scenic Hudson* case, which granted an organization "standing to sue" based on its members' "aesthetic, conservational, and recreational" interest. *Scenic Hudson* also required a federal agency to consider and weigh alternatives based on scenic values as well as ones representing economic interests. Armed with this new concept of standing, in 1969 attorneys working with the Sierra Club challenged plans of Walt Disney to build a gigantic ski resort in the Mineral King Valley, adjacent to Sequoia National Park. Following victory in the suit, the Sierra Club began work to set up its own environmental law team as a separate 501(c)(3) organization. Since its founding in 1971, SCLDF has served not just as legal staff to the Sierra Club for generating its own docket of litigation, but as the environmental law firm for over 175 conservation organizations and citizens groups across the country. Clients have ranged from the Adirondack Council to the Hawaii Audubon Society, from Greenpeace USA to the Rainforest Action Network. Frederic Sutherland was executive director from 1980 until his death in 1991.

CURRENT PRIORITIES: Although its primary focus has been the protection of public lands in the West, SCLDF's agenda has expanded to include air and water pollution, hazardous wastes, and regulation of land uses in all parts of the country—with tentative steps toward the arena of international environmental law. The current SCLDF docket includes cases in the areas of wildlife and habitat, national forest planning, coasts and wetlands, other public lands, clean air, clean water, and public water rights. The largest current cases involve Pacific Northwest old-growth forests and the spotted owl, the Sand Island sewage treatment plant in Honolulu, the Tongass National Forest and the *Exxon Valdez* oil spill in Alaska, and water contamination by dioxin.

STRUCTURE: SCLDF has a twenty-four-member, self-recruiting board of trustees, most of whom are attorneys or other long-time leaders of the Sierra Club. Field offices have been maintained in Denver, Juneau, Honolulu, Seattle, and Washington, D.C.; new offices in New Orleans and Tallahassee were opened in 1991. The eighty-seven-member staff includes thirty-six attorneys. Michael Traynor is president and chief executive. In 1991 SCLDF helped form the Sierra Legal Defence Fund of Vancouver, which will litigate conservation issues in British Columbia.

RESOURCES: SCLDF's revenue for 1991 of $9.8 million was derived 62 percent from individual contributions, 16 percent from foundations, 10 percent from donated services, 6 percent from court-awarded fees and costs, and 6 percent from investments and book sales. Expenses of $9.7 million were divided 77 percent for programs, 4 percent for administration, and 19 percent for fundraising. The balance of $1.5 million was held in reserve to cover ongoing litigation. In 1991 SCLDF trustees launched a memorial Rick Sutherland Fund with personal contributions totaling $1 million, with a goal of a $5 million endowment to help support the organization.

PUBLICATIONS AND SERVICES: Contributors receive *In Brief: A Quarterly News-letter on Environmental Law.* Tom Turner, staff writer for SCLDF, has written the official history in the coffee-table format *Wild by Law: The Sierra Club Legal Defense Fund and the Places It Has Saved* (1990), which includes over a hundred color photographs by Carr Clifton of lands protected by SCLDF. An annual report is available from the San Francisco headquarters. □

LEAGUE OF CONSERVATION VOTERS

1707 L STREET, NW, SUITE 550

WASHINGTON, DC 20036

(202) 785-8683

FOUNDED: 1970   CONTRIBUTORS: 17,300 mail; 67,000 in New England canvass
BUDGET: $750,000   STAFF: 8
TAX STATUS: PAC

The League of Conservation Voters (LCV) is the leading electoral action arm of the environmental movement.

BACKGROUND: LCV was founded in 1970 by Friends of the Earth as a political action committee (PAC). To solicit contributions from the public, not just FOE members, LCV reorganized to become a "nonconnected" or independent PAC. Unofficially, major activist environmental organizations coordinate electoral strategy through LCV, which gives direct contributions to candidates, organizes press conferences, and runs radio ads for candidates (featuring such celebrities as Robert Redford), and hires organizers—the "Greencorps"—to provide assistance for campaigns in the field and conduct door-to-door canvasses in key states.

STRUCTURE: LCV's twenty-two-member, self-recruiting board includes directors that not coincidentally are associated with the Sierra Club, the National Audubon Society, The Wilderness Society, the Izaak Walton League, the National Parks and Conservation Association, Defenders of Wildlife, Environmental Action, the Environmental Defense Fund, the Natural Resources Defense Council, Friends of the Earth, and other groups. The board decides which issues to use to rate legislators, and which candidates to support in election campaigns. From its founding in 1970 through the 1984 elections, LCV was directed by Marion Edey. Alden Meyer moved from Environmental Action to serve as executive director from 1985 through 1987. Jim Maddy became executive director in 1988. On the state level, there are several "leagues of conservation voters" not formally associated with the national LCV; particularly active and effective groups are found in California, Florida, Oregon, and New York.

RESOURCES: In 1986 LCV raised nearly $3.8 million, placing in the top ten PACs nationally. In the 1988 presidential campaign cycle LCV raised over $3.3 million, a figure that dropped to just under $2 million in the 1990 cycle.

PUBLICATIONS AND SERVICES: LCV publishes the *National Environmental Scorecard* every two years, rating U.S. senators and representatives by their voting records on key environmental bills before Congress. □

LAND AND WILDLIFE PRESERVATION

While the Sierra Club, Friends of the Earth, Greenpeace, and others redefined environmental activism during the 1960s and 1970s, noncontroversial programs of land and wildlife conservation also found support growing rapidly. The warning "once it's gone, it's gone forever" began to sink in—across the political spectrum. Conservatives naturally prefer private ownership over public control, and liberals are willing to support effective means—public or private—to save wildlife habitat. Ducks Unlimited (founded in 1937) has long drawn support from waterfowl hunters for wetlands protection. The Nature Conservancy (1951), the World Wildlife Fund (1961), and various national and local land trusts have attracted thousands of new members and donors eager to save critical areas from development. In the 1980s international causes from African wildlife to tropical rain forests attracted special attention from the land and wildlife protection groups.

The Nature Conservancy

THE NATURE CONSERVANCY

1815 N. LYNN STREET

ARLINGTON, VA 22209

(703) 841-8781

FOUNDED: 1951   Members: 600,000
BUDGET: $255 million   STAFF: 1,200
TAX STATUS: 501(c)(3)

PURPOSE: "To preserve plants, animals, and natural communities that represent the diversity of life on Earth by protecting the lands and water they need to survive."

SLOGAN: "Conservation through private action."

Staffed by MBAs, lawyers, and "scientists doing a poet's work," as the *Wall Street Journal* put it, The Nature Conservancy (TNC) raises large amounts of money to buy and administer biologically important lands ("the last of the least, and the best of the rest," as they like to say). The most businesslike and the least political of the conservation organizations (*Outside* magazine calls it "the pin-striped real estate broker of the environmental movement"), the Conservancy does not involve itself with government regulation or corporate abuse of the environment. Since purchasing its first preserve in 1955, TNC has acquired 5.5 million acres of "forests, marshes, prairies, mountains, deserts and islands" in fifty states and Canada. Of this, TNC has retained

around 60 percent (some 1,300 preserves), the world's largest private system of nature sanctuaries, managed by staff and volunteer land stewards. The remainder has been sold to federal and state agencies for preservation. TNC has also compiled the country's most complete computerized inventory of critical wildlife habitat.

BACKGROUND: The disappearance of America's wild lands concerned conservationists long before the cause became popular. Victor Shelford, an animal ecologist at the University of Chicago, helped form the Ecological Society of America in 1915—with 50 members. With Shelford's leadership, the scientists began to list untouched natural areas, publishing an inventory in 1926. Activists within the Ecological Society formed a committee to lobby Congress to protect wilderness areas, but the Society's majority put a higher priority on scientific work and abolished the committee in 1944. Undeterred, in 1946 the activists formed an independent Ecologists Union of 158 members to take action to preserve endangered natural areas (half the members worked for the U.S. Forest Service, and the rest were mostly university scientists). George Fell, a botanist member from Illinois, proposed a system of state natural area preserves, to be acquired by purchase or donation. Fell was persuaded to move to Washington, D.C., to open an office for the Union. To attract a wider membership, the Union changed its name to The Nature Conservancy (after the British organization of the same name) in the fall of 1950. TNC bought its first piece of land in 1955, sixty acres in the Mianus

River gorge, thirty miles north of New York City.

TNC has two basic methods of work: buying and holding land for its own preserves, and buying vital land when it comes on the market from its revolving fund and turning it over to the state or federal government once they have appropriated the funds. In buying land, the Conservancy often obtains a complete or partial tax-deductible charitable gift from individuals or corporations, thus leveraging its money up front into a much more valuable acquisition. After selling land to the government for preservation, the money is rolled back into the revolving fund. TNC's motto could be "leverage and rollover, leverage and rollover."

At the start, TNC was proud to preserve any pretty piece of land. Robert Jenkins, the Conservancy's top scientist, changed the focus first to preserving "little islands of biological diversity" and then to preserving entire ecosystems—to provide long-run sustainable habitat for diverse species. Over the 1970s TNC accomplished many major land deals—acquiring Santa Cruz Island off southern California, most of the Virginia barrier islands, the Santee Hunt Club in South Carolina, and the Old Mashomack Hunt Club on Shelter Island, New York. Most of these deals were made without substantial publicity, leading to the Conservancy's reputation of "all action, no talk."

During the 1980s, TNC received the biggest gifts ever made on behalf of the environment. The Richard King Mellon Foundation gave over $50 million from 1976 to 1990, supporting the "Rivers of the Deep South" program—preserving endangered bottomland hardwood forests along five rivers flowing into the Gulf of Mexico—and the "National Wetlands Conservation Project." The now dissolved Goodhill Foundation established by Katherine Ordway, heiress to the 3M fortune, provided $43 million over ten years for a nationwide state-by-state "Natural Areas Conservation" program. Since 1980 the Conservancy has bought more land than the U.S. Fish and Wildlife Service, which is charged with land acquisition under the Endangered Species Act of 1973. Recognizing that conservation of critical areas requires a broader relationship with the federal government, the Conservancy developed cooperative agreements with the Department of Defense, the Bureau of Land Management, and the Forest Service. The Conservancy also has served as a broker for big deals, doing the tax analysis that helped convince the Prudential Insurance Company to donate 120,000 acres of North Carolina wetlands and forest, worth $50 million, to the U.S. Fish and Wildlife Service. In 1990 the Conservancy scored a coup with its purchase of the Gray Ranch, 500 square miles in the southwestern boot heel of New Mexico, the largest private conservation acquisition ever.

Pat Noonan led TNC from 1974 to 1980, during its transition to big-time land deals. William Blair was president during the big project era from 1981 to 1986. Frank Boren, a California real estate developer, was president from 1987 through 1989. John Sawhill, former president of New York University and a federal executive in the Nixon, Ford, and Carter administrations, became president and chief executive of the

Conservancy in 1990. The only major internal uproar developed over the Latin American program, prompting thirty-four staff to resign in 1987 to form a new organization, Conservation International.

CURRENT PRIORITIES: TNC's highly praised Natural Heritage biological inventory program works state by state to identify exemplary ecosystems and critical habitat for rare and endangered species. Based on a model developed in South Carolina in 1974, the Natural Heritage Program has spread to all fifty states. A detailed computerized data base, the "Biological and Conservation Data System," helps track and prioritize vital acreage. When the identified land goes up for sale, the Conservancy works to secure it for state or federal ownership or for its own preserves. TNC is helping establish similar heritage data base programs for Canada and Central and South America—the start of an international inventory of the earth's natural resources and species. In conjunction with this project, the Conservancy's "Parks in Peril" program for Latin America aims to save twenty critical parks and preserves annually until the year 2000. TNC cooperates with Conservation International and the World Wildlife Fund in debt-for-nature swaps in Latin America.

TNC announced its "Last Great Places" initiative in 1991, to preserve an initial dozen large-scale bioreserves, entire ecosystems containing both core natural areas and the surrounding buffer zone. Of the first twelve Last Great Places, eight are in the United States (including the Florida Keys, the Virginia Coast Reserve, the Tallgrass Prairie Preserve, and California's Nipomo Dunes) and four are in Latin America (including reserves in Ecuador, Mexico, Panama, and Paraguay). Not only do these ecosystems include unprecedentedly large tracts of land, they also involve complex ownership and management relations that may pull TNC further into political controversy than it has ventured before. The initiative may eventually involve seventy-five large bioreserves, forty within the United States.

MEMBERS: Individual contributors have increased substantially over the past decade, from 100,000 in 1980 to 200,000 in 1985 to 600,000 in 1990. The largest group is from California.

STRUCTURE: TNC's officers and board of governors is elected by members from a nominated slate at an annual conference (most members vote by proxy). Four regional offices are maintained in Boston, Chapel Hill, Minneapolis, and Boulder, and there are field offices in forty-eight states. The Latin American program is run from the national office in Arlington, Virginia.

RESOURCES: TNC's budget distinguishes between operating and capital accounts. For 1991, operating revenue totaled $173 million and capital additions totaled $82 million. Expenditures totaled $163 million for programs, and $61 million for capital allocations. Fund-raising and membership development cost $22 million (10 percent), and administration $18 million (8 percent). TNC's fund balances total $737 million, representing the land value of its preserves, revolving funds for land preservation, and endowments.

PUBLICATIONS AND SERVICES: Membership begins at $15 and includes the magazine *Nature Conservancy* six times a year, with an *Annual Report* in the November/December issue. TNC affinity VISA and MasterCard are available. The early history of TNC is traced in the thirtieth-anniversary issue of *The Nature Conservancy News* (July/August 1981). For a humorous look at the art of the land deal, see David E. Morine, *Good Dirt: Confessions of a Conservationist* (Globe Pequot, 1990), by the Conservancy's former vice president for land acquisition. In gratitude for the generosity of this foremost woman conservationist, TNC has published *Katherine Ordway: The Lady Who Saved the Prairies* (1990). □

**WORLD WILDLIFE FUND AND
THE CONSERVATION FOUNDATION**

1250 24TH STREET, NW

WASHINGTON, DC 20037

(202) 293-4800

FOUNDED: WWF, 1961; CF, 1948
MEMBERS: 1 million   BUDGET: $55 million
STAFF: 245   TAX STATUS: 501(c)(3)

PURPOSE: "To preserve the diversity and abundance of life on earth and the health of ecological systems."

The panda logo of the World Wildlife Fund (WWF) must be the best-known insignia of any conservation organization. It also symbolizes WWF's ability to capture the public's imagination with popular programs. WWF is devoted to the preservation of endangered species and their habitats on a world scale, and is the largest single American source of international conservation project grants. In 1990 WWF completed a merger with The Conservation Foundation (CF), a respected think tank. CF and WWF have been home to many moderate Republican conservationists.

BACKGROUND: The Conservation Foundation was founded in 1948 by Fairfield Osborn, energetic official of the New York Zoological Society and author of *Our Plundered Planet* (Little, Brown, 1948), one of the first widely read warnings on the dangers of world population growth and environmental destruction. CF has been a source of independent policy analysis on such issues as pollution, wetlands conservation, and use of public lands—emphasizing solutions that harmonize economic growth with environmental concerns.

With the sponsorship of Prince Philip of the United Kingdom and Prince Bernhard of the Netherlands, World Wildlife Funds were established in 1961 in the United States, the United Kingdom, the Netherlands, and Switzerland to protect endangered significant wildlife habitats in Latin America, Africa, and Asia. Leaders of WWF and CF have been well-connected politically. WWF founding trustee Russell Train— now chairman of the board—also served as the first chairman of the Council on Environmental Quality and as the second administrator of the Environmental Protection Agency under President Nixon. William Reilly, president of CF from 1973 and WWF from

1985 to 1989, was named director of the Environmental Protection Agency by President Bush. The current president and chief executive is Kathryn Fuller, an attorney who helped found the wildlife section at the U.S. Department of Justice and who led WWF's wildlife trade-monitoring program from 1982 to 1985. Since its founding, the U.S. WWF has carried out over 1,600 conservation projects in 107 countries.

CURRENT PRIORITIES: Besides its well-publicized campaign to help China save the panda (with limited results at best), WWF has programs of preservation for tropical forests, parks and habitats, primates, endangered and migratory species, and marine ecosystems. WWF also supports conservation education and training in the Caribbean and in Latin America, public information and education in the United States, and TRAFFIC, an international program to monitor the global trade worth more than $5 billion annually in wildlife and wildlife products. WWF dropped its support for controlled ivory harvesting and came out in 1989 for a world ban on ivory trade, prompting President Bush to sign a moratorium on commercial imports of African elephant ivory. CF priorities include studies of environmental quality, land and resource management, and environmental dispute resolution.

MEMBERS: Under Reilly's leadership membership leaped from 58,000 in 1981 to 200,000 in 1984 to 1 million in 1990; the budget went from $10 million to $50 million.

STRUCTURE: WWF and CF are governed by a thirty-six-member, self-recruiting board of directors. The board is packed with notables from the elite worlds of politics, philanthropy, and science: Oscar Arias Sanchez, former president of Costa Rica; former governors Thomas Kean (New Jersey) and Richard Lamm (Colorado); scions of wealth Anne Bass, Julie Packard, and Marshall Field; and Harvard zoologist Edward O. Wilson (who even discovered a new species of ant—*Pheidole fullerae*—in a potted palm in the office of WWF president Kathryn Fuller).

WWF is the U.S. affiliate of the World Wide Fund for Nature, headed by Prince Philip of the United Kingdom (whose passion for hunting has drawn fire from animal rights activists). The "international WWF family" (headquartered in Gland, Switzerland) includes organizations in 23 countries with over three million members and combined annual budgets of over $130 million. The international headquarters is financed by the elite "1001 Club"— European royalty, shipowners, bankers, and oil, mining, and chemical industry tycoons. The international WWF network has funded over 4,000 projects in 130 countries.

RESOURCES: During its 1991 fiscal year WWF and CF raised a total of $55 million—derived from individual contributions (59 percent), foundations (9 percent), corporations (2 percent), investment income (6 percent), government grants and contracts (11 percent), royalties and other income (3 percent), contributed advertising (2 percent), and other sources (8 percent). Expenses of $55 million in 1991 were allocated for programs (89 percent), administration (3 percent), and fund-raising (8 percent). WWF and CF has a $29.6 million endowment. In 1991 WWF made grants totaling $12.9 million to 407 conservation projects in sixty-three countries.

PUBLICATIONS AND SERVICES: WWF membership starts at $15 and includes the newsletter *Focus* six times a year; a summary annual report appears in the January/February issue. A full-blown annual report is available from the national office. CF publishes an extensive list of research reports. The *World Wildlife Fund Atlas of the Environment*, by Geoffrey Lean, Don Hinrichsen, and Adam Markham (Prentice Hall, 1990), is comprehensive and well designed. WWF also sponsors travel programs emphasizing wildlife observation to locations around the world. WWF affinity VISA and MasterCard are available. WWF's TRAFFIC program sponsors a hotline to report commercial trade in endangered species: (800) 634-4444. □

COMPUTER NETWORKS

During the 1980s environmentalists entered the age of computer communications. Most bulletin board services (FidoNet) and commercial services (CompuServe) have conferences discussing environmental topics. Several environmental organizations have private networks through commercial services, although Greenpeace set up its EnviroNet with public access. The most extensive computer network, EcoNet/PeaceNet, has been set up by International Global Communication, which links activists on five continents.

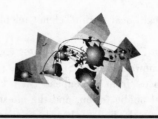

ECONET/PEACENET

INSTITUTE FOR GLOBAL COMMUNICATIONS

18 DEBOOM STREET

SAN FRANCISCO, CA 94107

(415) 442-0220

FOUNDED: 1984   SUBSCRIBERS: 6,000
BUDGET: $1 million   STAFF: 18
TAX STATUS: 501(c)(3)

EcoNet is a worldwide communications network of environmental activists and organizations.

Started in 1984 as a project of the Farallones Institute in northern California, EcoNet was absorbed and merged with PeaceNet (another project launched at the same time in the San Francisco area) in 1987 by the Institute for Global Communications (IGC), a project of the Tides Foundation in San Francisco. IGC's telecommunications visionaries work to connect activists in all corners of the earth. The IGC systems include EcoNet, PeaceNet, ConflictNet, and LaborNet serving the United States, and link up with related networks in the Association for Progressive Communications including GreenNet in Britain, The Web in Canada, Pegasus in Australia, Alternex in Brazil, FredsNaetet in Sweden, GlasNet in Russia, and Nicarao in Nicaragua. Over 6,000 individuals and organizations throughout the United States use IGC's electronic mail, conference, and data base systems, connecting with the network through local Sprint/Telenet telephone numbers.

On EcoNet you can monitor legislative news from the Sierra Club, press releases from Greenpeace, an Earth First! public forum, and the latest entries on the bulletin boards on over 150 environmental conference topics from Antarctica and climate to rain forests, recycling, and toxic wastes. If you're looking for project funding, you can check the directory of environmental grant-makers. The Environmental Press Service posts samples, with the full service available by subscription.

On PeaceNet you can monitor legislative news from Council for a Livable World and Friends Committee on National Legislation, respond to urgent action alerts from Amnesty International or CARNET for Central America, and follow the monthly actions of 20/20 Vision. SANE/FREEZE, Women's International League for Peace and Freedom, War Resisters League, Physicians for Social Responsibility, The Greens, and Foundation for Global Community (formerly Beyond War) maintain conferences. Bulletin boards cover topics including Central America, the Middle East, human rights, nuclear weapons testing, United Nations activities, and Third World development.

Access to telex, fax, MCI Mail, HandsNet, Internet, UseNet, and other services are available through electronic gateways. And the price is a bargain: a $15 sign-up fee and $10-a-month subscription fee (which includes an hour of off-peak connect time). IGC operates under the 501(c)(3) umbrella of the Tides Foundation in San Francisco. □

PEACE AND FOREIGN POLICY ORGANIZATIONS

2.
PEACE AND FOREIGN POLICY

American foreign policy is shaped and constrained by powerful opposing currents of internationalism and isolationism. Historian Arthur Schlesinger, Jr., suggests the American approach to foreign affairs swings like a pendulum between extroversion and introversion, intervention and isolationism, moralism and pragmatism. This oscillating pattern holds true up to the end of World War II, until the beginning of the Cold War. By 1947 isolationism had disappeared, for all practical purposes, and the old dualism was supplanted by a contest among three forces—best summarized as owls, hawks, and doves. With the disintegration of the Soviet empire by the end of 1989, the Warsaw Pact in 1990, and Soviet Union itself in 1991, the old pattern of internationalism versus isolationism is returning, in an updated form.

Isolationism was traditionally associated with the political Right, and linked with nativism, racism, and opposition to immigration. In its most reputable form, isolationism was identified with Senator Robert Taft of Ohio, son of President William Howard Taft. In its disreputable form, isolationism was manifested in the America First Committee (AFC), formed in 1940 to oppose the Roosevelt administration's intervention against the Axis powers. AFC disbanded a few days after the Japanese attack on Pearl Harbor in 1941 and the U.S. declaration of war against Japan and Germany. After World War II, the end of conservative isolationism was symbolized by the conversion to internationalism of Michigan senator Arthur Vandenberg, the ranking Republican on the Senate Foreign Relations Committee. Abandoning his long-standing opposition to foreign entanglements, Vandenberg supported ratification of the United Nations Charter in 1945, and the Truman doctrine of military aid to Greece and Turkey to combat Communist insurgencies, and the Marshall Plan of economic aid to revive Europe in 1947. After the Cold War, conservative isolationism was revived in 1992 by presidential spokesman and television political commentator Patrick Buchanan, who adopted the slogan "America First!" in his campaign for the Republican presidential nomination.

Five years after the end of World War II, the Cold War had been firmly embedded with the consolidation of Communist regimes in Eastern Europe by 1947, the victory in China of Mao Tse-tung's Communist army over Chiang Kai-shek's Nationalists in 1949, the formation of the North Atlantic Treaty Organization (NATO) in 1949 and its counterpart Warsaw Treaty Organization, and the outbreak of war in Korea in 1950. For the next forty years owls, hawks, and doves contended over the direction of American foreign policy, as the United States and the Soviet Union developed vast nuclear weapons arsenals. The foreign policy establishment (the owls) pursued a policy objective of "containment" of Communism, maintaining a wide influence through its organizations of moderate discourse, including the Council on Foreign Relations, the Foreign Affairs Association, the World Affairs Councils, and the United Nations Association. A new range of peace organizations (the doves) emerged in the 1970s, seeking one variety or another of "disarmament" as a policy objective. In reaction, the resurgent Right (the hawks) developed its own advocacy groups and think tanks emphasizing the Soviet threat and reviving its traditional policy objective of "rollback."

THE PEACE MOVEMENT

The peace movement in the United States has four substantial accomplishments to its credit in the period since World War II: (1) It pushed the Kennedy administration to begin arms control negotiations with the Soviet Union in the early 1960s, ending atmospheric nuclear testing and proving that arms control treaties would be widely popular; (2) it turned public opinion against the Vietnam War in the late 1960s, forcing a U.S. military withdrawal; (3) partly as a consequence of Vietnam, but also through renewed organizing, it prevented massive direct intervention by U.S. military forces in the Third World—particularly in Nicaragua and El Salvador, and possibly in southern Africa—until the Gulf War in 1990; and (4) it swung popular opinion so strongly behind nuclear arms control that Ronald Reagan had little choice in his second term but to work with Mikhail Gorbachev to lower nuclear stockpiles and end the Cold War. Surprisingly, the peace movement has often conspired with its critics in refusing to acknowledge these achievements.

The peace movement has been a complex and shifting coalition among several distinct political and ethical traditions as well as organizations with roots in different eras and representing the experiences of diverse political generations. Important intellectual currents include religious and secular pacifists; Marxists of assorted varieties, some apologists for Communism in one variant or another; and liberals of several types, including world federalists, arms controllers, and people who simply thought our military adventures were bad foreign policy. Current generations of activists had formative experiences varying from the struggle against Nazism and fascism from the 1930s through World War II, the birth of the United Nations and onset of the Cold War, the opposition to the Vietnam War in the context of the social movements of the 1960s and early 1970s, and the 1980s of Ronald Reagan, which extended from fears of nuclear Armageddon to the end of the Cold War.

Unlike issues raised by other domestic social movements, questions of foreign policy involve nations and leaders whose responses are framed beyond the borders of our political system. Since World War II the peace movement has sought an end to the superpowers' arms race, an end to armed intervention in less-developed countries, and an end to support for repressive regimes of allies. The question to the peace movement—and not just from reactionaries—was short but not simple: "What about the Russians?" Peace organizations and coalitions were not always of one mind on the questions posed by Communist regimes in the Soviet Union and elsewhere. Where did blame rest for the Cold War and the arms race—with the United States, the Soviet Union, or both equally? Did the Soviet Union (or China, or Cuba) represent the fulfillment of the socialist tradition or its perversion? Should moves toward disarmament be taken unilaterally by the United States, or only bilaterally together with the Soviet Union? Was it the responsibility of the peace movement to be concerned for human rights in the Soviet bloc, or just in countries allied with the United States? For the moderate majority of the American public, the peace movement as a whole never developed completely consistent or convincing responses to such questions. With the Cold War in the past, peace activists now face a new challenge—defining a positive program for common security in a polycentric world facing resurgent nationalism.

THE RISE AND FALL OF THE HAWKS

Reorganizing after Barry Goldwater's defeat in the 1964 presidential campaign, conservatives had been on the defensive during Richard Nixon's administration in the late 1960s and early 1970s, unhappy with Henry Kissinger's detente with the Soviet Union and his opening to the People's Republic of China. Disoriented again by Watergate, they regrouped with a clear opponent in President Jimmy Carter from 1976 to 1980. Old Right groups like the American Security Council built coalition networks. Many Democrats who had opposed George McGovern and sat out his campaign in 1972—some supporters of former Senator Henry Jackson of Washington state, others allies of the AFL-CIO leadership—became neoconservatives and worked together with hard-line Republicans in the Committee on the Present Danger, asserting that the Soviet Union was outpacing the United States in the arms race. Midge Decter organized neoconservatives in the Committee for the Free

World. The far Right fought over who would revive the U.S. Committee for World Freedom, the affiliate of the World Anti-Communist League. Together these organizations produced a clamor for a military buildup, which indeed began in 1978 during Carter's last two years as president.

The Reagan years, capped by the dramatic events in the Soviet Union at the end of the 1980s, surprisingly led to the virtual collapse of the hawks' organizations. The Old Right's American Security Council failed to enlist a new generation of activists. The neoconservative Committee for the Free World disbanded after a rancorous annual meeting in 1990, mocked even by the *Wall Street Journal* for "refusing to concede victory." The Committee on the Present Danger, which justified the arms buildup of the first-term Reagan administration, was focused exclusively on the Soviet Union and ran out of dangers. Howard Phillips downplayed his Conservative Caucus, which tried to organize a "Freedom Fighters International" in the mid-1980s, to start a new political party on the Right. Specialized single-interest lobbies like High Frontier dropped from view as "Star Wars" development was pared from the defense budget. The rear guard battle on the Strategic Defense Initiative (SDI) and military preparedness is currently being fought by the Heritage Foundation and other conservative think tanks. Patrick Buchanan began to forge a right-wing isolationism uniting paleoconservatives and libertarians. And back at the foreign policy establishment, "realists" were arguing against "globalists" that the United States should place scant hope in international institutions and devote little effort to encouraging democracy in the developing world.

AFTER THE COLD WAR

From John Kennedy's "missile gap" to Ronald Reagan's "window of vulnerability," American presidents spent three decades exaggerating American weaknesses and overplaying Soviet strengths. In retrospect it's clear that the Soviet Union's command economy had exhausted its potential for growth by the early 1970s, and was unable to make the transition to a high-technology, postindustrial system capable of providing its citizens with consumer goods and services comparable to

Western Europe, Japan, and the United States. Sharply rising oil prices beginning in 1973, which provided the Soviet Union with a $200 billion windfall up to 1985, disguised the Soviet economy's stagnation and allowed it to prop up its Eastern European satellites and participate in Third World military adventures.

The Brezhnev period in the Soviet Union—now called the "era of stagnation"—ran from the ouster of Nikita Khrushchev in 1964 to Leonid Brezhnev's death in 1982, and lingered on through the brief reigns of Yuri Andropov and Konstantin Chernenko, ending only in 1985 with the selection of Mikhail Gorbachev as general secretary of the Soviet Communist party. Gorbachev astonished Reagan's hard-line advisers by saying yes to his most extreme arms reduction proposals, writing an end to the arms race. Gorbachev's policies of *glasnost* and *perestroika* introduced reform in the Soviet Union and led to the collapse of Communist regimes in Eastern Europe in late 1989 and the reunification of Germany in the fall of 1990. The failed coup against Gorbachev in August 1991 led to independence for the Baltic states and a new Commonwealth of Independent States—and created a fresh diplomatic climate by the beginning of 1992.

How will the peace movement respond? Isolationism is a strong temptation. Until the Vietnam War, peace activists and the Left generally had been internationalists. Influenced by Vietnam and revolutionary movements in Latin America and Africa, leftists revived variations on the Leninist theory of imperialism, arguing that advanced capitalist economies require exploitation of the Third World. The simplistic conclusion drawn from this analysis is that U.S. influence or intervention abroad is always suspect and probably harmful. Influencing activists far beyond Marxist-Leninist circles, this outlook comes close to what conservatives like to call "blame America first." It minimizes the capacity of other governments to commit mischief, and exaggerates the power of the United States over events far from its shores. By feeding conspiracy theories of shadowy secret teams manipulating events, this outlook also minimizes the power of peace activists to impact world affairs, and points toward a withdrawal from the practical politics of foreign policy. The Gulf War in early 1990 was an unhappy start for the post–Cold War era, and pushed the peace movement further toward isolationism. Many peace activists expressed an increased cynicism toward international institutions and turned away from foreign policy toward domestic issues. Right and Left isolationism have an odd symmetry, as Charles Krauthammer has noted: Conservative isolationists fear the world would corrupt America, and progressive isolationists fear America would corrupt the world.

Winding down the Cold War presents an unprecedented opportunity for international cooperation on disarmament, regional conflict resolution, the environment, human rights, and Third World development. But first there's still a long "end game" for the peace movement to wrap up: a test ban treaty to prevent development of new generations of "modernized" nuclear weapons; preventing proliferation of nuclear weapons; disarming existing nuclear weapon stockpiles; eliminating chemical and biological weapons; cleaning up the hazardous radioactive waste from decades of weapons production in the United States and the former Soviet Union; stopping the arms trade in conventional weapons. Beyond disarmament, peace activists need a positive program of international institutions to reclaim the old World Federalist vision of a "new world order"—including U.N. reform and implementation of the Universal Declaration of Human Rights. Examples of constructive new directions include the Socialist International's Brandt report on North/South development issues, and Gro Harlem Bruntland's report for the U.N. on world environmental challenges. By early 1992 peace organizations were beginning to respond, broadening their missions to encompass human rights, global environmental protection, and sustainable development in the Third World. That agenda should occupy peace activists and organizations well into the twenty-first century.

1963: Limited Test Ban Treaty. Trilateral agreement among the U.S., USSR, and U.K. to prohibit testing nuclear devices in the atmosphere, in outer space, or under water. Now signed by 114 additional countries.

1968: Nuclear Non-Proliferation Treaty. Multilateral agreement signed and ratified by the U.S., USSR, U.K., and 138 nonnuclear weapon states to prevent the spread of nuclear weapons; Review Conference in 1995.

1972: Biological Weapons Convention. Multilateral agreement between the U.S., USSR, U.K., and 108 other countries banning biological weapons.

1972: Antiballistic Missile (ABM) Limitation Treaty (Strategic Arms Limitation Talks—SALT I). Bilateral treaty ratified by the U.S. and USSR limiting each side's anti-ballistic missile (ABM) systems.

1972: SALT I Interim Agreement. Bilateral agreement between the U.S. and USSR freezing the number of strategic ballistic missile launchers at 1972 levels for a five-year period, with modernization allowed.

1974: Threshold Test Ban Treaty. Bilateral agreement between the U.S. and USSR, ratified in 1990, prohibiting underground nuclear weapons tests with yields above 150 kilotons.

1975: Helsinki Accords. Multilateral agreement among thirty-five countries, including the U.S., USSR, and most European countries, negotiated by the Conference on Security and Cooperation in Europe (CSCE), providing for cooperation in human rights, economics, and security, and codifying postwar European boundaries.

1979: Strategic Arms Limitation Treaty (SALT II). Bilateral unratified agreement between the U.S. and USSR setting equal aggregate ceilings on strategic offensive weapon systems and qualitative restraints on existing and future strategic systems.

1987: Intermediate-Range Nuclear Forces (INF) Treaty. Bilateral ratified treaty between the U.S. and USSR requiring both to eliminate all intermediate-range missiles, shorter-range missiles, and associated equipment, with monitored compliance.

1990: Conventional Forces in Europe Treaty. Multilateral treaty between the U.S. and its fifteen NATO allies and the USSR and its five former Warsaw Pact allies to limit tanks, armored vehicles, artillery, attack helicopters, and combat airplanes in Europe.

1991: Strategic Arms Reduction Treaty (START). Bilateral treaty between the U.S. and USSR to reduce the number of warheads for long-range nuclear weapons.

Source: Arms Control Association, *Arms Control and National Security* (1989), for data through 1987; *The Defense Monitor*, for updates through 1990.

OWLS: THE FOREIGN POLICY ESTABLISHMENT

The organization of a foreign policy establishment by such groups as the Council on Foreign Relations (CFR), founded in 1921, was an effort to seek a larger role for the United States in world affairs, an active and interventionist stance to combat the persistent streak of American isolationism. CFR strongly supported U.S. entry into World War II, and became a leading force in developing a response to the superpower rivalry that followed it. George Kennan coined the term "containment" in a famous 1947 article in CFR's journal *Foreign Affairs*. This strategy led to long-term political, economic, and military pressure on the USSR, limiting the likelihood of all-out war by a series of negotiations on strategic nuclear weapons and on conventional forces in Europe. Fighting was largely limited to wars in the Third World, often fought by proxy forces. The consensus on the meaning of containment gave way during the Vietnam War as fighting bogged down and domestic opposition mounted.

As CFR members argued over Vietnam, foreign policy was becoming less the province of the economic and social establishment and more the territory of a professional elite. CFR membership was expanded and broadened, and a range of new foreign policy think tanks began to develop contending strategies. CFR chairman David Rockefeller organized the Trilateral Commission in 1973 to have a more elite international body to discuss relations among North America, Western Europe, and Japan. The Carnegie Endowment for International Peace swung from the center to a moderate-liberal stance, and established a rival journal, *Foreign Policy*. The Foreign Policy Association aimed its annual "Great Decisions" program on critical foreign policy issues at a wide range of upper-middle-class business, professional, and educational leaders in communities across the country. Staff who set up the Arms Control and Disarmament Agency during the Kennedy and Johnson administrations founded the Arms Control Association to promote the arms control agenda. The two leading membership organizations of the owls, CFR and the United Nations Association of the USA, are sketched in the following profiles.

COUNCIL ON FOREIGN RELATIONS

58 E. 68TH STREET

NEW YORK, NY 10021

(212) 734-0400

FOUNDED: 1921   MEMBERS: 2,790
BUDGET: $11.5 million   STAFF: 118
TAX STATUS: 501(c)(3)

PURPOSE: "Improving understanding of American foreign policy through the free exchange of ideas."

The apex of the foreign policy establishment is the Council on Foreign Relations (CFR), an organization of 2,790 members drawn from national economic, political, media, and academic elites.

BACKGROUND: The Council was organized in 1921 by President Woodrow Wilson's friend and associate, Edward M. House. The Council hosts "off the record" meetings with guest speakers (often heads of governments and foreign ministers), conducts studies, and publishes books and reports. Officially, CFR does not take any position on questions of foreign policy; nevertheless, its discussions and publications help build consensus among foreign policy influentials. CFR also recruits and recognizes young talent—Henry Kissinger launched his career in the mid-1950s by directing a CFR study on nuclear weapons and foreign policy. Since the Vietnam War and the rise of a professional foreign policy elite fragmented the post–World War II "containment" consensus, CFR has become, as I. M. Destler, Leslie Gelb, and Anthony Lake write, "an institution that reflects rather than shapes policy debates, and one that now confirms status rather than confers legitimacy."

MEMBERS: Essentially a white male club of the eastern establishment for its first fifty years, since 1971 CFR has sought to increase membership in underrepresented categories including women, minorities, labor leaders, and scientists —as well as recruit people who are younger or live beyond the East Coast. New CFR members are elected by the board of directors. Members—2,790 in 1991—are classified in relation to the northeastern seaboard: "Resident" members (967) live or work within fifty miles of City Hall in Manhattan, and "Washington" members (772) live or work within fifty miles of the Capitol. All other members are "nonresident" (901), although Boston is counted separately (150). The average age of Council members is fifty-eight.

STRUCTURE: In the interest of greater openness, members of the twenty-five-person board of directors, elected by the general membership, are now limited to three consecutive three-year terms, and must retire at age seventy. CFR opened a Washington office in 1977, presently a suite of rooms within the new headquarters of the Carnegie Endowment for International Peace. In an outreach program begun in 1938, CFR established Committees on Foreign Relations, affiliated membership organizations now active in thirty-seven major cities across the country and involving a total of 3,885 members drawn from regional professional, government, academic, and media leaders. Peter G. Peterson has been chairman of the board since 1985 (a position held by John J. McCloy from 1953 to 1970, and by David Rockefeller from 1970 to 1985). Peter Tarnoff is president and chief executive; John Temple Swing is executive vice president.

RESOURCES: CFR had an operating budget of $11.5 million in 1991. The Council has net assets of $51 million, including investments and its elegant Harold Pratt House headquarters.

PUBLICATIONS AND SERVICES: CFR publishes a newsletter, *Council Briefings*, and its prestigious journal, *Foreign Affairs* (circulation 115,000), available by subscription. The CFR Press publishes an extensive list of books and critical issue studies. CFR's *Annual Report* provides a thorough listing of the year's meetings, studies programs, staff, fellows, publications, membership, by-laws, and finances. For a balanced history, see Robert D. Schulzinger, *The Wise Men of Foreign Affairs: The History of the CFR* (Columbia University Press, 1984). From the left, see Laurence H. Shoup and William Minter, *Imperial Brain Trust: The CFR and U.S. Foreign Policy* (Monthly Review Press, 1977). For a current take from the far right, see James Perloff, *The Shadows of Power: The CFR and the American Decline* (Western Islands, 1988). □

UNITED NATIONS ASSOCIATION OF THE UNITED STATES OF AMERICA

485 FIFTH AVENUE

NEW YORK, NY 10017-6104

(212) 697-3232

FOUNDED: 1964   MEMBERS: 20,000
CHAPTERS: 171   BUDGET: $4 million
STAFF: 39   TAX STATUS: 501(c)(3)

PURPOSE: "Strengthening the U.N. system and enhancing U.S. participation in international institutions."

The United Nations Association of the United States of America (UNA-USA) promotes its agenda of public education, policy analysis, and international dialogue through a national network of chapters, divisions, and affiliated organizations. UNA-USA sponsors the annual U.N. Day (October 24) in communities across the country, and makes a special effort to reach young people through its Model U.N. program, which involves 60,000 high school and college students each year.

BACKGROUND: Although it is heir to a longer tradition, UNA-USA dates its founding to 1964, when it was created by a merger of the American Association for the U.N. (AAUN) and the United States Committee for the U.N., which promoted U.N. Day. The AAUN was the successor to the League of Nations Association (LNA) founded in 1923 and disbanded in 1945. UNA-USA also absorbed a conference group of national organizations supporting the U.N. Clark Eichelberger directed LNA and then AAUN from 1934 to 1964; Porter McKeever took over as director of the new UNA-USA. Edward C. Luck is the current president and chief executive.

CURRENT PRIORITIES: In 1966 UNA-USA issued its report on a major study of U.S.-China relations, funded by the Ford Foundation, which supported admission of the People's Republic of China to the U.N. (controversial at the time, the report paved the way for President Nixon's historic visit to China in 1972). Recent studies by UNA-USA include reform of U.N. management and decision-making, an assessment of the contentious UNESCO (the U.N. Educational, Scientific, and Cultural Organization), and reform of the U.N. Disarmament Commission. UNA-USA's policy studies division also fosters international dialogue through its "parallel studies program," in which nongovernmental leaders from the U.S., the USSR, Japan, and the People's Republic of China work to resolve bilateral and multilateral issues.

MEMBERS: UNA-USA has some 20,000 members in 171 chapters and divisions, and also counts 130 associated groups in its Council of Organizations—including unions, churches, and a variety of public interest groups. Although the top levels of the organization are composed of the foreign policy establishment, at the grassroots UNA-USA groups often attract political liberals willing to confront isolationists for whom the U.N. is a radical venture in world government.

STRUCTURE: UNA-USA is supervised by a 30-member board of governors (half are CFR members) elected from a 120-member board of directors (a third are CFR members). A national convention is held twice in each five-year period. UNA-USA is a member of the World Federation of United Nations Associates.

RESOURCES: UNA-USA's revenue of $4 million in 1989 came from corporations (22 percent), foundations (35 percent), individuals (35 percent), and other sources (8 percent). Expenditures of

$3.7 million supported programs (63 percent), and management and fund raising (37 percent).

PUBLICATIONS AND SERVICES: Membership is $25 and includes the bimonthly newspaper *The InterDependent* (circulation 20,000). The Washington office publishes the newsletter *Washington Weekly Report*, available by subscription. □

DOVES: THE PACIFIST TRADITION

Christian pacifism has been an important current of opposition to war in the United States, particularly through the historic peace churches—Mennonites, Brethren, and Religious Society of Friends (Quakers). Quakers in particular have influenced social reform far out of proportion to their modest numbers, providing leaders for the movements for abolition of slavery, woman suffrage, prison reform, and humane treatment of the mentally ill—in addition to the peace movement. In this century Quakers have been leaders in the Fellowship of Reconciliation (FOR) and, of course, the American Friends Service Committee (AFSC).

Pacifists opposed U.S. intervention in World War I, but after the war supported efforts to build new international institutions to promote peace—the League of Nations being the most ambitious effort. FOR, AFSC, War Resisters League (WRL), and Women's International League for Peace and Freedom (WILPF) all date their founding in the period from 1914 to 1923—the final efforts of progressive era optimism and moralism applied to foreign

affairs. Although they had moments of wider influence between the world wars, pacifist groups have functioned more as "prophetic minorities," believing in the necessity of a radical reconstruction of society, and demanding an intense commitment from members.

THE FELLOWSHIP OF RECONCILIATION

P.O. BOX 271

NYACK, NY 10960

(914) 358-4601

FOUNDED: 1915 MEMBERS AND CONTRIBUTORS: 15,000 CHAPTERS: 75 BUDGET: $1.3 million STAFF: 30 TAX STATUS: 501(c)(3)

PURPOSE: "To explore the power of love and truth for resolving human conflict; . . . opposition to war . . . based on a commitment to the achieving of a just and peaceful world community, with full dignity and freedom for every human being."

Members of the Fellowship of Reconciliation (FOR) combine the spirit of love with the tactics of active nonviolence as they campaign against militarism, war, racism, and injustice. As the U.S. affiliate of International FOR, the group is part of the world's largest religious pacifist organization.

BACKGROUND: In August 1914 an ecumenical peace conference brought 150

Christians to Switzerland on the eve of the First World War. When fighting broke out, participants scattered to their homelands. As they parted at the Cologne railway station, British Quaker Henry Hodgkin and Friedrich Siegmund-Schultze, pacifist chaplain to the German kaiser, vowed never to sanction war or violence. This vow inspired the birth of the International Fellowship of Reconciliation (IFOR) four months later in a meeting at Trinity College, Cambridge. Hodgkin, elected chair of the British FOR, came to New York in 1915 to meet with 68 men and women who founded FOR in the United States. An initial campaign protested the harsh treatment of conscientious objectors imprisoned during the war in such places as Fort Leavenworth. Continued pressure for the rights of conscientious objectors resulted in provisions for alternative service in the Selective Service Act of 1940.

As the leading voice of Protestant pacifism in America, FOR was concerned from the start with wider issues of social justice. FOR member Roger Baldwin was central to the founding in 1916 of the National Civil Liberties Bureau, which became the ACLU. A. J. Muste—then a Boston FOR leader—played a prominent role in the 1919 textile strike in Lawrence, Massachusetts, and helped found Brookwood Labor College in Katonah, New York, in 1921, where he worked as education director for twelve years. FOR helped organize the National Conference of Christians and Jews in 1923. During the Depression decade of the 1930s, with wars and militarism spreading in Europe and Asia, absolute pacifism was less easy to maintain. Theologian Reinhold Nie-

buhr, an FOR board member, abandoned pacifism in 1934. FOR supported industrial union organizing and shared leadership of the peace movement, opposing U.S. involvement when the Second World War broke out in Europe in 1939—a popular position until the United States was attacked by Japan at Pearl Harbor in December 1941. FOR stood by its principles of Christian pacifism, and many members served time in Civilian Public Service camps or in prison as conscientious objectors. FOR protested the internment of Japanese Americans on the West Coast, and assisted the families evacuated to relocation camps. FOR member Gordon Hirabayashi refused to register for evacuation—and over forty years later won a federal lawsuit to vacate his criminal conviction.

A. J. Muste, whose activities had taken him in and out of socialist organizations in the 1930s, became executive secretary of FOR in 1940 and initiated an emphasis on nonviolent direct action. The Indian practice of nonviolence had been brought to the attention of FOR leaders by a follower of Mahatma Gandhi studying at Columbia University, Krishnalal Shridharani, in his book *War Without Violence* (Harcourt, Brace, 1939; rpt., Garland Publishing, 1972). FOR leaders decided to check its relevance to the struggle for racial justice by allowing three of its staff—two blacks, youth secretary Bayard Rustin and James Farmer, and one white, George Houser—to put Gandhian techniques to the test. As Taylor Branch notes in *Parting the Waters*, (Simon & Schuster, 1988), "by example the hard-drinking, cigar-smoking, woman-chasing Shridharani taught the wide-eyed young Americans that Gandhian politics did not require a life of dull asceticism." In the midst of a popular war, FOR concluded its most fruitful arena for success might be race relations.

Farmer and Houser formed the first chapter of the Congress of Racial Equality (CORE) in Chicago in 1942, with FOR providing their salaries and expenses for several years. CORE led the first efforts to desegregate restaurants, theaters, and swimming pools in such cities as Chicago, Denver, St. Louis, and Los Angeles. Strongly influenced by the sit-down strikes of the CIO, the first CORE "sit-ins" were called "sit-downs." Houser directed CORE until 1955, when he left to become executive director of the American Committee on Africa, another FOR project. Under Farmer's leadership, CORE would become one of the central components of the civil rights movement in the 1960s. In 1947 FOR and CORE cosponsored the first interracial team of "freedom riders" (including Bayard Rustin and George Houser) on the "Journey of Reconciliation," taking buses across state lines in the upper South to test a Supreme Court decision declaring segregation in interstate travel to be unconstitutional. When the historic Montgomery bus boycott began in 1955, FOR sent Reverend Glenn Smiley to work beside Reverend Martin Luther King, Jr., and dispatched Reverend James Lawson, a black minister who had spent a year in jail as a conscientious objector during the Korean War and three years in India studying Gandhian civil disobedience, to work in Nashville as its first southern field secretary. Smiley and Lawson, together with King, established nonviolence as the touchstone of the civil rights movement.

During the Cold War anticommunism of the 1950s, FOR opposed collaboration with communists, but encouraged dialogue. In the popular front of the mid-1930s, pacifists, socialists, and communists had cooperated uneasily in the peace movement. Following Germany's invasion of the USSR, communists switched positions and bitterly denounced the pacifists. FOR concluded that communists were not opposed to war and totalitarianism in principle, and in 1946 adopted a policy opposing association with communist organizations. Nevertheless FOR defended the civil liberties of communists and opposed the Smith Act prosecutions of Communist party leaders. In the interest of dialogue, FOR leaders A. J. Muste and John Swomley opened discussions with John Gates and other dissident Communist party members. FOR rented Carnegie Hall in 1956 for a public debate between Muste and socialist Norman Thomas (a long-time FOR member) on one hand and Communist party secretary Eugene Dennis and W.E.B. Du Bois on the other, with Roger Baldwin moderating. Also in the 1950s FOR launched a six-year "food for China" program in response to famine, sending tens of thousands of miniature bags of grain to President Eisenhower with the inscription, "If thine enemy hunger, feed him."

As the Vietnam War expanded in the 1960s, FOR formed the International Committee of Conscience on Vietnam, bringing together 10,000 clergy in forty countries. Alfred Hassler, former editor of *Fellowship* and FOR's executive secretary since 1960, established contact with the pacifist movement in Vietnam and sponsored a world tour by Buddhist leader and monk Thich Nhat Hanh. Hassler was increasingly at odds with FOR's executive committee over participation in the various anti–Vietnam War coalitions and their call for immediate U.S. withdrawal; although his sharpest critics resigned in 1971, Hassler retired from FOR in 1974 to work exclusively for International FOR. Richard Deats, on the staff since 1972, has been a central figure for FOR in the last decade in various roles from executive secretary to, presently, coordinator of the U.S.-USSR reconciliation program. Doug Hostetter has been executive director since 1987.

CURRENT PRIORITIES: After Vietnam, disarmament resurfaced as a primary goal. FOR launched a national effort with the American Friends Service Committee in 1977 to close the Rocky Flats Weapons Plant in Colorado. As the Cold War deepened under the Reagan administration in the early 1980s, FOR helped initiate the Nuclear Weapons Freeze Campaign and emphasized U.S.-USSR reconciliation. IFOR established branches throughout Latin America known as *Servicio Paz y Justicia* (SERPAJ's Adolfo Perez Esquivel from Argentina was awarded the Nobel Peace Prize in 1980). IFOR's workshops in the Philippines helped train nonviolent resistance groups contributing to the peaceful "people's power" overthrow of Ferdinand Marcos in 1986. Since the Gulf War in 1991, FOR has emphasized counteracting anti-Arab stereotypes, humanitarian aid to war victims, an alternative energy policy,

and redirecting national priorities toward human needs.

MEMBERS AND CONTRIBUTORS: FOR has 7,500 currently active members who have signed its "Statement of Purpose," and another 7,500 contributors, numbers that have remained steady in recent years.

STRUCTURE: FOR is governed by a thirty-member national council with representatives elected at-large and from each of six regions by the membership. There are seventy-five chapters in twenty-six states and Washington, D.C. The college and seminary program helps campus activists set up FOR chapters. FOR is affiliated with Catholic, Jewish, Buddhist, and various Protestant denominational peace fellowships across the country. Shadowcliff, an old mansion overlooking the Hudson River at Nyack (just twenty miles from New York), has been FOR headquarters since 1956, when it was purchased at a bargain price with the help of a timely bequest. International FOR, which has affiliates in thirty countries, is headquartered near Amsterdam, The Netherlands; the executive director from 1976 to 1992 was Jim Forest (editor of *Fellowship* in the early 1970s).

RESOURCES: The bulk of FOR's $1.3 million budget comes from the membership, with some gifts from church groups. A few grants are received from foundations.

PUBLICATIONS AND SERVICES: The magazine *Fellowship* (circulation 6,100), available for a $15 subscription, is published eight times a year. FOR's publications department sells a range of books on nonviolence, peace, and civil rights. Early FOR leaders wrote several historical sketches in issues of *Fellowship* during 1990, the seventy-fifth-anniversary year. □

WOMEN'S INTERNATIONAL LEAGUE FOR PEACE AND FREEDOM

1213 RACE STREET

PHILADELPHIA, PA 19107

(215) 563-7110

FOUNDED: 1915   MEMBERS: 15,000
BRANCHES: 100   BUDGET: $800,000
STAFF: 11   TAX STATUS: 501(c)(4): Women's International League for Peace and Freedom; 501(c)(3): Jane Addams Peace Association

PURPOSE: "The achievement by peaceful means of those political, economic, social, and psychological conditions throughout the world which can assure peace, freedom, and justice for all."

The Women's International League for Peace and Freedom (WILPF) is the U.S. section of the international organization of the same name. WILPF as an organization has never been strictly pacifist, although many members have been. Reaching its heyday in the 1930s, it took three decades to recover from the loss of members during World War II. In recent years, however, WILPF has begun to bridge the generation gap and attract younger women. Today it carries on a seventy-five-year tradition combining feminism, a quest for peace through international institutions, and a commitment to social justice.

BACKGROUND: Following the start of World War I in Europe in August 1914, two European suffrage and peace leaders, Emmeline Pethick-Lawrence of England and Rosika Schwimmer of Hungary, came to the United States to rally antiwar activity. Crystal Eastman, a feminist and socialist labor lawyer in New York, put them in touch with Jane Addams, the social worker who opened Hull House in Chicago. Addams called a national women's meeting in Washington, D.C., in January 1915—which established the Women's Peace Party (WPP), with Addams as president. In April delegates from the WPP traveled to The Hague in Holland for a congress of 1,400 women from twelve countries. The congress formed a committee that became the Women's International League for Peace and Freedom in 1919. Jane Addams held the office of international president from 1915 to 1929.

Most WILPF founders believed that women's voting and participating in public life would bring an end to war. Women in the United States and most European countries won the right to vote shortly after the end of World War I, and the movement for women's rights lost momentum. WILPF's feminist focus faded, and despite some disillusionment with the resurgence of militarism its women continued working for peace, emphasizing support for the League of Nations. Two WILPF founders, Jane Addams and Emily Green Balch, remain the only American women awarded the Nobel Peace prize.

Addams received the prize in 1931, four years before her death. Balch lost her faculty position of twenty-five years at Wellesley College due to her activism against World War I and went on to serve as WILPF's international general secretary from 1919 to 1923 and again from 1933 to 1936. Balch's book *Occupied Haiti*, (Writers Publishing, 1927), the product of a mission to that country in 1926, led to an investigation resulting in the withdrawal of U.S. Marines. She was awarded the Nobel Peace Prize in 1946.

The rise of European fascism and the onset of World War II brought conflict to WILPF ranks. Some members were staunch pacifists while others—particularly in the French and German sections—wanted to give active support to revolutionary movements. Sections had autonomy to define their own positions. The U.S. section opposed participation in the war, and many members dropped out—some because the organization was too pacifist, others because it was not pacifist enough. Many central European members went into exile, were imprisoned in concentration camps, or died during the war. Following the war Mildred Scott Olmsted, executive secretary of the U.S. section from 1934 to 1966, rallied international members to rebuild the organization. The United Nations provided a new focus. WILPF participated in the San Francisco conference that founded the U.N. in 1945, and has had consultative status as a nongovernmental organization (NGO) at the U.N. since 1948.

The 1950s were hard for WILPF, which had opposed the formation of NATO in 1948–49 and the Korean War, which began in 1950—unpopular positions, particularly in the European countries that felt most threatened by the Cold War. WILPF was attacked during the McCarthy era, but maintained its open membership while pointing out it had no sections in communist countries. As concern with radioactive fallout from atmospheric nuclear weapons testing grew in the late 1950s, WILPF's approach of education and lobbying did not express the urgency felt even by many of its own members. A new organization, Women Strike for Peace, stole some of WILPF's thunder—and activists—by mobilizing thousands of women for demonstrations in November 1961. When the Limited Test Ban Treaty was signed in August 1963, Women Strike for Peace declined and many members went back to WILPF. Many members actively supported the civil rights movement, and Reverend Martin Luther King, Jr., gave the keynote address at WILPF's biennial meeting in 1965.

The first of many seminars with Soviet women, initiated by Olmsted, took place in 1961 at Bryn Mawr College. Because of the ongoing association with the Soviet Women's Committee, WILPF has been accused by conservatives of being "fellow travelers" with communists. In 1968, as WILPF held its international congress in Denmark, Czechoslovakia was invaded by Soviet and Warsaw Pact tanks. WILPF expressed its criticism to Soviet observers, but thereafter felt that maintaining its relationship with the Soviet Women's Committee and the Soviet-backed World Peace Council was more important than public criticism of the USSR. The Vietnam War dominated WILPF's attention by the late 1960s. WILPF joined the various antiwar mobilizations, and in 1968 led a national women's demonstration of 5,000 women in Washington demanding that Congress end the war—called the Jeannette Rankin Brigade, in honor of its long-time member, the first woman elected to the U.S. House of Representatives (1917), and the lone congressional vote against entry into World Wars I and II. WILPF's position on the Vietnam War, which shifted from calling for a negotiated peace to "out now," proved controversial. Executive director Jo Graham resigned in 1967, believing that WILPF's stance supported armed liberation movements rather than peaceful and democratic change—the return of an old tension in the organization.

WILPF's eighteenth international congress was held in New Delhi, India, in 1970, its first meeting in the developing world. During the 1970s the organization became more involved with women in Southeast Asia, the Middle East, and Latin America. The United Nations Decade for Women drew WILPF into greater contact with the Third World. In 1985 WILPF played a major part in the NGO forum at the Decade for Women conference in Nairobi, Kenya, which brought together fourteen thousand women from 159 countries to set goals for the advancement of women by the year 2000. The meeting of First and Third World women proved an exciting event for participants, making clear the links between development, social justice, and peace.

Jane Midgely, formerly WILPF's legislative director in Washington, D.C., and author of WILPF's *Women's Budget*, served as executive director from 1986 to 1992. The hiring of Midgely

clearly reflected a decision to empower a younger generation of members. The end of the Cold War and the demise of the Soviet Union should remove the "fellow traveler" issue, always a stronger tendency at the international office in Geneva. International secretary general Edith Ballantyne retired in spring 1992, after expressing her faith in socialism and Marxism and her frustration that "50 or more years of struggle may have been in vain." Fresh winds will be blowing through WILPF, but where they will carry the organization depends on the direction steered by the membership.

CURRENT PRIORITIES: WILPF's 1991–94 plan of action is centered on the theme of economic justice and contains five programs: (1) use of WILPF's *Women's Budget* by branches to call for shifting the federal budget toward education, health care, nutrition, and housing; (2) a campaign for a Comprehensive Test Ban Treaty in coordination with international WILPF; (3) "undoing racism" activities; (4) "women vs. violence" events, with an emphasis on developing a peace and justice treaty between women of North and Latin America; and (5) "undoing sexism/women's empowerment" workshops. During 1992 and 1993 WILPF and its Central and South American affiliates are conducting a campaign for the Women's Peace and Justice Treaty of the Americas.

MEMBERS: WILPF's membership reached 15,000 by 1937 but declined as Germany grew more aggressive under the Nazis and the United States was drawn into World War II. By the end of the war membership was down to 5,000. Many of WILPF's members are from the political generations of the 1930s, 1940s, and 1950s, giving it an image as an organization of older women. (Many potential recruits among younger women were drawn into the women's movement in the 1970s and into more narrowly focused organizations such as Women's Action for Nuclear Disarmament in the 1980s). A substantial contingent of younger women joined in the past decade, and by 1990 membership stood at 15,000. A small number of members are men. A biennial national congress brings members together in odd-numbered years; an international congress is held every three years.

STRUCTURE: A national board of from twenty-seven to thirty-six women is elected to two-year terms by the membership to represent the four regions. While the majority of members are white, women of color are represented on the board, reflecting WILPF's continuing commitment to diversity. WILPF's 501(c)(3) affiliate, the Jane Addams Peace Association (JAPA), shares the New York office. WILPF's staff of eleven women is concentrated in its Philadelphia headquarters, although it maintains an office at the U.N. in New York City and a legislative office in Washington, D.C. The office of the international WILPF is in Geneva, Switzerland. There are some 50,000 members in twenty-eight national sections (the U.S. section is the largest). Sections in Spanish-speaking countries are known as *Liga Internacional de Mujeres Pro-Paz y Libertad* (LIMPAL).

RESOURCES: The bulk of the income for WILPF's $500,000 budget comes from membership dues, contributions, and subscriptions. JAPA has a budget of $300,000, also contributed primarily by the membership, for educational activities.

PUBLICATIONS AND SERVICES: Membership is $35 and includes *Peace and Freedom* (circulation 10,000) six times a year. *Program & Legislative Action* is available to activists by subscription, as is *Pax et Libertas*, a quarterly published by the international office. The WILPF hotline posts legislative updates on PeaceNet. There are two organizational histories, both available from the national office: Gertrude Bussey and Margaret Tims's *Pioneers for Peace: WILPF 1915–1965* (1965; Alden Press, 1980), emphasizing the international structure; and Catherine Foster's *Women for All Seasons: The Story of the WILPF* (University of Georgia Press, 1989), which gives more attention to the U.S. section and recent events. □

AMERICAN FRIENDS SERVICE COMMITTEE

1501 CHERRY STREET

PHILADELPHIA, PA 19102

(215) 241-7000

FOUNDED: 1917   CONTRIBUTORS: 100,000
BUDGET: $25.6 million   STAFF: 390
TAX STATUS: 501(c)(3)

PURPOSE: "AFSC is a Quaker organization supported by individuals who care about social justice, peace, and human service. Its work is based on a profound Quaker belief in the dignity and worth of every person, and a faith in the power of love and nonviolence to bring about change."

The American Friends Service Committee (AFSC) confounds categories: Launched as a relief organization, it has evolved to include international assistance for reconstruction and sustainable development, domestic advocacy for the poor and powerless, and education and action for peace and against war, militarism, and the nuclear arms race. Woven deeply through the fabric of the organization is the Quaker belief there is that of God in every person, and one must avoid polarizing or dehumanizing people in situations of conflict.

BACKGROUND: Twenty-four days after the start of World War I in 1917, fourteen American Quakers led by Rufus Jones founded the AFSC in Philadelphia to provide conscientious objectors with constructive alternatives to military service. Working with British Friends, AFSC volunteers provided food and medical care for civilian victims in France and Russia during the war, and after the armistice in Germany, Poland, and Austria as well. (AFSC's symbol since 1917, the eight-pointed red and black star, was first used by the British Quaker Relief Fund during the Franco-Prussian War in 1870). In 1927 AFSC launched a peace mission to Nicaragua following a U.S. invasion, beginning a presence in Central America that continues to this day.

AFSC's work followed human disasters rather than natural ones. Clarence Pickett, executive secretary from 1929 to 1950, helped guide the organization toward providing relief around domestic struggles for social justice. Quakers were often accepted where partisan organizations of the Left were not. AFSC provided winter survival help in 1929 for striking textile workers in North Carolina. In 1931 they fed 40,000 undernourished children of unemployed and striking coal miners in Appalachia. AFSC lent a hand to the disenfranchised in settlement houses, reform schools, and schools for Indians, blacks, and isolated mountain children.

AFSC began by aiding war victims, regardless of political affiliation, providing refugee relief in the Spanish Civil War in 1937 and medical aid to Chinese civilians in 1941. During World War II, AFSC vigorously protested the internment of Japanese Americans, and provided alternative service for conscientious objectors in mental hospitals, conservation programs, and schools. AFSC, together with the British Friends Service Council, was awarded the Nobel Peace Prize in 1947 for "silent help from the nameless to the nameless." AFSC's domestic community relations programs have emphasized the poor and powerless, and those denied recognition and rights. Support for farm workers began in 1955, with a focus on union organizing drives and national boycotts to win rights for farm workers. In the 1960s programs aided desegregation campaigns (James Reeb, an AFSC worker, was killed during a protest in Selma, Alabama). AFSC has given strong support to Native American struggles for treaty rights, health care, and education.

AFSC's peace education division has

expanded the initial concern for conscientious objectors to a wide-ranging program for disarmament and human rights. In 1955 AFSC published *Speak Truth to Power*, a study of pacifist alternatives to the arms race supporting unilateral disarmament initiatives by the United States. During the Vietnam War in the 1960s and 1970s, AFSC's international division conducted aid programs in South Vietnam, spending over $2 million at its Quong Ngai medical and prosthetic center alone; token amounts of medical aid were given to North Vietnam and the National Liberation Front. Stewart Meacham, head of the peace education division, played a leadership role with various antiwar coalitions, stirring some controversy among Quakers. Draft counseling was an important service on the home front. After the war and the overthrow of the Pol Pot regime, AFSC was one of the first organizations to go into Cambodia to work on agricultural projects, rebuilding schools, and fitting artificial limbs. From 1979 to 1982 the peace education division, led by Terry Provance, helped initiate the Nuclear Weapons Freeze Campaign, carrying resolutions to hundreds of New England town meetings.

AFSC began work in the Middle East in 1948, supporting a secure state of Israel and providing refugee relief to Palestinians in the Gaza Strip. AFSC continues to work with Palestinians in Gaza, the West Bank, and Lebanon, supporting their right to self-determination and advocating a comprehensive peace settlement. AFSC has published two major studies and position statements on the Arab-Israeli-Palestinian conflict, *Search for Peace in the Middle East* (1970) and *A Compassionate Peace* (1982). Intent on seeing the apartheid system dismantled, for fifteen years AFSC has supported economic sanctions on South Africa. AFSC staff have picketed ships unloading cargo from South Africa, published a guide to U.S. corporations doing business in South Africa, and nonviolently challenged corporations, banks, and individuals not to provide financial support to apartheid.

CURRENT PRIORITIES: *International division* programs emphasize development projects promoting self-reliance in Central America (Guatemala, Honduras, El Salvador, and Nicaragua) and South America (Chile and Brazil), Southeast Asia (Laos and Cambodia), and sub-Saharan Africa (Mali, Guinea-Bissau, and Mozambique). Palestinian refugees are the focus of programs in the Middle East. *Peace education division* work includes draft and military counseling for young people, activity given added urgency by the Persian Gulf War in 1990–91. Throughout the 1980s AFSC worked to broaden the disarmament constituency beyond white professionals, involving people of color by building relationships with social justice groups. *Community relations division* domestic programs include work with the homeless, farm workers, and immigrants—including sanctuary for Central American refugees. Human rights issues addressed include women's issues, gay rights, prison reform, and opposition to apartheid.

CONTRIBUTORS: AFSC is not a membership organization. Primarily through direct-mail solicitation, the number of contributors has grown to 100,000. An estimated 80 to 85 percent of the donors are non-Quakers (of the 200,000 Quakers worldwide, 110,000 live in the United States, and many of these are evangelicals at odds with the social activism of the AFSC).

STRUCTURE: The AFSC Corporation has 164 Quaker members, half appointed by Yearly Meetings of American Friends and half nominated at-large. (Quaker groupings supporting the AFSC include the Friends General Conference, based in Philadelphia, and the Friends United Meeting, based in Richmond, Indiana—home of Earlham College; the Evangelical Friends Alliance cut ties with the AFSC in the 1920s). The actual oversight of the AFSC is governed by a 31-member board of directors (all Quakers designated from the corporation membership) plus 9 regional representatives to the board, which sets policy and reviews programs. The board also hires the executive secretary. Asia Bennett, who served from 1980 to 1992, was the first woman to hold that position; Kara Newell was hired as executive secretary in 1992. Field staff have substantial decision-making authority, and many program priorities percolate up from the local level through the Quaker consensus-oriented discussion process. The Philadelphia staff began organizing a union in 1988 and signed its first contract in 1990 —a symptom of conflict over staff reductions, control, and communication.

The national office is located in Friends Center, an attractive brick complex shared with the Philadelphia Yearly Meeting and other Quaker organizations. There are nine regional offices—each with its own executive committee—in Atlanta, Baltimore, Cambridge, Chicago, Des Moines, New York City, Pasadena, San Francisco, and Seattle. In addition, there are some thirty-five project offices in the United States, plus programs in twenty-two foreign countries.

RESOURCES: AFSC received $25.6 million in revenue in 1991, derived from contributions (57 percent), bequests (19 percent), earnings on investments (14 percent), program service fees (8 percent), and other sources (2 percent). Income has not kept up with inflation, resulting in a cut of some fifty staff positions since 1987. Expenditures of $25.6 million in 1991 supported overseas programs (30 percent), peace education programs (17 percent), community relations programs (22 percent), other special programs (7 percent), management and support services (14 percent), and fund-raising (9 percent).

Of the 390 U.S. staff members, some 170 work in the national office, 189 work in regional offices for domestic programs, and 31 work abroad for international programs (additional local staff work for programs in Gaza, Mali, and Guinea-Bissau). The vast majority (85 percent) of the AFSC staff is non-Quaker—a result primarily of the small numbers of Quakers and a strong emphasis on affirmative action hiring.

PUBLICATIONS AND SERVICES: Contributors of $20 or more receive the *Quaker Service Bulletin* three times a year. The national office also sells books and pamphlets and publishes an occasional feminist newsletter, *Listen Real Loud.* Local offices publish their own newsletters and distribute books, pamphlets, films, and related materials. The controversies among Quaker religious bodies, the AFSC, and Guenter Lewy are debated in *Quaker Service at the Crossroads* (1988), edited by Chuck Fager and published by his Kimo Press, P.O. Box 1361, Falls Church, VA 22041. □

WAR RESISTERS LEAGUE

339 LAFAYETTE STREET

NEW YORK, NY 10012

(212) 228-0450

FOUNDED: 1923   MEMBERS: 15,000
LOCAL GROUPS: 20   BUDGET: $400,000
STAFF: 8   TAX STATUS: 501(c)(4): War Resisters League; 501(c)(3): A. J. Muste Memorial Institute

PURPOSE: "Believing war to be a crime against humanity, the War Resisters League advocates Gandhian nonviolence to create a democratic society free of war, racism, sexism, and human exploitation."

The War Resisters League (WRL) is the Fellowship of Reconciliation's secular sister, an organization for nonreligious pacifists, advocating militant nonviolent resistance to confront injustice. Long a haven for feisty anarchists and socialists, WRL has attracted a younger generation influenced more by feminism and the nonviolent direct-action protests of the civil rights and anti-nuclear movements.

BACKGROUND: WRL has its roots in the Anti-Enlistment League, formed in 1915 by Jessie Wallace Hughan and the Reverend John Haynes Holmes to rally war resisters opposed to American involvement in World War I. After the war, European conscientious objectors formed War Resisters International (WRI) in 1921 in the belief that wars would end when substantial numbers of people declared in advance that they would not fight ("wars will cease when men refuse to fight"). In 1923 Hughan drew together representatives of the Women's Peace Union, the Women's Peace Society, and the Fellowship of Reconciliation (FOR) to launch the WRL for resisters, particularly anarchists and socialists, who did not feel comfortable in a religious organization like FOR. Hughan's dream was to transform a largely unorganized group of individual objectors into a vital anti-war movement. In the early years Hughan was the financial mainstay of the WRL.

In the 1930s WRL led annual "No More War" parades in New York and saw its enrollments grow from 1,000 in 1928 to 13,000 in 1938, with 800 contributing members. Pacifists warned against the rise of fascism—although they had no clear strategy to oppose it —and in 1933 WRL's Rev. John Holmes joined Rabbi Stephen Wise in leading the first public demonstration against German anti-Semitism.

During World War II, WRL shifted its efforts from enrolling people opposed to war to moral and legal assistance to conscientious objectors. WRL broke with the peace churches over support for the official Civilian Public Service camps for conscientious objectors, in the belief that such support helped the government administer conscription. In prisons and in camps, militant pacifists experimented with fasts, work strikes, and other tactics of noncooperation, forging experience and interpersonal bonds that would build a new movement centered on nonviolent direct action in the Gandhian tradition.

After the war, the influx of militant war resisters radicalized WRL, and replaced the old leadership. Abe Kaufman, who had been the organization's lone staffer since 1928, resigned in 1947 and was replaced by Roy Kepler, a staunch advocate of direct action. In 1947, in the first demonstration of its kind, 400 men burned their draft cards or sent them to the White House. In 1948 WRL helped launch the Central Committee for Conscientious Objectors to counsel conscientious objectors and draft resisters. In the San Francisco area, WRL members led by Lewis Hill established the Pacifica Foundation in 1946 and its first listener-sponsored FM radio station, KPFA, in Berkeley in 1949.

As the Cold War began to limit the appeal of militant pacifism in the 1950s, WRL targeted civil rights as an area for nonviolent action. Activists Jim Peck and Igal Roodenko (who remained on the staff until his death in 1991) took part in the first "freedom ride" in the South organized by FOR and the Congress of Racial Equality (CORE) in 1947. In 1956 Bayard Rustin was employed by WRL (after leaving FOR) to work closely with the Reverend Martin Luther King, Jr., while members joined sit-ins, marches, voter registration drives, and other actions for civil rights in the North as well as the South.

The threat of nuclear war also could rally large numbers of people by 1960. At a time when schoolchildren were being taught to "duck and cover" under their desks, WRL began cosponsoring civil disobedience during a nationwide civil defense alert in 1955. The number of arrests in New York's City Hall Park grew from 28 in 1955 to 1,000 in 1960, after which the mandatory drills were called off. WRL members helped form the Committee for Nonviolent Action (CNVA) in 1958; A. J. Muste from the WRL executive committee served as national chair of CNVA. CNVA sponsored several spectacular civil disobedience campaigns—sailing the *Golden Rule* into the Pacific nuclear testing zone in 1958, and staging the Omaha Action and Polaris Action protests at missile and submarine bases in 1959 and 1960 and the San Francisco–Moscow Walk for Peace (1960–61), which took the message of unilateral disarmament to the Soviet Union for the first time. CNVA merged into WRL following Muste's death in 1967.

In 1960, David McReynolds joined the WRL staff, bringing with him a decade of experience in the Socialist party, honed writing and speaking abilities, and a strong personality that would influence the organization for the next thirty years (continuing as a leader of the Socialist party, McReynolds ran as its candidate for president in 1980). In a tribute to McReynolds celebrating his thirty years with WRL, staffer Wendy Schwartz noted he had been WRL's "chief policy-maker—the person with the knowledge and ideas and recommendations who challenges the rest of us to learn and think hard . . . He has helped create a rational political program out of the concept of pacifism, previously dismissed as a wish of the good-hearted naive. . . . He has remained steadfastly a pacifist and Socialist, irritatingly rigid in his commitment to nonviolence and social justice."

In December 1964 WRL cosponsored the first major demonstration against the Vietnam War, in New York City. McReynolds authored WRL's position on the war, calling for immediate and unconditional U.S. withdrawal. While FOR was split on participation in antiwar coalitions with communist groups and continued to favor the "third force" Buddhist neutralists in South Vietnam, McReynolds became a leader of the mobilizations as a WRL representative and gradually came to support a victory of the National Liberation Front, although without endorsing its use of violence. There was less dissent in WRL than in FOR on participation in coalitions with groups supporting revolutionary violence, although one member of the WRL executive committee, vice-chairman Charles Bloomstein, did resign over the issue in 1967. McReynolds visited Vietnam twice during the war, to the South in 1966 and to the North in 1971. During the war WRL promoted tax resistance, draft resistance, and nonviolent blockades of induction centers. WRL also endorsed the week-long 1971 May Day demonstrations. After Vietnam, WRL campaigned for nuclear disarmament. It initiated the Continental Walk for Disarmament and Social Justice in 1976, involving 10,000 people and twenty march routes from San Francisco to Washington, D.C. WRL supported the antinuclear demonstrations in the late 1970s at Seabrook, New Hampshire; Shoreham, New York; and the Pentagon.

CURRENT PRIORITIES: In 1989 WRL issued "A Platform for Disarmament" to guide its work toward the elimination of war, the foundation of international justice, shifting priorities to meeting human needs, and supporting human rights. WRL continues education on national budget priorities and war tax resistance by promoting the "Alternative Revenue System" and its "1040 EZ Peace" form, a means of channeling contributions to peace groups. Draft counseling and draft resistance remain important activities of WRL's youth and militarism program. A well-publicized "No War Toys" campaign protests the advertising and sale of war toys, particularly during the Christmas holiday.

MEMBERS: Members are asked to make the following pledge: "WRL affirms that war is a crime against humanity. We therefore are determined not to support any kind of war, international or civil, and to strive nonviolently for the removal of all causes of war." Supporters grew from 3,000 in 1964 to 15,000 in 1973 during the Vietnam War and remain close to this level today. WRL sends a monthly "key list" mailing, available by subscription, to some 300 local organizers and activists. The WRL Track Club, serving both recreational and fund-raising purposes, competes in New York City races and has been known to appear in the Marine Memorial Marathon in Washington,

D.C. Each summer WRL holds a ten-day training program for organizers in the nonviolent movement.

STRUCTURE: The membership elects two decision-making bodies: the National Committee, twenty-one members representing five geographic regions elected by the membership plus one member from each local, which meets twice a year and sets major goals; and the Executive Committee, a group of twenty-one members who meet monthly in New York City, responsible for day-to-day activities. Members of each group serve three-year terms, with one-third elected each year. Executive Committee members also serve as part of the National Committee. A New England regional office is in Norwich, Connecticut. There is a national conference every other year (as a break from workshops, participants play a traditional anarchists versus socialists softball game). WRL is a member of War Resisters International with sections in twenty-five countries; an international conference is held every three years.

RESOURCES: The League depends on member contributions for its modest $400,000 budget, and receives occasional grants through the A. J. Muste Memorial Institute.

PUBLICATIONS AND SERVICES: WRL has a keen appreciation for the power of the press. *Liberation* magazine (published from 1956 to 1977) started as a WRL project and became an important forum for the New Left of the 1960s under editor David Dellinger. *WIN* magazine (published from 1965 to 1983), a joint project of WRL and the New York–based Workshop in Nonviolence, appealed to the youth culture of the New Left. As a successor to these efforts, in 1984 WRL began publishing a new membership magazine, *The Nonviolent Activist* (circulation 14,000) eight times a year, available for a $15 subscription. WRL sells pamphlets and resources—including the popular WRL Peace Calendar—by mail order. WRI News, announcements and information from War Resisters International, is posted on PeaceNet. Publications include a wide-ranging guide to the techniques of organizing, the *WRL Organizer's Manual*, and the *WRL Guide to War Tax Resistance* (1986). □

DOVES: FROM WORLD GOVERNMENT TO ARMS CONTROL

After World War II, the founding of the United Nations presented an opportunity to establish world law and international mechanisms for conflict resolution—a "new world order" as its advocates put it. Several world federation and world law organizations came together to form the United World Federalists in 1947, with hopes of strengthening the U.N. charter, or establishing an altogether new and more encompassing world organization. That dream was set aside with the outbreak of the Cold War, as the mutual vetoes of the United States and the USSR on the Security Council prevented the U.N. from becoming an exclusive peacekeeping power. The realistic short-range goal would have to be arms control agreements. *Saturday Review* editor Norman Cousins led the world federalists, but also founded the National Committee for a Sane Nuclear Policy (SANE) in

1957, bringing together pacifists and world government advocates for the more modest goal of limiting nuclear arms. Radical pacifists formed the Committee for Nonviolent Action, which sponsored the 1958 voyage of Captain Albert Bigelow's *Golden Rule*, which attempted to sail into a nuclear testing zone in the Pacific. The Student Peace Union, founded in 1959, began to win a following on college campuses. Women Strike for Peace was organized in 1961 by Dagmar Wilson, and picketed the U.N. and the White House for disarmament and a test ban treaty. Dr. Bernard Lown and Dr. Victor Sidel started Physicians for Social Responsibility in Boston in 1961 to address the medical effects of nuclear war and work for the test ban treaty. Also in Boston, Leo Szilard and fellow nuclear scientists organized the Council for a Livable World in 1962 to support candidates for the U.S. Senate who would back nuclear arms control. SANE and the other groups won a major victory with the Limited Test Ban Treaty in 1963, but momentum was lost after the assassination of John Kennedy in November 1963. Lyndon Johnson's expansion of the U.S. intervention in Vietnam soon engaged the full energy of the peace movement, and little attention was given to checking the accelerating nuclear arms race from the mid-1960s through the late 1970s.

WORLD FEDERALIST ASSOCIATION

418 7TH STREET, SE

WASHINGTON, DC 20003

(202) 546-3950

FOUNDED: 1947 MEMBERS: 8,500
CHAPTERS: 70 BUDGET: $500,000
STAFF: 10 TAX STATUS: 501(c)(3): World Federalist Association; 501(c)(4): Campaign for U.N. Reform

PURPOSE: "The abolition of war and the protection of the global environment through a system based on world law, limited in accord with the principle of federalism, in which global institutions could resolve conflicts peacefully and provide security and justice."

The World Federalist Association (WFA) is the leading organization of "one worlders," promoting the idea of world peace through world law. An influential component of the liberal mainstream just after World War II, world federalism declined as the Cold War flourished in the 1950s. Although world federalists adopted the arms control agenda, other organizations with greater appeal emerged in the 1960s. With the collapse of the Soviet bloc and talk of a "new world order" in the air at the beginning of the 1990s, WFA finds more receptive ears for its program of "transforming the United Nations into a democratic world federation capable of ensuring peace, economic progress and environmental protection."

BACKGROUND: WFA's predecessor, the United World Federalists (UWF), was formed in February 1947 at a convention in Ashville, North Carolina, which merged five organizations, led by World Federalists USA and Americans United for World Government. Sam Levering, a Quaker activist, served as the first interim director, followed by Upshur Evans as executive director and Cord Meyer, Jr., as president. Believing the United Nations charter to be too weak to prevent wars among heavily armed sovereign states, the world federalists sought a stronger form of world government. After forty years of the Cold War, it is surprising to realize how widely the sentiment was shared. Many individuals who would become prominent in politics were UWF members in its early days, including Senators Alan Cranston and Thomas Dodd—and even Ronald Reagan and George Bush. In the late 1940s Robert Lee Humber persuaded twenty-three state legislatures, many in the South, to pass resolutions advocating world federal government. In 1949, congressional resolutions calling for developing the United Nations into a world federation were sponsored by 111 congressmen and 22 senators— the high-water mark for world government advocates. With the start of the Korean War in 1950, the movement was eclipsed. Cord Meyer left the president's position in 1951 to take a government position—as it turned out, with the Central Intelligence Agency (from which he would funnel money to the National Student Association and other liberal-left organizations). Membership fell from a peak of 40,000 to 20,000 in the 1960s to 8,500 by 1990.

During the 1950s and early 1960s many world federalists supported legislation that led to creation of the Arms Control and Disarmament Agency in 1961. Norman Cousins, editor of *Saturday Review*, became a central figure in the world federalist movement—serving as president of UWF, international president of the World Association of World Federalists, and president of the WFA from 1976 until his death in 1990. Cousins helped start the Committee for a Sane Nuclear Policy (SANE) in 1957, and tried to engineer a merger of SANE and UWF in 1964, but final agreement was not reached. In 1975 UWF shifted its educational programs to WFA, and Campaign for U.N. Reform was established as a lobbying wing.

CURRENT PRIORITIES: WFA supports creation of an International Criminal Court to try crimes against international criminal law, and an International Arms Control Verification agency. WFA's environmental program objectives include a U.N. Environmental Security Council with power to develop and enforce international environmental regulations, an enhanced International Court of Justice to adjudicate environmental disputes among nations, a global environmental fund to assist poor nations with technology and sustainable development, and U.S. ratification of the Law of the Sea Treaty.

STRUCTURE: WFA has a 104-member board of directors, half elected by the sixty chapters and half selected by the board itself; there is a 35-member executive committee, and an annual membership assembly. WFA field offices are maintained in Boston, Chicago, Los Angeles, New York, and Pittsburgh. Former Republican congressman and independent presidential candidate John Anderson was elected WFA president in 1991. Walter Hoffmann retired from WFA's executive director post in 1992; Tim Barner, a WFA leader from Pittsburgh, was hired as the new executive director. WFA is a member of the World Federalist Movement (WFM), headquartered in Amsterdam, which has members in thirty-three countries and affiliated organizations in fifteen countries. WFM is accredited to the United Nations, and has an office in New York. Actor Peter Ustinov was elected WFM president in 1991 at its international congress, which is held every four years.

PUBLICATIONS AND SERVICES: Membership is $30 and includes the quarterly national newsletter *World Federalist* (circulation 8,500) and a regional newsletter. Activist members can join the WFA ONE/21 Club, to write a letter or take one specific action a month to help achieve world government by the twenty-first century. You can get information on WFA from a toll-free telephone number: (800) HATE-WAR. An annual report is available from the national office. A source of continuing inspiration for world federalism is the detailed proposal for revising the U.N. Charter by Grenville Clark and Louis Sohn, *World Peace Through World Law* (1948; Harvard University Press, 3rd edition enlarged, 1966); see also Sohn's update in Clark and Sohn, *Introduction to World Peace Through World Law*, revised edition (1973; World Without War Publications, 1984). □

SANE/FREEZE:
CAMPAIGN FOR GLOBAL SECURITY

1819 H STREET, NW

WASHINGTON, DC 20006

(202) 862-9740

FOUNDED: 1957   MEMBERS: 130,000
CHAPTERS: 240   BUDGET: $1.5 million
STAFF: 16   TAX STATUS: 501(c)(4):
SANE/FREEZE: Campaign for Global Security;
501(c)(3): National SANE/FREEZE Education
Fund; PAC: SANE/FREEZE PAC

PURPOSE: "We share a vision of world peace: where the menace of nuclear weapons has forever been erased from our planet, where war has been abolished as a method of solving conflicts, where all human beings are assured the wherewithal to live in health and dignity, where no one is denied the opportunity to participate in making decisions that affect the common good."

SANE/FREEZE: Campaign for Global Security, the largest peace organization in the United States, is the product of a 1987 merger that promised to build a powerhouse for the peace movement. The plan was this: SANE, with its roots in the disarmament campaigns of the late 1950s and early 1960s, would provide its national structure, media savvy, and lobbying presence in Washington, D.C. The Freeze, launched at the beginning of the Reagan administration as a fresh campaign to end the arms race, would supply its grassroots activists. Financial problems (debt from the Freeze) and timing (thawing of the Cold War) have left the organization struggling to realize its potential.

BACKGROUND: On the first day of summer in 1957, Norman Cousins, editor of *Saturday Review* and a leader of the world federalist movement, and Clarence Pickett of the American Friends Service Committee brought together twenty-seven national leaders concerned about nuclear weapons proliferation and radioactive fallout from atmospheric nuclear weapons testing. The group chose the name National Committee for a Sane Nuclear Policy (SANE for short) after urging from psychoanalyst Erich Fromm. Although the group was rooted in two constituencies left of center (moderate pacifists and supporters of world government), SANE appealed to a wider public on the liberal side of the mainstream.

The new committee started by publishing the first of many full-page ads in *The New York Times* in November 1957 under the headline "We Are Facing A Danger Unlike Any Danger That Has Ever Existed." Thousands responded as the ad was reprinted across the country, starting a movement that surprised even the SANE leaders. Local committees sprang up in dozens of communities. By the summer of 1958, there were 25,000 members and 130 local chapters advocating a nuclear weapons test ban. From the start SANE received the support of influential sponsors including Eleanor Roosevelt, Linus Pauling, Albert Schweitzer, Cleveland Amory, Norman Thomas, and the Reverend Martin Luther King, Jr. Its popularity spread to Hollywood where

entertainer Steve Allen hosted the first meeting of a Hollywood SANE chapter, including such stars as Marlon Brando, Henry Fonda, Kirk Douglas, and Gregory Peck.

In May 1960 SANE held a major rally of 20,000 people in Madison Square Garden in New York, and a Hollywood concert with Harry Belafonte that drew 6,500 people. On the eve of the rally, while SANE was at the height of its early influence and prestige, the organization was thrown into crisis by Senator Thomas Dodd (D-Connecticut), a leading opponent of a nuclear test ban, who demanded that SANE purge its ranks of communists. He subpoenaed Henry Abrams, cochair of the West Side New York SANE and organizer of the rally at Madison Square Garden. Abrams took the Fifth Amendment, charging the hearings were attempting to discredit the movement to end the arms race.

Rather than defend the principle of open membership or Abrams's effective work, Cousins dismissed Abrams (who denied he was under the direction of any outside organization) from the New York SANE leadership. SANE established a policy that "membership in the Communist Party is incompatible with association with SANE." Dodd's attacks and SANE's response drove out half the New York chapters in protest of what they considered "McCarthyite" tactics by SANE's board.

The election of John Kennedy as president in November 1960 created hope that his New Frontier would be more open to peace initiatives than the administration of Dwight Eisenhower. In spite of the setbacks caused by Senator Dodd, SANE continued placing ads advocating a nuclear test ban as the United States and the USSR negotiated for thirty-six months in Geneva— through the Berlin Wall and Cuban missile crises. SANE was a major lobby behind the creation of the U.S. Arms Control and Disarmament Agency in September 1961. Finally in 1963 President Kennedy and Soviet premier Khrushchev signed the Limited Test Ban Treaty, prohibiting atmospheric testing of nuclear weapons. SANE played a crucial role in mobilizing popular support for Senate ratification. The treaty victory undercut the momentum of disarmament activism, and soon the Vietnam War captured the attention of peace activists.

The Vietnam War created a second period of contentious internal division in SANE, which was beset by the same conflicts over tactics and allies as other peace groups. Concerned to appear a model of "responsible" protest, SANE avoided the Students for a Democratic Society (SDS) rally in the summer of 1965, but planned its own march in Washington for November—when it brought a crowd of 35,000 mostly middle-class adults to hear speeches of moderate dissent (except for SDS president Carl Oglesby, who denounced Cold War liberalism). SANE was cautious, calling for negotiations among all parties to the war.

Controversy developed around an unlikely person—pediatrician Benjamin Spock, who had been recruited to SANE in 1962 (a spectacularly effective full-page ad on radioactive fallout proclaimed "Dr. Spock is worried"). Spock had agreed to cochair with Reverend Martin Luther King, Jr., the April 1967 Spring Mobilization to End the War in Vietnam, organized by A. J. Muste. The SANE board would not endorse the event, as it was "non-exclusionary," accepting everyone regardless of politics, tactics, or slogans. Many SANE chapters supported Spock and the April Mobilization, and a line was drawn between liberals and radicals within the organization. Norman Cousins and executive director Donald Keyes resigned believing the organization had become too radical; Spock resigned as cochair believing SANE to be too conservative.

Over the summer of 1968, SANE strongly supported Senator Eugene McCarthy's bid for the Democratic presidential nomination (won by Hubert Humphrey). By the fall of 1969 SANE had decided to support the October Vietnam Moratorium and the November march on Washington led by the New Mobilization Committee—in effect coming to support immediate unilateral withdrawal of U.S. forces. In 1972 SANE supported Senator George McGovern's unsuccessful presidential campaign to unseat Richard Nixon. Throughout the 1970s SANE lobbied for arms control, supporting the Anti-ballistic Missile (ABM) Limitation Treaty and the Strategic Arms Limitation Treaty (SALT I), and opposing the Trident submarine, Cruise missile, and B-1 bomber programs. After American troops returned from Vietnam, SANE like other peace groups lost membership, reaching a low of 6,000 in 1977. Merger discussions with the World Federalist Association, Clergy and Laity Concerned, and the Council for a Livable World did not bear fruit, and Sanford Gottlieb, executive director since 1967, resigned.

Thirty-year-old David Cortright, a GI

who had organized for peace within the army during the Vietnam War, was hired in 1977 to rebuild the organization. Cortright had worked at the Institute for Policy Studies (IPS), the leading think tank on the left in Washington, D.C. Cortright recruited IPS leader Marcus Raskin to the SANE board as well as IPS financial angel Cora Weiss, activist and heir to the cosmetic fortune of Samuel Rubin, and William Winpisinger, president of the International Association of Machinists (who agreed to be SANE's cochair, with economic conversion advocate Seymour Melman). Attracting foundation and union money to hire new staff, SANE focused on legislative issues: blocking funds for the B-1 bomber, ratifying the SALT II treaty, defeating the MX missile system, and promoting conversion of military industries to civilian purposes. SANE initiated the first door-to-door canvass campaign for peace in the nation, employing fifty full-time organizers who contacted a quarter of a million households. Membership rocketed from 17,000 in 1982 to 90,000 in 1984 and 150,000 by 1987, supporting a full-time staff of forty. Cortright pushed outreach to black and Hispanic leaders, recruiting Jesse Jackson to the SANE board and emphasizing opposition to Reagan's interventions in Central America.

Meanwhile, Randall Forsberg had launched the Freeze movement with a simple proposal. Her idea was to unite behind a basic first step: a bilateral, verifiable freeze in the production, testing, and deployment of nuclear weapons. Forsberg's 1980 "Call to Halt the Nuclear Arms Race" revitalized the peace movement. Assisted by the peace education staff of the American Friends Service Committee, activists promoted Freeze resolutions across New England. A loosely structured Nuclear Weapons Freeze Campaign was organized, with a national coordinating office in St. Louis. A CBS–*New York Times* poll in 1982 found that 72 percent of the American public favored a bilateral nuclear weapons freeze. By 1984, 370 cities, 71 city councils, 23 state legislatures, and 446 New England town meetings had passed Freeze resolutions.

The 1984 elections brought mixed results, returning Ronald Reagan to the White House, but increasing Democratic seats in the Senate by two. Voters exiting the polls revealed many had voted for Freeze resolutions *and* for Reagan, who had argued his Strategic Defense Initiative (dubbed "Star Wars" by opponents) would reverse the arms race. Freeze Voter, an independent PAC run by William "Chip" Reynolds, raised $3.5 million, supported a staff of 200, and mobilized 25,000 volunteers from Freeze supporters. Its candidates won in four of eight Senate contests and twenty-five of thirty-five House races. SANE PAC also ran its largest campaign to date in 1984, raising $250,000.

In his second term Reagan quickly outflanked the peace movement by calling for deep reductions in nuclear weapons in his summit meetings with Soviet premier Gorbachev in Geneva in 1985 and Reykjavik in 1986. The House had approved the Freeze resolution in 1983, but it failed to pass the Senate. After 1984, with Reagan seizing the initiative in arms control, media coverage of the Freeze movement declined and the issue faded from the public eye.

Freeze Voter continued through the 1986 campaign, when the Democrats regained control of the Senate, but disbanded after the 1988 elections.

Staff from SANE and the Freeze initiated merger talks in 1986. Local Freeze groups, with their consensus decision-making and distrust of strong leadership, were suspicious of SANE's top-down traditions. After lengthy discussions of structure and program, merger was ratified by the Freeze convention in December 1986 and by SANE's convention the following January; the merged organization held its first national convention in November 1987. SANE brought to the marriage a financially solvent national office, sophistication using the media, sustained lobbying experience, and an agenda beyond the nuclear weapons freeze. Although in financial disarray, the Freeze complemented SANE with a democratic grassroots structure and a politically active membership. The new organization would be headed by a president and two codirectors, Cortright of SANE and Carolyn Cottom of the Freeze. Leading candidates for president included former congressman Bob Edgar, a strong supporter of the Freeze movement, and Reverend William Sloan Coffin, pastor of Riverside Church in New York. Coffin, a close associate of SANE's Cora Weiss, was selected by the SANE/FREEZE executive committee and left Riverside Church in 1987.

The amount of Freeze debt that surfaced—some $300,000—surprised and dismayed the new leadership. Many staff from the merged national offices had to be laid off. Some local Freeze activists balked at joining the new organization. Even choosing a name proved contentious—the best that could be agreed upon after a poll of members and long debate was the lengthy "SANE/FREEZE: Campaign for Global Security." The codirector scheme proved unworkable. Cortright and Cottom resigned, and Nick Carter, a former Freeze staffer, was hired as the new executive director in 1988. Support for peace groups began to plummet with the signing of the Intermediate-Range Nuclear Forces (INF) Treaty in December 1987, and the fall of the Berlin Wall and collapse of Communist governments in Eastern Europe in 1989. Monica Green has been executive director since 1990.

CURRENT PRIORITIES: At its third annual congress in 1990 SANE/FREEZE identified priorities including: (1) a comprehensive test ban treaty, (2) a 50 percent cut in the U.S. military budget with reallocation of savings to domestic needs, (3) a permanent halt to the production of nuclear materials for weapons, (4) a 50 percent reduction in strategic nuclear warheads in the START treaty, (5) support for economic conversion projects, (6) deeper cuts in conventional forces in Europe, (7) a halt to chemical and biological weapons production, (8) opposition to U.S. military intervention abroad, and (9) promoting the concept of global security through international organizations.

MEMBERS: Integrating Freeze activists into the new organization wasn't easy; the decentralized Freeze never had a national membership, much less a membership list, until its last year. At its peak just after the merger, SANE/

FREEZE claimed 180,000 members; some 130,000 are current.

STRUCTURE: The national board has twenty-nine directors elected by the membership to represent state affiliates, with twenty-five at-large members selected by the board to include national figures and promote diversity (there's a goal of 50 percent representation of women and one-third of people of color). The national board hires the executive director and interprets policy. An annual national congress, with delegates chosen by congressional district by the membership, sets policy.

RESOURCES: Just before merging with the Freeze, SANE's annual budget peaked around $4 million. After merger the decline in membership and support has left SANE/FREEZE with a $1.5 million budget, from member dues and contributions, with some support from foundation grants. To reduce the inherited debt, SANE's headquarters (an old townhouse near Capitol Hill dubbed the Ben Spock building) was sold, and the office moved to rented space. From a peak of 40 full-time staff and 100 canvassers, the staff is down to 15 in Washington, D.C., and 1 in New York City, with 15 part-time fund-raisers plus canvassers.

PUBLICATIONS AND SERVICES: Membership is $25 and includes the quarterly *SANE/FREEZE News* (circulation 130,000). An annual Senate and House voting record and rating is compiled. The SANE/FREEZE Weekly Legislative Report is posted on PeaceNet. Message checks and a SANE/FREEZE affinity MasterCard are available. The

history of SANE to 1985 is told in Milton S. Katz's *Ban the Bomb* (Greenwood Press, 1986). Pam Solo relates the story of the Nuclear Weapons Freeze Campaign in *From Protest to Policy* (Ballinger, 1988). □

Council For A Livable World

COUNCIL FOR A LIVABLE WORLD

20 PARK PLAZA

BOSTON, MA 02216

(617) 542-2282

PEACEPAC

110 MARYLAND AVENUE, NE

WASHINGTON, DC 20002

(202) 543-4100

FOUNDED: 1962   CONTRIBUTORS: 40,000
BUDGET: $1.4 million (2-year cycle)   STAFF: 7
TAX STATUS: PACs: Council for a Livable World and PeacePac; 501(c)(3): CLW Education Fund

PURPOSE: "To combat the menace of nuclear war and strengthen national security through rational arms control."

The Council for a Livable World (CLW) is the leading political arm of the arms control movement.

BACKGROUND: The Council for a Livable World was founded in 1962 by the nuclear physicist Leo Szilard and other scientists who worked to create atomic weapons during World War II. CLW was designed for three functions: conducting research on disarmament, lobbying Congress for arms control, and electing sympathetic candidates to the U.S. Senate (because of the Senate's special role ratifying arms control agreements negotiated by the President). Szilard died in 1964, but by then CLW was firmly established. PeacePAC, headquartered in CLW's Washington office, was started in 1982 to raise money for House candidates.

CURRENT PRIORITIES: In Washington, CLW lobbies to influence arms control legislation and reduce the military budget, monitors voting records in the Senate, and conducts seminars providing technical and scientific information to Senators and their staffs. CLW supports a comprehensive nuclear test ban treaty and strategic arms cuts beyond the scheduled START reductions, and opposes the B-2 bomber, the MX missile rail system, the Midgetman missile, space weapons, and chemical weapons. CLW supports a 50 percent reduction in the military budget over the next five years, with economic conversion assistance to communities hit by military cutbacks.

CONTRIBUTORS: CLW has 40,000 contributors, 7,000 of whom take part in the "Grassroots Network" responding to legislative alerts by calling senators and congressmen. PeacePAC has 12,000 contributors. CLW pioneered the technique of "bundling" contributions—collecting checks made out directly to a candidate's campaign fund. By turning over a large number of checks to a candidate, CLW demonstrates the strength of support for arms control—and gets around the Federal Election Campaign Act's limitation on multicandidate PACs of giving no more than $5,000 per candidate per election ($10,000 for both a primary and general election).

STRUCTURE: CLW serves both as a lobbying organization and a PAC. CLW has a twenty-four-member board of directors, mostly from the Boston area, including scientists and other academics from MIT and Harvard. Jerome Grossman, president for many years, is now chairman of the board. John Isaacs, formerly the legislative director in the Washington, D.C., office, is president and chief executive. Wayne Jaquith directs the Boston office. PeacePAC shares a number of directors in common with CLW on its twelve-member board. The chair of PeacePAC is Robert Drinan, a Catholic priest who spent ten years in the House of Representatives; Suzy Kerr is executive director.

RESOURCES: In the 1984 election, CLW raised nearly $900,000 for candidates for the Senate. In the crucial 1986 elections, when the Democrats regained control of the Senate, CLW spent nearly $1.3 million; thirteen of the seventeen candidates it backed won. CLW raised $955,000 in the 1988 campaign cycle, and $1.4 million in the 1990 cycle. CLW helped organize an affiliated organization, PeacePAC, in 1982 to raise money for candidates for the House of Representatives. The CLW

Education Fund is a 501(c)(3) arm organized in 1980 to handle tax-deductible contributions for public education on the arms race; its annual budget is $450,000. PeacePAC raised $313,000 in the 1988 campaign cycle, and $400,000 in the 1990 cycle.

PUBLICATIONS AND SERVICES: CLW issues several mailings with fact sheets on endorsed candidates, and an annual summary of activity. PeacePAC publishes fact sheets on candidates and an annual election report, and rates House members on arms control votes. CLW maintains the "Nuclear Arms Control Hotline," with latest legislative information and lobbying suggestions: (202) 543-0006; hotline information is also posted weekly on PeaceNet. For a related collection of papers, letters, and documents, see *Toward a Livable World: Leo Szilard and the Crusade for Nuclear Arms Control*, edited by Helen S. Hawkins, G. Allen Greb, and Gertrud Weiss Szilard (MIT Press, 1987). □

DOVES REVIVED: NUCLEAR DISARMAMENT

Surprisingly, few lasting organizations (still active twenty-five years later) emerged directly from opposition to the Vietnam War in the 1960s and 1970s (two exceptions from Boston: the Union of Concerned Scientists, which developed out of the teach-ins; and Resist, which developed out of the draft resistance movement; one other, Clergy and Laity Concerned, emerged from the liberal religious community). Instead, the movement was built around coalitions of previously existing pacifist, Left, student, and disarmament groups. Mobili-

zation committees consisting of an uneasy alliance of pacifist groups, Communists, and Trotskyists coordinated major demonstrations, such as the October 1967 march from the Lincoln Memorial to the Pentagon (later described by Norman Mailer in *The Armies of the Night*). After President Nixon's invasion of Cambodia at the end of April 1970, peace activists split over tactics —the Trotskyist coalition would only support peaceful, legal demonstrations, and the Mobilization coalition wanted to add nonviolent civil disobedience to demonstrations. Movement leaders became exhausted by years of frenetic work, growing factionalism and disputes over tactics, and prosecutions such as the Chicago conspiracy trial. Other activists were being drawn into the growing women's movement and the new environmental movement.

When Jimmy Carter defeated Gerald Ford in the 1976 presidential elections, returning the Democrats to the White House, the peace movement had some reason for hope. Carter was committed to continue Nixon and Kissinger's policy of detente toward the Soviet Union and to a foreign policy that would require U.S. allies to live up to international agreements on human rights. Nixon had negotiated the Antiballistic Missile Limitation Treaty (SALT I) with the USSR in 1972, and Carter would push on to a SALT II agreement. The Helsinki Accords, negotiated in 1975 while Ford was president, established the Conference on Security and Cooperation in Europe (CSCE) as a forum for human rights and mutual security issues. But rather than following these issues closely, many peace activists were pulled in another direction.

The prospect of a nuclear power plant at Seabrook, New Hampshire, prompted the formation of the Clamshell Alliance in 1976 by pacifists in New England, many from the American Friends Service Committee (AFSC), committed to nonviolent direct action. Organized in affinity groups and using a consensus decision-making process, the Clams tried tactics of massive civil disobedience, resulting in many arrests. Unable to settle disputes over tactics that might lead to violence, the Clamshell Alliance broke apart. In California a similar Abalone Alliance attempted to block the Diablo Canyon nuclear plant near San Luis Obispo, but the movement faded after 1978 and 1981 blockades that failed to stop construction. Many activists shifted to the Livermore Action Group that conducted nonviolent civil disobedience from 1981 to 1984 against the Lawrence Livermore National Laboratory, which manufactured nuclear weapons. The protests were symbolic action, a combination of moral witness and public theater, more "expressive politics" than practical politics. Hoping to couple the antinuke energy with traditional disarmament and social justice activity, the old Vietnam "Mobe" activists pulled together a new Mobilization for Survival coalition in 1977, based on a four-point platform: "zero nuclear weapons, ban nuclear power, reverse the arms race, and meet human needs"; in 1986 they added "stop military intervention."

Carter's arms control efforts quickly ran into trouble. A second round of OPEC oil price increases produced serious inflation in the American economy. The Soviet Union increased its support for its Cuban army surrogates fighting in Angola and Ethiopia, and in 1979 invaded Afghanistan to intervene between two warring Communist factions who had seized the government in a coup. Carter imposed a grain embargo on the Soviet Union and canceled U.S. participation in the summer 1980 Moscow Olympics. The resurgent right wing successfully fought Senate ratification of the SALT II treaty concluded in 1979. Iranian revolutionaries held Americans hostage in the U.S. embassy after Ayatollah Khomeini ousted the Shah. Carter's presidency ended in disarray, and with the election of Ronald Reagan in 1980 the peace movement wasn't in very good shape either.

Reagan's rhetoric about the Soviet Union as "the evil empire" revived the peace movement much the way his appointment of James Watt as interior secretary lit a fire under environmentalists. Many peace activists who were students during the Vietnam War era found new vehicles in the 1980s to express their concerns as young professionals. Dr. Helen Caldicott had already begun her effort to revitalize Physicians for Social Responsibility in 1978, and helped form the Women's Party for Survival in Boston in 1980, a group that became Women's Action for Nuclear Disarmament (WAND) in 1983. The Jobs with Peace Campaign also got started in 1978, working to shift funds from the defense budget to meet human needs; its local referenda campaigns caught on during the 1980s. The Union of Concerned Scientists emphasized nuclear power safety issues during the 1970s, and shifted toward checking the nuclear arms race in the 1980s. "Social responsibility" groups expanded beyond physicians in the early 1980s to include lawyers, architects/designers/planners, educators, psychologists, computer professionals, and business executives. New organizations such as Beyond War and Peace Links reached out to a moderate professional and managerial heartland constituency uncomfortable with the "movement" style of peace activists. Widespread interest in citizen diplomacy led to exchanged visits of local officials and professionals and the establishment of sister city relationships, particularly with the Soviet Union and Central America.

PSR

PHYSICIANS FOR SOCIAL RESPONSIBILITY

1000 16TH STREET, NW, SUITE 810

WASHINGTON, DC 20036

(202) 785-3777

FOUNDED: 1961   MEMBERS: 30,000
CHAPTERS: 125   BUDGET: $2.1 million
STAFF: 21   TAX STATUS: 501(c)(3)

PURPOSE: "A national organization of health professionals working on issues related to nuclear weapons, environmental degradation, and federal budget priorities."

Nuclear war could be the ultimate epidemic. Physicians and other health professionals have an ethical responsibility to help prevent a nuclear holocaust. From a modest start in the early 1960s, Physicians for Social Responsi-

bility (PSR) came to life in the late 1970s and inspired a worldwide network, the International Physicians for the Prevention of Nuclear War (IPPNW), which won its leaders the Nobel Peace Prize in 1985. PSR's greatest achievement is establishing nuclear war prevention as a legitimate part of the professional practice of medicine.

BACKGROUND: What was to become Physicians for Social Responsibility began in 1961 with a small group of doctors (including Bernard Lown and Victor Sidel) meeting in Cambridge, Massachusetts, to hear British Nobel peace laureate Philip Noel-Baker talk about the dangers of nuclear war. Concerned about the growing stockpiles of nuclear weapons, the physicians began research on the medical effects of nuclear war, which was published in the *New England Journal of Medicine*. PSR's work influenced the passage of the 1963 Limited Test Ban Treaty.

As public interest in nuclear issues was displaced by the Vietnam War during the late 1960s and early 1970s, PSR maintained a low profile. In 1978 Dr. Helen Caldicott, an instructor of pediatrics at Harvard Medical School and assistant in medicine at Children's Hospital in Boston, was elected PSR president and gave the organization a second life. Caldicott, a dynamic speaker, toured the country with a catalyzing message on the dangers of nuclear war. Conflicts over style and direction led Caldicott to step down in 1983 and devote her energies to building Women's Action for Nuclear Disarmament (WAND).

PSR helped change conventional wisdom to the understanding that fighting a nuclear war is unacceptable. As a model for professional organizations, PSR inspired sister groups for educators, lawyers, psychologists, architects, engineers, planners, and computer experts. PSR's success owes something to the status of physicians, and particularly the respect their opinions have on matters of life and death. Most medical schools now offer some form of education regarding the effects of nuclear war, and the leading professional organizations, including the American Medical Association, the American Public Health Association, the American Psychiatric Association, and the National Medical Association, have passed resolutions urging doctors to become involved in the campaign to prevent nuclear war.

In 1980, Bernard Lown and his Soviet colleague Evgueni Chazov (the two cardiologists had met in the 1960s) formed International Physicians for the Prevention of Nuclear War (IPPNW). PSR was the model for the group that now has 150,000 physician members in affiliated chapters in forty-nine countries. IPPNW members drew up four guidelines: They agreed to restrict their focus to nuclear war, to base their efforts on their professional vows to preserve life and health, to involve physicians from East and West in circulating factual information throughout the world, and to avoid taking positions on specific policies of any government. In 1985, copresidents Lown and Chazov received the Nobel Peace Prize for the work of the IPPNW to educate the public about the devastating medical consequences of nuclear war. Some also saw it as a message to President Reagan and Soviet premier Gorbachev, who were scheduled to meet later that year to discuss arms control.

CURRENT PRIORITIES: PSR has three priority programs: (1) education on the health risks associated with the continued production and testing of nuclear weapons (prescriptions: a Comprehensive Nuclear Test Ban Treaty, closing down and cleaning up the Department of Energy's nuclear weapons facilities, and continued arms reduction agreements), (2) shifting excessive spending on the military budget to increased funding of health programs and other human services, and (3) its newest campaign, reducing environmental degradation from toxics and global warming. PSR will work to establish that environmental issues, like nuclear weapons, are important for health professionals to care about.

MEMBERS: PSR has two categories: full membership at $90 (open to all health professionals with doctoral degrees) and health staff and associates at $50 (student rates also available), and other supporters (PSR and IPPNW have both done extensive direct-mail fund-raising to the general public). From a peak of 60,000 in 1986 (25,000 full members and 35,000 supporters), PSR's support has declined some 50 percent to 30,000 in 1990 (12,000 full members and 18,000 supporters). There is an annual conference open to all members.

STRUCTURE: In 1991, PSR changed its governing structure, merging the board of directors with the House of Delegates, a group chosen democratically by region. The new forty-member board has many regional and chapter representatives. The executive director as of 1991 is Julia Moore, formerly deputy director of the Arms Control Association and communications vice president for World Wildlife Fund. Previous executives have included Tom Halstead, Jane Wales, and Maureen Thornton.

RESOURCES: PSR's $2.3 million revenue in 1991 was derived from member dues and contributions (77 percent), grants (14 percent), and other sources (9 percent). Expenses of $2.2 million covered program services (64 percent), fundraising (17 percent), and administration (19 percent).

PUBLICATIONS AND SERVICES: The newsletter *PSR Reports* (circulation 30,000) goes out three times a year to the whole membership. The *PSR Quarterly*, begun in 1991, is a scholarly journal (circulation 12,000), sent to full members in the health professions. The *PSR Monitor* (circulation 4,000) contains legislative information for members who join PSR's activist network. PSR maintains an arms control hotline: (202) 543-0006; PSR Bulletins are posted on PeaceNet. A PSR affinity MasterCard is available. □

UNION OF CONCERNED SCIENTISTS

UNION OF CONCERNED SCIENTISTS

26 CHURCH STREET

CAMBRIDGE, MA 02238

(617) 547-5552

FOUNDED: 1969 MEMBERS: 90,000
BUDGET: $4 million STAFF: 38
TAX STATUS: 501(c)(3)

PURPOSE: "To give scientists a voice in important decisions having to do with the impact of advanced technology on society."

The Union of Concerned Scientists (UCS) combines scientific research with analysis and advocacy on national energy policy and arms control. Backed by its research, UCS rallies the scientific community to sign declarations and appeals on issues of science policy. UCS makes excellent use of the media, op-ed columns, and expert testimony to publicize its positions.

BACKGROUND: A group of forty MIT professors and graduate students formed UCS around the March 1969 teach-ins on the Vietnam War. A position paper authored by professors Henry Kendall and Kurt Gottfried urged work on "survival problems": the nuclear arms race, chemical and biological warfare, air pollution, and nuclear power safety. In its first three years UCS actively opposed antiballistic missile systems (ABMs) and supported the ABM Limitation Treaty signed by the United States and the USSR in 1972.

UCS began raising questions about the safety of nuclear power plants in the early 1970s. After studies revealed serious design dangers, UCS sponsored a "Scientists' Declaration on Nuclear Power" in 1975 (signed by over 2,000 physicists, biologists, chemists, engineers, and other scientists), which called for a moratorium on new plant construction and a halt to reactor exports. Robert Pollard, a Nuclear Regulatory Commission project manager, resigned during a *60 Minutes* broadcast in a dramatic protest of poor attention to safety concerns, and joined the UCS staff in 1976 as its reactor safety specialist. In January 1979 UCS called for the immediate shutdown of sixteen of the seventy-two operating nuclear power plants in the United States, including the Three Mile Island plant, which would be damaged two months later by the worst accident in the history of the U.S. commercial nuclear power program. UCS also raised the issue of radioactive wastes with studies from 1975 to 1980. UCS has not opposed nuclear power absolutely, for ever and all time, but it does call for no further nuclear plants until issues of safety standards, radioactive waste disposal, and plutonium safeguards are resolved.

As President Jimmy Carter negotiated the SALT II treaty in the late 1970s, UCS revived its device of a scientists' manifesto with the "Scientists' Declaration on the Nuclear Arms Race," issued in 1977 and signed by over 12,000 scientists and engineers, calling for the United States and the Soviet Union to halt underground weapons testing and the testing and deployment of new weapons systems. The SALT II treaty was signed in 1979, but was never ratified by the Senate, being withdrawn by President Carter following the Soviet invasion of Afghanistan. UCS also actively opposed the MX missile deployment plans throughout the Carter and Reagan administrations.

As concern for arms control intensified during President Reagan's first term, UCS updated its arms race statement with the "Framework for a New National Security Policy" in 1982, calling for a comprehensive test ban, "no first use" of nuclear weapons, a bilateral nuclear weapons freeze, a nonproliferation policy, and massive reductions in nuclear arsenals. Forty-six Nobel laureates in science and medicine and over 500 members of the National Academy of Sciences endorsed the UCS "Framework." Leading the opposition to President Reagan's Strategic Defense Initiative proposal, UCS organized an "Appeal by American Scientists to Ban Space Weapons" in 1985 (signed by 57 Nobel laureates and more than 700 members of the National Academy of Sciences). UCS was generally credited as the leading lobby against the "Star Wars" proposals.

CURRENT PRIORITIES: *Energy program* priorities include global warming, national energy policy, transportation, and nuclear power safety. A "Scientists' Appeal on Global Warming" issued in 1990 is the centerpiece of UCS's energy policy campaign to reduce dependence on fossil fuels by energy efficiency and by clean and renewable energy sources. *Transportation* policy emphasizes fuel efficiency, alternative fuels, and increased funding for mass transit. *Arms control* programs include nuclear weapons, nuclear proliferation, European security, and arms control treaties. UCS has placed a priority on reducing U.S. and Soviet strategic nuclear weapons by 75 percent to 3,000 to 4,000 by 1995, and by 90 percent to 1,000 to 2,000 by the year 2000. In 1992 UCS initiated a new program on *population, consumption, and environmental degradation* to focus on air, water, and atmospheric pollution;

the poverty and oppression of women that underlie high fertility rates in developing countries; and energy conservation and recycling.

MEMBERS: UCS contributors, called sponsors, have remained relatively constant around 90,000 for the past few years. With its second track of energy and environmental issues, UCS has not experienced the decline felt by most peace groups. UCS maintains two activist networks: the Legislative Action Network for arms control, and the Scientist Action Network for global warming and other energy and environment issues.

STRUCTURE: UCS is governed by an eleven-member, self-recruiting board of directors. Physicist Henry Kendall of MIT has chaired the board since 1973 (in 1990 he shared a Nobel Prize for discovering quarks). UCS cofounder Victor Weisskopf, Manhattan Project group leader at Los Alamos (and professor emeritus of physics at MIT), remains a board member. Claudine Schneider, former Republican member of the House of Representatives from Rhode Island, recently joined the board. Howard Ris has been executive director since 1984. UCS maintains a headquarters in Cambridge; a Washington, D.C., legislative, lobbying, and media office; and a West Coast office in Berkeley, California, which works on transportation policy issues. In 1991 UCS joined representatives from over a dozen countries to form the International Network of Engineers and Scientists for Global Responsibility (INESGR), which will be headquartered in Berlin.

RESOURCES: UCS's $4 million in revenue in 1991 was received from public donations (63 percent) and foundation grants (30 percent), with the remainder from bequests, interest, publication sales, and other sources. Expenditures of $3.8 million covered program services (76 percent)—including energy policy (45 percent), arms control (17 percent), nuclear power (8 percent), and legislative programs (6 percent); administration (3 percent); and fundraising and communications (21 percent).

PUBLICATIONS AND SERVICES: Contributors of at least $15 receive the quarterly newsletter *Nucleus* (circulation 90,000). Members of the Scientist Action Network and Legislative Action Network receive the newsletter *Legislative Alert* monthly. UCS produces books, reports, briefing papers, videos, and brochures on energy and arms control issues, most aimed at the general-public audience. UCS has a toll-free legislative hotline: (800) 444-4827. □

JOBS WITH PEACE

For a Just Economy
In a Peaceful World

JOBS WITH PEACE CAMPAIGN

76 SUMMER STREET

BOSTON, MA 02110

(617) 338-5783

FOUNDED: 1978   MEMBERS: 17,000
CHAPTERS: 9   BUDGET: $500,000   STAFF: 7
TAX STATUS: 501(c)(3)

PURPOSE: "Jobs with Peace is a national campaign that seeks to redirect our tax dollars away from excessive military spending in order to fund jobs and social programs in education, transportation, housing, health care, human services, and other socially useful industries."

Jobs with Peace (JWP) wants to give a bigger slice of the federal budget pie to domestic programs and force the Department of Defense to tighten its belt. Its strategy is a progressive coalition of the peace, labor, civil rights, and women's movements. National JWP supports sustained campaigns in selected urban areas, expanding the constituency of the peace movement by targeting minority and working-class neighborhoods, reaching people who have to deal with economic survival issues on a day-to-day basis. JWP staff and volunteers walk precincts, hold neighborhood meetings, sponsor referendum drives, register voters, and lobby from the grassroots up. Local campaigns have autonomy to design their own action programs, with the national office providing resources and training.

BACKGROUND: JWP got its start in 1978 with a referendum campaign in San Francisco, advising the Congress to reduce military spending. Fueled by success, the idea took off. By 1986 the people of eighty cities had passed referenda calling for city governments to make public how much local tax money is spent on the military.

JWP sees the military economy as a major cause of the nation's economic decline. Over one-third of all research and development expenditures are directed to the military, with only minor spin-offs for civilian applications of new technology. An estimated half of all scientists and engineers work in the military economy, contributing little to the competitiveness of U.S. industry in the world consumer economy.

Local campaigns have composed many variations on the theme of capturing the peace dividend for civilian jobs and social programs. In 1984 Los Angeles JWP sponsored the first successful citizen initiative since 1939, becoming a model with its use of person-to-person organizing in minority communities. In Minnesota, JWP won the cooperation of the governor's office to launch a state economic task force to convert military facilities to civilian use as a spur to the economy. In Philadelphia, the campaign brought together a diverse coalition of local business, navy yard workers, and community organizations to press for conversion of the yard, which employed 11,000 and is scheduled to be shut down. Boston JWP created a high school curriculum called "Books not Bombs," with lessons on the economy, military spending, and nuclear war. In 1987, with 72 percent of the vote, Boston voters passed a referendum directing the city to lobby Congress for a transfer of 9 percent of the federal military budget into a national housing program.

The 1988 presidential election campaign brought JWP to the national spotlight along with the ACLU, when the Republican Bush-Quayle ticket criticized Democratic contender Michael Dukakis for sitting on the JWP advisory board. Dukakis waffled during a campaign debate, stating he did not agree with the JWP goal of reducing military spending by 25 percent.

CURRENT PRIORITIES: JWP supports economic conversion of military facilities to socially useful production, retaining and creating jobs for local residents. The "Build Homes not Bombs" program works with housing activists to connect the military budget to the lack of affordable housing. JWP helped organize the Common Agenda Coalition, formed in 1990 by forty peace, social justice, and environmental groups working to cut the military budget in half and redirect spending to social needs. The Coalition conducts actions around the country, including demonstrations on Tax Day, April 15, and sponsors local referenda on cutting the military budget to fund social needs. The Coalition, with leadership from JWP, is carrying out an extensive Voter's Pledge Campaign around the 1992 elections. JWP supported the April 1992 National Save Our Cities March, and supports dismantling the budget "walls" to allow spending defense savings on domestic programs.

MEMBERS: National JWP assists chapters in 9 cities: Baltimore; Boston; Los Angeles; Milwaukee; Minneapolis; Pittsburgh; Philadelphia; Chester, Pennsylvania; and New Bedford, Massachusetts. There are some 9,000 local members in the urban chapters. JWP also helps affiliated organizations in 100 additional cities. JWP has enjoyed a steady growth in national contributors from 3,000 in 1984 to 8,000 in 1991.

STRUCTURE: In 1991 JWP streamlined its governing body from a thirty-member coordinating committee to a fifteen-member national governing board. One person from each of the nine local campaigns sits on the board, and additional at-large members are selected. Jill Nelson was the first executive director and served until 1991; Ann Wilson was hired as executive director in 1991 after working for JWP as an organizer in Milwaukee and as national cochair. George Pillsbury, a founder of the Funding Exchange network, works as director of development.

RESOURCES: National JWP receives 40 percent of its $500,000 annual budget from grants, 35 percent from major donors, and 25 percent from members through direct-mail and local campaigns. The national office has seven staff, and each of the nine local chapters has from one to four staff and its own budget.

PUBLICATIONS AND SERVICES: Contributors of $25 or more receive the *Jobs with Peace Campaign Report* (circulation 17,000) twice a year. □

WOMEN'S ACTION FOR NEW DIRECTIONS

691 MASSACHUSETTS AVENUE

BOSTON, MA 02258

(617) 643-6740

FOUNDED: 1980   MEMBERS: 10,000
CHAPTERS: 50   BUDGET: $392,000   STAFF: 8
TAX STATUS: 501(c)(4): Women's Action for New

Directions; 501(c)(3): WAND Education Fund;
PAC: WAND PAC

PURPOSE: "To empower women to act politically to reduce violence and militarism and redirect military resources toward human and environmental needs."

When Dr. Helen Caldicott toured the country speaking out on the nuclear crisis as president of Physicians for Social Responsibility, she was struck by the way women reacted differently than men to the threat of nuclear war. She became convinced that if the arms race were to be stopped, it would be women who would stop it. She inspired the creation of Women's Action for Nuclear Disarmament (WAND), which drew fresh circles of women activists into the peace movement during the 1980s. Reflecting new priorities for redirecting military spending toward human needs in the post–Cold War world, the organization changed its name to Women's Action for New Directions in 1992.

BACKGROUND: Helen Caldicott and a group of women gathered in a Newton, Massachusetts, living room in 1980 and created the Women's Party for Survival (WPS). (Caldicott is Australian, and the choice of an alternative political party reflected her experience of parliamentary systems, in which minor parties can tip the balance of power.) The WPS would aid women in becoming active in their own communities through local chapters.

The group's first demonstration was organized on Mother's Day in 1980 by women in Boston and San Francisco —reclaiming suffragist Julia Ward Howe's original intention of honoring women working for a peaceful world. Smaller actions followed on Mother's Day in 1981. As the antinuclear movement grew in 1982, marked by the publication of Jonathon Schell's best-seller, *The Fate of the Earth* (Knopf, 1982), and the rally of nearly one million people in New York City in June 1982, it became clear that the group needed a different structure. WPS was reorganized as Women's Action for Nuclear Disarmament, a nonprofit advocacy organization rather than a political party. Caldicott helped build WAND by her inspirational speaking tours across the country. Her TV appearances on the *Merv Griffin* and *Donahue* shows brought in nearly 20,000 letters, and WAND was off and running.

By 1984, WAND's PAC had become an effective player in the election of sympathetic candidates such as Senators Tom Harkin and John Kerry. WAND's Education Fund began publishing fact sheets, posters, and other materials and WAND began a speaker-training program, empowering women to take leadership in the antinuclear movement. After the 1984 election victory of President Reagan, Caldicott admitted to suffering from extreme burnout. To analyze the new political context facing the movement for arms control and disarmament, the WAND Education Fund authorized a study of media and public opinion, published in 1986 as "Turnabout: The New Realism in the Nuclear Age." Among other recommendations, the analysis urged peace activists to emphasize the cost of the arms race, rather than invoke fears of an impending nuclear apocalypse (the staple of Caldicott's jeremiads). In 1986 Caldicott announced her "retirement" from the movement, returning to Australia with her husband, fellow physician and peace activist Bill Caldicott. She returned to speaking in the United States in 1989, addressing environmental themes more than nuclear war. She continues raising funds for WAND and maintains her seat on the national board, although she does not participate in regular board meetings or policy planning.

CURRENT PRIORITIES: WAND continues its Mother's Day for Peace programs. Affiliates host events honoring women in their local communities who have worked for peace, while the national office sponsors annual Helen Caldicott awards. Noted recipients include singer Judy Collins and Carl Sagan, astronomer and theorist of "nuclear winter."

WAND has initiated a Women Legislators' Lobby, in which women state legislators lobby to redirect national priorities from the military budget toward programs and policies reflecting women's values and concerns, emphasizing housing, education, health, and the environment. WAND PAC assists congressional candidates, male and female, with strong records of support for arms control. The WAND Education Fund works to give the peace movement more visibility through the media, including a billboard campaign in fifty cities in 1991.

MEMBERS: WAND's members are primarily women who had not been active previously in the peace or social justice movement. Membership grew rapidly during WAND's first years, peaking around 22,000 in 1986, and then dropping to a stable level around 10,000.

WAND has always welcomed men, and a small number are members. WAND Action sends monthly action alerts to members who commit to writing or calling legislators.

STRUCTURE: Twelve women are elected by the membership to the WAND board of directors; five are chosen by regions. Eight directors sit on the separate board of the WAND Education Fund. The board hires WAND's executive director and sets policy. WAND has had three executive directors—Diane Aronson from 1980 to 1987, Calien Lewis from 1987 to 1990, and Marjorie Smith since 1990. A national conference is held every two years.

RESOURCES: WAND's combined revenue of $376,000 in 1990 ($213,000 to WAND and $163,000 to WAND Education Fund) came from member contributions, fund-raising events, and foundation grants. Expenditures of $349,000 went for program services (76 percent) and administration and fundraising (24 percent). A surplus of $27,000 was used to reduce a deficit to just under $20,000. WAND PAC in 1990 concentrated its support on eight women congressional candidates.

PUBLICATIONS AND SERVICES: Membership is $35 and includes the quarterly *WAND Bulletin* (circulation 10,000). Books and educational materials are available from the national office. Caldicott's books include *Nuclear Madness: What You Can Do* (1978; Bantam, 1982), *Missile Envy: The Arms Race and Nuclear War* (Morrow, 1984), and *If You Love This Planet* (Norton, 1992). □

PROFESSIONALS' COALITION FOR NUCLEAR ARMS CONTROL

1616 P STREET NW, SUITE 320

WASHINGTON, DC 20036

(202) 332-4823

FOUNDED: 1984   CONTRIBUTORS: 6,000
BUDGET: $350,000   STAFF: 5
TAX STATUS: 501(c)(4): Professionals' Coalition
for Nuclear Arms Control; 501(c)(3):
Professionals' Coalition Education Fund

PURPOSE: "A lobbying coalition of professionals, committed to stopping the arms race."

The Professionals' Coalition is the lobbying arm of the leading professionals' arms control organizations.

BACKGROUND: The Professionals' Coalition for Nuclear Arms Control (PCNAC) was formed in 1984 by the Union of Concerned Scientists, Physicians for Social Responsibility, and Lawyers Alliance for Nuclear Arms Control (now Lawyers Alliance for World Security, LAWS) as a joint lobbying arm. Smaller organizations— including Psychologists for Social Responsibility, Architects/Designers/ Planners for Social Responsibility, and Business Executives for Nuclear Age Concerns (BENAC)—are affiliates. In 1989 the Professionals' Coalition Education Fund absorbed the training institute and voter education fund of Freeze Voter, the political and lobbying arm of the Freeze campaign (which did not join

the SANE/FREEZE merger). PCNAC now conducts national and regional training institutes for citizen lobbying and election work.

CURRENT PRIORITIES: PCNAC's lobbying concentrates on: (1) supporting the "Budget for a Strong America" campaign, which advocates cuts in military funding of $100 billion over three years; (2) opposing SDI and antisatellite and antiballistic missile "Star Wars" systems; (3) opposing nuclear weapons with first-strike capabilities, such as the Midgetman and the MX missile rail-garrison proposal; (4) opposing the B-2 stealth bomber; (5) obtaining a Comprehensive Test Ban Treaty.

STRUCTURE: The board of directors has nine members, the president plus two representatives of the four core member organizations. David Cohen (former president of Common Cause) is president and lobbyist, and Victoria Almquist is executive director.

RESOURCES: PCNAC's budget of $350,000 is derived from individual contributions (40 percent), grants from such foundations as W. Alton Jones and Ploughshares (50 percent), and contributions from member organizations.

PUBLICATIONS AND SERVICES: Contributors receive a newsletter, *The Professional* (circulation 7,000), published three or four times a year. PCNAC publishes an annual analysis of arms control votes in Congress, ranking each member of the House of Representatives and the Senate. PCNAC also publishes helpful citizen activist manuals on lobbying, the media, and coalition building. □

20/20 VISION NATIONAL PROJECT

30 COTTAGE STREET

AMHERST, MA 01002

(413) 549-4555

FOUNDED: 1986   MEMBERS: 10,000
CHAPTERS: 75 chapters serving 150
congressional districts   BUDGET: $450,000
STAFF: 10   TAX STATUS: 501(c)(4): 20/20
Vision National Project; 501(c)(3): 20/20 Vision
Education Fund

PURPOSE: "To enable citizens to communicate effectively with policymakers to improve world security, end the arms race, and reduce the risk of nuclear war."

The idea is simple: For $20 a year, you spend twenty minutes a month taking a single action described on a postcard you receive from 20/20 Vision, designed for maximum impact on elected officials. Local district projects, run by a core group of five or more volunteers, communicate with members and tailor actions to district policymakers.

BACKGROUND: Amherst peace activist Lois Barber started 20/20 Vision in her western Massachusetts congressional district to provide concerned but busy people with a specific and manageable way to keep the pressure on lawmakers. Barber's project came to the attention of California activist and entrepreneur Jeremy Sherman, founder of The Body Shop store chain in the United States, who had also been look-

ing for ways to engage people in convenient and effective lobbying action. From his background in business, Sherman saw the potential for "franchising" the project in congressional districts across the country. Working together, Barber and Sherman formed the 20/20 Vision National Project, which organized 20 districts in its first year and 55 more the next. Over 500 volunteers coordinate lobbying efforts from the 75 chapters covering 150 congressional districts.

CURRENT PRIORITIES: 20/20 Vision selects its topics for action in cooperation with seventeen peace and environmental organizations, including all the usual suspects: Council for a Livable World, Friends of the Earth, Greenpeace Action, Jobs with Peace Campaign, National Toxics Campaign Fund, Peace Links, Physicians for Social Responsibility, Professionals' Coalition for Nuclear Arms Control, SANE/FREEZE, Sierra Club, Union of Concerned Scientists, Women's Action for New Directions, and Women's International League for Peace and Freedom. Typical examples of monthly actions are calling a senator's office to express opposition to the B-2 stealth bomber, writing a congressman to delete funding for the SDI/Star Wars program from the defense budget, and contacting legislators to fund environmental cleanup of military facilities.

STRUCTURE: 20/20 Vision National Project has a fifteen-member, self-recruiting board of directors, including Barber, Sherman, Wayne Jaquith of Council for a Livable World, Brent Blackwelder of Friends of the Earth, and Ed Snyder, former director of the

Friends Committee on National Legislation; five core group coordinators are also members. The National Project has two offices, one in Amherst directed by Lois Barber, and one at 1000 16th Street, NW, Washington, DC 20036; telephone (202) 728-1157. A monthly legislative update is posted on PeaceNet by the Washington office. Information on how to join is available from a toll-free telephone number: (800) 669-1782. □

HUMAN RIGHTS
ORGANIZATIONS

3.

RIGHTS AND
LIBERTIES

CIVIL LIBERTIES

The basic liberties we have come to expect in the United States
are defined and protected primarily in the Bill of Rights, the
first ten amendments to the Constitution, and certain subsequent amendments. These rights as we now know them did
not exist until the twentieth century, when the Supreme Court
extended most of the restrictions on the federal government to
the states through its interpretation of the equal protection
clause of the Fourteenth Amendment. The expansion of the
freedoms of speech, assembly, and association was led by the
labor movement in the course of its efforts to organize unions,
and by such notable allies as the American Civil Liberties
Union (ACLU) and the National Association for the Advancement of Colored People (NAACP). The Jehovah's Witnesses
established the legal foundations of the separation of church
and state during the 1930s and 1940s, and the ACLU has carried many such cases since. The ACLU has also pushed out
the boundaries for the freedom of expression, fighting literary
and artistic censorship.

American advocates of democracy have read the Constitution and the Bill of Rights in the context of the Declaration of

Independence, with its ringing assertion "that all men are created equal, that they are endowed by their Creator with certain unalienable rights, that among these are life, liberty, and the pursuit of happiness." Viewed in this light, the Constitution is an imperfect document, with its acceptance of slavery and failure to enfranchise women. If the Declaration of Independence is part of the American compact, however, then we can understand the development of rights through amendment and interpretation of the Constitution as an unfolding process of attaining the democratic vision inherent in the Declaration. From a beginning in which only white men with property could vote, rights were extended to all white men in the Jacksonian era; to black men with the Thirteenth, Fourteenth, and Fifteenth amendments from 1865 to 1870; to women with the Nineteenth Amendment in 1920; to American Indians with the citizenship act of 1924; to poor people with the abolition of the poll tax with the Twenty-fourth Amendment in 1964; and to people between eighteen and twenty-one years of age with the Twenty-sixth Amendment in 1971.

All these rights were won through struggle. The very existence of the Bill of Rights was the result of the Anti-Federalist pressure from traders, artisans, and backcountry farmers. The Civil War was necessary to abolish slavery, establish due process and equal protection of the laws, and win the right to vote for former slaves through the Thirteenth, Fourteenth, and Fifteenth amendments. A long woman suffrage campaign from the end of the Civil War to 1920 was necessary to win women's right to vote. And securing the freedoms of speech, assembly, and religion as we now know them took a less visible but vital series of campaigns in the streets and in the courts during the first half of the twentieth century.

The First Amendment reads "Congress shall make no law . . ."—in other words, it does not restrict state or local governments. Until this century, the Supreme Court consistently upheld the absolute authority of local officials to regulate or restrict speech and assembly as they saw fit. A key case was presented by the Reverend William Davis, who was arrested for preaching in Boston Common in 1894. In *Davis* v. *Massachusetts* (1897) the Supreme Court affirmed the ruling of the Massachusetts Supreme Court, which had ruled that a city can forbid speech in its park with the same authority a homeowner can forbid it in his house. The Industrial Workers of the World carried out a series of free speech campaigns between 1909 and 1915, usually ending in mass arrests and repression. Socialists, labor organizers, and other dissenters continued to assert their right to free speech. In a critical test, the Congress of Industrial Organizations (CIO) attempted to explain the new National Labor Relations Act in 1935 by passing out literature and holding outdoor meetings in Jersey City. Mayor Frank Hague announced he was the law, and ran the organizers out of town. The Supreme Court ruled in *Hague* v. *CIO* (1939) that streets, parks, and public places were open and protected for public discussion—without explicitly overruling the *Davis* decision.

Several controversial cases with unpopular defendants brought about the crucial constitutional interpretation that "incorporated" most of the protections of the Bill of Rights into the Fourteenth Amendment's prohibitions against a state denying any person "due process of law" or "the equal protection of the laws." In *Gitlow* v. *United States* (1925), ACLU attorney Walter Pollak defended Communist party member Benjamin Gitlow, arrested during the 1919 "Red scare" under New York's Criminal Anarchy Act. Although his conviction was affirmed and the act held constitutional, in his opinion for the Court conservative Justice Edward Sanford held that the freedom of speech and of the press are among the personal rights and liberties protected by the "due process" clause of the Fourteenth Amendment against impairment by the states. In two cases emerging from the Scottsboro trials—also argued by Pollak—the Supreme Court ruled in *Powell* v. *Alabama* (1932) that the Sixth Amendment required a person charged with a capital crime be provided legal counsel at his trial, and in *Patterson* v. *Alabama* (1935) that excluding blacks from Alabama juries had deprived Patterson of the equal protection of the law guaranteed by the Fourteenth Amendment.

Jehovah's Witnesses provided a series of important cases on the freedom of speech and religion by their confrontational public proselytizing and their refusal to salute the flag, recite the pledge of allegiance, or serve in the armed forces. In *Cantwell* v. *Connecticut* (1940) the Supreme Court ruled that the "free exercise" of religion clause in the First Amendment was incorporated by the Fourteenth Amendment, thus protecting a Jehovah's Witness's right to proselytize. And in 1943 in *West Virginia* v. *Barnette*, the Supreme Court upheld the right of Jehovah's Witness children to refuse to salute the flag, reversing in the middle of World War II its earlier decision in the *Gobitis* case.

The controversy over First Amendment protections and the place of religion in American public life has continued for the past several decades. In *Everson* v. *Board of Education* (1947) Justice Hugo Black wrote, "The First Amendment has erected a wall between church and state." During the 1940s and 1950s this "wall" was primarily a concern of Catholics, who wanted public support for parochial schools. Then with two cases the Supreme Court effectively "disestablished Protestantism as the nation's unofficial religion," in the words of ACLU historian Samuel Walker: *Engle* v. *Vitale* (1962), in which the Court declared public school prayer unconstitutional, and *School District* v. *Schempp* (1963), brought by atheist Madalyn Murray O'Hair, in which it declared public school Bible reading unconstitutional. Consequently in the 1960s and 1970s the focus of controversy shifted to Protestant fundamentalists, who wished to preserve prayer and Bible reading in the public schools and objected to the teaching of material (such as scientific evolution) that contradicted their religious beliefs. People for the American Way was formed in 1980 to oppose efforts of fundamentalists to keep religion in the public schools, require teaching of "scientific creationism" as an alternative approach to evolution, and ban certain books from classrooms and libraries. Fundamentalists charged the civil libertarians had enshrined a new religion—secular humanism—in public education.

AMERICAN CIVIL LIBERTIES UNION

132 W. 43RD STREET

NEW YORK, NY 10036

(212) 944-9800

FOUNDED: 1920 MEMBERS: 280,000
AFFILIATES: 51 state affiliates (including D.C.);
218 local chapters BUDGET: $22.2 million
STAFF: 160; 350 nationally, including affiliates
TAX STATUS: 501(c)(4): American Civil Liberties
Union; 501(c)(3): ACLU Foundation

PURPOSE: "To maintain and advance civil liberties including the freedoms of association, press, religion, and speech, and the rights to the franchise, to due process of law, and to equal protection of the laws for all people throughout the United States and its possessions . . . sought wholly without political partisanship."

The American Civil Liberties Union (ACLU) is the nation's leading civil liberties and civil rights organization, handling some 6,000 cases annually, assisted by 2,000 volunteer attorneys in addition to the national and affiliate staff. The ACLU handles more cases on sex discrimination, reproductive rights, and minority voting rights than any other organization in the nation. With active chapters across the country, the ACLU is a vigilant presence in every state. In effect the largest nongovernmental law firm in the country, the ACLU appears before the Supreme Court more often than any organization except the U.S. Justice Department.

ACLU cases have defined the freedoms of speech and religion, and have helped extend due process of law to all Americans.

BACKGROUND: As fighting began in Europe in 1914, a group of Progressive-era social reformers and pacifists organized the American Union Against Militarism (AUAM) to oppose U.S. entry into the war. When Woodrow Wilson led the United States into the war in 1917, two AUAM board members, social worker Roger Baldwin and labor lawyer Crystal Eastman, organized a civil liberties bureau of the AUAM to defend conscientious objectors (Baldwin was born into a wealthy Boston family; his aunt Ruth Standish Baldwin was a founder of the National Urban League). The ensuing controversy led them to split from the AUAM and form the independent National Civil Liberties Bureau (NCLB), which defended war resisters and other dissenters tried under the Espionage Act of 1917. Baldwin refused the draft and was sentenced to a year in prison. Freed in 1919, he set about reorganizing the NCLB as the ACLU, chartered in January 1920. The initial constituency of the ACLU drew from three distinct groups: social workers associated with Eastman and Baldwin; Protestant clergy preaching the social gospel and influenced by socialism, including Norman Thomas, John Haynes Holmes, and Harry Ward; and conservative lawyers who believed the Constitution protects free speech and due process, including Albert DeSilver and Quaker pacifist L. Hollingsworth Wood.

During the early 1920s the ACLU took principled positions protesting Boston mayor James Curley's banning

Ku Klux Klan meetings and actions of Cleveland and Toledo city officials banning Henry Ford's anti-Semitic publications. But its most celebrated case was the "monkey trial" of Tennessee teacher John Scopes in 1925, the ACLU's first involvement in freedom of religion issues. Clarence Darrow and Arthur Garfield Hays, both members of ACLU's national committee, defended Scopes; William Jennings Bryan assisted the prosecution, and died a week after the trial. Scopes was convicted and fined $100; on appeal the Supreme Court upheld the statute but reversed Scopes's conviction on a technicality. The case was a publicity circus, but raised the question of religion and public education. Also in the 1920s Morris Ernst and Arthur Garfield Hays led the ACLU into cases opposing censorship of the arts. Hays defended H. L. Mencken in a case that made "banned in Boston" famous, and Ernst, who was also counsel for Planned Parenthood, in 1933 successfully challenged a ban on James Joyce's *Ulysses* by the U.S. Customs Service.

During its first two decades, the ACLU found many volatile free speech issues involving labor organizing. In Los Angeles in 1923, author Upton Sinclair was arrested on "Liberty Hill" as he read the First Amendment to striking marine transport workers; Sinclair went on to organize the ACLU's first affiliate, the Southern California CLU. During the mid-1930s the ACLU fought Jersey City mayor Frank Hague in a series of highly publicized battles over free speech and labor's right to organize. When Boss Hague banned a CIO rally in 1937, the ACLU sought an injunction against the ban, received it

from a federal district court, and was upheld by the Supreme Court in *Hague* v. *CIO* in 1939.

In a series of important cases during the 1930s and 1940s, the ACLU won its most significant and far-reaching victories for civil liberties and civil rights by obtaining rulings from the Supreme Court that the Fourteenth Amendment, in effect, incorporated or extended most of the protections of the Bill of Rights to cover actions by the states as well as the federal government. The cases typically involved controversial defendants: In *Gitlow* v. *U.S.*, a founder of the Communist party had been convicted under New York's criminal anarchy statute; in an appeal handled for the ACLU by Walter Pollak, the Supreme Court upheld the wartime conviction and the constitutionality of the statute, but suggested that the due process clause of the Fourteenth Amendment protected the fundamental freedoms of speech and of the press.

War brought another major test for civil liberties. Following the Japanese attack on Pearl Harbor in December 1941 and a declaration of war by the U.S. Congress, in February 1942 President Roosevelt signed Executive Order 9066 ordering the evacuation and relocation of 120,000 Japanese Americans from the West Coast to detention camps (Japanese Americans in Hawaii were not affected). After internal controversy the ACLU opposed the evacuation and detention on procedural grounds, and became the only organization in the country to object to this violation of civil liberties (even the Japanese American Citizens League urged cooperation with the government at the time). The ACLU took on two of the four cases involving Japanese Americans objecting to relocation, *Korematsu* and *Hirabayashi*.

The ACLU's relationship with the Communist party had presented problems throughout the 1930s. William Z. Foster, a leading Communist, served four terms on the ACLU board during the 1920s, and Communist journalist Anna Rochester served one term. After 1928 the Communist party shifted to a militant left-wing position, organizing dual unions and denouncing socialists as "social fascists." The ACLU soured on the Communist party in 1930 when five of its organizers, out on bail facing criminal charges from the textile strike in Gastonia, North Carolina, fled to the Soviet Union—costing the ACLU bail fund $28,500. When the Communist party shifted its line again in 1935 to the Popular Front, it began to cooperate with the ACLU in the Scottsboro Defense Committee and the Angelo Herndon case. Several left-wing ACLU board members, including attorney Abraham Isserman, journalist Mary Van Kleeck, and labor organizers Elizabeth Gurley Flynn and Robert Dunn, drew closer to the Communist party—which Flynn joined openly in 1936. Baldwin's views, which had evolved from anarchism in 1917 to a pro-union socialism in the 1920s, shifted toward the left as the Depression deepened in the 1930s. But an event in 1934 returned Baldwin to the side of his socialist allies on the ACLU board: Communists tried to break up a Socialist party rally at Madison Square Garden, outraging Norman Thomas and John Haynes Holmes, who began a campaign to oust any Communists from the ACLU leadership.

The Nazi-Soviet Pact in August 1939, which led to the partition of Poland between Germany and the Soviet Union and the absorption of the Baltic states into the Soviet Union, was the final disillusionment for Baldwin and brought him firmly into the anticommunist camp on the ACLU board. In 1940 the ACLU adopted a resolution stating that although there would be no political test for membership, "the personnel of its governing committees and staff is properly subject to the test of consistency in the defense of civil liberties in all aspects and all places," thus excluding members of organizations supporting the totalitarian governments of the Soviet Union and of Fascist and Nazi countries. Harry Ward resigned as chair and was replaced by John Haynes Holmes.

When the board asked Elizabeth Gurley Flynn to resign, she refused and the board called a special meeting to hear the charges against her. At this "trial," Flynn defended her public membership in the Communist party and sought to justify her faith in Stalin and the Soviet Union. After a long debate the members present voted to remove Flynn from the board. The action did little to placate the ACLU's critics on the right, and remained a subject of controversy within the organization for decades. The 1940 antitotalitarian resolution was finally rescinded in 1968, and Flynn was posthumously reinstated to the board in 1976.

In 1938 the House created the Special Committee on Un-American Activities to investigate domestic Fascists and Communists, chaired by Martin Dies and known as the Dies Committee (and later tagged as HUAC, for House

Un-American Activities Committee). Baldwin, Hays, and Morris Ernst worked with Dies Committee staff to clear the ACLU of charges it was a Communist front. Ernst began a lengthy secret correspondence with the FBI that continued until 1964, seeking to assure J. Edgar Hoover that the ACLU remained anticommunist (ACLU members were astonished when the letters came to light in the 1980s). Although keen to keep itself free of any subversive taint, the ACLU consistently defended the freedoms of speech and association for radicals. The ACLU opposed the Smith Act prosecution in 1941 of twenty-nine members of the Trotskyist Socialist Workers party (SWP) in Minneapolis. Encouraged by Teamsters Union leadership following a SWP-led strike, the prosecution was cheered on by the Communist party, in an extraordinarily shortsighted position, as their top twelve leaders would be indicted under the Smith Act in July 1948. Filing briefs against the Smith Act prosecutions, and in the appeal of the convictions in the *Dennis* case, the ACLU cautiously added a disclaimer that it opposed single-party states whether Fascist or Communist. ACLU affiliates led the fights against loyalty oaths for public employees, which became law in most states between 1949 and 1951.

The ACLU began a new era when Baldwin retired in 1950 after thirty years as executive director. Believing that support for civil liberties would inevitably be limited to a small elite, Baldwin never made a vigorous effort to expand the ACLU membership, which stood at 9,000 in 1950. Baldwin's successor, economist Patrick Malin, sensed wider support for civil liberties across the land and quickly began a campaign to recruit new members—which succeeded beyond anyone's expectations, increasing membership to 30,000 by 1955 and 60,000 by 1960. Along with Malin's membership drive, the ACLU board encouraged the development of staffed affiliates, and revised its constitution and bylaws in 1951 to give affiliates representation. The biennial conference was established to give the rank-and-file members a voice, completing a transition from an autonomous self-selecting board to a complex democratic structure. At the first biennial conference in 1954, the members and affiliates voted down all three variations of anticommunist resolutions proposed by the board. The old socialist anticommunist bloc on the board faded as Norman Thomas and Morris Ernst distanced themselves from the organization and as staunch anticommunist staff resigned. The board refused to renominate its chief critic on the left, Corliss Lamont, who withdrew to work with his Emergency Civil Liberties Committee. The old Cold War ideological disputes subsided, and the ACLU entered a new period of expansion.

The year 1954 marked a new beginning for the country as well. The U.S. Senate censured Joseph McCarthy, ending his campaign of defamation against New Deal liberals and progressives. The Supreme Court rendered its unanimous decision in *Brown* v. *Board of Education*, ruling segregated schools to be unconstitutional. As the civil rights movement gathered steam following the Montgomery bus boycott in 1955, the ACLU began to defend hundreds of cases at the local and state levels throughout the South in the early 1960s. Following Malin's death in 1962, another Quaker, John Pemberton, Jr., was hired as executive director and served until 1970 through a turbulent decade in which civil rights dominated legal activity. The ACLU had always had a close association with the NAACP; beginning with James Weldon Johnson in the 1920s, leading NAACP officials including Thurgood Marshall and Roy Wilkins were represented on the ACLU board. Advancing this commitment to civil rights, the ACLU biennial meeting in 1964 established a southern regional office, and Chuck Morgan, a charismatic southern populist, was hired as director and began the ACLU's "Operation Southern Justice." Morgan shifted ACLU's customary practice of filing *amicus* briefs to providing direct representation in school desegregation cases and defending arrested civil rights demonstrators.

In 1968 the ACLU was drawn into two convulsive controversies, the teachers' strike in New York City and the mounting opposition to the Vietnam War. The New York CLU entered the dispute over a Ford Foundation–funded experimental program for community control of schools in the Ocean Hill–Brownsville neighborhood of Brooklyn. When the local school board ordered the involuntary transfer of several teachers and administrators, the union struck the entire New York school system, pitting the largely white and Jewish teachers union against black community leaders and leaving a legacy of mistrust and hostility. NYCLU director Aryeh Neier and associate director Ira Glasser blamed union leader Albert Shanker and the citywide board of ed-

ucation. The issues split progressive ranks, with writers Nat Hentoff and Dwight MacDonald defending community control, and socialist Michael Harrington and union democracy leader Herman Benson defending the union.

Opposition to the Vietnam War escalated along with the conflict, and as demonstrations became more militant the federal government response grew more repressive. In January 1968 the Justice Department indicted Dr. Benjamin Spock and four other Boston antiwar activists who had organized Stop the Draft Week in October 1967 with a "call to resist illegitimate authority." The ACLU board was split between moderates who believed the organization should not go beyond free speech issues and activists who would use the Spock case to challenge the constitutionality of the war. After long and acrimonious discussion, the ACLU board voted to defend war resisters, but without taking a stand on whether the war was unconstitutional or whether U.S. troops had committed war crimes. As historian Samuel Walker notes, "neoconservative critics saw the Spock case as the point at which the ACLU abandoned civil liberties for a 'political' agenda." After the Ohio National Guard killed four students at Kent State University in May 1970, the ACLU board disavowed moderation and declared that the war in Vietnam and Cambodia was a violation of the war powers clause of the Constitution. Some members quit, but many more joined, doubling the membership between 1970 and 1972 to 180,000.

With Richard Nixon elected president in 1968 and Earl Warren retired as Chief Justice in 1969, the ACLU reassessed its strategy. Supported by the larger affiliates, Aryeh Neier moved from the NYCLU to replace John Pemberton as ACLU executive director in 1970. Neier strengthened the organization's lobbying presence on Capitol Hill, and obtained major grants from liberal foundations for special projects in prisoners' rights, reproductive rights, and voting rights. Chuck Morgan moved from Atlanta to become Washington office director in 1972, emphasizing legislative approaches to protecting civil liberties as an alternative to litigation before an increasingly conservative Supreme Court. As the implications of the Watergate scandal became clear, the ACLU was the first national organization to call for President Nixon's impeachment, with a full-page ad in *The New York Times* in October 1973:

The organization's most costly stand on civil liberties principles was the Chicago CLU's defense in 1977 of the right of Nazis to march in the majority Jewish community of Skokie, Illinois (it wasn't the first time—the ACLU defended American Nazi George Lincoln Rockwell in 1960). Several traditional ACLU allies—including the American Jewish Congress, the Anti-Defamation League, and the National Lawyers Guild—supported Skokie. Court cases dragged on for two years, receiving frequent national publicity. In the end the ACLU prevailed, and the Nazis opted to stage brief marches in downtown Chicago and Marquette Park. The controversy cost the ACLU many Jewish supporters (membership dropped by 25,000), and plunged the organization into a financial crisis with a 1978 deficit of $500,000. An emergency development campaign

brought in record contributions and new members that more than replaced the losses. But the travail of the 1970s and the administrative requirements of the expanded organization took its toll on the top staff, particularly the passionate activists of the 1960s. Washington office director Chuck Morgan resigned in 1976 in a dispute over his comments on the presidential race, and Norman Dorsen was elected ACLU president later that year. Dorsen engineered the resignation of Mel Wulf, legal director for fifteen years, and Neier resigned in 1978 (eventually helping form and direct Human Rights Watch), turning the leadership over to his former assistant, NYCLU director Ira Glasser.

Glasser has presided over the ACLU during a backlash against the rights revolution of the 1960s and 1970s. It's a remarkable credit to the ACLU that conservatives have not rolled back the recently empowered "enclaves of the silent": students, women, gays and lesbians, the handicapped, the mentally retarded, and prisoners. The *Griswold* case in 1965, which established the right to privacy, proved to be a vital precedent for the Supreme Court's protection of the right to abortion in *Roe* v. *Wade*. It was Robert Bork's opposition to right to privacy arguments and related protections for civil rights that drew the ACLU into the battle over his nomination to the Supreme Court. The ACLU changed its policy of neutrality on judicial nominations and led the successful coalition that blocked Bork's confirmation by the Senate in 1987.

Conservative critiques of the ACLU have taken two directions: Traditional conservatives argue that the ACLU was guided by left-wing politics from the start; and neoconservatives, who were often members until the 1970s, argue the ACLU was a courageous, nonpartisan defender of civil liberties until the 1960s, when it was corrupted by New Left enthusiasms. In this view, the ACLU was no longer defending classic civil liberties, but inventing new rights and supporting discrimination in the name of affirmative action and a new agenda of equality—abandoning common sense and the public interest in the process. Conservatives of both types hold that extending freedom of expression beyond political speech to artistic expression ends with defending obscenity and pornography, which undermine community standards of decency, civility, and social order. Libertarians applaud the ACLU's opposition to censorship, but join other conservatives in rejecting affirmative action and the notion of economic rights.

CURRENT PRIORITIES: The ACLU's greatest impact comes from its often unheralded ongoing work, organized into several projects: (1) the *Voting Rights Project* has filed lawsuits against some 180 jurisdictions since passage of the Voting Rights Act of 1965, and has been responsible for the election of hundreds of black officials in the South; recently the project has turned its attention to electoral procedures that discriminate against Latinos and American Indians in the West and Southwest; (2) the *Reproductive Freedom Project* handles more cases challenging restrictions on women's rights to reproductive freedom than any other organization—yet the ACLU has also defended the rights of abortion pro-

testers; (3) the *Women's Rights Project* has given special attention to the employment rights of pregnant women; (4) the *Lesbian and Gay Rights Project* fights for legal protection to lesbian and gay family relationships; its related *AIDS and Civil Liberties Project* combats discrimination against people with HIV and AIDS; (5) the *National Prison Project* works on prison reform, racial disparities in sentencing, and prisoners' rights; (6) the *National Security Project* works to eliminate government secrecy, surveillance, and other anti-libertarian practices dating from the Cold War era—yet also defended Oliver North's Fifth Amendment rights, challenging his conviction in the wake of the Iran-Contra hearings; (7) the *Children's Rights Project* has challenged state foster care programs to improve child welfare services and speed children's return to parents or placement in adoption; (8) the *Capital Punishment Project* advocates for the abolition of the death penalty; (9) the *Privacy and Technology Project* explores the threat to individual privacy posed by new computer data banks and other high-tech developments; and (10) the *Immigration and Aliens' Rights Task Force* has opposed efforts of the Immigration and Naturalization Service to deport people seeking political asylum. Out at the leading edge of emerging issues, the Southern California CLU has pushed the idea of economic rights for the poor—assuring all Americans decent housing and a job with a living wage. A majority of the ACLU board views this as a political question, not a civil liberties issue, but support for a "bill of economic rights" has been growing.

MEMBERS: ACLU ranks peaked at 275,000 in 1977 before its defense of Nazis' right to march in Skokie, dropped to 200,000 in 1979, and worked back up to 250,000 before George Bush attacked Michael Dukakis in the 1988 presidential election campaign for being "a card-carrying ACLU member." Civil libertarians determined to become "card-carrying members" added thousands to the ACLU rolls, totaling 280,000 by 1991.

STRUCTURE: The ACLU is governed by an 81-member board of directors, including one representative from each of 51 state affiliates (including D.C.) and 30 at-large members elected by affiliate and national boards in a population-weighted vote. An 11-person executive committee acts for the organization between the quarterly board meetings. Nadine Strossen is president. Every two years 400 delegates from the affiliates convene for a four-day meeting called "The Biennial" to recommend organizational and civil liberties policies to the board of directors; any recommendations rejected by the board may be submitted to the membership in a referendum that may overrule the board. The ACLU maintains regional offices in Atlanta and Denver, and a legislative office in Washington, D.C. The ACLU Foundation was established in 1966, and is governed by a self-recruiting board. Affiliate boards are elected by all ACLU members within a state. Each affiliate is autonomous, has its own staff, and decides what cases and issues it will emphasize.

RESOURCES: In 1989 the ACLU and the ACLU Foundation had combined revenue of $22.2 million, $10 million for the

ACLU and $12.2 million for the Foundation. Revenue comes from individuals (60 percent), foundations (25 percent), court-awarded attorneys' fees (11 percent), and other sources (4 percent). ACLU expenses of $8.4 million went for programs (79 percent), fundraising (19 percent), and administration (2 percent). Foundation expenses of $10.3 million went for programs (74 percent), fund-raising (7 percent), and administration (19 percent). About half the national dues revenue ($4.7 million in 1989) goes to support affiliates, which also raise money independently for their organizations and foundations. The ACLU bought its headquarters office, named for Roger Baldwin, in 1979.

PUBLICATIONS AND SERVICES: Membership begins at $20 and includes the newspaper *Civil Liberties*, published six times a year, and state and local newsletters. *Civil Liberties Alert* is a quarterly national legislative newsletter, available on request to members who actively participate in legislative lobbying, from the ACLU Washington Office, 122 Maryland Avenue NE, Washington, DC 20002; (202) 544-1681. An extensive list of publications is available by catalog order, including a series of handbooks on the rights of various groups from authors, crime victims, gay people, older persons, parents, prisoners, and students; and the voluminous *Policy Guide of the ACLU*. An annual report is available. Peggy Lamson presents a portrait of the ACLU's leading figure based on personal interviews in *Roger Baldwin: Founder of the ACLU* (Houghton Mifflin, 1976). Samuel Walker's *In Defense of American Liberties: A History of the*

ACLU (Oxford University Press, 1990) provides a detailed organizational history by an ACLU board member. For an attack by the ACLU's leading conservative critic, see William A. Donohue, *The Politics of the American Civil Liberties Union* (Transaction Books, 1985). For a study of the Skokie controversy, see James L. Gibson and Richard D. Bingham, *Civil Liberties and Nazis: The Skokie Free-Speech Controversy* (Praeger, 1985). To commemorate the 200th anniversary of the Bill of Rights, executive director Ira Glasser wrote *Visions of Liberty: The Bill of Rights for All Americans* (Arcade, 1991). □

PEOPLE FOR THE AMERICAN WAY

2000 M STREET, NW

WASHINGTON, DC 20036

(202) 467-4999

FOUNDED: 1980   MEMBERS: 290,000
BUDGET: $6.6 million   STAFF: 60
TAX STATUS: 501(c)(3): People for the American Way; 501(c)(4): People for the American Way Action Fund

PURPOSE: "To defend the values of pluralism, individuality, freedom of thought, expression and religion, a sense of community, and tolerance and compassion for others."

People for the American Way (PFAW) takes on the religious Right and allied conservatives over schoolbook censorship, artistic freedom, abortion rights, and judicial appointments. As a self-styled "non-partisan constitutional liberties organization," PFAW uses TV ads, op-ed columns, and lawsuits to defend the separation of church and state.

BACKGROUND: PFAW was founded by Norman Lear, the famous writer-producer of television sitcoms *All in the Family, Maude,* and *Mary Hartman, Mary Hartman.* Researching a possible movie on an evangelical minister, Lear was screening videos of Reverend Jerry Falwell's *Old Time Gospel Hour* and Reverend Pat Robertson's *700 Club* when he became so alarmed he dropped the movie and produced a one-minute television commercial on religious intolerance. Antipathy to Falwell's "Moral Majority" movement fueled Lear's creation of PFAW and provided its first target. When Falwell changed the organization's name to Liberty Federation in 1984, he gave Lear credit for an effective campaign against him. Lear recruited John Buchanan, a former Baptist minister and eight-term Republican congressman from Alabama defeated by the New Right in 1980, to chair the PFAW board and speak widely for the organization.

PFAW grew very rapidly and achieved great fund-raising success. Their skilled use of TV—paid ads as well as newsroom video feeds—brought them into the public eye. Staff writers create about 60 newspaper opinion pieces per year, sent out to 1,700 newspapers; staff also produce weekly radio commentaries. PFAW is well known for its 1987 major media campaign to successfully defeat the nomination of Robert Bork to the Supreme Court. The campaign featured Gregory Peck denouncing Bork for defending poll taxes and literacy tests.

PFAW has won important cases battling the religious right in the schools. In 1984, the group helped defeat a constitutional amendment allowing school prayer. That same year they convinced the Texas State Board of Education to repeal a ten-year-old ban on covering the theory of evolution in textbooks. PFAW sponsored a two-year letter-writing and petition campaign aimed at Doubleday publishers, because their high school biology text didn't mention evolution. They won a new edition with an extensive treatment of the subject. PFAW paid for the school board defense in censorship cases in Alabama and Tennessee, both of which it won at the appeals court level. As the televangelist scandals of the late 1980s forced the New Right to switch from relying on high-profile national leaders to building a grassroots network, PFAW shifted its own emphasis toward mobilizing the grassroots.

CURRENT PRIORITIES: PFAW's program plan for 1992 emphasizes four areas: (1) *Fighting bigotry and intolerance*, including projects to improve communication across racial lines in public high schools and on college campuses; (2) *preserving free expression*, including project Artsave, supporting artists facing censorship; combating attacks on films, videos, music, and other aspects of popular culture; and fighting the censorship of books in the public schools; (3) *protecting constitutional liberties*, including defending reproductive rights, civil rights, religious liberty, and

the separation of church and state; and Court Watch, a project to research nominations for appointment to the federal judiciary; and (4) *renewing democratic values*, including First Vote, a project to interest young people in politics and have them leave high school "with a diploma in one hand and a voter registration card in another," as PFAW's Sanford Horwitt says.

MEMBERS: PFAW membership grew rapidly in its first years, reaching a quarter million by 1986, and 290,000 by 1991.

STRUCTURE: PFAW has a sixty-member, self-recruiting board of directors, including Lear and Buchanan, Julius Chambers of the NAACP Legal Defense and Educational Fund, David Cohen of the Professionals' Coalition for Nuclear Arms Control, former Congress members Father Robert Drinan and Barbara Jordan, Stanley Scheinbaum, and Marge Tabankin (sixteen PFAW directors also sit on the board of the PFAW Action Fund). Anthony Podesta was the founding executive; Arthur Kropp has held the executive position of president since 1987.

RESOURCES: PFAW in 1991 had revenue of $4.5 million and expenditures of $4.2 million. The PFAW Action Fund had revenue of $2.1 million and expenditures of $2 million. The combined PFAW and PFAW Action Fund revenue derived from membership contributions (44 percent), special donations (23 percent), foundation grants (12 percent), special events (14 percent), and other sources (7 percent). Combined expenditures were divided among programs (66 percent), fund-raising (18 percent), and administration (16 percent).

PUBLICATIONS AND SERVICES: Membership is $20 and includes the quarterly newspaper *The Forum* (circulation 290,000). PFAW also publishes *Right Wing Watch* (circulation 5,000), a monthly newsletter that monitors the political and religious right, available for a $15 subscription. *The Activist*, which focuses on a specific topic for action, is available to members on request. Each year PFAW puts out a Censorship Report, documenting books that have been banned by schools. An affinity VISA card is available. □

HUMAN RIGHTS: AN INTERNATIONAL PERSPECTIVE

The idea of human rights has an ancient pedigree, dating from the Stoics of ancient Greece and running through St. Thomas Aquinas to such English political philosophers as Richard Hooker, Thomas Hobbes, and John Locke. Milestone charters include the English Magna Charta (1215), forced by the barons from King John; the English Bill of Rights (1689), developed by Parliament to establish a limited monarchy; the American Declaration of Independence (1776); the French Declaration of the Rights of Man and Citizen (1789); and the U.S. Bill of Rights (1791). Our contemporary framework of international law on human rights is of more recent vintage, dating from the ratification in 1945 of the United Nations Charter, Articles 1 and 55 of which establish the purpose of protecting human rights and fundamental freedoms.

The United Nations established a Commission on Human Rights to draft the Universal Declaration of Human Rights, which was passed unanimously by the General Assembly in December 1948. The declaration contains the basic civil and political rights: the right to life, liberty, and security of person; freedom from slavery and torture; freedom from discrimination and equal protection of the law; the presumption of innocence until proven guilty; freedom of thought, conscience, and religion; and freedom of opinion and expression. The declaration also contains economic, social, and cultural rights: social security, education, work, equal pay for equal work, and an adequate standard of living.

In order to establish these rights more clearly in international law as binding treaty obligations and to provide enforcement mechanisms, the General Assembly approved two covenants in 1966 that may be ratified by individual countries —the International Covenant on Civil and Political Rights (with an Optional Protocol), and the International Covenant on Economic, Social and Cultural Rights. The covenants provide for periodic reporting and interstate complaint procedures, based on the techniques developed by the International Labor Organization (an organization established in 1919 by the Versailles Peace Treaty ending World War I, and which now operates as a specialized agency of the U.N.). The periodic reports are reviewed by a committee of experts who assess whether a government is fulfilling its obligations under the covenants. Similar processes are followed by the numerous regional covenants, including the European Convention for the Protection of Human Rights and Fundamental Freedoms (1953); the American Convention on Human Rights (1969) adopted by the Organization of American States; and the African Charter on Human and People's Rights (1981) adopted by the Organization of African Unity.

A number of additional treaties have developed significant mechanisms of cooperation and monitoring, and several recent declarations have expanded the vision of human rights. The Helsinki Agreement (1975) among European states surprised its critics by having a strongly positive impact on human rights in Eastern Europe, as has the Conference on Security and Cooperation in Europe's statement on Cooperation in Humanitarian and Other Fields (1989). Other important agreements include United Nations Conventions on Genocide (1951), the Elimination of All Forms of Racial Discrimination (1969), and Discrimination Against Women (1979); the Declaration on the Elimination of Intolerance and of Discrimination Based on Religion or Belief (1981); the Convention Against Torture and Other Cruel, Inhuman or Degrading Treatment or Punishment (1984); and the United Nations Declarations on the Right of Peoples to Peace (1984), and on the Right of Development (1986).

International treaty mechanisms are usually cumbersome and can be subject to political obstruction. Private, non-governmental organizations are playing a vital role in publicizing violations of human rights. Amnesty International mobilizes its members on behalf of prisoners of conscience around the world. Human Rights Watch takes a wider scope of monitoring violations of civil and political rights through its Helsinki Watch, Americas Watch, Asia Watch, Africa Watch, and Middle East Watch committees. Freedom House publishes an annual survey on freedom in countries throughout the world. Cultural Survival has staked out the special niche of safeguarding the rights of the scattered indigenous peoples—also termed tribal peoples or national minorities.

AMNESTY INTERNATIONAL USA

322 EIGHTH AVENUE

NEW YORK, NY 10001

(212) 807-8400

FOUNDED: 1961   MEMBERS: 385,000
GROUPS: 410 local and 2,800 student
BUDGET: $31 million   STAFF: 90
TAX STATUS: 501(c)(3)

PURPOSE: "A worldwide movement of people working for the release of all prisoners of conscience, for fair and prompt trials for all political prisoners, and an end to torture and the death penalty."

Amnesty International USA (AIUSA) is the U.S. section of the global movement supporting prisoners of conscience— defined as people detained anywhere for their beliefs, color, sex, ethnic origin, language, or religion, provided they have not used or advocated violence. Volunteers who write letters and send telegrams are the heart of the program. Amnesty International (AI) was awarded the Nobel Peace Prize in 1977 for "securing the ground for freedom,

for justice, and thereby also for peace in the world." In three decades the organization has adopted over 42,000 prisoners, and helped free 38,000.

BACKGROUND: In November 1960, British human rights attorney Peter Benenson was angered by a newspaper report of two Portuguese students jailed for raising their glasses in a public toast to freedom. Benenson wondered if the Portuguese government could be moved by a barrage of letters to release these prisoners. He initiated a newspaper appeal in May 1961 calling for a voluntary association, Appeal for Amnesty, to assist eight political prisoners —and inspired people from six countries to meet and form Amnesty International. Among the influential founders was Irish jurist and diplomat Sean MacBride, the only person to have won both the Nobel (1974) and Lenin (1977) peace prizes. The methods of work adopted by the new organization are still in use today. Supporters were encouraged to form groups based in schools, churches, or neighborhoods. Groups adopted particular prisoners and wrote letters to the prisoners, their families, and the governments responsible. AI members advocate only for prisoners in other countries, never in their own.

AI's first internal controversy began

in 1964. South African Congress leader Nelson Mandela had been adopted as a prisoner of conscience in 1962. When the South African government convicted him of sabotage in 1964, the AI group supporting Mandela decided it could not continue to support him as a prisoner of conscience, because he endorsed violent opposition to apartheid. In fact, an organizational poll of all members found the majority believing AI should not adopt prisoners of conscience who used or advocated violence.

In 1966, reports of British torture in the Persian Gulf colony of Aden led to another major controversy. Benenson and others alleged that AI had been penetrated by British Intelligence and was not able to act independently on this case. In its wake, the five-man executive committee kicked out Benenson, abolishing his post as president and creating in its stead a new position of director general (later secretary general).

U.S. section membership had been relatively low during AI's first two decades. AIUSA's executive director John Healey produced an infusion of youthful energy with the "Conspiracy of Hope" concert tour in 1986, bringing U2, Sting, Bob Dylan, Joan Baez, Bryan Adams, Peter Gabriel, and Jackson Browne to six U.S. cities. Membership nearly doubled, to 300,000. In 1988 Healey organized a six-week, five-continent "Human Rights Now!" tour to publicize the fortieth anniversary of the U.N. Universal Declaration of Human Rights and recruit a new generation of members. Bruce Springsteen, Tracy Chapman, Youssou N'dour of Senegal, Sting, and Peter Gabriel donated their time and performed for over a million people. Reebok Foundation, the charitable arm of the sport shoe manufacturer, agreed to pick up any unpaid bills for the $23 million tour.

Although AI has won widespread respect from the political left and right for its nonpartisan approach (from the early days, local groups adopted three prisoners, one each from a Communist, noncommunist, and non-aligned country), it is not without criticism. Some human rights advocates fault AI for a casework approach that fails to focus on the absence of political rights (free elections, freedom of the press) and economic rights (free trade unions, freedom of enterprise) that underpin a society that needs to hold political prisoners. For several years gay and lesbian rights groups stepped up their efforts to pressure AI to add sexual orientation to its list of unjust grounds for imprisonment, and advocate for persons incarcerated only because they are homosexuals. AIUSA supported the idea, along with some Western European sections, but many Third World participants viewed homosexuality as immoral and blocked the change. At the 1991 international council meeting in Yokohama, Japan, the AI governing body adopted a resolution that recognized as prisoners of conscience gay men and lesbians jailed for their identity or conduct.

CURRENT PRIORITIES: AI celebrated its thirtieth anniversary in 1991 and launched a campaign to stop the special horrors suffered by women prisoners, including rape and repetitive strip searching. AI continues its campaign to end torture by the turn of the century, with its "8-point program for the pre-vention of torture," including training for law enforcement officials and pros-ecution of people responsible for in-humane acts against individuals in custody. AI is also mounting a cam-paign to pressure the government of Peru, where atrocities by the military and the Shining Path guerrillas con-tinue at a high level. Previous special campaigns have focused on capital pun-ishment, children, and the arms trade.

MEMBERS: AIUSA's membership grew rapidly in the late 1980s, from 75,000 in 1981 to 125,000 in early 1986 (Amnes-ty's twenty-fifth anniversary) to 250,000 by the end of 1987, following the suc-cessful "Conspiracy of Hope" human rights rock concert tour. The world rock tour "Human Rights Now!" in 1988 boosted the membership to near 400,000. There are over 1 million mem-bers worldwide.

AIUSA offers several ways to partic-ipate: (1) some 400 *local groups*, usually ten to twenty-five people, are commu-nity based; they work for individual prisoners, or conduct special cam-paigns aimed at countries with patterns of human rights violations; (2) some 2,700 *student groups*, based in colleges and high schools, work on special coun-try campaigns and urgent actions, and help educate the campus community on human rights; (3) the *Urgent Action Net-work* whose 15,000 members telegram, fax, telex, or airmail letters to assist persons in extreme danger; special groups—academics, journalists, law-yers, business people, trade unionists, religious congregations, women—work on behalf of colleagues imprisoned abroad; (4) *professional networks* of medical, legal, education, religious, and union members help imprisoned colleagues and use special skills and contacts through programs organized by the national office; (5) *individuals* who don't join a community or student group can send letters as part of the 25,000-member Freedom Writers Net-work, whose participants receive three prisoner cases to advocate for each month.

STRUCTURE: Headquartered in New York, AIUSA has five regions, with of-fices in Washington, D.C.; Somerville, Massachusetts; Atlanta; and Chicago. The western region has offices in San Francisco and Los Angeles. The Urgent Action Network, coordinated by Scott and Ellen Harrison, works out of Nederland, Colorado. The twenty-four-member board of directors is elected to two-year terms by the membership. A board member can serve a maximum of six years.

AI, headquartered in London, has forty-seven national sections and mem-bers in 150 countries. Each year 200 delegates from the national sections at-tend the International Council, which determines long-term policy and cur-rent priorities. The Council selects an International Executive Committee, which oversees the work worldwide.

RESOURCES: AIUSA's $31 million in rev-enue in 1991 derived 64 percent from individuals, 27 percent represented do-nated services for public service an-nouncements and professional art, and the remainder came from foundation grants, bequests, conference fees, spe-cial events, and literature sales. Ex-penses of $31 million went for program services (76 percent), administration (5 percent), and fund-raising (19 percent).

PUBLICATIONS AND SERVICES: Membership is $20 and includes the newspaper *Amnesty Action* (circulation 400,000), published six times a year, with one issue containing an annual report. The annual *Amnesty International Report* details its findings on human rights abuses around the world. Many other special reports, such as *Torture in the Eighties*, are also published. For the organizational history, see Jonathan Power, *Amnesty International: The Human Rights Story* (McGraw-Hill, 1981). *The Amnesty International Handbook* (Hunter House, 1991) provides a thorough guide to AI's history, policies, structure, and avenues for member involvement. Urgent Action Alerts are posted on many computer networks including PeaceNet, FidoNet, and UseNet. □

HUMAN RIGHTS WATCH

485 FIFTH AVENUE

NEW YORK, NY 10017

(212) 972-8400

FOUNDED: 1975   BUDGET: $5.2 million
STAFF: 65   TAX STATUS: 501(c)(3)s: The Fund for Free Expression, and Helsinki Watch

PURPOSE: "To monitor the human rights practices of governments: murder, disappearances, kidnapping, torture, imprisonment or other reprisals for non-violent expression or association; exile, censorship, denial of the right to assemble peaceably, denial of freedom of movement, deprivation of political freedom, violation of due process of law, and discrimination on racial, gender, ethnic or religious grounds."

Human Rights Watch (HRW) is the umbrella organization (formed in 1988) for the Fund for Free Expression (founded in 1975) and five regional divisions: Helsinki Watch (1979), Americas Watch (1981), Asia Watch (1985), Africa Watch (1988), and Middle East Watch (1989). Each regional Watch division collects information on human rights abuses in countries in its area, sending fact-finding missions to meet with government officials, opposition leaders, local human rights groups, victims of abuse, and witnesses to abuses. The Watch committees publish reports and publicize violations of human rights, and strongly defend local human rights monitors. HRW also monitors violations of the rules of war in sustained armed conflicts, covering both governments and rebel forces. HRW generates international protests against human rights violations, and pressures the U.S. government and other international groups (such as the Organization of American States and the United Nations) to respond to abuses.

BACKGROUND: Robert Bernstein, then president and chief executive of Random House, established the Fund for Free Expression in 1975. Together with Wall Street attorneys Orville Schell and Adrian DeWind, Bernstein founded Helsinki Watch in 1979 in response to persecution of citizens in the Soviet Union and Czechoslovakia (including Vaclav Havel's Charter 77) for organizing groups to monitor the Helsinki accords. Aryeh Neier, executive director of the American Civil Liberties Union from 1970 to 1978, joined as executive director and has played a central role in developing the full Human Rights Watch program.

Americas Watch was launched in 1981 on the same model to counteract the human rights approach of the Reagan administration—a selective plan in which human rights violations by "hostile totalitarian" governments would be treated more severely than those by "friendly authoritarian" governments. Americas Watch is the only committee to draw fire from conservatives, who called it too harsh on the government of El Salvador, a U.S. "friend" fighting a civil war against guerrilla insurgents, and too lenient on the government of Nicaragua, an "enemy" under attack by the U.S.-sponsored contras. Watch committees to cover Asia, Africa, and the Middle East were formed in the late 1980s.

In 1987 Human Rights Watch was created as a governing umbrella for all the Watch groups. Each Watch group has its own staff and advisory committee. There are executive directors for each committee: Jeri Laber for Helsinki Watch, Juan Méndez for Americas Watch, Sidney Jones for Asia Watch, Rakiya Omaar for Africa Watch; Aryeh Neier is overall director for Human Rights Watch, and Holly Burkhalter directs the Washington office.

CURRENT PRIORITIES: HRW continues its programs around the world under its mandate to protect human rights. New activities include a women's project and a prison project. In 1991, the group campaigned against the granting of "most favored nation" trading status with China, due to its record of human rights abuses.

STRUCTURE: The Fund for Free Expression is the primary financial vehicle for the Watch committees; some foundation grants are received by Helsinki Watch, which was founded as a separate organization. HRW's sixteen-member executive committee oversees the work of the committees; Robert Bernstein is the chairman and Adrian DeWind the vice-chairman, with other members including Jack Greenberg, Jeri Laber, and Aryeh Neier. HRW has its headquarters in New York, offices in Los Angeles and Washington, D.C., and overseas offices in London, Hong Kong, and El Salvador.

RESOURCES: HRW's $5.2 million budget in 1991 was derived 85 percent from foundations and 15 percent from individuals. Program funds are divided roughly evenly among the five Watch committees, with the budget for Helsinki Watch a bit larger and that of Middle East Watch a bit smaller than the others.

PUBLICATIONS AND SERVICES: Contributors receive the *Human Rights Watch* newsletter (circulation 7,000) four times a year. The individual Watch committees put out their own newsletters (available by subscription), sometimes as often as weekly. In addition, each group regularly publishes lengthy, documented reports on conditions in individual countries. The *Human Rights*

Watch World Report, published by Yale University Press, is an annual review of the countries monitored by HRW. An *HRW Annual Report* is available, summarizing the activities of each committee by country, and listing staff and the year's publications. A complete publications catalog is also available. □

CULTURAL SURVIVAL

11 DIVINITY AVENUE

CAMBRIDGE, MA 02138

(617) 495-2562

FOUNDED: 1972   MEMBERS: 20,000
BUDGET: $2.2 million   STAFF: 24
TAX STATUS: 501(c)(3)

PURPOSE: "To help indigenous peoples retain their rights and culture as they learn to live with the modern world."

Cultural Survival (CS) mixes activism and scholarship to defend and assist tribal peoples and ethnic minorities around the world—combining the activities of a human rights group, an environmentally sensitive development organization, and a marketing agent.

BACKGROUND: When modern industrial societies encounter small-scale traditional cultures, the indigenous peoples too often have been dispossessed or annihilated. Cultural Survival was founded in 1972 by anthropologist David Maybury-Lewis and other Harvard University social scientists to help once remote and isolated tribal societies survive the encroachment of the outside world. CS aims to help indigenous societies maintain cultural continuity in the midst of change and have some say in determining their futures.

CURRENT PRIORITIES: Although it is active on five continents, CS has placed a major emphasis on the tribal peoples of the Americas, particularly Indians in the rain forests who have become victims of government and corporations in the development process. Connecting environmental and human rights issues, CS promotes a form of federalism that would allow limited regional autonomy within the nation-state, with an emphasis on land and resource rights and sustainable economic development. In 1989 CS began Cultural Survival Enterprises as a trading arm to promote sustainably produced nontimber forest products—including the highly successful Rainforest Crunch nut brittle and Rainforest Crunch ice cream (sold by Ben and Jerry's).

STRUCTURE: CS has a ten-member board of directors, most associated with Harvard University, with Maybury-Lewis as president. Pam Solo, veteran peace activist, was named executive director in 1990.

RESOURCES: CS's 1991 revenue of $2.1 million came from foundations (61 percent), individual contributions (21 percent), net income from product sales (4 percent), grants from the U.S. Agency for International Development (USAID) (3 percent), and other sources. Expenditures of $2.2 million supported programs and product sales (85 percent), fund-raising (6 percent), and administration (9 percent).

PUBLICATIONS AND SERVICES: Membership begins at $25 and includes the monthly bulletin *Action for Cultural Survival;* a $45 membership also includes the quarterly magazine *Cultural Survival* (circulation 20,000). The publications catalog distributes the materials of ten organizations. For an excellent survey on indigenous peoples, see Julian Berger, *Report from the Frontier: The State of the World's Indigenous Peoples* (Zed Books and Cultural Survival, 1987). Maybury-Lewis was anthropological adviser to the 1992 public television series *Millennium: Tribal Wisdom in the Modern World.* □

WORKERS' RIGHTS

Independent farmers and artisans were the foundations of Jefferson's vision of democracy in the United States. As the journeyman artisan was squeezed by an expanding mercantile capitalism, crafts were broken down into tasks that could be completed by less-skilled workers and laborers. Initial forms of workingmen's associations and unions emerged in the 1790s and early 1800s. The industrial manufacturing system took root in the United States during the Civil War, and the number of wage earners increased from 1.5 million in 1860 to 5.5 million by the turn of the century. The expansion of industry and the campaign for an eight-hour day prompted the organization of the National Labor Union in 1866 by William Sylvis; the Knights of Labor in 1869, which grew under Terence Powderly's leadership to over 700,000 members in 1886; and the American Federation of Labor (AFL) for craft unions by Samuel Gompers in 1886. A radical rival to the AFL, the Industrial Workers of the World, was organized in 1905, but its growth was checked by World War I and the Red scare that followed.

The AFL followed a tradition of voluntarism, looking to the power of organized labor to protect workers by making and enforcing contracts with corporations—not considering the state to be a reliable ally in defending workers' rights. Corporations moved to make the state their ally, seeking injunctions against strikes under the Sherman Anti-Trust Act of 1890—which had been passed to break up the power of corporate industrial monopolies. And in the case of *Hitchman Coke and Coal Co.* v. *Mitchell,* the Supreme Court upheld labor contracts that forbid union activity (the infamous "yellow dog" contract). John L. Lewis, president of the United Mine Workers (UMW—actually an industrial union within the AFL) came to support labor legislation, including the Anti-Injunction (Norris–La Guardia) Act, which prohibited federal injunctions in labor disputes and outlawed "yellow dog" contracts, and Section 7(a) of the National Industrial Recovery Act (NIRA), which recognized the right of employees to organize and bargain collectively. When Title I of NIRA was held unconstitutional, its labor guarantees were written into the National Labor Relations (Wagner) Act of 1935. The first minimum wage was established by the Fair Labor Standards Act of 1938.

John L. Lewis led the UMW and the new industrial union–organizing committees out of the AFL in 1935 and founded the Congress of Industrial Organizations (CIO), which proceeded to organize unions in the steel, auto, rubber, oil, and other major industries. CIO membership rose from 1.5 million in 1937 to 2.8 million in 1941; AFL membership jumped from 2.5 million to 4.5 million over the same period. After World War II, business took the offensive to blunt the power of organized labor with the Labor Management Relations (Taft-Hartley) Act of 1947, passed over President Truman's veto. In response to the business offensive, labor moved toward greater unity. Walter Reuther became president of the United Auto Workers and then the CIO in 1952; that year George Meany succeeded William Green as president of the AFL. In December 1955 the two federations merged to form the AFL-CIO. In 1959 Congress passed the Labor-Management Reporting and Disclosure (Landrum-Griffin) Act to secure the democratic rights of union members.

The International Labor Organization (ILO), established in 1919, develops international agreements to protect the rights of workers. Now functioning as a specialized agency of the United Nations, the ILO monitors the implementation of conventions and evaluates complaints by labor, employers, and governments. Cold War conflicts between the United States and the Soviet Union limited the effectiveness of the ILO (the United States actually withdrew from the ILO between 1978 and 1980). Over the last decade the ILO has been increasingly effective in securing the rights of labor in Eastern Europe (particularly Solidarity in Poland) and elsewhere. The United States has ratified only a few of the ILO conventions, and the Economic Policy Council of the United Nations Association of the USA has recommended U.S. ratification of the conventions on freedom of association, the right to bargain collectively, and equality of treatment and elimination of discrimination in employment.

KEY LABOR LEGISLATION, 1931–1959

1931: Davis-Bacon Act. Required payment of prevailing wage rates to laborers and mechanics employed by contractors and subcontractors on public construction.

1932: Anti-Injunction (Norris—La Guardia) Act. Prohibited federal injunctions in labor disputes, and outlawed "yellow-dog" contracts.

1933: National Industrial Recovery Act. Section 7(a) guaranteed the right of employees covered by National Recovery Act (NRA) agreements to organize and bargain collectively through representatives. (Title I of NIRA was declared unconstitutional by the Supreme Court in *Schecter* v. *U.S.* in 1935.)

1935: National Labor Relations (Wagner) Act. Protected the right of workers to organize and elect representatives for collective bargaining.

1938: Fair Labor Standards Act. Established minimum wage and limited child labor.

1947: Labor Management Relations (Taft-Hartley) Act. Title 14(b) established the ability of states to pass "right to work" laws banning "union shops," establishments requiring union membership as a condition of employment.

1959: Labor-Management Reporting and Disclosure (Landrum-Griffin) Act. Required reporting of union business matters, protected democratic rights of union members, and banned secondary boycotts.

Source: U.S. Department of Labor, *Important Events in American Labor History, 1778–1978.*

Although unions and professional associations are beyond the scope of *The Activist's Almanac*, we present profiles of two progressive groups that concentrate on internal democracy and participation in unions generally (the Association for Union Democracy and the Labor Education and Research Project), and one conservative organization that defends individuals who oppose membership or participation in unions (the National Right to Work Committee). Union women address common concerns through the Coalition of Labor Union Women (CLUW), founded in 1974, which has some 20,000 members and seventy-five chapters around the country. Joyce Miller of the Amalgamated Clothing and Textile Workers is president, and Clara Day of the Teamsters is executive vice president. Contact CLUW, 15 Union Square, New York, NY 10003; (212) 242-0700. In 1992 the Institute for Global Communications, sponsor of EcoNet and PeaceNet, developed LaborNet, a computer network for labor activists.

ASSOCIATION FOR UNION DEMOCRACY

500 STATE STREET, 2ND FLOOR

BROOKLYN, NY 11217

(718) 855-6650

FOUNDED: 1969   CONTRIBUTORS: 3,000
BUDGET: $200,000   STAFF: 4
TAX STATUS: 501(c)(3)

PURPOSE: "Advancing the principles and practices of internal democracy in the U.S. labor movement."

The Association for Union Democracy (AUD) works to protect and enforce the democratic rights of union members. Pro-labor and pro-union, AUD believes the union movement can be a powerful force for progress only if unions practice internal democracy and protect the rights of their members.

BACKGROUND: In 1959 former toolmaker and machinist Herman Benson started publishing a newsletter with the help of socialist leader Norman Thomas to support unionists who were fighting to democratize their unions or were battling to free them from mobster control. Following the murder of Painters union reformers Dow Wilson and Lloyd Green in San Francisco in 1966, Thomas and Benson formed a Citizens Committee to call for a federal investigation of the murders and racketeering in the painting industry. Supporters of the Citizens Committee formed the AUD in 1969 to serve as a permanent organization to defend union democracy. AUD has been the leading organization supporting the democratic rights of union members—regardless of their politics—under the Labor-Management Reporting and Disclosure Act of 1959 (the Landrum-Griffin Act).

CURRENT PRIORITIES: AUD has supported numerous union democracy campaigns, including Miners for Democracy in the United Mine Workers, Steelworkers Fight Back, Teamsters for a Democratic Union, and the Teamster Fair Election Project. AUD has sponsored the Women's Project for Union Democracy since 1985, designed to increase involvement and influence of women in unions, and help women mobilize unions to support pay equity, parental leave, day care, health and safety, and freedom from harassment.

MEMBERS: AUD's 3,000 members include unionists, labor educators, attorneys, and other supporters. Periodic national and regional meetings bring supporters together.

STRUCTURE: AUD has a 12-member, self-recruiting board of directors; Judith Schneider is president and Herman Benson is secretary-treasurer. Prominent members have included Joseph Rauh and Victor Reuther. Attorney Susan Jennik has been executive director since 1989, when Benson stepped down.

PUBLICATIONS AND SERVICES: Benson still edits *Union Democracy Review* (circulation 3,000), which members receive six times a year. AUD publishes various handbooks and pamphlets, including *Democratic Rights of Union Members:* *A Guide to Internal Union Democracy.* □

LABORNOTES

LABOR EDUCATION AND RESEARCH PROJECT

7435 MICHIGAN AVENUE

DETROIT, MI 48210

(313) 842-6262

FOUNDED: 1976   CONTRIBUTORS: 8,000
BUDGET: $300,000   STAFF: 8
TAX STATUS: 501(c)(3)

SLOGAN: "Let's put the movement back in the labor movement."

The Labor Education and Research Project (LERP) publishes the newsletter *Labor Notes* and holds an annual convention that has become the leading forum for left-leaning rank-and-file activists from a variety of unions. Critical of bureaucratic union leadership, LERP opposes nonadversarial approaches to labor-management relations and supports a radical vision of social unionism.

LERP emphasizes support for rank-and-file militants against both corporate management and the "labor bosses." LERP associates helped initiate Teamsters for a Democratic Union (TDU), which has led a twenty-year struggle for democracy in the International Brotherhood of Teamsters. LERP leaders continue informal ties with the American socialist group Solidarity (an organization of former Trotskyists that publishes the journal *Against the Current*), the British shop steward movement and the Labor Party left, the British *New Left Review*, and Verso Press.

Labor Notes has held a national conference in Detroit for rank-and-file union activists, usually every other year, since 1981—the 1989 and 1991 meetings each attracted over a thousand participants. LERP has made a major effort to criticize Quality of Work Life (QWL) and Team Concept, based on Japanese labor relations and work organization methods.

STRUCTURE: LERP has an eighteen-member, self-recruiting board of directors. Kim Moody has been executive director of LERP since its founding.

PUBLICATIONS AND SERVICES: The monthly *Labor Notes* (circulation 8,000), edited by Jim Woodward, is available for a $10 subscription. LERP sells pamphlets and books by its associates, including Nick Parker, *Inside the Circle: A Union Guide to QWL* (South End Press, 1985); Mike Parker and Jane Slaughter, *Choosing Sides: Unions and the Team Concept* (South End Press, 1988); and Dan LaBotz, *A Troublemakers Handbook: How to Fight Back Where You Work—and Win* (Labor Notes, 1991). See Kim Moody, *An Injury to All: The Decline of American Unionism* (Verso, 1988), for a left perspective on rank-and-file insurgency and the labor movement since World War II. □

National Right to Work Committee

NATIONAL RIGHT TO WORK COMMITTEE
8001 BRADDOCK ROAD
SPRINGFIELD, VA 22160
(703) 321-9820

FOUNDED: 1955   MEMBERS: 170,000
BUDGET: $9.8 million   STAFF: 90
TAX STATUS: 501(c)(4): National Right to Work Committee; 501(c)(3): National Right to Work Legal Defense and Education Foundation

PURPOSE: "All Americans must have the right but not be compelled to join labor unions."

The National Right to Work Committee (NRTWC) advocates for the right of individuals to refuse to join unions, which states can protect under Section 14(b) of the Taft-Hartley Act, and for the right of union members to refuse to support lobbying and political activities of their union. A reliable member of the traditional conservative coalition, NRTWC under the leadership of Reed Larson has skillfully used lobbying, litigation, and public relations to limit the power of organized labor.

BACKGROUND: NRTWC was founded in 1955 by Congressman Fred Hartley (of the Taft-Hartley Act) and a group of small businessmen and blue-collar railroad employees who were or had been members of the railroad "brotherhoods"—the Brotherhood of Locomotive Engineers, the Brotherhood of Trainmen, and other railroad unions.

The term "right to work" was borrowed from a 1941 editorial in the *Dallas Morning News* by journalist William B. Ruggles, who defended the right of individuals to work without joining unions if they so chose. Section 14(b) of the 1947 Taft-Hartley Act permits states to shield individuals from compulsory union ("closed shop") provisions of labor contracts. Twenty-one states have enacted "Right-to-Work" laws that allow individuals to reject union membership in jobs covered by union contracts, although they may have to pay a fee for union representation services.

One of NRTWC's biggest battles with organized labor came in 1965 when the AFL-CIO attempted to use its influence with President Lyndon Johnson to try to repeal Section 14(b) of Taft-Hartley. The legislation passed the House, but was foiled in the Senate when Larson persuaded Everett Dirksen (R-Illinois) to filibuster. In 1968 NRTWC stopped an executive order by President Johnson that would have granted "agency shop" status for unions representing all federal employees. Again in 1969 labor attempted to write "agency shop" provisions covering 750,000 postal workers into the Postal Reorganization Act, and again labor was thwarted by an amendment guaranteeing postal workers the right to decline to join a union even in "closed shop" states. The "common situs" picketing bill in 1975 would have allowed construction unions to shut down an entire construction site if any subcontractor employed nonunion labor. President Ford indicated he would sign the bill if it passed Congress; a strenuous lobbying campaign led by

NRTWC changed his mind, and Ford vetoed the bill.

The election of President Jimmy Carter in 1976 revived labor's hopes for passing "common situs" without a veto. Another major publicity campaign by NRTWC included full-page ads in several dozen newspapers around the country, and resulted in defeat of the bill in the House by a 217–209 vote. As an alternative, the AFL-CIO devised the Labor Law Reform Act of 1977, backed by the Carter administration. After the bill passed the House, NRTWC and its allies generated a massive grassroots lobbying campaign, leading to a defeat for the Reform Act in the Senate.

In 1949 the National Labor Relations Board (NLRB) ruled in *Union Starch and Refining Co.* that under the 1947 Taft-Hartley law, employees can be required to pay union fees but cannot be forced to join the union. The Supreme Court upheld this interpretation of "agency shop" contracts in *NLRB* v. *General Motors* in 1963 (unions are limited to charging "agency fees" for employees in a bargaining unit who do not want to join the union). In 1975 NRTWC's Legal Defense Foundation started litigating the case of Harry Beck and nineteen other telephone company employees who objected to the Communications Workers of America using their dues to support Hubert Humphrey for president in 1968. NRTWC promoted the case with an ad campaign in such magazines as *The New Republic* and *The New York Review of Books*, appealing to civil libertarians. The NRTW LDEF supported Beck's claim that workers who do not join the union should not have to pay fees for anything more than the union's cost of contract negotiation, administration, and handling grievances, excluding the cost of a union's political activities. Unions can legally use "soft money," staff and resources, to support political candidates with such in-kind services as telephone banks, publicity, printing, mailings, and get-out-the-vote drives. The Supreme Court upheld Beck and NRTW LDEF in *Beck* v. *Communication Workers of America* in 1988.

CURRENT PRIORITIES: NRTWC is emphasizing an educational campaign to inform workers of their right to refuse to pay full union fees, and is pressuring the NLRB to force unions to inform members of their right to refuse to pay fees for lobbying and political activities (in 1992 President Bush signed an executive order requiring federal contractors to so notify their workers). The NRTW LDEF carries a legal docket of some 300 cases, half of which deal with teachers and the National Education Association (NEA). NRTWC sponsors the Concerned Educators Against Forced Unionism (CEAFU), a coalition of professional educators.

MEMBERS: NRTWC claims 1.7 million members and supporters; current contributors number around 170,000.

STRUCTURE: NRTWC has a thirty-five-member, self-recruiting board of directors. Conservative New York investment banker Shelby Collum Davis is chairman of the board, which includes several blue-collar workers and union members. The NRTW Legal Defense and Education Foundation was formed in 1968 to provide legal services for individuals opposing compulsory unionism; it has a ten-member, self-recruiting board of trustees, all from the business community. Reed Larson—known as "Mr. Right to Work"—started on the staff of Right to Work in Kansas and has headed NRTWC since 1959; he serves as president of both the Committee and the Foundation. There is also a Right to Work PAC, for which Larson serves as treasurer, but it is an independent political action committee, not a "separate, segregated fund" of NRTWC. It is not restricted to taking money only from NRTWC members—anyone can contribute.

RESOURCES: In 1991 NRTWC had revenues of $6.1 million from dues and contributions, and expenses of $5.7 million, divided 76 percent for programs, 21 percent for fund-raising, and 3 percent for administration. The NRTW LDEF had revenue of $3.9 million and expenditures of $4.4 million, divided 83 percent for legal programs and 17 percent for management and fund-raising. In the 1990 campaign cycle, RTW PAC raised $400,000.

PUBLICATIONS AND SERVICES: Contributors receive the monthly *National Right to Work Newsletter* (circulation 135,000); the NRTW LDEF also sends its contributors *Foundation Action* (circulation 40,000) six times a year. □

THE RIGHT TO KEEP AND BEAR ARMS

Second Amendment: A well regulated militia, being necessary to the security of a free State, the right of the people to keep and bear arms, shall not be infringed.

In a population of some 250 million in the United States in 1990, there may be 150 million privately owned firearms—very roughly 50 million each of rifles, shotguns, and handguns. Seventy million households own guns. A staff report to the National Commission on the Causes and Prevention of Violence summarized the situation in 1969 in terms that remain descriptive today: "About half of all American homes have a firearm, and many have more than one. Firearms ownership is highest in the South and lowest in the East. Ownership of rifles and shotguns is higher in rural areas and towns than in large cities, but handgun ownership is highest in towns and large cities." The two primary purposes for owning a gun are sport and protection, with rifles and shotguns predominating for sport and handguns leading for protection.

In round figures, there may be as many as one million gun-related crimes a year. Handguns are used in 70 percent of crimes involving firearms. In 1990 there were over 15,000 murders with guns in the United States, two-thirds of all murders. Another 15,000 people committed suicide with guns, over half of all suicides (men are twice as likely as women to commit suicide with a gun). There were also some 2,000 accidental deaths by guns, about 2 percent of the total accidental deaths. Handguns account for about 22,000 deaths per year, about two-thirds of the total deaths by guns. Estimates of firearms injuries run from 100,000 to 200,000 per year. This level of gun violence is the highest of any Western industrialized country, which provokes responses across the full spectrum from "something must be done!" to "nothing can be done"—as noted by James Wright, Peter Rossi, and Kathleen Daley, authors of *Under the Gun* (Aldine, 1983). Does gun control do any good? Can guns be regulated without infringing the "right of the people to keep and bear arms?"

The framers of the Bill of Rights believed a militia of citizen soldiers to be the best defense against the tyranny of a professional standing army, which the colonists had experienced under the English. The Second Amendment aimed to protect the right of the states to maintain an armed citizen militia against any effort by the federal government to abolish such militias in favor of a standing federal army. "Militia" in 1789 clearly meant "the people in arms" rather than a body like today's National Guard, yet the Supreme Court has consistently held that the Constitution does not protect an individual right to own and use any variety of firearm. Surprisingly, James Madison's original draft added a right of religious conscientious objection, no doubt in deference to the Pennsylvania Quakers: "No person religiously scrupulous of bearing arms shall be compelled to render military service in person."

Numerous state laws regulate the sale, ownership, and use of firearms. One of the first and most significant was New York's Sullivan Act of 1911, which required a license for the possession of a handgun; amended many times, it is still in force. The first federal legislation regulating guns was the National Firearms Act of 1934, which prohibited submachine guns, silencers, and sawed-off rifles and shotguns (a response to gangsterism flourishing after Prohibition in the "roaring twenties" and the early days of the Depression). The Federal Firearms Act of 1938 required the licensing of firearms manufacturers and dealers. The assassination of President John Kennedy in 1963, the urban riots of the mid-1960s, and the assassinations of Robert Kennedy and Reverend Martin Luther King, Jr., in 1968 provoked a searching discussion of new legislation. The Gun Control Act of 1968 banned imports of cheap pistols ("Saturday night specials") and surplus military weapons, and prohibited the interstate sale of all firearms. Federal gun laws are under the jurisdiction of the Bureau of Alcohol, Tobacco and Firearms of the Department of the Treasury (the "revenuers" renowned for breaking up moonshine stills and bootlegging operations). The Consumer Product Safety Commission is explicitly forbidden from regulating firearms, so no federal agency prevents unsafe firearms from being sold.

The Supreme Court has held consistently that states and the federal government may regulate firearms. In *United States* v. *Miller*, the Supreme Court in 1939 upheld the National Firearms Act of 1934, commenting that a sawed-off shotgun owned by an individual has no relationship to the preservation of a well-regulated militia. The Supreme Court has ruled that the Second Amendment applies only to the federal government, not the states, and that the contemporary counterpart of the militia is the National Guard, not the people in arms.

The Wall Street Journal suggests the gun issue reflects a divided population: "cosmopolitan America" (urban, educated, upper middle class, liberal) and "bedrock America" (small town, rural, lower middle and working class, conservative). As the writer put it, the dispute over gun control can best be seen as a contest between two alternative world views, "a skirmish in the larger battle over the nation's cultural values" (parallel to the splits over abortion and capital punishment). The National Rifle Association speaks for "bedrock America," with the more extreme gun advocates clustered in such groups as Citizens Committee for the Right to Keep and Bear Arms and Gun Owners of America. Handgun Control, Inc., represents urban professionals with a liberal Republican tilt, and the traditional Democratic liberal alliance is assembled in the church-connected Coalition to Stop Gun Violence.

NATIONAL RIFLE ASSOCIATION OF AMERICA

1600 RHODE ISLAND AVENUE, NW

WASHINGTON, DC 20036

(202) 828-6000

FOUNDED: 1871 MEMBERS: 2.7 million
CLUBS: 15,000 BUDGET: $96.7 million
STAFF: 550 TAX STATUS: 501(c)(4)s: National Rifle Association, and NRA Institute for Legislative Action; 501(c)(3)s: The NRA Foundation, Firearms Civil Rights Legal Defense Fund, International Shooter Development Fund, National Firearms Museum Fund, and NRA Special Contribution Fund; PAC: NRA Political Victory Fund

PURPOSE: "To protect and defend . . . the inalienable right of the individual American citizen . . . to acquire, possess, transport, carry, transfer ownership of, and enjoy the right to use arms."

The National Rifle Association of America (NRA), organized in 1871 to promote marksmanship, was for many years an organization of sport shooters, hunters, and gun collectors concerned primarily with competitions, training, and gun safety. Most members became involved through local hunting and gun clubs. As gun control legislation became popular in the 1960s in response to social turmoil and violence, a segment of the NRA membership made opposition to all restrictions on firearms ownership a top priority, and won control of the organization in 1977. With aggressive publicity and recruitment, membership expanded rapidly. Since then a major portion of NRA's resources has been directed toward electing and lobbying public officials on the state and national levels. Customarily aligned with police, NRA hurt itself during the 1980s by supporting "cop-killer bullets" and semiautomatic firearms. With traditional allies defecting and public patience with gun violence wearing thin, NRA's image has been wounded. NRA may not be running out of ammunition, but it is no longer the invincible political gunslinger of years past.

BACKGROUND: The National Rifle Association of America was organized in 1871 by former Union Army officers to promote marksmanship and the popular sport of match shooting: General Ambrose Burnside (of sideburns fame) served as the first president. NRA declined in the 1880s along with interest in competitive long-range shooting, as trap shooting with shotguns became more popular. The Spanish-American War renewed interest in the rifle, and NRA revived with it, launching a new marksmanship program in 1900. Congress established a National Board for the Promotion of Rifle Practice in 1903, and authorized the sale of surplus arms and ammunition to rifle clubs in 1905. NRA became the primary vehicle for such sales through its member clubs. Drawn to its new benefactor, NRA moved its headquarters to Washington, D.C., in 1908, the same year it organized the first American Olympic shooting team to win a Gold Medal. World War I provided another boost to NRA,

as Congress authorized subsidies to civilian rifle practice through the National Defense Act of 1916.

Although NRA did oppose New York State's Sullivan Act requiring permits for pistols in 1911, and successfully lobbied against including gun registration provisions in the National Firearms Act of 1934, fighting gun laws was a minor NRA activity (the official NRA history, published in 1967, devotes twenty-four chapters to marksmanship programs and one chapter to legislation). After World War I, NRA made a concerted effort to expand its constituency by adding sportsmen and hunting clubs. NRA membership before World War II peaked in 1940 around 50,000; after the war, with rifle sales reestablished, membership soared to 300,000 by 1948. After rifle sales were suspended in 1949, membership declined slightly and held around 250,000 for several years, reviving in 1957 when Springfield rifles were offered for sale, and jumping again in 1963 to 600,000 as the M-1 carbine was put on the market. Membership leaped to one million in 1968 in response to the Federal Gun Control Act. Gun sales were suspended by the Defense Department, and membership slowly declined during the 1970s to 900,000.

In the mid-1970s some old-guard members argued that NRA's image as a sportmen's organization could be restored by moving the headquarters out of Washington to Colorado, and by emphasizing hunting and shooting. The new hard-liners, whose first priority is to lobby against all gun control proposals, called the old guard a bunch of environmentalists and bird-watchers soft on gun control. They staged the "revolt in Cincinnati" at the 1977 NRA convention, ousting the old-guard board members and executive vice president Maxwell Rich, and selecting leaders committed to fighting all forms of gun control.

The insurgents' choice was Harlon Carter, a former official of the U.S. Border Patrol and NRA board member from 1951 to 1969, and the first director of NRA's Institute for Legislative Action (ILA) from 1975 to 1976. An outstanding marksman in his own right, Carter held forty-four national shooting records for pistol, military rifle, and small-bore rifle. Carter was installed as executive vice president in 1977, and during his tenure until 1985, membership tripled to three million, and the budget increased to $66 million. Over several years, however, Carter failed to get NRA's McClure-Volkmer bill through Congress, and Washington newspapers began playing up his murder conviction (overturned on a technicality) as a young man. Ray Arnett, the former National Wildlife Federation board member who worried about *Ranger Rick* magazine turning children against hunting, was named to replace Carter in 1985.

Arnett succeeded in getting an amended McClure-Volkmer Act passed in 1986, but hard-liners saw a partial defeat—interstate handgun sales remained forbidden, and all sales of machine guns and armor-piercing bullets were banned. Accused of using NRA facilities for private hunting trips and shooting at an endangered species of bird from a motorboat, Arnett in turn lost his position in 1989 to J. Warren Cassidy, who remains NRA's current executive vice president.

When the smoke had cleared from the 1980s, NRA had lost several shoot-outs: More police were alienated by NRA's opposition to the banning of armor-piercing ("cop-killer") bullets; Maryland voters in 1988 refused to repeal a law that allowed banning of cheap handguns; and California passed the Assault Weapons Control Act of 1989 to limit semiautomatic weapons. NRA also offended conservatives by refusing to support Robert Bork's nomination to the Supreme Court in 1987.

CURRENT PRIORITIES: NRA's primary policy focus is opposition to all forms of restrictions on guns, including (1) firearms licensing and registration, (2) restrictions on semiautomatic firearms, (3) waiting periods for the purchase of firearms, (4) restrictions on armor-piercing ammunition, (5) restrictions on plastic guns, (6) restrictions on "Saturday-night specials," (7) handgun bans and other firearms prohibitions, and (8) disruption or banning of hunting. In search of positive ways to combat crime, NRA supports stronger law enforcement, tougher prosecutors and judges, and more prisons. Alarmed by the success of local and state laws limiting gun purchases, NRA began its CrimeStrike advertising campaign in 1992—emphasizing self-defense against armed criminals.

MEMBERS: After the Cincinnati revolt in 1977 and a new emphasis opposing gun control legislation, membership soared from 900,000 into the millions. From a peak of 3 million in the mid-1980s, NRA membership was down to around 2.3 million in 1990, and has since rebounded to some 2.7 million in 1992. Recent recruitment campaigns have targeted women as potential new members, with controversial ads emphasizing pistols in self-defense for women. NRA membership is available at a variety of dues levels, beginning at $25. Voting rights are extended to Annual Members who have held continuous membership for at least five years, or who join as Life Members (a one-time $500 fee). The *NRA Member Guide*, a booklet giving a thorough outline of NRA structures and services, is distributed as a magazine insert to new members.

STRUCTURE: NRA is governed by a seventy-five-member board of directors elected in groups of twenty-five for three-year terms by voting members. A bylaws booklet is available. The NRA board designates its members to serve on the boards of the ILA and NRA's various 501(c)(3)s. There are over 15,000 NRA-affiliated shooting, hunting, law enforcement, and other specialty clubs on the local level (clubs must include at least 50 percent NRA members). State associations are active in every state, and are served by a network of field representatives in twenty-one area offices. NRA also operates the National Firearms Museum at its national headquarters in Washington, the Whittington Center for shooting competitions near Raton, New Mexico, and the U.S. Olympic Shooting Center in Colorado Springs. NRA is recognized by the United States Olympic Committee as the national governing body for the sport of shooting.

RESOURCES: NRA had revenue of $87.1 million in 1991, derived from membership dues (60 percent), contributions (14 percent), advertising (8 percent), interest and dividends (7 percent), and other (11 percent). Expenses of $96.7 million went for lobbying through the Institute for Legislative Action (20 percent), publications (16 percent), general operations (13 percent), membership recruitment and administration (31 percent), general administration (11 percent), and public affairs (9 percent). NRA ran a deficit of nearly $9.6 million in 1991. NRA has net assets in excess of $100 million. The NRA Political Victory Fund, the political action committee, raised $4.7 million in the 1986 campaign cycle, $4.6 million in the 1988 cycle, and $3.7 million in the 1990 cycle.

PUBLICATIONS AND SERVICES: Members receive either *The American Rifleman* (circulation 1.4 million) or *The American Hunter* (circulation 1.3 million). Specialized publications available by subscription include *NRA Action*, a monthly tabloid published by the NRA Institute for Legislative Action; *The Badge* (circulation 145,000), a monthly newsletter sent free to police officers and agencies; *Shooting Sports USA*, for competitive shooters; *InSights*, for junior members; *Man at Arms*, for gun collectors; and the *NRA Training Supplement*, for shooting instructors. NRA conducts training in firearms safety and marksmanship, and conducts special camps for advanced competitive shooters. Members may also buy insurance, obtain an affinity credit card, and invest in The Reserve Fund, a U.S. government bond fund. The house history is *Americans and Their Guns*, compiled by James B. Trefethen and edited by James E. Serven (Stackpole Press, 1967). On the 1977 conservative insurgency within NRA, see Joseph P. Tar-

taro, *Revolt at Cincinnati* (Hawkeye, 1981), a pamphlet reprinting a series from *Gun Week*. NRA has a computer bulletin board, Gun Talk, open to members for a $15 annual fee; connect via computer at (703) 719-6406, or telephone (800) GUN-TALK to sign up. □

HANDGUN CONTROL

ONE MILLION STRONG . . . working to keep handguns out of the wrong hands.

HANDGUN CONTROL, INC.

1225 EYE STREET, NW, ROOM 1100

WASHINGTON, DC 20005

(202) 898-0792

FOUNDED: 1974   MEMBERS: 180,000
BUDGET: $9 million   STAFF: 28
TAX STATUS: 501(c)(4): Handgun Control, Inc.;
501(c)(3): Center to Prevent Handgun Violence;
PAC: Handgun Control Voter Education Fund

PURPOSE: "To keep handguns out of the wrong hands."

Handgun Control, Inc. (HCI), is the leading lobby for controls on the sale and ownership of handguns and semi-automatic weapons. Under the leadership of Pete Shields and now Sarah Brady, HCI has been the predominant antagonist of the National Rifle Association's efforts to keep gun sales and ownership unrestricted. HCI's board and community activists include many people whose families have been victims of handgun violence.

BACKGROUND: Pete Shields was a conservative Republican, a marketing manager for DuPont, living in Wilmington, Delaware, when his son Nick be-

came the last victim of San Francisco's infamous "Zebra" killers in 1974. Through a friend, Shields met Mark Borinsky, a victim of armed robbery who founded the National Council to Control Handguns (NCCH) in 1974, and his volunteer lobbyist, retired CIA staffer Ed Welles. Shields took a leave of absence from DuPont in 1975 to work with NCCH, and in late 1976 formally retired and became executive director and later chairman of NCCH (renamed Handgun Control, Inc., in 1978, to avoid confusion with NCBH, the National Coalition to Ban Handguns).

As a conservative Republican and daughter of an FBI agent, Sarah Brady is another unlikely crusader for handgun control. She took up the cause after her husband, James Brady, press secretary to Ronald Reagan, was shot in the head from a .22-caliber pistol in 1981 by John Hinckley, Jr., who was attempting to assassinate the President. Despite a history of mental disorders, Hinckley had no trouble purchasing the handgun in a Texas pawnshop. James Brady spent several years in painful physical therapy, regaining limited mobility and speech. Sarah Brady joined the board of HCI in 1985, and has become a well-publicized witness before congressional committees on handgun legislation. Signing the direct-mail appeals of HCI, she has also been a formidable fund-raiser. Since Shields became chairman emeritus, Sarah Brady has emerged as HCI's most effective public representative.

HCI had high hopes for the administration of President Jimmy Carter, who had campaigned supporting handgun control legislation. Carter, however, was beset by troubles and never invested his dwindling political capital in gun control issues. With the election of Ronald Reagan in 1980, the National Rifle Association (NRA) decided the time was ripe to roll back the federal Firearms Control Act of 1968. The modified McClure-Volkmer Act that finally passed Congress in 1986 allowed interstate purchases of rifles and shotguns but not handguns, and banned machine guns entirely, thus giving both HCI and NRA a partial victory. HCI has given support to many state and local handgun and assault weapon control initiatives, including California's unsuccessful Proposition 15 in 1978; the ordinance banning handguns passed by Morton Grove, Illinois; a referendum in 1988 that upheld Maryland's ban on "Saturday night specials"; and California's 1989 Assault Weapons Act.

CURRENT PRIORITIES: In 1987 HCI began pushing the "Brady bill," which simply requires a seven-day waiting period for handgun purchases. Jim Brady has joined Sarah in presenting testimony before Congress. The Brady bill got a big boost in 1991 when former president Ronald Reagan endorsed it on the tenth anniversary of the attempt on his life. The bill passed both the House and the Senate in 1991, but did not become law. HCI would also ban assault weapons and high-capacity ammunition magazines, and strengthen requirements for federal licenses to sell guns.

MEMBERS: HCI claims some 1.7 million contributors since its founding. Around 180,000 are current supporters, up from 100,000 in 1985. Members interested in speaking, writing, and organizing in their home communities can join the Handgun Control Network and receive the newsletter *Network News* every six weeks.

STRUCTURE: HCI has a twenty-one-member board of directors, mostly self-recruiting. Following an NRA complaint filed with the Federal Elections Commission, HCI reorganized its board to accommodate membership representation. Each year members are given the opportunity to nominate and vote for one director. An annual meeting is open to all supporters. Charles Orasin has been the chief executive since 1974, currently with the title president. The HCI political action committee was renamed the Voter Education Fund in 1990.

RESOURCES: HCI's budget of $7.3 million in 1990 included $4.5 million for program services (62 percent) and $2.8 million for administration and fundraising (38 percent). Income of $7.6 million for 1990 was derived largely from membership dues and other contributions. The Center to Prevent Handgun Violence received $1.7 million in contributions and spent $1.3 million on education and research (76 percent) and $400,000 (24 percent) on support services. The Handgun Control Voter Education Fund (a PAC) raised $300,000 in the 1986 campaign cycle, $254,000 in the 1988 cycle, and $322,000 in the 1990 cycle.

PUBLICATIONS AND SERVICES: Members receive the newsletter *Progress Report* twice a year. The Center to Prevent Handgun Violence issues the *Legal Action Report* to its supporters. The HCI legislative hotline is (202) 898-0796. Pete Shields describes his work with HCI in *Guns Don't Die—People Do* (Arbor House, 1981). □

4.

RACE AND
ETHNICITY

From the beginning, race has been at the heart of the deepest divisions in the United States and the greatest challenges to its democratic vision. Africans were brought to the continent in slavery, American Indian nations were subjected to genocidal wars of conquest, northwestern Mexico was invaded and annexed, Asians were imported as laborers then subjected to exclusionary laws. Black historian W.E.B. Du Bois wrote that the history of the twentieth century would be the history of the color line, predicting that anticolonial movements in Africa and Asia would parallel movements for full civil and political rights for people of color in the United States.

During the 1920s and 1930s social scientists worked to replace the predominant biological paradigm of European racial superiority (common in social Darwinism and eugenics) with the notion of *ethnicity*—which suggested that racial minorities could follow the path of white European immigrant groups, assimilating into the American mainstream. Gunnar Myrdal's massive study, *An American Dilemma*, in 1944 made the case that the American creed of democracy, equality, and justice must be extended to include blacks. Nathan Glazer and Daniel Moynihan argued in *Beyond the Melting Pot* in 1963 for a variation of assimilation based on cultural pluralism, in which various racial and ethnic groups retained some dimension of distinct identity. Following the civil rights movement's victories, neoconservatives began to argue in the 1970s that equal opportunity for individuals should not be interpreted as group rights to be achieved through affirmative action in the sense of preferences or quotas.

African Americans: The abolitionist movement used the Civil War to press first for the Emancipation Proclamation in 1863, freeing slaves in the Confederate states, and then for the Thirteenth Amendment, abolishing slavery in 1865. A program of Reconstruction under occupation by the Union army protected the right of freed slaves to vote, and radical governments including black officials took office. The Freedmen's Bureau coordinated efforts to set up schools for blacks and establish a system of free labor for their employment, but efforts at land reform were cut short and a sound economic foundation for free blacks was not achieved. The Panic of 1873 and subsequent depression undercut the economic revival of the South. Bargaining for a majority in the electoral college after the indecisive presidential election of 1876, Republican Rutherford Hayes agreed to withdrawal of federal troops from the South in 1877, assuring a return to white supremacy. The Reconstruction era constitutional amendments (the Thirteenth, Fourteenth and Fifteenth) were insufficient by themselves to guarantee the protection of rights to southern blacks.

Independent black institutions—churches, clubs, benevolent societies, schools—survived, but gains in civil rights were rolled back after 1877 as the "Jim Crow" system of legal segregation was tightened in the South. Mob rule was commonplace; there were 4,742 documented cases of lynchings in the United States between 1882 and 1964—3,445 blacks and 1,297 whites (most of the whites were lynched before 1900). Lynchings didn't drop below 10 per year until 1936. The Supreme Court's ruling in *Plessy* v. *Ferguson* in 1896 endorsed "separate but equal" as the legal basis of segregation.

Two contrasting approaches to black development were advanced by Booker T. Washington (1856–1915) and W.E.B. Du Bois (1868–1963). Washington advocated uplift of Negroes through education and industrial training, acknowledging the strength of systematic segregation by avoiding efforts for political and social equality in the South. Washington interested northern white philanthropists in supporting his programs, including Tuskegee Institute, and appealed to the southern planter-industrialist class to see common interests in preparing blacks to work in southern industry. Washington's ideas influenced the founders of the National Urban League (NUL) in 1910, established to provide assistance to blacks in northern cities, and would find echoes in later movements for black separatism and black nationalism—including the rapid rise and fall of Marcus Garvey's United Negro Improvement Association in the 1920s and both leftist nationalist and black Muslim movements from the mid-1960s forward.

Du Bois rejected accommodation and urged protest and agitation for political and social equality. In 1905 he organized the Niagara Movement to restore black Americans' political and civil rights, under attack since the end of Reconstruction, and counter the vocational self-help programs of Booker T. Washington with a movement for equal rights. Du Bois was a cofounder of the National Association for the Advancement of Colored People (NAACP) in 1909, the first editor of its magazine *The Crisis*, and organizer of the first Pan-African Congress in 1919. Both the NAACP and the NUL were creations of the progressive era. The progressive white cofounders of the NAACP and the NUL, living primarily in New York, were often from families with an abolitionist background. Many would become prominent leaders of other progressive era organizations, including the Fellowship of Reconciliation and the American Civil Liberties Union.

To an extent, the NAACP and NUL reflected political and economic alternatives, but they also represented a division of labor within a broader vision of political, social, and economic equality—the NAACP emphasizing political agitation and legal action for racial equality, and the NUL emphasizing employment opportunities. The NUL not only promoted vocational guidance and training, it strongly supported an end to employment discrimination. For the first half of the twentieth century, the primary vehicle for the continuing black freedom movement was the NAACP, which conducted a three-decade campaign against lynching and began the legal work that would culminate in the Supreme Court's decision in *Brown* v. *Board of Education* in 1955 that overturned *Plessy*'s "separate but equal" doctrine and set the stage for the civil rights movement of the mid-1950s and 1960s.

The vast migration of nearly five million African Americans from the South to the North and West between 1910 and 1960 created a new political opportunity structure for the civil rights movement. Blacks went from being nonvoters in the South to voters in the North, and under the influence of Roosevelt's New Deal began to switch allegiance from the Republicans to the Democrats with the election of 1936. Reflecting this growing political influence, A. Philip Randolph (a socialist and president of the Brotherhood of Sleeping Car Porters) brought together several black civil rights groups in his March on Washington movement in 1940. The threat of the march prompted Roosevelt to issue Executive Order No. 8802 in June 1941, banning discrimination in defense industries and in government, and also setting up a Fair Employment Practices Committee. Black voters made the difference in several key states—including Illinois, Ohio, and California—for Truman's upset victory in the presidential election of 1948.

Following the Supreme Court's decision in *Brown* in 1954, the border southern states began desegregating school systems, but the Deep South waited to see what the federal government would do about enforcing the ruling. The civil rights movement began with the Montgomery bus boycott, initiated when Rosa Parks was arrested for not surrendering her seat to a white passenger. Parks had been a state and local NAACP leader for several years, and had recently attended a workshop at the Highlander Folk School where participants discussed what they could do to foster change in their communities. Her associate in the Montgomery NAACP, E. D. Nixon (a sleeping car porter and member of Randolph's union), helped mobilize local ministers while Jo Anne Robinson, president of the Women's Political Council and teacher at Alabama State College, mimeographed leaflets calling for a boycott. Local ministers formed the Montgomery Improvement Association, and selected newcomer Reverend Martin Luther King, Jr., as president. The year-long bus boycott ended with victory, and sparked the organization in 1957 of the Southern Christian Leadership Conference (SCLC), an association of ministers committed to furthering the civil rights movement.

In the fall of 1957 the attention of the world was drawn to

the effort to integrate Central High School in Little Rock, Arkansas. Arkansas NAACP president Daisy Bates led the legal strategy resulting in nine black students entering the school, protected from mobs by federal troops. Tactics for the next stage of the movement were being developed by James Lawson and Glenn Smiley, two ministers on the staff of the Fellowship of Reconciliation, who began working with King and the SCLC in 1958 to conduct workshops on nonviolent direct action. Independently of each other, groups of black college students in Nashville and Greensboro began lunch-counter sit-ins in early 1960, and the movement spread quickly. The SCLC's staffer Ella Baker called a meeting of students involved in the sit-ins, and some 300 showed up at Shaw University in Raleigh over Easter weekend in 1960, and ended by forming a new organization, the Student Nonviolent Coordinating Committee (SNCC).

The three legs of the civil rights movement in the South were the local NAACP chapter network, the black churches, and the black colleges. Each had its own organizational form—the NAACP, SCLC, and SNCC. But other organizations also played important roles, particularly the Congress of Racial Equality (CORE), led by James Farmer. CORE and the Fellowship of Reconciliation (FOR) had sponsored an integrated bus trip through four upper southern states in 1947, called the "Journey of Reconciliation." Reviving that idea, Farmer decided to challenge segregated transportation by a "Freedom Ride" through the Deep South in 1961. In Birmingham the Freedom Riders were attacked by a mob, with police complicity, in an event that received international press coverage, but Freedom Riders persisted throughout the summer. As southern resistance to integration stiffened, A. Philip Randolph led a coalition of civil rights groups that called for a March on Washington in August 1963 to demand passage of the Civil Rights Act. Randolph's colleague Bayard Rustin—who had served on the staff of FOR, SCLC, and the War Resisters League—served as the deputy director of the march, which drew a quarter-million people to the reflecting pool between the Washington Monument and the Lincoln Memorial.

Mississippi proved to be a heartland of segregationist resistance. President Kennedy had to federalize the state National Guard to protect James Meredith, who enrolled at Ole Miss

(University of Mississippi) in 1962. In June 1963 the NAACP's state field director Medgar Evers was assassinated at his home in Jackson; President Kennedy was killed in Dallas in November. The NAACP, SCLC, SNCC, and CORE worked together under the umbrella of the Conference of Federated Organizations (COFO) to conduct a Freedom Vote mock election in 1963 and sponsor the Mississippi Summer Project in 1964. Freedom Summer began with the kidnapping and murders of project volunteer Andrew Goodman and two civil rights workers, Michael Schwerner and James Chaney. President Johnson signed the Civil Rights Act in July 1964. The Mississippi volunteers persisted, and the summer ended with the Mississippi Freedom Democratic party's widely publicized unsuccessful challenge to the regular white delegation to the Democratic party convention in Atlantic City (future delegations would be integrated). It took further demonstrations, violence by police at the Edmund Pettus Bridge in Selma, Alabama, and the march from Selma to Montgomery early in 1965 to build pressure for Congress to pass the Voting Rights Act.

A watershed event in the civil rights movement occurred with the sixteen-day "walk against fear" from Memphis to Jackson announced in June 1966 by James Meredith, the first black student at the University of Mississippi. Meredith was shot from ambush and hospitalized on the second day of his march, and SCLC and SNCC leaders agreed to take up his march. At evening rallies and during the march, Stokely Carmichael raised the slogan "Black Power"; SCLC and SNCC led competing chants of "Freedom Now!" and "Black Power!" Separatist sentiment in SNCC pushed young whites out of the movement—back to campuses and the anti–Vietnam War movement. The rise of black nationalism strained relations between black movement leaders and old allies, including many Jews who had long been strong civil rights supporters. Women were prompted to reexamine their roles in the civil rights struggle—reflections that gave a powerful push to the emerging women's liberation movement.

Several of the organizations that emerged in the 1950s and 1960s—including CORE, SCLC, and SNCC—either failed to survive the next decade or continued with diminished influence. CORE and SNCC both moved entirely to black nationalism, SNCC disintegrating and CORE reduced to marginality.

Indeed King's program had foundered when he entered the North, with his Chicago campaign outmaneuvered by Mayor Daley. The Poor People's Campaign attempted to address the roots of poverty, but ended in disarray. After King's assassination in Memphis in 1968, SCLC never regained more than regional influence.

Bayard Rustin urged the movement in another direction with his influential *Commentary* article "From Protest to Politics" in 1965, away from protest demonstrations and into politics at every level. In the end, Rustin's logic and advice prevailed; there were 7,500 black elected officials in 1991, who remain an important focus of black political activity. The Congressional Black Caucus (twenty-seven black Representatives, including two women) is the most progressive group of elected officials in American public life. Black elected officials now have a think tank, the Joint Center for Economic and Political Studies, directed by Eddie Williams. The Leadership Conference on Civil Rights, organized in 1950, has emerged as the powerful Washington umbrella lobby organization for the movement. Whitney Young and Vernon Jordan pulled the National Urban League firmly into the civil rights coalition, and the NUL's research department serves as another black think tank. Several black officials have emerged as powerful elected officials in majority white jurisdictions—Tom Bradley as mayor of Los Angeles, David Dinkins as mayor of New York, and Douglas Wilder as governor of Virginia. Jesse Jackson's Rainbow Coalition pointed the way toward a revival of interracial progressive populism, particularly during his presidential primary campaign in 1988. There are approximately thirty-one million African Americans in the United States (12 percent of the population in 1990).

American Jews: American Jews have made contributions to social reform and Left politics far out of proportion to their numbers (variously counted from 4.3 million to 6 million, around 2 percent of the population in 1990). Recently they have also contributed to the vital core of neoconservative intellectuals. German Jews were predominant among early immigrants, settling widely across the South and West as well as in the East. Over 2 million Eastern European Jews—mostly from Russia—were among the 35 million immigrants who came to the United States between 1885 and 1920. Jews were prominent among early socialist and labor leaders: Morris Hillquit of the Socialist party, Sidney Hillman of the Amalgamated Clothing Workers, and David Dubinsky of the International Ladies Garment Workers Union (ILGWU). American Jews have taken a leading role in fighting discrimination, helping found the NAACP and the National Urban League (Joel and Arthur Spingarn and Kivie Kaplan together served as presidents of the NAACP for sixty years, from 1915 to 1975). The 1913 trial of Leo Frank in Georgia (and his subsequent lynching in 1915) fueled development of the Anti-Defamation League of B'nai B'rith (ADL); rooted in the experience of anti-Semitism by Jewish Americans, ADL has opposed all varieties of bigotry in America. The American Jewish Committee (founded 1906) and the American Jewish Congress (1918) are two other important organizations promoting civil rights. Before the end of World War II, Jews were restricted by informal enrollment quotas in private colleges, and few Jews could obtain tenured faculty appointments in American colleges and universities (giving "quotas" a repugnant resonance to this day). Jews also had very limited access to professional firms, businesses, and private clubs controlled by non-Jews. The war against Nazism awakened most Americans to the danger of anti-Semitism, which declined sharply in the postwar period. Nevertheless, the resurgence during the 1970s and 1980s of Klan groups, the Aryan Brotherhood, skinhead gangs, and other extremists has kept the ADL busy researching hate groups and promoting legislation combating hate crimes.

Just as black nationalism was pushing many whites out of the civil rights movement, the importance of Israel became highlighted for American Jews by the Six-Day War in June 1967. Faced with an Egyptian naval blockade and an Arab alliance, Israel destroyed the air forces of its Arab neighbors and occupied Egypt's Sinai Peninsula and Gaza Strip, Jordan's West Bank, and Syria's Golan Heights. In October 1973 Egypt and Syria staged a coordinated attack that left Egypt with a foothold in the Sinai—and led eventually to the Camp David accord between Israel and Egypt brokered by President Jimmy Carter, and the 1979 peace treaty that returned Sinai to Egypt. Despite disagreements over Israeli policy toward the Palestinians in the Occupied Territories and the basis for an eventual peace settlement, most American Jews maintain a strong commitment to Israel's survival. Support remained strong for the powerful lobby, American Israel Political Affairs Committee (AIPAC), as well as various political action committees supporting U.S. military and economic assistance to Israel. Despite their economic prosperity, a majority of American Jews remain committed to liberalism, the Democrats, and an inclusive vision of social justice.

American Indians: There are some 1.8 million American Indians (less than 1 percent of the population in 1990), who belong to at least 500 tribes (the number currently recognized by the federal government), 307 in the lower forty-eight states and 197 in Alaska. Understanding the unique situation of Native Americans requires a look at the complex field of Indian law, which has oscillated between sovereignty and dependency in its view of tribal rights. As Europeans colonized North America, they recognized Indian tribes as independent societies capable of defining political and legal relationships through treaties. In a series of Supreme Court opinions written from 1823 to 1832, Chief Justice John Marshall described Indian tribes as quasi-sovereign "domestic dependent nations" subject to federal authority but free of state control. The reality of the unequal relationship would be another matter. Andrew Jackson was elected president in 1828 and proposed a program of voluntary removal of Indians east of the Mississippi to lands in the West. The Indian Removal Act of 1830 compelled Indians to move, with the Cherokee walking the "Trail of Tears" from Georgia to Oklahoma under harsh conditions, and the Choctaw abandoning many millions of acres of traditional lands.

Reversing its position on quasi-sovereignty, the federal government adopted a policy of assimilation with the General Allotment (Dawes) Act of 1887, establishing individual ownership of tribal lands and resulting in millions of acres shifting from Indian to white ownership. Between 1887 and 1934 Indian lands were reduced from 138 million to 48 million acres, of which 20 million acres were arid and economically useless. In a new series of cases between 1882 and 1903, the Supreme Court interpreted tribes as societies without power, essentially wards of the federal government.

As a New Deal reform, Interior Department critic John Collier was named commissioner of Indian Affairs, and supported the Indian Reorganization (Wheeler-Howard) Act of 1934 (IRA), which ended the allotment policy and fostered Indian self-government by authorizing tribal councils with formal, federally approved constitutions and bylaws. Indian traditionalists objected to the Anglo-American form of tribal government under the IRA; when votes were taken, 181 tribes accepted IRA provisions and 77 tribes (including the Navajo) rejected the act. Reversing field again after World War II, the federal government adopted a policy of termination in 1954, arguing that Indians would do better without federal regulation and paternalism. Termination was halted in 1958, and during the 1960s and 1970s tribes benefited from a new round of federal antipoverty and economic development programs. Frustration with federal policy led Indians to seize Alcatraz Island in San Francisco Bay in 1969; the occupation ended with no clear gains in 1971. The militant American Indian Movement briefly occupied Bureau of Indian Affairs offices in Washington in 1972, and staged a major campaign in Wounded Knee, South Dakota, in 1973—but failed to oust the elected tribal leaders after battles with the FBI. From the federal legal services program the Native American Rights Fund emerged in 1970 to become the leading authority on Indian law and the primary legal force behind the movement to reclaim the doctrine of tribal sovereignty and confront continuing problems of poverty, discrimination, and racism.

Hispanic Americans: There are 22.3 million people in the United States of Hispanic descent (nearly 9 percent of the population in 1990), of whom 13.4 million (60 percent) are of Mexican heritage. Hispanics (or Latinos, as some activists prefer) have been difficult to organize as a unified constituency because of their diversity of national backgrounds and the scattered geographic locations of different groups. Mexican Americans are concentrated in the southwestern states of California, Texas, New Mexico, Arizona, and Colorado. Puerto Ricans on the mainland (2.5 million) live primarily in New York and New Jersey. Cuban Americans (1.2 million) are concentrated in south Florida around Miami, and in New Jersey. Illinois is home to both Mexican Americans and Puerto Ricans.

Other Central and South Americans (2.6 million) are scattered on the East and West coasts.

The League of United Latin American Citizens (LULAC) was founded in 1929 in Texas as a Mexican American organization emphasizing education for citizenship; in recent years it has reached out to include other Latinos in its membership. LULAC has never established a strong lobbying office in Washington. The American GI Forum was founded in Texas by Mexican American veterans in 1948 to work for civil rights and voter registration. Political action and voter registration was also emphasized in California by the Community Service Organization (CSO) formed in the early 1950s and the Mexican American Political Association (MAPA) founded in 1958, and in Texas by the Political Association of Spanish Speaking Organizations (PASSO). The Chicano movement of the mid-1960s developed around student organizations inspired by several new organizing efforts—Cesar Chavez's United Farm Workers in California; Reies Tijerina's land grant movement in northern New Mexico, Alianza Federal de Mercedes; and Rudolfo "Corky" Gonzalez's Crusade for Justice in Denver. Young Chicanos organized La Raza Unita party in Texas and the Chicano Moratorium in Los Angeles during the late 1960s, evoking a vision of the legendary land of Aztlan in the U.S. Southwest. What remains of this period are numerous influential community organizations in cities throughout the Southwest, and the National Council of La Raza (NCLR) established as a coordinating body, lobby, and think tank in 1968. The Mexican American Legal Defense and Education Fund (MALDEF) was also founded in 1968, and a corresponding Puerto Rican Legal Defense and Education Fund (PRLDEF) in 1972. The Cuban American National Foundation (CANF) of Jorge Mas Canosa is patterned after the American Israel Political Affairs Committee's successful lobbying for Israel; CANF is concerned primarily with U.S. policy toward Cuba, and is strongly anti-Castro and pro-Republican.

Asian Americans: Some 7.3 million people of Asian or Pacific Island descent (just under 3 percent of the population in 1990) live in the United States. The widespread stereotype of the "model minority" overlooks the vast variety of individual backgrounds, diverse cultures, languages, educational traditions, and economic classes of at least ten major national or ethnic clusters: Chinese (themselves divided by long-time residents and recent arrivals, dialect groups, and background from the mainland, Taiwan, or Hong Kong), Japanese, Korean, Filipino, Asian Indian (also divided by religion and culture—Hindu, Muslim, and Sikh), Vietnamese, Cambodian, Hmong, Laotian, and Thai. Pacific Islanders include Polynesians, Melanesians, and others. Of the Asian Americans, 23 percent are Filipino, 19 percent Chinese, 11.7 percent Japanese, 11.2 percent Asian Indian, and 10.9 percent Korean. About 40 percent of all Asian Americans (2.4 million) live in California.

The Japanese American Citizens League (JACL) is the Asian American organization with the longest participation in the liberal civil liberties and civil rights network. JACL's sensitivity to civil liberties was heightened during World War II, when many Japanese Americans were evacuated from the West Coast and relocated to internment camps. JACL has led a movement for redress, which obtained an act of Congress in 1983, providing each former internee with $20,000 in compensation. The Asian American Legal Defense and Education Fund was organized in New York in 1974.

Arab Americans: There are some 2.5 million Arab Americans (1 percent of the population in 1990). The first wave arrived with the great immigration around the beginning of the century, mostly Christians from Lebanon and Syria who sought assimilation. A second wave arrived after World War II, from throughout the Middle East, most ethnically conscious and with a greater proportion of Muslims. Many have settled in Dearborn and Detroit, Michigan. Organizations include the National Association of Arab Americans (NAAA) led by David Sadd, the American-Arab Anti-Discrimination Committee (ADC) headed by former South Dakota senator James Abourezk, and the Arab American Institute founded by James Zogby in 1985.

NATIONAL ASSOCIATION FOR THE ADVANCEMENT OF COLORED PEOPLE

4805 MOUNT HOPE DRIVE

BALTIMORE, MD 21215-3297

(410) 358-8900

FOUNDED: 1909   MEMBERS: 400,000
BRANCHES: 2,200   BUDGET: $13.3 million
STAFF: 132   TAX STATUS: 501(c)(3)s: NAACP
and NAACP Special Contribution Fund

PURPOSE: "To improve the political, educational, social and economic status of minority groups; to eliminate racial prejudice; to keep the public aware of the adverse effects of racial discrimination; and to take lawful action to secure its elimination."

The National Association for the Advancement of Colored People (NAACP) has been the leading membership organization striving to secure equal justice for African Americans. Launched in an era of increasing repression, the NAACP fought against lynching for decades and, beginning in the 1930s, mounted an aggressive challenge to the legal structures limiting voting rights and supporting segregated education, housing, and employment. The NAACP's litigation and lobbying assisted a series of judicial and political victories that, in tandem with the direct-action tactics of the civil rights movement in the 1950s and 1960s, brought about a revolution in race relations in the United States. The NAACP's presence in thousands of cities and towns provided a base of local leadership for the movement—as it continues to do today.

BACKGROUND: Americans of all races were shocked in the summer of 1908 when whites rioted in Springfield, Illinois, the birthplace of Abraham Lincoln, looting and burning homes in black neighborhoods, lynching two black men, and injuring scores of residents. W.E.B. Du Bois, Ida B. Wells-Barnett, Mary Church Terrell, and other black leaders joined in issuing the "Lincoln Day Call" on February 12, 1909 (the 100th anniversary of Abraham Lincoln's birth), with a group of white radicals and socialists including Henry Moskowitz, Mary White Ovington, William English Walling, and Oswald Garrison Villard (grandson of abolitionist William Lloyd Garrison and publisher of the *New York Evening Post* and later *The Nation*). The "Call," from which the founding of the NAACP is dated, announced a meeting to create a national interracial organization to defend the rights of Negroes. The first meeting was held in New York City on May 31 and June 1. At the second annual conference in May 1910, Du Bois was hired as the director of publicity and research, and began work on the organization's official publication, *The Crisis*, which first appeared in November.

As widespread mob violence continued into the 1910s, the NAACP began a campaign against lynching and led efforts to pass a federal antilynching law. The organization's 1919 report, *Thirty Years of Lynching in the United States, 1889–1918*, noted that 3,224 men and women had been lynched in that period. Over 50 blacks were being lynched each year—more than one per week on average—until 1923. Walter White was the key NAACP staff on the campaign, investigating lynching and riots, and writing numerous articles in the black press and the book *Rope and Faggot: A Biography of Judge Lynch* (Knopf) in 1929—the year he became NAACP director. With the NAACP rallying support, antilynching bills passed the House in 1922, 1937, and 1940, but all were blocked by Senate filibusters. Nevertheless, the campaign against lynching helped the NAACP build alliances with a wide range of civil liberties, labor, women's, and liberal organizations—including the ACLU, the YWCA, the American Federation of Labor, the Women's International League for Peace and Freedom, and religious groups from Quakers to Methodists to the American Jewish Committee. Only with passage of the Civil Rights Act of 1968, providing sanctions for violating the civil rights of citizens, has there been a federal law penalizing lynching.

The NAACP legal committee was active from the start, and became effective under the leadership of attorney and board member Arthur Spingarn. The NAACP came to the defense of the Negro soldiers of the 24th Infantry in Houston, who were tried for murder after they had fired on mobs attacking them in the riots of September 1917, killing eighteen whites. Of the soldiers tried, thirteen were hanged, and the NAACP continued defending the remaining forty-one soldiers until the last was released from prison in 1938. The NAACP was in and out of the defense of the Scottsboro Boys, nine black

males ages thirteen to twenty, arrested in 1931 and convicted of raping two white women on a freight train; all but the youngest were sentenced to death. Although the NAACP had lined up Clarence Darrow and Arthur Garfield Hays as defense attorneys, the Communist party persuaded the boys to be defended by its International Labor Defense (ILD). Eventually the NAACP and the ILD joined in a common Scottsboro Defense Committee, and none of the young men were executed.

In 1935 the NAACP board approved a program aimed at overcoming segregation, a shift in strategy from the largely defensive stance against lynching and violence toward a systematic legal offensive that would challenge discrimination in education, employment, voting, and military service. Legal adviser Charles Hamilton Houston arranged for young attorney Thurgood Marshall to join the NAACP staff in 1936. Initially the legal campaign worked within the "separate but equal" doctrine, seeking cases dealing with unequal salary scales for black and white teachers, and blacks seeking admission to law schools and other graduate professional programs available at white state colleges but not offered at traditionally black colleges in the state. The protracted litigation required substantial financial support, and fundraising was hindered by the NAACP's lack of "charitable and educational" status, denied by the Internal Revenue Service because of the NAACP's lobbying throughout the 1920s and 1930s for a federal antilynching law. In 1939 the NAACP board agreed to incorporate a separate NAACP Legal Defense and Educational Fund (known as the

LDF or "Inc. Fund"), which would qualify for tax-deductible contributions. The LDF was set up in 1940 with a common board with the NAACP, but in 1941 began including board members who were not on the NAACP board. Some competition for funds between the LDF and its parent soon developed.

As World War II approached in 1940, the NAACP pushed to end discrimination in the armed forces; Benjamin Davis was promoted to brigadier general, the first black man to reach this rank. In 1941 A. Philip Randolph and Walter White met at the White House with President Roosevelt and other officials to discuss the threatened March on Washington to protest discrimination in employment; to avoid the march Roosevelt issued Executive Order No. 8802, banning discrimination in industries receiving government contracts, and setting up the Committee on Fair Employment Practices. In the courts, the NAACP widened its legal strategy to win voting rights by attacking white primaries, the poll tax, and other barriers to registration.

After World War II the momentum for change was accelerating. President Harry Truman addressed the NAACP's 1947 convention, promising an attack on discrimination; he won reelection in 1948 with the help of three states—Ohio, California, and Illinois—in which black voters provided a crucial margin of support. Truman issued Executive Order No. 9980, prohibiting racial discrimination in the federal service, and in 1949 issued an executive order ending segregation in the armed services. In 1948 Du Bois left the NAACP for a second time, splitting from the leadership by his endorsement of Henry Wal-

lace for president and his opposition to the Marshall Plan. And in 1948 the NAACP board endorsed Thurgood Marshall's recommendation that the legal program undertake a direct assault on the "separate but equal" doctrine and push for the elimination of segregation. Litigation was succeeding, slowly preparing a foundation for overturning the old *Plessy* ruling; the NAACP had won thirty-four out of thirty-eight cases it had brought before the Supreme Court by 1952.

On May 17, 1954, the Supreme Court handed down its unanimous ruling in *Brown* v. *Board of Education*, overturning the "separate but equal" doctrine and ruling that segregated educational systems were inherently unequal, and thus a denial of the equal protection clause of the Fourteenth Amendment. The ruling prompted resistance in the South, where White Citizens Councils were established and several states attempted to outlaw the NAACP. As the civil rights movement flowered, its roots were in local black churches and NAACP chapters. Although new organizations like Martin Luther King, Jr.'s Southern Christian Leadership Conference (SCLC) and the Student Non-violent Coordinating Committee (SNCC) took the lead in militant demonstrations and voting rights campaigns, the NAACP frequently provided local leaders and even martyrs. Montgomery NAACP secretary (and former Alabama state secretary) Rosa Parks launched the Montgomery bus boycott in 1955 by refusing to move to the back of a public bus. Arkansas NAACP president Daisy Bates led the 1957 campaign in which nine students desegregated Little Rock's Central

High School under the protection of federal troops. When Robert Moses began work in Mississippi for SNCC, his first contacts were local NAACP leaders like Amzie Moore, C. C. Bryant, and E. W. Steptoe. Mississippi NAACP leader Medgar Evers and NAACP attorney Constance Baker Motley planned James Meredith's effort to integrate the University of Mississippi in the fall of 1962 (Evers was assassinated in June 1963). Long after the protest leaders from other organizations had returned home, it was often the NAACP attorneys who dealt with the legal fallout.

There is no doubt the civil rights movement suffered from conflicts between NAACP director Roy Wilkins, who took the more conservative legal approach, and others, particularly Martin Luther King, Jr., and the SNCC leaders, who favored direct action. Where the NAACP made a crucial contribution was shepherding civil rights legislation through the Congress. The NAACP's veteran lobbyist Clarence Mitchell, who joined the staff in 1946 and directed its Washington office from 1950 to 1978, saw that rapid progress in desegregation could be made following implementation of the President's executive order integrating the armed services. In 1950 Mitchell and Wilkins, together with Joseph Rauh of the Americans for Democratic Action, organized the Leadership Conference on Civil Rights, a coalition including the major Jewish organizations, churches, and labor unions. Mitchell began working with Rep. Adam Clayton Powell to attach an antisegregation amendment (which became known as the Powell Amendment) to bills of all sorts, from the Railway Labor Act to federal housing and education acts. Mitchell helped achieve a legislative breakthrough with the Civil Rights Act of 1957, a weakened bill, but the first since the Civil War era. Over the next decade he would help lobby through Congress such major achievements as the Civil Rights Act of 1964, the Voting Rights Act of 1965, and the Housing Act of 1968, earning the title of "lion in the lobby."

The NAACP has been fortunate to have four very able black men who served long terms as executive secretary: James Weldon Johnson (1920–1928), writer and poet (in 1900 he wrote Lift Ev'ry Voice and Sing; set to music by his brother, the song came to be known as the "Negro National Anthem"); Walter White (1929–1955); Roy Wilkins (1955–1977), formerly the editor of The Crisis; and Benjamin Hooks (1977 to date). The organization also benefited from a series of white long-term presidents: Moorfield Story (1910–1915); Columbia University literature professor Joel Spingarn (1915–1940); his brother, attorney Arthur Spingarn (1940–1966); and Boston industrialist Kivie Kaplan (1966–1975)—who also served to anchor the strategic alliance between blacks and Jews. Joel Spingarn established the Spingarn Medal in 1913, the NAACP's most distinguished award, for "an American Negro of highest achievement"; awardees have included Marian Anderson, Richard Wright, Paul Robeson, Thurgood Marshall, Ralph Bunche, Langston Hughes, and Rosa Parks.

The NAACP that greeted incoming director Benjamin Hooks in 1977 had more than its share of problems.

Hooks, named a member of the Federal Communications Commission by President Nixon in 1972, inherited an organization with declining membership and finances and subject to a $1.2 million judgment in damages for its support of a boycott in Port Gibson, Mississippi. The organization had been feuding with its independent offspring, the NAACP Legal Defense and Educational Fund, which had been upstaging its parent in fund-raising. The dispute was finally resolved through litigation, which allowed the "Inc. Fund" to retain the NAACP title in its name. On appeal the Port Gibson damage claim was dismissed.

Hooks's next challenge came from board chair Margaret Bush Wilson, an attorney who also sat on the board of Monsanto Chemical and got the NAACP to support the oil industry during the energy crisis of the 1970s. Wilson was soon at odds with Hooks and suspended him from office in 1983. The board rallied behind Hooks, reinstating him and asking Wilson to resign. She refused, but was not reelected at the end of her term in 1983. Much as Wilkins and Mitchell had fought successfully to oppose President Nixon's nominations of Clement Haynesworth and G. Harrold Carswell to the Supreme Court, Hooks joined the effort that blocked Senate confirmation of President Reagan's nomination of Robert Bork. Hooks and the Leadership Council failed, however, to block Clarence Thomas's nomination to the Supreme Court by President Bush in 1991. In 1992 the sixty-seven-year-old Hooks announced his resignation, following an NAACP board meeting in which president Hazel Dukes and former Georgia state senator Julian Bond were not reelected as directors. Board chairman William Gibson appeared to be in a strong position to influence the selection of a new executive director to lead the NAACP into a challenging new era.

Critics charge the NAACP is out of touch with the issues that affect African Americans in their daily lives. Conservatives like Clint Bolick charge that few African Americans benefit from affirmative-action programs, and that the poor are more concerned about drugs, crime, education, welfare dependency, and teenage mothers. Further, the NAACP has an aging leadership who have not recruited enough people in the twenty to forty age group. The leadership responds that the NAACP *is* dealing with social problems within the black community—the breakup of the black family, teenage pregnancy, the AIDS crisis, the destruction of the black community and the black male by crime and lack of jobs—and that its defense of affirmative action is necessary to redress the systematic impact of generations of discrimination. During the 1980s the NAACP launched two major initiatives in employment and education, Operation Fair Share, and the Second Emancipation program to deal with the problems of black children.

CURRENT PRIORITIES: NAACP programs are coordinated by departments: (1) The *Economic Development Department* works to provide blacks jobs and purchase contracts through Fair Share agreements, signed with fifty-six companies since 1982—including General Motors, Chrysler, Walt Disney Productions, Coors Brewing, McDonald's,

Hardee's, and Wendy's—and with seventeen public sector agreements since 1985; (2) the *Education Department* conducts teacher preparation workshops and administers the NAACP scholarship program—separate units run the ACT-SO program (Academic, Cultural, Technological and Scientific Olympics), which encourages black youth to compete in these areas, and the Back-to-School/Stay-in-School program; the New York NAACP sponsors Project Excellence, an ambitious parent participation program; (3) the *Voter Education Department* concentrates on voter registration, and reapportionment and redistricting issues following the 1990 census; (4) the *Labor Department* works closely with the AFL-CIO unions and with issues of workplace discrimination generally; (5) the *Legal Department* litigates in the areas of voting rights, police misconduct, and discrimination in employment, education and housing; (6) the *Armed Services and Veterans Affairs Department* continues the NAACP's long struggle for equal opportunity in the military; (7) the *Housing Department* works on enforcement of fair housing laws, and on affordable housing programs with the Federal Home Loan Bank Board and the Resolution Trust Corporation; (8) the *Youth and College Division* works with some 500 local youth and college branches nationwide; and (9) the *Prison Department* works on education, job development, and rehabilitation with some thirty-eight branches established in prisons in sixteen states.

MEMBERS: A crucial period of growth for the NAACP took place during World War II, as the number of branches tripled and membership increased from 50,000 in 1940 to 450,000 in 1946; the NAACP had become a mass organization, with much of the expansion taking place in the southern states. Membership peaked at 535,000 during the height of the civil rights movement in 1963, then declined during the late 1960s and the 1970s to a plateau at the current 400,000. At-large membership for $25 was introduced to reach NAACP supporters by direct mail.

STRUCTURE: The NAACP has a sixty-four-member board of directors, of which twenty-one are elected by the seven regions, eighteen are elected at-large, seven are elected by youth councils, and eighteen are elected by the board. As the NAACP was originally a 501(c)(4), the NAACP Special Contribution Fund (SCF) was established in 1964 as a tax-deductible arm after the Legal Defense and Educational Fund was forced by the IRS to establish a completely separate board of directors. The SCF is governed by a board of trustees of between twenty and fifty-nine members, elected by the NAACP board. The NAACP switched its status to a 501(c)(3) organization in 1981, when the IRS clarified the amount of lobbying that can be conducted by charitable and education organizations. And just in time—the organization's fiscal crisis commanded a shift to the charitable classification for its greater fund-raising potential. A separate Crisis Publishing Company, Inc., puts out the NAACP's monthly magazine, *The Crisis*. As the cost of office space skyrocketed, the NAACP moved its headquarters from New York City to Brooklyn in 1982, and then to Baltimore in 1986—purchasing its first permanent office.

RESOURCES: The NAACP had income of $6.8 million in 1990, including 47 percent from membership dues and the rest from various fund-raising activities. Expenditures of $7.4 million were divided to support programs (82 percent), administration (15 percent), and fund-raising (3 percent). The deficit was covered by a surplus from 1989. The NAACP Special Contribution Fund received income of $6.5 million in 1990 and spent $6.3 million, of which 77 percent supported programs and 23 percent supported administration and fund-raising. Crisis Publishing Company, Inc., which now breaks even for annual operations, has an accumulated deficit of nearly $1.2 million.

PUBLICATIONS AND SERVICES: Members receive the monthly magazine *The Crisis* (circulation 300,000), published since 1910. A year-by-year chronology of key events, "Highlights of NAACP History, 1909–1988," was published in the eightieth-anniversary issue of *The Crisis* (January 1988). No definitive history of the NAACP has been written, but see Langston Hughes, *Fight for Freedom: The Story of the NAACP* (Norton, 1962), and Robert L. Zangrando, *The NAACP Crusade Against Lynching, 1909–1950* (Temple University Press, 1980). The usually hostile relationship between the NAACP and the U.S. Communist party is traced in Wilson Record, *Race and Radicalism: The NAACP and the Communist Party in Conflict* (Cornell University Press, 1964). For the biography of Clarence Mitchell, Jr., the NAACP's Washing-

ton bureau director from 1950 to 1978, see Denton L. Watson, *Lion in the Lobby* (Morrow, 1990). □

NATIONAL URBAN LEAGUE
500 E. 62ND STREET
NEW YORK, NY 10021
(212) 310-9000

FOUNDED: 1910   AFFILIATES: 114
BUDGET: $26 million   STAFF: 120
TAX STATUS: 501(c)(3)

PURPOSE: "To secure equal opportunity for Blacks and members of other minority groups in all areas of American life."

The National Urban League (NUL) is an interracial social service organization founded in the Progressive era in response to conditions facing black migrants to urban areas in the North. The historic leader in pushing business and industry to employ blacks, NUL continues to provide job training and placement, and has taken new initiatives for education and career development, youth, health, housing, and social welfare. During the 1960s NUL shifted away from an exclusive emphasis on social services and positioned itself as a moderate member of the civil rights coalition.

BACKGROUND: NUL dates its founding to a meeting in May 1910 at which white and black leaders of various associations for Negro improvement in New

York formed the Committee on Urban Conditions. Two individuals central to the new organization were sociologist and social worker George Edmund Haynes, the first black to earn a Ph.D. at Columbia University, and Ruth Standish Baldwin, widow of a young railroad mogul who was one of the closest white friends of Booker T. Washington. Ruth Baldwin, who convened the meeting to form the new Committee, was a model Progressive era reformer—pacifist, socialist, Smith College trustee, and later a patron of Highlander Folk School in Tennessee (her nephew Roger Baldwin became a founder of the American Civil Liberties Union). The Committee consolidated with two other organizations to form the National League on Urban Conditions Among Negroes (NLUCAN) in 1911 (the name was changed to National Urban League in 1917). Ruth Baldwin served as the League president until 1915, and George Haynes was hired as the League's executive secretary from 1911 to 1918.

Other NUL founders composed a register of progressive racial reformers. Prominent white NUL board members included Quaker attorney L. Hollingsworth Wood, who served as NUL president from 1915 to 1941; Paul Cravath, whose father was a Fisk University president; New York banker and reformer Algernon Frissell, a supporter of Hampton Institute; Chicago social-work dean Sophonisba Breckenridge, from the family prominent in Kentucky politics; and the socialist Unitarian minister John Haynes Holmes. Whites on the NUL board included a wide range of viewpoints from social workers to more conservative business leaders. In general, NUL board members were less radical than the NAACP's board, and more likely to favor Booker T. Washington's approaches than W.E.B. Du Bois's, although several individuals served on both boards.

In the first years of NUL, George Haynes promoted training blacks for social work, conducted sociological surveys, and encouraged community organization. Eugene Kinckle Jones, who joined NUL as field secretary in 1911, became executive secretary in 1917 and increasingly emphasized vocational guidance. Under Jones the Urban League movement began to flourish, and NUL established affiliates throughout cities in the North, typically funded through local Community Chests (forerunners to the contemporary United Ways). Blacks began mass migrations to the North around 1914, and streamed into industry with the onset of the First World War, overwhelming the capacity of the fledgling Urban League affiliates. Gains in employment made during the war were largely wiped out by 1921 in the "return to normalcy," with some exceptions in the mining, auto, steel, and meat packing industries. In 1925 NUL created a Department of Industrial Relations, and hired T. Arnold Hill to increase opportunities for black employment in industry and to work with the American Federation of Labor (AFL) to abolish discrimination within its craft unions, with little success.

After the stock market crash of 1929 and the loss of jobs during the Depression of the 1930s, NUL began to give attention to employment opportunities for blacks within the New Deal's government programs. Jones spent nearly four years on leave from the NUL studying Negro problems with the Commerce Department, and Hill served as a consultant on Negro affairs to the Works Progress Administration and the National Youth Administration (NYA) in 1939. Two NUL board members served in President Roosevelt's "Black Cabinet," Robert Vann as special assistant to the attorney general, and Mary McLeod Bethune as director of Negro Affairs for the NYA. Along with the NAACP, NUL cooperated, albeit reluctantly, with A. Philip Randolph's plan to rally 100,000 Negroes for a March on Washington in 1941. When it became clear to Roosevelt that the plan was no idle threat, he issued Executive Order 8802, banning employment discrimination in defense industries.

When Jones stepped down because of illness at the end of 1941, he arranged for his position to go to Lester Granger, a social worker who had headed NUL's Workers' Bureau. As the liaison with local League Workers' councils, Granger had encouraged and supported the antidiscrimination program of the Committee for Industrial Organization (CIO) as it broke away from the AFL in 1935. When Granger took over in 1941, NUL had a staff of nine, a budget of $52,000, and thirty-seven affiliates. Not a membership organization, NUL had no mass following and none of the legal victories the NAACP could claim. Bickering between Granger and NAACP director Roy Wilkins ended the era of cooperation between the organizations and established a rivalry that would defy attempts at mediation. After Wood resigned as president after twenty-six years in 1941, presidents rotated after one or two terms, and Granger effectively took control of the organization,

handpicking presidents from the largely white board of trustees and dominating NUL for nearly twenty years.

NUL experienced constant financial crisis and was barely solvent during the 1940s and 1950s. Local Leagues, and their Community Chest funders, came under increasing attack from racists following the Supreme Court's *Brown* decision in 1954. Granger, a supporter of President Eisenhower, responded very cautiously to the growing pressures for integration from the civil rights movement. Black members of the NUL board, believing white corporate executives and Granger were taking too conservative a stance, moved to reorganize the board to include representation from local Leagues. Theodore Kheel, the respected president of the Urban League of Greater New York, became NUL president in 1956 determined to bring harmony to the board and end arguments between NUL and the NAACP. Rather than oust Granger directly, Kheel eased him out by waiting until he reached mandatory retirement in 1961.

Kheel was looking for a vigorous leader in tune with the climate of the new era of the civil rights movement. He supported Whitney Young, Jr., who had worked for Urban League affiliates in St. Paul and Omaha, and had come to the national job from a position as dean of the Atlanta University School of Social Work. Finding the financial situation worse than he expected, Young launched an "operation rescue," which attracted large grants from major foundations and corporations. Young led NUL to participate in the March on Washington in 1963 in support of the pending civil rights bill. Young helped engineer the selection of Bayard Rustin as the march director, and mediated with the Kennedy administration to plan march logistics acceptable to both the movement and the government.

The urban riots of the late 1960s made Whitney Young and NUL even more attractive to the white business establishment, as Nancy Weiss describes, a "safe, respectable, experienced" alternative to black militants. At the same time, Young embraced a moderate version of black power at a CORE convention in July 1968, making headlines and rallying support from black nationalists. Young bolstered the NUL budget and expanded its operations with job training grants worth millions of dollars from the Department of Labor under the Manpower Development and Training Act, predecessor of the current Job Training Partnership Act. At the height of his influence, Young died in a swimming accident in 1971 at an international conference in Lagos, Nigeria, at age forty-nine. His biographer Nancy Weiss summarizes the loss: "He bridged the gulf between the ghetto and the power structure in ways that no other black man of his generation was able to duplicate."

Vernon Jordan, Jr., succeeded Young as executive director in 1972. Jordan was closely identified with the civil rights movement, having worked as an attorney in Atlanta and field secretary for the Georgia NAACP—in 1961 he helped desegregate the University of Georgia by physically forcing a path through an angry mob for student Charlayne Hunter (now a reporter for PBS's *MacNeil-Lehrer Newshour*). He was executive director of the Voter Education Project of the Southern Regional Council from 1964 to 1968, and the United Negro College Fund from 1970 until moving to NUL. Jordan began a voter registration program at NUL, and built up the Washington office research staff to take on issues of black unemployment. Under Jordan's leadership in 1974 NUL began publication of its annual *State of Black America* report. Jordan was shot in an attempted assassination in May 1980; he recovered, and left NUL for a private legal practice at the end of 1981.

John Jacob, executive vice president under Jordan, has been president since 1982. Under Jacob, NUL has emphasized black self-help, taking on four critical problems—teenage pregnancy, single female–headed households, crime, and voter apathy—and cosponsoring a "Black Family Summit," bringing educators, social workers, and community activists together to develop strategies to preserve the black family. The NUL Research Department has become an important black think tank, and Jacob draws on its research for his weekly newspaper column, "To Be Equal."

CURRENT PRIORITIES: Major NUL program areas include employment and job training, education, youth, and health and social welfare. *Employment, training, and job placement* have been central to NUL's work since its founding. Local NUL affiliates raised over $15 million in United Way funding for employment services, and added over $30 million in support through the Job Training Partnership Act (JTPA). Overall in 1990, the NUL network trained 250,000 people for employment and placed 89 percent in jobs. NUL also funded twenty-three local Leagues to operate Seniors in Community Service programs, providing employment to low income people over age fifty-five, with $11.8 million from the U.S. Department of Labor. *Education programs* center on NUL's National Education Initiative to improve equity and access to quality education through programs promoting parent involvement, community mobilization, pre-college math and science, tutoring, mentoring, guidance and counseling; some 300,000 students are directly involved. NUL's Black Executive Exchange Program (BEEP) connects corporate executives and government professionals to historically and predominantly black colleges to inform students on current issues in business and government. *Youth programs* include efforts aimed at African American adolescent males, a Stop the Violence program, and the NUL Incentives to Excel and Succeed (NULITES) program. *Health and social welfare programs* include a National AIDS Initiative, a program to assist Aid to Families with Dependent Children (AFDC) recipients, and a national fair housing outreach program. Including all programs, NUL provided direct services to over 1.5 million people in 1990.

STRUCTURE: NUL has a sixty-member, self-recruiting board of trustees, predominantly corporate executives. The 114 affiliates are independent organizations, active in thirty-four states and D.C. NUL's headquarters building in New York City is shared and jointly owned with the United Negro College Fund. Regional offices are maintained in Atlanta, Chicago, and Los Angeles,

with research and government relations departments in the Washington, D.C., office. Regional assemblies and an annual mid-winter meeting bring together NUL affiliate board and staff members. The NUL annual conference is a major event, typically attracting some 20,000 corporate executives, local business leaders, government employees, and community service workers.

RESOURCES: NUL had revenue of $26 million in 1990, including $13.6 million in government grants and contracts (52 percent); $5.9 million in contributions (23 percent) from corporations, foundations, and individuals; $2.4 million in donated equipment, materials, and services (9 percent); $1.25 million from affiliate dues (5 percent); and $1.3 million in interest and dividends (5 percent); and $1.6 million (6 percent) from other sources. Expenses of $24.6 million included $19.7 million for programs (80 percent), and $4.9 million for administration and fund-raising (20 percent). The proportion of NUL support from government grants dropped from 75 percent in 1980 to 62 percent in 1987 and 52 percent in 1990.

PUBLICATIONS AND SERVICES: Since 1975, NUL's annual report on *The State of Black America* has been an important collection of essays on the condition of African Americans. NUL also publishes *Urban League News*, *The Quarterly Economic Report on the African-American Worker*, and *Runta: The NUL Research Department Fact Sheet*, primarily for distribution to local affiliate staff and boards. For NUL's sixtieth anniversary, Guichard Parris (NUL's director of public relations under Granger and Young) and Lester Brooks wrote an organizational history through 1960, *Blacks in the City: A History of the National Urban League* (Little, Brown, 1971). Jesse Thomas Moore, Jr., covers the same ground in a more analytical vein in *A Search for Equality: The National Urban League, 1910–1961* (Pennsylvania State University Press, 1981). Nancy J. Weiss interprets NUL's early years in a book based on her dissertation, *The National Urban League 1910–1940* (Oxford University Press, 1974), and has written a very readable biography of NUL's leader for the crucial decade of the 1960s, *Whitney M. Young, Jr., and the Struggle for Civil Rights* (Princeton University Press, 1989). □

ANTI-DEFAMATION LEAGUE OF B'NAI B'RITH

823 UNITED NATIONS PLAZA

NEW YORK, NY 10017

(212) 490-2525

FOUNDED: 1913   BUDGET: $38.3 million
STAFF: 400   TAX STATUS: 501(c)(3)s: Anti-Defamation League of B'nai B'rith, ADL Foundation, and ADL Foundation Common Fund

PURPOSE: "To stop the defamation of the Jewish people; to secure justice and fair treatment for all citizens alike."

The Anti-Defamation League (ADL) leads the fight against anti-Semitism; promotes understanding among racial, religious, and ethnic groups; employs research, fact-finding, education, and law to counter prejudice; confronts threats to the security of the Jewish community and to democracy; and advocates for Israel.

BACKGROUND: ADL was founded in 1913 to counter defamation of the Jewish people, in an atmosphere darkened by the Leo Frank trial and lynching in Georgia. From a group of volunteers using two desks in a Chicago law office, ADL has grown into a powerful nationwide organization with international offices. Overt anti-Semitism was common in the 1920s and 1930s. ADL challenged the Ku Klux Klan, and helped to diminish its power through education and legislation. ADL acted to halt quotas limiting university enrollment and employment of Jews and other minorities. ADL participated actively in the civil rights struggles of the 1960s, campaigning for legislation banning discrimination in housing and employment. ADL also worked to reduce anti-Jewish sentiment within the Catholic church; relations between leaders of the two religions have greatly improved since Vatican II in 1965.

According to ADL polls, anti-Semitism peaked in 1945, a time when there was a general unwillingness to rescue European Jews from the Nazis. In recent times, overt anti-Semitism has greatly decreased—however, ADL audits have shown a yearly increase of anti-Semitic actions through the 1980s and into the early 1990s. ADL has drafted legislation, now adopted by forty states, mandating stiffer penalties for hate crimes. ADL backed the federal Hate Crimes Statistics Act (HCSA), and monitors its implementation. The group also monitors extremism and the activities of groups like the White Aryan Resistance (WAR) and the skinheads. In partnership with Morris Dees of the Southern Poverty Law Center, ADL successfully sued white supremacists Tom and John Metzger and WAR for their role promoting the violence that inspired three skinheads to beat to death Ethiopian immigrant Mulugeta Seraw in Portland, Oregon. Dees and ADL won a $12.5 million verdict (a record for such cases) in 1990 for Seraw's family.

CURRENT PRIORITIES: ADL works in six program areas: (1) confronting anti-Semitism—monitoring the growth of extremism and the number of anti-Semitic incidents; (2) reducing prejudice —through the "World of Difference" project, which produces materials used in the schools to teach children to live in a multicultural world and respect differences of color, creed, ethnicity, and gender; (3) advocating for Israel—clarifying the Jewish community's concerns; (4) strengthening interreligious relations—working with Catholic and Protestant churches to uproot anti-Semitism in Christian doctrine; (5) remembering the holocaust—developing in-service training for teachers, and preserving Holocaust records and memorabilia; and (6) representing Jews around the globe—emphasizing defending endangered communities of Jews in Eastern Europe and the former Soviet Union.

STRUCTURE: The ADL national commission of 150 members meets once a year in June. A smaller executive committee meets twice a year. The current national director is Abraham Foxman, on the ADL staff since 1965, who succeeded long-time director Nathan Perlmutter in 1987. The ADL Foundation was established in 1976 to administer endowments and restricted gifts; there is also an ADL Foundation Common Fund established in 1982 to support ADL and other charitable organizations. ADL has five major divisions: Civil Rights, Communications, Community Service, Intergroup Relations, and International Affairs. For each division there is an advisory committee of lay people. ADL has thirty-one regional offices across the United States, all of which take complaints and respond to cases of prejudice. A Washington office monitors federal agencies and provides testimony on pending legislation. An annual leadership conference in Washington, D.C., provides briefings and opportunities to talk to legislators on Capitol Hill. There are overseas offices in Jerusalem, Paris, and Rome. Half the staff of 400 work in the New York headquarters.

RESOURCES: ADL's income of $38.3 million in 1990 came from individual and corporate contributions (85 percent) with the remainder from restricted grants, publication sales, and investment income. Expenditures of $36.6 million went for program services (73 percent), management (8 pecent), and fund-raising (19 percent). (These financial figures consolidate the ADL, ADL Foundation, and ADL Foundation Common Fund). Over half the program services funds help support the thirty-one staffed regional offices.

PUBLICATIONS AND SERVICES: The *ADL on the Front Lines* (circulation 100,000) is published monthly. The League has a publications catalog of multicultural human relations materials for schools. The ADL Civil Rights Division publishes an annual *Audit of Anti-Semitic Incidents*, numerous studies of specific hate groups, and a comprehensive report, *Hate Groups in America: A Record of Bigotry and Violence*, revised edition (1988). □

LEGAL EAGLES

With initial grants from the Ford Foundation, several organizations were formed in the late 1960s and early 1970s on the model of the NAACP LDF (also known as the "Inc. Fund"), including, among the most successful, the Mexican American Legal Defense and Education Fund (MALDEF), the Puerto Rican Legal Defense and Education Fund (PRLDEF—pronounced "pearl-deaf"), the Native American Rights Fund (NARF), and the Asian American Legal Defense and Education Fund (AALDEF). The relationship with the "Inc. Fund" is close: both PRLDEF and AALDEF also have offices at 99 Hudson Street in New York City (as does the NOW LDEF).

NAACP LEGAL DEFENSE AND EDUCATIONAL FUND

99 HUDSON STREET, SUITE 1600

NEW YORK, NY 10013

(212) 219-1900

FOUNDED: 1940; independent of NAACP since 1957 CONTRIBUTORS: 25,000

BUDGET: $11.9 million STAFF: 87

TAX STATUS: 501(c)(3)

PURPOSE: "The principal legal arm of the civil rights movement, serving members of all organizations and unaffiliated individuals."

The NAACP Legal Defense and Educational Fund (which uses the abbreviated initials LDF—and is also informally known as the "Inc. Fund") is the pioneer "legal defense fund." Its litigation resulted in a series of Supreme Court cases, culminating in *Brown* v. *Board of Education*, which destroyed the legal basis of segregation in the United States. The LDF model's success has inspired similar organizations working on behalf of other ethnic groups, women, the disabled, the environment, and animals. LDF continues an extensive program of litigation aimed at eliminating continuing discrimination in education, employment, housing, health care, voting, and criminal justice.

BACKGROUND: Although the NAACP Legal Committee under the leadership of attorney Arthur Spingarn had been involved in litigation and legal defense work for many years, the LDF began to take shape when the NAACP hired Thurgood Marshall on its staff in 1936. The board of directors had approved a new emphasis on attacking discrimination in education, employment, housing, voting, and service in the armed forces. Marshall set out to develop a series of precedent-setting cases that would undermine the legal foundation of segregation established by the Supreme Court's "separate but equal" doctrine in *Plessy* v. *Ferguson* (1896).

Ideal plaintiffs were not always easy to come by. One of the first important cases involved Lloyd Gaines, president of the senior class at Lincoln University in Missouri, who wanted to attend law school. Missouri's state law school refused his application, and the NAACP sued on his behalf. On appeal to the Supreme Court, the NAACP won a ruling in *Missouri ex rel. Gaines* v. *Canada* (1938) that Missouri's refusal to provide a law school for blacks was "a denial of equal protection." The decision made significant law, but Gaines dropped from sight and his right to attend law school was not developed further.

Discrimination in voting limited black political power throughout the South, and LDF attacked in three areas: white primaries, the poll tax, and barriers to registration. In a case from Texas, the Supreme Court ruled in *Smith* v. *Allright* (1944) that black citizens had the right to vote in Democratic primaries. LDF won another significant victory concerning transportation in *Morgan* v. *Virginia* (1946), when the Supreme Court held that a state law requiring separation of races on motor carriers could not be applied to inter-state passengers. And LDF made a breakthrough against housing segregation when the Supreme Court ruled against restrictive covenants in *Shelley* v. *Kramer* (1948).

Returning to education, LDF filed several cases involving students seeking admission to graduate programs. The university level was a good place to begin the legal attack, as southern states had not gone to the considerable expense to establish "separate but equal" law and other graduate and professional schools. In 1946 George McLaurin sued for admission to an education doctoral program at the University of Oklahoma, and Heman Sweatt sued to attend law school at the University of Texas. Undermining but not overruling *Plessy*, the Supreme Court decided in *Sweatt* v. *Texas* (1950) and *McLaurin* v. *Oklahoma State Regents* (1950) that the separate educations the men were offered were not equal, given the specific situations and the intangible elements involved. Surprisingly, the U.S. government had filed a brief asking the court to reverse *Plessy*. With the victories in *Sweatt* and *McLaurin* and the federal shift, Marshall was confident it was time for a direct assault on segregation in elementary and secondary education.

Having learned that a single plantiff or case could fall victim to various human and legal mishaps, Marshall began to cultivate several lawsuits concerning elementary and secondary school systems. Cases from South Carolina, Kansas, Delaware, Virginia, and the District of Columbia were grouped together under *Brown* v. *Board of Education of Topeka*, and arguments were heard in 1952 by a Supreme Court that had been greatly transformed by President Roosevelt's appointments. Dwight Eisenhower was elected president in 1952, and appointed Earl Warren as chief justice in 1953 following the death of Fred Vinson. A second hearing of oral arguments was held in late 1953. Warren wrote the unanimous decision the Court delivered in May 1954 overturning segregated education. Implementing the Court's decision was another matter. Although the border southern states began desegregating in fall 1954, other southern states called for gradual adjustment. The Supreme Court issued its implementation decree for Brown in 1955, ordering the states to "make a prompt and reasonable start toward full compliance" and proceed "with all deliberate speed." Obtaining enforcement of desegregation would occupy LDF for the next two decades.

Jack Greenberg, an LDF attorney who made his first Supreme Court appearance during *Brown*, became the second director of LDF in 1961 when Thurgood Marshall was appointed to the U.S. Court of Appeals by President Kennedy (President Johnson appointed Marshall as solicitor general in 1965 and named him to the Supreme Court in 1967). Greenberg led LDF during the 1960s as it worked to enforce school desegregation, voting rights, and equal opportunity in employment and housing. LDF had to challenge all the efforts to evade the *Brown* decision, winning Supreme Court decisions against public support for segregated private schools in *Griffin* v. *County School Board of Prince Edward County* (1964), "freedom of choice" plans that didn't result in desegregation in *Green* v. *County School Board of New Kent County, Virginia* (1968), and simple stalling by Mississippi school districts in *Alexander* v. *Holmes County Board of Education* (1969). An important question was whether busing should be mandated to overcome de facto segregation resulting from assigning children to neighborhood schools where there were long-standing patterns of residential segregation. The Supreme Court approved a court-imposed pupil assignment plan requiring bus transportation in *Swann* v. *Charlotte-Mecklenburg Board of Education* (1971).

During the 1980s the NAACP and the NAACP LDF got into an embarrassing public feud over LDF's use of the NAACP initials. LDF was begun as a program of the NAACP in 1939, but incorporated as a separate 501(c)3 charitable organization in 1940, with a board of directors identical with the NAACP's, as a means to raise tax-deductible contributions for the NAACP's legal work. As the campaign for a federal antilynching law had been a centerpiece of its first thirty years, the IRS had classified the NAACP as a lobbying organization, a 501(c)4. LDF began adding directors not on the NAACP board as early as 1941, but continued to function under the direction of the NAACP until 1957, when the IRS (responding to conservative political pressure following the *Brown* decision in 1954) objected to the close association. LDF established a completely separate board and staff in 1957—and gradually the two organizations began to compete for financial support and for credit for accomplishments in civil rights litigation. The NAACP board voted in 1965 to ask LDF to drop its use of NAACP, but then withdrew its threat to go to court. In 1979 the board revoked its 1939 resolution that authorized LDF to use the NAACP initials. When the financially weakened NAACP shifted its tax status to (c)(3) in 1981, following an IRS rules clarification, it realized it was in direct competition with the independent LDF for charitable contributions.

In 1982 NAACP initiated a trademark infringement suit to stop LDF from using the NAACP initials. The NAACP won an injunction against use of the initials by LDF in 1983, but on appeal the decision was reversed in 1985—under the doctrine of "laches," which requires a timely response to the trademark violation. By not following up on its concern from 1966 through 1978, the court ruled, the NAACP had let LDF spend much money and effort to build up its goodwill through use of the initials, and the NAACP had delayed assertion of its claim for an unreasonable period of time.

During the 1970s LDF won several significant court victories in areas other than education. In *Griggs* v. *Duke Power* the Supreme Court ruled that tests for employment or promotion must be job related if they have a differential racial impact. After a seven-year effort to have capital punishment declared a violation of the Eighth Amendment's prohibition of cruel and unusual punishment, the Supreme Court ruled in *Furman* v. *Georgia* that capital punishment cannot be arbitrarily and capriciously applied. There were no executions in the United States for over a decade. In 1984 LDF selected as its third director Julius Chambers, formerly president of the board and the attorney who had argued the *Swann*

case regarding busing to achieve school desegregation in Charlotte, North Carolina.

CURRENT PRIORITIES: The NAACP LDF maintains programs of litigation in seven areas: (1) education, continuing to emphasize integration of schools; (2) poverty and justice, advocating for low-income housing and the right to adequate education and health care; (3) fair employment, emphasizing the advancement of minorities and women in the workplace; (4) voting rights, including restrictive voter registration systems, discriminatory judicial election practices, and at-large election systems in local governments; (5) fair housing, emphasizing testing for housing discrimination; (6) capital punishment, in which LDF staff are chief counsel for some two dozen death row inmates, seeking to have courts address issues of racial bias in capital trials; and (7) administration of criminal justice, focusing on police misconduct and racially motivated violence.

STRUCTURE: LDF has an 85-member, self-recruiting board of directors, including such figures as Mary Frances Berry, Yvonne Braithwaite Burke, Ossie Davis, Adrian DeWind, Marian Wright Edelman, John Hope Franklin, Jack Greenberg, Charles Hamilton, Nicholas Katzenbach, Jacob Sheinkman, Cyrus Vance, Roger Williams, and Andrew Young. William T. Coleman, Jr., former U.S. secretary of transportation, has been chairman of the board since 1978. Robert Preiskel has been president of the board since 1985. In addition to its New York headquarters, LDF maintains a Washington office, which follows new civil rights statutes, educational reform, and civil rights enforcement; and a western regional office in Los Angeles, opened in 1987, which follows housing, employment, and voting rights issues. LDF has 28 staff attorneys, and calls upon the services of over 400 cooperating attorneys.

RESOURCES: LDF's $12.4 million revenue in its 1990–91 fiscal year came from public support (78 percent) and from court-awarded fees and investment income (23 percent). Total expenses of $9 million were divided among program services (76 percent), administration (4 percent), and fund-raising (20 percent). LDF does not accept government funds. The Ford Foundation committed a $5 million challenge grant to the LDF endowment campaign, which aims to raise an initial $15 million, and $25 million by the year 2000. LDF also administers the Herbert Lehman Education Fund, which provides some 170 scholarships to black undergraduates and 135 to law students; and the Earl Warren Legal Training Program, which gives some 155 scholarships to black law students. "The Committee of 100" is a group of celebrities and other prestigious individuals who support fund-raising.

PUBLICATIONS AND SERVICES: LDF's quarterly newsletter *Equal Justice* (circulation 4,000) is available on request. LDF's long desegregation campaign is described in Minnie Finch, *The NAACP: Its Fight for Justice* (Scarecrow Press, 1981), and Mark V. Tushnet, *The NAACP's Legal Strategy against Segregated Education, 1925–*

1950 (University of North Carolina Press, 1987). The story of *Brown* v. *Board of Education* is told in rich detail by Richard Kluger, *Simple Justice* (Knopf, 1976). □

MEXICAN AMERICAN LEGAL DEFENSE AND EDUCATION FUND

634 S. SPRING STREET, 11TH FLOOR

LOS ANGELES, CA 90014-1974

(213) 629-2512

FOUNDED: 1968   BUDGET: $4.8 million
STAFF: 60   TAX STATUS: 501(c)(3)

PURPOSE: "Promoting and protecting the civil rights of Hispanics in the United States."

The Mexican American Legal Defense and Education Fund (MALDEF) is the leading legal advocate for Mexican Americans and other Hispanics on such issues as education, employment, voting rights, and immigrants' rights. MALDEF also conducts significant programs of leadership development and law student scholarships for Hispanics.

BACKGROUND: Pete Tijerina was an attorney and civil rights chairman for the League of United Latin American Citizens' Council in San Antonio, Texas, in the mid-1960s, traveling the state responding to discrimination against Chicanos. Frustrated by the lack of Mexican Americans on jury lists despite a Supreme Court mandate in *Her-*

nandez v. *Texas*, Tijerina concluded the Southwest needed a legal defense organization modeled after the NAACP LDF. Jack Greenberg, director of LDF, brought Tijerina together with the Ford Foundation to discuss a proposal that led in 1968 to a $2.2 million grant over five years to the newly organized MALDEF, which would cover five states— Texas, New Mexico, Arizona, California, and Colorado. As executive director, Tijerina recruited Mario Obledo, Texas assistant attorney general, to direct litigation as MALDEF's general counsel.

MALDEF quickly began to win victories for Mexican Americans in jury representation, equal treatment and access to education, employment, and voting rights. Tijerina raised scholarship funds to match funds for law students in the Ford Foundation grant. To enhance its national visibility and effectiveness, MALDEF moved its headquarters to San Francisco in 1970, with Mario Obledo as president and general counsel, while Tijerina remained in San Antonio and returned to private practice, later becoming a Texas appellate court judge. In the midst of the Chicano movement (and the student, anti-war, and feminist movements) of the late 1960s and early 1970s, MALDEF under Obledo often had a confrontational tone as the organization attacked discrimination and police brutality.

As the temper of the mid-1970s began to shift from public protest to the long-term, stubborn struggle against patterns of inequality, MALDEF needed to develop a strong organizational and financial structure. Obledo resigned in 1973, and was appointed by Governor Jerry Brown as California's secretary of health and welfare. Vilma Martinez became the first woman heading a national civil rights law organization when she was hired at age twenty-nine to head MALDEF in 1973. Martinez, who had worked for the NAACP LDF, expanded funding sources; focused MALDEF's legal work on class-action suits on bilingual education, employment discrimination, and political access; and initiated a Chicana Rights Project. In a major political victory with long-term consequences, MALDEF's research and testimony helped persuade the Congress to add the "Hispanic Amendments" to the Voting Rights Act in 1975, when the legislation was up for its ten-year review and renewal. Under the amendments, MALDEF's Voting Rights Project forced the courts to replace at-large elections with single-member districts, giving Mexican Americans representation in local government across the Southwest. Court-supervised redistricting plans have provided Mexican Americans greater access to state legislatures. After eight years as president, Martinez resigned in 1982 to return to Los Angeles and to serve on the University of California Board of Regents, to which she had been appointed by Governor Brown. Joaquin Avila served as president and general counsel from 1982 to 1985, as MALDEF expanded its Leadership Development Project and became more involved with immigration issues, opposing the Simpson-Mazzoli bill before Congress.

Antonia Hernandez joined MALDEF in 1981 as associate counsel of the Washington, D.C., office, where she worked with Avila on the extension of the Voting Rights Act in 1982; in 1985 she was appointed president and general counsel following Avila's resignation. Two years later Hernandez had to fight for her job when the board's executive committee, unhappy with her fund-raising and staff promotions, surprised everyone by firing her and hiring Toney Anaya, who had just finished a term as governor of New Mexico. Hernandez, backed by the staff, held her ground and refused to give up her office, claiming she could only be fired by the full board of directors. Hernandez won a court restraining order, and a special meeting of the board of directors in March 1987 voted 18 to 14 to retain her as president and general counsel.

CURRENT PRIORITIES: MALDEF emphasizes seven program areas: (1) *Education* continues as a major focus of MALDEF litigation, with important cases in the courts of Texas, California, and Illinois seeking equal allocation for resources to schools with large numbers of Hispanic students; (2) *employment* cases include class-action lawsuits under Title VII of the Civil Rights Act and monitoring private and public employers' affirmative-action programs; (3) *political access* lawsuits challenge at-large representation systems that exclude Hispanics from local office—in *Gomez* v. *City of Watsonville*, MALDEF won a precedent-setting case for nine western states after four years of litigation that was appealed all the way to the Supreme Court; (4) the *census and redistricting* campaign follows up on the 1990 census undercount of minorities and seeks redistricting plans that provide greater Hispanic representation;

(5) *immigration rights* remains a central concern, contesting the Immigration and Naturalization Service (INS) arrests and detentions, assisting immigrant workers with legalization programs, and keeping the pressure on the national civil rights coalition for a liberal federal immigration policy; (6) *language rights* cases center on the right to use Spanish in courts; and (7) the *leadership development* program concentrates on preparing Hispanics for decision-making positions on local boards and commissions.

STRUCTURE: MALDEF moved its headquarters to Los Angeles in 1985 when Antonia Hernandez took over as president and general counsel. MALDEF has a forty-member, self-nominating board of directors, chaired by Frank Herrera, Jr., from San Antonio. To encourage fresh perspectives, members are limited to two consecutive two-year terms. The staff of sixty includes twenty-two attorneys. MALDEF maintains field offices in Washington, D.C., Chicago, San Antonio, and San Francisco, and a program office in Sacramento. It leaves the New York area to the Puerto Rican Legal Defense and Education Fund (PRLDEF).

RESOURCES: MALDEF's fiscal 1991 revenue of $4.8 million was derived from foundation grants (45 percent), special events (14 percent), individual and corporate contributions (13 percent), professional fees and awards (24 percent), and other sources (4 percent). Expenditures of $4.8 million went for litigation (68 percent), community education and services (15 percent), public policy and research (7 percent), and management and fund-raising (10 percent). MALDEF has launched an $8.5 million capital campaign to purchase and renovate an office building in downtown Los Angeles for its headquarters and as a nonprofit center.

PUBLICATIONS AND SERVICES: Contributors receive the newsletter *MALDEF*. The National Leadership Program publishes the newsletter *Leading Hispanics* twice a year. An annual report is available. □

Native American Rights Fund

NATIVE AMERICAN RIGHTS FUND

1506 BROADWAY

BOULDER, CO 80302

(303) 447-8760

FOUNDED: 1970   CONTRIBUTORS: 32,000
BUDGET: $6.3 million   STAFF: 46
TAX STATUS: 501(c)(3)

PURPOSE: "The protection of Indian rights."

Native American Rights Fund (NARF) is the only legal services organization serving Indians of all tribes throughout the country.

BACKGROUND: NARF began in 1970 as a project of California Indian Legal Services (CILS), one of several such organizations for Indians launched by the federal Office of Economic Opportunity during the "War on Poverty" in the 1960s. Following its experience with the

NAACP LDF and MALDEF, the Ford Foundation hoped to create an organization to litigate key cases in Indian law. Ford Foundation staff met with CILS director Monroe Price and his attorneys David Getches and Robert Pelcyger to prepare a planning grant for CILS to develop a national Indian law firm. NARF was established in 1971 in Boulder, a more central location, with Getches as the founding director; the Ford Foundation provided a $1.2 million three-year grant to get programs under way.

The federal Legal Services Program also saw NARF as the vehicle to provide backup legal assistance to the local programs it was funding on Indian reservations and in urban areas, and began funding NARF's Indian Law Support Center (ILSC) in 1972. And with help from the Carnegie Corporation and the National Clearinghouse for Legal Services in 1972, NARF established the National Indian Law Library (NILL), now a national resource for federal Indian law and tribal law. John Echohawk served as executive director from 1973 to 1975, Tom Fredericks held the job from 1975 to 1977, and in 1977 Echohawk returned to the position, which he has held to date.

From its first days NARF initiated precedent-setting cases. In *Pyramid Lake Paiute* v. *Morton*, NARF defended the water rights of the Paiutes in Nevada from a Bureau of Reclamation irrigation project directed at non-Indian farmland—and saved Pyramid Lake in the process. NARF pressed the federal government to file *U.S.* v. *Nevada and California* to renegotiate water rights, and *U.S.* v. *Washington* to protect fishing rights of Indian tribes in the Pacific Northwest. NARF attorneys successfully pressed President Nixon to restore federal tribal status of the Menominee of Wisconsin in 1973, and won federal tribal recognition for the Passamaquoddy of Maine in 1975.

CURRENT PRIORITIES: NARF's board defined five priority areas: (1) *the preservation of tribal existence*, including tribal sovereignty, economic development, and federal recognition and restoration; (2) *the protection of tribal natural resources*, including land and water rights, and hunting and fishing rights; (3) *the promotion of human rights*, including education, health, housing, welfare, and the protection of traditional Native American religions and associated sacred objects and sites; (4) *the accountability of governments to Native Americans*, including the proper conduct of trust responsibilities, proper enforcement of laws and regulations, and recognition of unique tribal rights and immunities; and (5) *the development of Indian law*, via the collecting, indexing, and distribution of materials through NILL and backup legal assistance through ILSC.

STRUCTURE: NARF has a thirteen-member, self-recruiting board of directors composed exclusively of Native Americans from throughout the country, presently chaired by Richard Hayward of Connecticut. In addition to its headquarters in Boulder, NARF maintains offices in Washington, D.C., and Anchorage, Alaska. NARF has eighteen lawyers on staff.

RESOURCES: NARF revenue of $6.3 million in 1991 was derived from government grants (44 percent), foundation grants (22 percent), individual contributions (18 percent), legal fees (6 percent), and other sources (10 percent). Expenditures of $5.9 million included litigation and client services (72 percent), the National Indian Law Library (5 percent), and management and fundraising (23 percent). In 1991 NARF launched a campaign to raise a $5 million endowment over five years.

PUBLICATIONS AND SERVICES: Contributors receive the quarterly bulletin *NARF Legal Review*. NARF publishes resources on Indian law and tribal economic development. An annual report is available. □

5.

GENDER AND SEXUALITY

The cultural meanings we give to gender and sexuality constitute a complex web connecting male and female power, status,
and identity; women's rights; birth control and abortion; homosexuality; family policy; and population policy. All these
elements are bound up in the emergence of the women's movement, the related movement and countermovement for reproductive rights including abortion, the gay and lesbian rights
movement, and the backlash on the Right that emphasizes
traditional family values.

THE WOMAN SUFFRAGE MOVEMENT AND ITS HERITAGE

Among the U.S. delegation to the World Anti-Slavery Convention in London in 1840 were two women, Quaker minister Lu-
cretia Mott and Elizabeth Cady Stanton, wife of a prominent
abolitionist. The convention refused to seat women as delegates, so Mott and Stanton had to watch from the gallery.
Resolving to improve the status of women, Mott and Stanton
called a Woman's Rights Convention at Seneca Falls, New
York, in 1848. The meeting, attended by some 300 women and

men, produced a "Declaration of Principles" including a resolution calling for the franchise for women. National woman's rights conventions were held throughout the 1850s, drawing Susan B. Anthony with her exceptional organizational skills into the leadership.

After the Civil War, abolitionists pushed at all costs to pass the Fourteenth and Fifteenth amendments granting rights and the vote to the slaves freed by the Thirteenth Amendment. The woman's rights movement split in 1869 into two groups: the American Woman Suffrage Association (AWSA), led by Lucy Stone, which backed the Fifteenth Amendment giving black males the vote; and the National Woman Suffrage Association (NWSA), led by "irreconcilables" Susan B. Anthony and Elizabeth Cady Stanton, which opposed the Fifteenth Amendment because it did not grant women the vote. The two groups also split on strategy, with the AWSA undertaking "realistic" efforts for state laws enfranchising women, while the NWSA directed its activity toward a national constitutional amendment. Victories in western states—women won the vote in Wyoming in 1869 and Utah in 1870—paved the way for wider suffrage gains.

Women's organizations were beginning to flourish generally —Young Women's Christian Association (YWCA) groups were organized in several eastern cities in the 1860s, and the formidable Women's Christian Temperance Union (WCTU), led by Frances Willard, was founded in 1874. The forerunner of the American Association of University Women (AAUW) was launched in 1882. The General Federation of Women's Clubs was organized in 1890, and the National Association of Colored Women was founded in 1896 under the leadership of Mary Church Terrell. Unity between the AWSA and the NWSA was finally forged with the encouragement of Alice Stone Blackwell, and the two groups merged into the National American Woman Suffrage Association (NAWSA) in 1890. Elizabeth Cady Stanton was chosen as its first president. Susan Anthony and the first generation of feminist leaders were aging, and she arranged to pass on the NAWSA presidency to Carrie Chapman Catt in 1900. When Catt resigned to deal with family matters and lecture internationally, Anna Howard Shaw—another younger representative of second generation feminists— stepped in as NAWSA president.

Although there were additional state victories during the first decade of the century, little was happening on the federal front—no floor debate on woman suffrage had been held in Congress since 1887. That began to change with the arrival of Alice Paul, a young Quaker who had gone to study in England and became involved with Emmeline Pankhurst's Women's Social and Political Union—jailed for protest activity, she had gone on a hunger strike and been force-fed. Paul chaired the Congressional Committee of NAWSA and created fresh momentum for a federal suffrage amendment. In 1913 she and Lucy Burns created a separate national organization, the Congressional Union, to press a vigorous campaign for the federal suffrage amendment—a goal the NAWSA felt was premature. Carrie Catt returned as NAWSA president in 1915, and began a campaign to convince Woodrow Wilson to support the woman suffrage amendment. Alice Paul and the Congressional Union, on the other hand, formed the National Women's Party to contest the 1916 election in the twelve states where women could vote for president.

Following the end of World War I, woman suffrage bills were passed in England and most Canadian provinces. The NAWSA mounted an all-out campaign for the federal woman suffrage amendment in 1918. Carrie Catt had received a bequest in 1914 of over $1 million to be used to further the cause of woman suffrage from Mrs. Frank Leslie, publisher of *Leslie's Weekly*. After considerable litigation and a settlement, Catt finally received the money in 1917, in time to employ some 200 women organizers for the final campaign. The NAWSA had to fight opposition from political machines, the brewing and liquor industries (who feared temperance), the Catholic hierarchy, and corporate interests who were alarmed by the progressive implications of the new federal income tax (authorized by the Sixteenth Amendment in 1913) and direct popular election of U.S. senators (as provided by the Seventeenth Amendment in 1913). After the 1918 elections, the Nineteenth Amendment granting women the vote finally received the required two-thirds majority in the House and Senate in May 1919, and ratification by three-fourths of the states (thirty-six of forty-eight) was completed in August 1920.

The NAWSA created the National League of Women Voters (LWV) in 1920 to carry on the work of educating women and the public on civic issues. Unsatisfied by the suffrage victory, Alice Paul maintained the National Women's Party to promote an Equal Rights Amendment (ERA), which she believed was essential to attaining equality for women. Paul's small, elite, sectarian, and divisive organization sustained the idea of the ERA for the several decades when feminism was in abeyance —and when most influential women and women's organizations opposed the ERA in favor of protective labor legislation for women, and an alliance with the labor movement and, later, the civil rights movement.

The absence of an explicitly feminist movement did not mean that women were not making gains during the 1920s and 1930s. The Federation of Business and Professional Women (BPW) was organized in 1919, grew into a powerful force for women's rights, and became an early supporter of the ERA. Women worked on the unsuccessful campaign for a child labor amendment, but did succeed in obtaining passage of the Sheppard-Towner Act in 1921, providing matching federal funds for state maternal and child health programs. The Children's Bureau was established in 1912, and the Women's Bureau in 1920, both housed in the Department of Labor and providing footholds for women in the federal bureaucracy (Mary Anderson was chief of the Women's Bureau from 1920 to 1944; Julia Lathrop was chief of the Children's Bureau from 1912 to 1921; Grace Abbott from 1921 to 1934, followed by Katherine Lenroot from 1934 to 1949). During the New Deal administration of Franklin Roosevelt, over two dozen women were appointed or elected to influential positions in Washington agencies or the Democratic party structure, and formed a loose network fostered by Eleanor Roosevelt. Frances Perkins became the first woman in a president's cabinet as secretary of labor from 1933 to 1945, and Mary Dewson became an important leader of the Democratic National Committee's Women's Division. The women's network had substantial influence over social welfare policy in the New Deal agencies—Jane Hoey, for example, served as director of the Bureau of Public Assistance from 1936 to 1953—and established an impressive record of government service.

THE NEW WOMEN'S MOVEMENT

During World War II women were called upon to replace men in factories, as "Rosie the Riveter" became the model of the patriotic woman working in a defense plant. As men were demobilized after the war, women were expected to give up their jobs and take up homemaking—as many did, raising the children of the baby boom generation through the 1940s and 1950s. Women continued to move into the work force, but in traditional occupations: as secretaries in the expanding pink-collar office force, and in such helping professions as teaching, nursing, and social work. At the same time women were achieving a higher level of education that prepared them for positions beyond the traditional job roles. The availability of the Pill resulted in a decline in fertility after 1964, as women planned children around education and work (it also opened up potential for greater sexual freedom). In this context Betty Friedan's best-seller, *The Feminist Mystique*, caught fire in 1963.

Not that there hadn't been progress for women in the early 1960s. In 1961 Esther Peterson, a former lobbyist for the AFL-CIO and then director of the Women's Bureau, successfully lobbied President Kennedy to set up the President's Commission on the Status of Women, chaired by Eleanor Roosevelt. The Commission published *American Women* in 1963, making mild recommendations to improve women's situation. With support from the Department of Labor and the AFL-CIO, Congress passed the Equal Pay Act of 1963, requiring equal pay for equal work. And in 1964 sex discrimination was made an illegal practice under Title VII of the Civil Rights Act; Rep. Howard Smith (D-Virginia) introduced the amendment, pushed by Rep. Martha Griffiths (D-Michigan) and Katharine St. George (R-New York), adding "sex" as a conservative tactic to reduce support for the bill—although as a long-time Alice Paul ally and supporter of the ERA, Smith didn't want black men to have an advantage over white women if the civil rights bill were to pass. The amendment was opposed by the Women's Bureau coalition but supported by ERA backers, and the Civil Rights Act passed as amended. The Equal Employment Opportunity Commission remained a strong supporter of protective legislation for women, and made little effort to enforce the prohibition against sex discrimination.

Betty Friedan and women's rights supporters used the occasion of the Third National Conference of the Commissions on the Status of Women in June 1966 to propose a new civil rights group, the National Organization for Women (NOW) to fight for enforcement of the sex provision of Title VII. NOW held its founding convention in October 1966, electing Friedan as president and a board of directors including professionals who worked in federal and state government, universities, business, and labor unions. With encouragement from the National Women's Party, NOW endorsed the ERA in 1967 and soon became its leading advocate (although that meant leaving an office provided by the United Auto Workers). NOW also supported abortion rights and federally funded child care, and divisions over these positions and priorities led to individuals leaving to form the Women's Equity Action League (WEAL) to focus on economic issues, and the National Women's Political Caucus (NWPC) to focus on electoral activity. While remaining part of the progressive women's rights coalition, traditional women's groups—LWV, AAUW, and BPW—were being overshadowed by the new wave of feminist organizations.

Much as the abolition movement helped inspire woman suffrage supporters in the nineteenth century, the civil rights struggle of the late 1950s and 1960s helped inspire a younger, more radical generation of women activists, many of whom were associated with the emerging New Left. Women who were resisting the sexism of male leadership in the civil rights work of the Student Nonviolent Coordinating Committee (SNCC) and the community organizing projects of Students for a Democratic Society (SDS) began meeting in 1967 in small groups to discuss their experiences. Out of these "consciousness-raising" groups emerged a decentralized women's liberation movement, using the insight "the personal is political" to examine and explore the grounds of oppression in their personal as well as organizational power relationships. Even as the "sisterhood is powerful" message was taking hold, the movement was fragmenting into a variety of competing perspectives, including radical feminism and socialist feminism. After 1970, lesbian separatism helped foster the development of women's services and cultural activities. Over the next decade feminists created a range of local women's institutions that flourish to this date: rape crisis hotlines and counseling centers, battered women's shelters, women's health clinics, and other women's projects—newspapers, bookstores, coffeehouses, and entertainment.

THE EQUAL RIGHTS AMENDMENT

1. Equality of rights under the law shall not be denied or abridged by the United States or by any State on account of sex.

2. The Congress shall have the power to enforce, by appropriate legislation, the provisions of this article.

3. This amendment shall take effect two years after the date of ratification.

The ERA battle: Support for the ERA had been growing with little controversy. The Republican party platform had endorsed the ERA since 1940, and the Democratic party since 1944, despite labor opposition. The ERA had been endorsed by Presidents Johnson and Nixon, and the Presidential Task Force on the Status of Women. The Women's Bureau and several unions reversed their opposition and supported the ERA. Beginning in 1970 hearings were held in the Senate and House, and the ERA passed the House in 1971 and the Senate in March 1972. Supporters of the ERA had seven years to persuade the legislatures of thirty-eight states to ratify, but little concerted effort was mounted at first because it looked like clear sailing—in 1972 alone twenty-two states ratified. Then the opponents emerged, the most effective of which was Phyllis Schlafly's Stop ERA, formed in 1972 (incorporated in 1975 as Eagle Forum). By the end of 1975, thirty-four states had ratified, but then none in 1976 and only one in 1977. Meanwhile three states had voted to rescind ratification, an action with unclear constitutional impact. When it was evident in 1978 that ERA supporters could not get thirty-eight state ratifications by 1979, they got Congress to pass a three-year extension to 1982. All the opponents had to do was deny ratification in thirteen states—and Illinois and Utah proved decisive, with opposition from Schlafly influential in Illinois and the Mormon church in Utah. The ERA drive was defeated.

What went wrong? Schlafly and other opponents argued that the ERA would result in drafting women for combat, require federal funds to be used for abortions, mandate equal rights for homosexuals, remove powers from the states, and even establish unisex toilets. Sympathetic analysts like Jane Mansbridge conclude that ERA would have little direct impact on women's rights and economic position, given the liberal interpretations the courts have given to the Equal Pay Act, Title VII of the Civil Rights Act, Title IX of the Education Amendments of 1972, and state ERA laws. The ERA's impact would be largely symbolic, and would probably have some influence on court and legislative actions over time. Consequently both the ERA's backers and opponents had reason to exaggerate its effects to mobilize their constituencies. Mansbridge notes that ERA supporters emphasized its impact when they should have minimized it to build a broad consensus. Public opinion supported protection of women's equal rights, but not an upheaval in family life. Opponents simply had to raise enough doubts about the ERA's impact to doom support in a quarter of the states. Mary Frances Berry emphasizes that not enough groundwork was done in the states to assure solid support for the ERA.

NATIONAL ADVOCATES

THE LEAGUE
OF WOMEN VOTERS

LEAGUE OF WOMEN VOTERS OF THE U.S.

1730 M STREET, NW

WASHINGTON, DC 20036

(202) 429-1965

FOUNDED: 1920   MEMBERS: 105,000
BUDGET: $5.5 million   STAFF: 45
LOCAL LEAGUES: 1,150; 50 state Leagues plus D.C., Puerto Rico, and the Virgin Islands
TAX STATUS: 501(c)(4): League of Women Voters of the U.S.; 501(c)(3): LWV Education Fund

PURPOSE: "To promote political responsibility through informed and active participation of citizens in government and to act on selected governmental issues."

The League of Women Voters of the U.S. (LWV) is the descendant of the National American Woman Suffrage Association (NAWSA) that won passage of the Nineteenth Amendment in 1920. Not a women's rights organization, LWV has emphasized good government, voter education and registration, internationalism, and support for a generally progressive set of issues that shifts over time. Given the number of women in public life who got their start with LWV, the organization probably has done more than any other group to prepare women in the skills necessary for success in politics. Recently LWV is best known for its sponsorship of presidential debates. Although it has not grown significantly in recent years, LWV has a vital network of active members in local chapters and state organizations across the country.

BACKGROUND: When the National American Woman Suffrage Association held its last, jubilant convention in February 1920, six months before ratification of the Nineteenth Amendment, president Carrie Chapman Catt called for the creation of a National League of Women Voters to promote citizen education for the entire electorate. The first president of the new League was Maude Wood Park, who had lobbied the women's suffrage amendment through Congress in the two years prior to ratification. (The organization changed its name to League of Women Voters of the U.S. in 1946).

Although the League does not support or oppose candidates for public office, it has always aimed at influencing legislation and public policy. Among the issues supported by the first League convention were collective bargaining, child labor laws, a minimum wage, compulsory education, and equal rights for women in government and industry. The first legislative victory for the League was the passage over bitter opposition of the Sheppard-Towner Act by Congress in 1921, providing federal support for maternal and child care programs.

During the decade of the Depression in the 1930s, the League supported many New Deal programs: the Social Security Act, the Food and Drug Act, U.S. membership in the International Labor Organization, and the child labor provisions in the Wages and Hours Act. As federal programs increased, the League pushed for merit system employment, supporting legislation that moved numerous federal jobs from the spoils system to the Civil Service.

In international affairs the League rejected isolationism, supporting ratification in 1929 of the Kellogg-Briand Pact, which renounced war as an instrument of international policy, and supporting in 1932 U.S. membership in the League of Nations. The League also supported U.S. membership in the World Court, and in 1937 began its support for each renewal of the Trade Agreements Act, consistently supporting expansion rather than restriction of trade. As World War II began in Europe, the League opposed neutrality and supported collective security against the Axis powers. Toward the end of the war, the League waged a vigorous educational campaign on behalf of the Dumbarton Oaks proposals for the establishment of the United Nations. The League continues to advocate a foreign policy based on support of the U.N. system, freer world trade, and foreign aid to improve the lives of people in developing countries.

In the postwar period the League supported domestic federal reorganization acts, and state and local Leagues studied budgets and revenues related to public education, child welfare, housing, urban renewal, local planning, and police services. The witch-hunts of Senator Joseph McCarthy prompted a study of federal loyalty and security programs and eventually led to a League position emphasizing the protection of individual civil liberties. During the civil rights movement of the 1960s the League examined the problems of discrimination and poverty and gave strong support to programs for equal opportunity and access to employment, education, and housing. In international affairs, the League's 1969 convention called for normalization of relations with the People's Republic of China and an end to U.S. opposition to representation of China in the U.N.

The 1970s brought women's issues back onto the League agenda; the 1972 convention overwhelmingly endorsed the Equal Rights Amendment, and the League has worked at both local and national levels on ERA ratification campaigns. Growth of the environmental movement led to League positions on air and water quality, waste management, power plant siting, energy conservation, and hazardous substances. The Watergate affair led to League support for the campaign financing reforms in the Federal Election Campaign Act of 1974. In keeping with its historic commitment to extending the franchise, the League has lobbied for exten-

sions of the Voting Rights Act of 1965 and for full voting rights and representation in Congress for residents of the District of Columbia.

CURRENT PRIORITIES: The League groups its programs into four areas: government, international relations, natural resources, and social policy. Under government, the League's goal is "an open governmental system that is representative, accountable, responsive; that protects individual liberties established by the Constitution; and that assures opportunities for citizen participation in government decision making." Internationally, the League's goal is "to promote peace in an interdependent world through cooperation with other nations, the strengthening of international organizations, arms control measures and the resolution of conflict without the use of military force." Regarding natural resources, the League's goal is "to promote the wise management of resources in the public interest and an environment beneficial to life." In social policy, the League's goal is "to promote social and economic justice, secure equal rights for all and combat discrimination and poverty." Specific policy objectives are formulated and educational and lobbying programs developed for each of these four program areas.

MEMBERS: The increasing participation of women in the work force and the competing attraction of other organizations in the women's and peace movements have resulted in the League's membership declining over the past few years to its current level around 105,000 from a peak of 157,000 in 1969. Although the League has attempted to shed its image as the "mother hen of politics" by emphasizing its activist character, it has had difficulty attracting younger women (the average age of members is now over fifty). Although the League elevated men from associate to full membership status in the 1970s, only a small percentage of members are men. In attempting to attract men, the League may be competing with such organizations as Common Cause, which occupies similar political terrain, as well as a variety of single-interest groups in the environmental, peace, and civil liberties arenas.

STRUCTURE: LWV was originally a federation of state Leagues, governed by a board of state League presidents. In 1944 LWV changed its bylaws to reconstitute itself as a unitary organization of local Leagues; membership is joint in the local and national LWVs. Local and state Leagues are separate organizations recognized by the national LWV. National policy is set in the delegated biennial convention. LWV has a fourteen-member board of directors elected by the League biennial convention. The League president (a volunteer office) is elected for a two-year term, with a second term possible for a maximum of four years; the current president is Susan Lederman. LWV's first male executive director, Grant Thompson, served from 1986 to 1989; the current executive director is Gracia Hillman.

The LWV Education Fund was established in 1957 as a 501(c)(3) organization for educational activities and tax-deductible contributions. LWVEF has the same fourteen-member board as LWV. LWVEF sponsored presidential debates in 1976, 1980, and 1984—a national version of the nonpartisan candidate forums conducted by local and state Leagues.

RESOURCES: LWV had 1991 revenue of $2.7 million, and expenditures of $2.7 million, including program (69 percent) and administration and fund-raising (31 percent. The LWVEF had revenue of $2.6 million, and expenditures of $2.8 million, including program (70 percent) and administration and fund-raising (30 percent).

PUBLICATIONS AND SERVICES: Membership begins at $20 and includes the quarterly magazine *The National Voter* (circulation 154,000). *Report from the Hill*, a legislative newsletter published six times a year, is available by subscription. The Education Fund publishes an outstanding series of pamphlets, among the best written and most informative topical guides to public policy questions published by any organization, available from the League's annual catalog of publications. The publication *In League* provides a handbook of organizational details. The official history is Louise M. Young, *In the Public Interest: The League of Women Voters, 1920–1970* (Greenwood Press, 1990). There are two useful biographies of the LWV founder: Jacqueline Van Voris, *Carrie Chapman Catt: A Public Life* (Feminist Press, 1987), and Robert Booth Fowler, *Carrie Catt: Feminist Politician* (Northeastern University Press, 1986). □

NATIONAL ORGANIZATION FOR WOMEN

1000 16TH STREET, NW, SUITE 700

WASHINGTON, DC 20036-5705

(202) 331-0066

FOUNDED: 1966 MEMBERS: 250,000
CHAPTERS: 750 BUDGET: $6.9 million
STAFF: 32 TAX STATUS: 501(c)(4): National
Organization for Women; 501(c)(3): NOW
Foundation; PACs: NOW PAC, and NOW Equality
PAC

PURPOSE: "To bring women into full participation in the mainstream of American society now."

The National Organization for Women (NOW) is the leading voice of feminism in the United States, although it can no longer define by itself the agenda of the women's movement. Throwing its resources behind the drive to ratify the ERA and to elect a female vice president on the Democratic ticket, NOW suffered two serious defeats in the early 1980s, but rebounded to help lead the fight for abortion rights. Increasingly alienated from conventional politics, NOW has called for the formation of a new party, choosing to be an outside agitator rather than an inside player.

BACKGROUND: NOW emerged from a meeting in July 1966 by 28 women associated with the state Commissions on the Status of Women, who were frustrated at the federal government's unenergetic approach to their concerns. Led by Betty Friedan, who had written

"National Organization for Women" on a paper napkin during the final federal commission banquet, the group called a meeting in October at which the organization's bylaws and statement of purpose was adopted by the 300 women and men attending. Friedan was elected president of NOW, a post she held for the next four years. Envisioned as an "NAACP for women," NOW aimed initially at obtaining enforcement by the Equal Employment Opportunities Commission of Title VII of the Civil Rights Act of 1964, which included a prohibition against discrimination on the basis of sex.

For the first three years, NOW's administrative structure was minimal. From a temporary location at the Center for Continuing Education at the University of Wisconsin, it moved to Detroit, where it was housed with the Women's Committee of the United Auto Workers (UAW), and then to Chicago (after NOW's endorsement of the ERA caused a split with the UAW). By 1969 NOW had suffered three splits over abortion rights and the ERA. (In one, Elizabeth Boyer left to form the Women's Equity Action League to work on economic issues.) Over half the membership was concentrated in the New York chapter.

The women's liberation movement moved into the national media spotlight with NOW's "Strike for Equality" called for August 26, 1970, the fiftieth anniversary of the Nineteenth Amendment. Three issues formed the focus of the strike: abortion on demand, twenty-four-hour child care centers, and equal opportunity in employment and education. The numbers of people who responded to the August 26 events surprised even the organizers—25,000 took part in New York, 10,000 in Los Angeles, and 15,000 in Chicago. Membership in NOW chapters jumped along with participation in local women's groups. By 1974 NOW had increased from 14 to over 300 chapters and had grown from 1,000 to 40,000 members.

Wilma Scott Heide served as NOW president from 1970 to 1974, a period of rapid growth for the women's movement. Heide opened a lobbying office in Washington, D.C., in 1973, which became the national office. NOW was pulled along by the radicalization of women's liberation. During 1969 and 1970 Friedan had warned of the threat to NOW's image posed by lesbians—"the lavender menace"—but by 1973 NOW had organized a task force on sexuality and lesbianism and passed a resolution opposing discrimination based on sexual orientation.

Controversy between a narrow focus on economic rights and a more radical approach crystallized again in the election of attorney Karen DeCrow as NOW president in 1974. Running under the slogan, "Out of the mainstream into the revolution," DeCrow was reelected at the Philadelphia convention in 1975. DeCrow worked to heal rifts in the organization, championed gay rights and abortion rights, and led NOW toward a national campaign for ratification of the Equal Rights Amendment. Growth to 60,000 members led to revision of the bylaws to provide for a delegated convention, which met in Detroit in a spirit of unity in 1977 and elected Eleanor Smeal president. Smeal has been NOW's dominant figure ever since.

The ERA was in trouble, and Smeal directed all NOW's resources to get the ERA ratified by key state legislatures. NOW sponsored a pro-ERA march in Washington in July 1978, which helped persuade Congress to pass a three-year extension of the deadline for ratification. NOW waged major campaigns to have the ERA ratified in Illinois, Florida, North Carolina, Oklahoma, and Virginia—five of the fifteen states that had not passed the ERA by 1979. Paid staff coordinated the efforts of volunteers sent to the targeted states. But by June 30, 1982, no more states had ratified, and NOW had built up a deficit of nearly $1.7 million.

By the NOW convention of 1982 in Indianapolis, Ronald Reagan had been president for two years. At the end of her two-consecutive-term limit, Smeal supported as her successor NOW's executive vice president, former English professor Judy Goldsmith. She was challenged by Sonia Johnson, who had joined NOW three years earlier after being excommunicated from the Mormon church for her feminist views. Goldsmith prevailed by emphasizing her administrative experience and her continued commitment to political action. Building working alliances with black, Hispanic, and other women's groups, Goldsmith developed a multi-issue agenda with program staff working on economic concerns, reproductive rights, lesbian rights, and minority rights as well as the ERA. Goldsmith also led NOW into the thick of politicking around the Democratic party presidential nominations for the 1984 campaign. Six of seven Democratic contenders appeared at the annual NOW convention in Washington in 1983 to seek its endorsement. Goldsmith called for a woman as a vice presidential candidate in 1984, and Walter Mondale selected Geraldine Ferraro as his running mate. NOW PAC brought a $4 million campaign fund into the elections.

With the landslide defeat of the Mondale-Ferraro ticket in November 1984, the luster was off Goldsmith's strategy of practical politics. Smeal decided to challenge her former protégé in a bitterly contested election at the New Orleans NOW convention in 1985. Attacking Goldsmith's moderate image and her behind-the-scenes style of leadership, Smeal promised to lead the women's movement "back to the streets" and also capture the allegiance of a new generation of women on college campuses. Smeal's inspirational and militant oratory (with which, as Ellen Goodman says, she can "Cuisinart an opponent") swung an almost evenly divided convention to her side, and won her a third term as NOW president.

After two years in office Smeal surprised the organization by not running for reelection; instead she left to form the Fund for the Feminist Majority. Smeal threw her support behind NOW's political director, seventy-something Molly Yard, as her successor. Yard easily won election as NOW's president in the Philadelphia national conference in August 1987, which also saw NOW give a rousing welcome to Rep. Patricia Schroeder of Colorado, who was considering a run for the Democratic presidential nomination. In the end, Schroeder decided not to campaign for the nomination, and NOW sat out the election, weary of being blamed as a "special interest" albatross around the neck of the Democrats.

George Bush campaigned for president against the right to abortion, and after his election supported the Reagan administration's brief to the Supreme Court requesting it overturn the *Roe* v. *Wade* decision and allow the states to regulate abortion. NOW had planned to revive its ERA campaign with a march in the spring of 1989, but the forthcoming Supreme Court decision on abortion shifted the emphasis. NOW was a prominent sponsor of the April 1989 March for Women's Equality/Women's Lives, which drew over 300,000 women to Washington, D.C. The march failed to influence the outcome of the *Webster* v. *Reproductive Health Services* decision, which increased States' power to regulate abortion, but it energized organizations defending the right to abortion. Another march on Washington, "Mobilize for Women's Lives," in November put the focus on abortion rights. NOW took the hard line: its banners read "Keep Abortion Legal," while the National Abortion Rights Action League (NARAL) took the libertarian position, which emphasized "Pro-Choice" and the question "Who Decides?"

The Mondale-Ferraro ticket went down to defeat in 1984 on its own, but NOW received a piece of the blame for making the Democrats appear to be pandering to highly visible special interest groups. Pat Schroeder's decision not to run for the Democratic presidential nomination in 1988 added to NOW's disillusionment with Democratic party politics. At the 1989 NOW convention, a casual comment threatening to form a third party produced a spontaneous groundswell of enthusiasm. Criticism from Washington pundits (as well as colleagues in NARAL and the National Women's Political Caucus) prompted NOW to set up a Commission for Responsive Democracy to conduct hearings across the country on how to improve the two-party system. In 1991 the Commission voted 26 to 4 to recommend that NOW, together with other constituencies, help launch a new political party free from what it sees as the hypocrisy and corruption of the major parties. NOW set up a working group of six coconveners including Smeal, Ireland, Christic Institute director Sara Nelson, United Farm Workers leader Delores Huerta, and African American political figures Mel King of Boston and Monica Faith Stewart of Chicago. Presently functioning as the 21st Century party, the new party is independent of NOW.

Planning to retire in 1992, Yard suffered a stroke and was succeeded by vice president Pat Ireland in 1991. An articulate and energetic attorney, Ireland presented a fresh image as NOW reached out to a new generation of young feminists. But controversy wasn't long in surfacing, as conservative groups from Beverly LaHaye's Concerned Women for America to Phyllis Schlafly's Eagle Forum stepped up their attacks on NOW as being dominated by lesbian activists. Late in 1991 Ireland gave a widely publicized interview to the gay magazine *The Advocate* in which she acknowledged a close relationship with a woman with whom she shares her Washington apartment, as well as maintaining her marriage with her husband, who lives in Miami. The interview fueled the controversy, instigated by organizations on the right, over whether NOW is representative of

American women. Although it sponsored efforts to develop the new party, NOW leaders are taking care not to position the organization too far from the political mainstream. NOW's political action committees gave full support to several Democratic women running strong U.S. Senate campaigns in the 1992 primaries and general election. Any decision by the Supreme Court to restrict abortion rights would undoubtedly result in renewed support for NOW from its substantial constituency. NOW's leadership helped turn out a record number of 750,000 demonstrators in Washington, D.C., in support of abortion rights in April 1992.

CURRENT PRIORITIES: NOW has established four priority issues: (1) reproductive rights and defending the right to abortion; (2) ratification of the Equal Rights Amendment; (3) combating racism and supporting civil rights; and (4) lesbian and gay rights. Other areas of concern include economic rights, older women's rights, homemakers' rights, political rights, violence against women, discrimination in education, child care, and health care. In an effort to involve a younger generation of women, NOW held the first young feminist conference with 750 participants in February 1991.

MEMBERS: NOW's membership peaked at 250,000 in 1982 at the height of the ERA campaign, then dropped to 150,000 by the mid-1980s after the drive failed and the Mondale-Ferraro ticket went down to defeat. Following the *Webster* decision in 1989, NOW was flooded with new members, raising the current total back to 250,000.

STRUCTURE: There are 750 chapters in all fifty states and D.C. NOW is governed by a board of directors chosen by the nine regions and elected by members in good standing for at least two years. Women of color constitute 25 percent of the board, and NOW has a strong affirmative action policy to involve people of color at the chapter and state levels and on the staff. A delegated annual convention sets policy and elects officers. State organizations run their own lobbying campaigns and political action committees.

RESOURCES: NOW's budget for 1990 projects revenue of $6.9 million, derived 70 percent from membership dues, 22 percent from contributions, and 8 percent from other sources. Expenditures of $6.9 million were divided 16 percent for regions, states, and chapters; 13 percent for projects and programs; 42 percent for membership development; 9 percent for fund-raising; 4 percent for communications; 11 percent for administration, 4 percent for other expenses, and $50,000 for debt retirement. NOW PAC raised $271,000 in the 1990 campaign cycle, up from $162,000 in the 1988 cycle. In 1992 NOW PAC supported the many progressive women running for Congress as Democrats.

PUBLICATIONS AND SERVICES: Membership is $40 and includes *National NOW Times* six times a year, and the state and chapter newsletters. The national office publishes an *Issues Policy Manual*, which details the stands the organization has taken on dozens of issues through resolutions at its annual conferences, and an *Administrative Policy Manual*, containing organizational bylaws and a variety of procedural rules. You can organize your own consciousness-raising groups with *NOW Guidelines for Feminist Consciousness-Raising.*

NOW offers members nondiscriminatory comprehensive health insurance, term life insurance, and a medicare supplement plan, all underwritten by Consumers United Insurance Company of Washington, D.C., the largest employee-owned and managed insurance company in the United States. NOW feminist message checks are available. □

NATIONAL WOMEN'S POLITICAL CAUCUS

1275 K STREET, NW, SUITE 750

WASHINGTON, DC 20005

(202) 898-1100

FOUNDED: 1971   MEMBERS: 70,000
CAUCUSES: 330   BUDGET: $2 million
STAFF: 12   TAX STATUS: 501(c)(4): National
Women's Political Caucus; 501(c)(3): NWPC
Leadership Development, Education and
Research Fund; PAC: NWPC Campaign Support
Committee

PURPOSE: "To move women into elected and appointed office at all levels of government."

As the National Women's Political Caucus (NWPC) says, "there is no substitute for a seat at the table." NWPC works in a bipartisan manner to identify, recruit, train, and elect feminist women to public office. With a goal of gender-balanced government representing the interests of women (who compose 53 percent of the population), NWPC has declared the 1990s to be "The Decade of Women in Politics," setting the stage for a new century of progress. NWPC avoids strident rhetoric and polarizing stances, concentrating on being, as it claims, "practical, pragmatic, mainstream, and effective."

BACKGROUND: NWPC was formed in July 1971 at a conference of 300 women to support the election and appointment of women to public office, to promote political party reform, and to support women's issues and feminist candidates across party lines. The immediate impact of NWPC owed much to the well-known group of women leaders who were part of the original national council: author and founding NOW president Betty Friedan; Congresswomen Bella Abzug and Shirley Chisholm; writers and editors Gloria Steinem and Shana Alexander; Lady Bird Johnson's White House press secretary Liz Carpenter; Nixon White House aide Jill Ruckelshaus; NOW president Wilma Scott Heide; National Council of Negro Women president Dorothy Height; Indian rights leader LaDonna Harris; Mississippi civil rights leader Fannie Lou Hamer; United Auto Workers vice president Olga Madar; and former Republican National Committee vice-chair Elly Peterson.

This initial group of leaders was heavily liberal, Democratic, and East Coast. Nevertheless NWPC managed to attract women from many regions of the country and retain representation from Republican women. New leaders emerged, including Frances "Sissy" Farenthold of Texas. The 1971 founding conference had developed a broad list of women's issues that were considered nonbinding guidelines for state and local Caucuses. In 1977 the Caucus, through its Campaign Support Committee, adopted national endorsement guidelines that remain in effect today: A candidate endorsed by the Caucus must support the Equal Rights Amendment, the 1973 Supreme Court decision in *Roe* v. *Wade* favoring choice on abortion, and publicly funded child care.

CURRENT PRIORITIES: NWPC emphasizes increasing the number of women in Congress and state legislatures. There were two women among the 100 members of the U.S. Senate in 1991, the same number as in 1971. There were 29 women (including one nonvoting delegate) among the 435 members of the House of Representatives, up from 13 in 1971. NWPC state and local Caucuses focus on electing women as governors (3 in 1991) and state legislators, who have increased from 5 percent in 1971 to 12 percent in 1981 to 18 percent in 1991, for a total of 1,359 women in state legislatures in 1991. With the election of the first woman to the Louisiana state senate in 1991, women now sit in each of the ninety-nine state legislative chambers. Women mayors have increased from 7 in 1971 to 151 in 1991.

NWPC expresses its strong commitment to civil rights and liberties in a declared dedication to the "eradication of sexism, racism, anti-Semitism, ageism, violence, poverty, discrimination against the disabled and discrimination on the basis of religion, and to ensuring reproductive freedom and freedom of sexual orientation." In recent years NWPC has emphasized recruiting and electing women of color to office, and is pleased that there are now six women of color in the U.S. House of Representatives.

NWPC organizes election-year "win with women" campaigns that recruit qualified women candidates; train candidates, campaign managers, and volunteers to organize, raise money, and get out the vote; and support endorsed candidates with financial contributions, technical assistance, and volunteers. Special training programs are aimed at women of color, first-time candidates, and candidates for state legislatures.

MEMBERS: NWPC's 70,000 members participate in national, state, and local Caucus activities. Governing members include all those elected to the boards of local and state Caucuses.

STRUCTURE: NWPC's governing board includes a representative from each of the 330 Caucuses. The national steering committee meets quarterly, and a delegated convention meets every two years. Recent presidents have included Irene Natividad and Sharon Rodine; former Missouri lieutenant governor and U.S. Senate candidate Harriet Woods was elected president at the NWPC's twentieth anniversary convention in 1991. An advisory board of noted women in politics includes Bella Abzug, Shirley Chisholm, Midge Costanza, Coretta Scott King, Sharon Percy Rockefeller, Jill Ruckelshaus, Patricia Schroeder, Gloria Steinem, and Maxine Waters. Jody Newman is executive director.

RESOURCES: NWPC revenues are derived 41 percent from corporate, union, and foundation contributions; 23 percent from membership dues; 28 percent from direct-mail solicitations; and 8 percent from special events. The NWPC Campaign Support Committee raised $54,000 in the 1986 campaign cycle, $57,000 in the 1988 cycle, and $31,000 in the 1990 cycle. Most of the action is at the local and state Caucus levels.

PUBLICATIONS AND SERVICES: Members receive the quarterly newsletter *Women's Political Times*. NWPC publishes a *National Directory of Women Elected Officials* and other materials on political campaigning, congressional voting records, and women in appointed offices. ☐

LEGAL EAGLES OF THE WOMEN'S MOVEMENT

Several women's organizations have established related organizations or internal departments to conduct litigation on behalf of women's rights. Perhaps foremost is the NOW Legal Defense and Education Fund; the American Association of University Women Legal Advocacy Fund and the Women's Equity Action League are also active in court cases. The Women's Legal Defense Fund litigates class-action suits, in addition to functioning as a legal services organization for women in the District of Columbia. The American Civil Liberties Union also carries a docket of women's rights cases.

NOW LEGAL DEFENSE AND EDUCATION FUND

99 HUDSON STREET

NEW YORK, NY 10013

(212) 925-6635

FOUNDED: 1970   BUDGET: $1.8 million
STAFF: 20   TAX STATUS: 501(c)(3)

PURPOSE: "To bring about true equality for women."

BACKGROUND: The National Organization for Women organized the Legal Defense and Education Fund (NOW LDEF) in 1970 on the model of the NAACP LDF to advance economic rights and justice for all women. Following the enactment of Title IX of the Education Amendments of 1972, NOW LDEF started its Project on Equal Education Rights (PEER) to conduct workshops, develop manuals, and initiate programs to obtain equal sports opportunities for girls and equal training in all areas including science, math, and computers. PEER's Project Sister (Stay in School to Earn Rewards) works to prevent teen pregnancy and dropping out.

In the area of family law, NOW LDEF has emphasized the economic value of the homemaker in calculating alimony awards for women in divorce proceedings. Similar calculations on the cost of child raising emphasize the need for adequate child support awards for single women raising children; NOW LDEF pushed for the Family Support Act of 1988 and monitors state child support guidelines. NOW LDEF has argued for "delayed discovery" and extensions of the statute of limitations in childhood sexual abuse cases.

NOW LDEF strongly supports reproductive choice, and provides technical assistance for state legislative advocacy in the wake of the *Webster* decision. NOW LDEF has gone to court to keep blockaders from shutting down clinics providing abortions, winning suits against Operation Rescue in New York City, Maryland, Virginia, and D.C. Its civil damage judgments against Operation Rescue virtually put the original group out of business, forcing it to reorganize as Operation Rescue National.

CURRENT PRIORITIES: NOW LDEF focuses on the following: (1) *workplace issues*, including equal opportunity on the job, nontraditional jobs, and sexual harassment; (2) *economic supports*, particularly unisex insurance rates and fair and equal distribution of pensions at the time of divorce; (3) *Project on Equal Education Rights* (PEER), supporting equity for girls in such areas as science, math, computers, and sports; (4) *family law*, including fair evaluation of a homemaker's work in divorce settlements, family violence, and support for children; (5) *reproductive choice*, including the right to bear children, the right to use contraception, and the right to abortion; and (6) *court reform*, aimed at eliminating gender bias in the court system, conducted through the National Judicial Education Program to Promote Equality for Women and Men (NJEP).

STRUCTURE: NOW LDEF has a twenty-four-member, self-recruiting board of directors. Three NOW board members serve on the NOW LDEF board: LDEF president Phyllis Segal, Patricia Ireland, and Molly Yard. Helen Neuborne is executive director. NOW LDEF is not only modeled after the NAACP LDF, it is headquartered in the same New York City building.

RESOURCES: NOW LDEF's 1991 revenue of $1.8 million was derived from individual donors (38 percent), foundations (25 percent), corporations (10 percent), special events (24 percent), and other sources (3 percent). There were over 280 corporate donors and 20 foundation grantors in 1989. Expenditures of $1.8 million included legal research and litigation (44 percent), public information and education (16 percent), PEER program (11 percent), program development (1 percent) management (16 percent), and fund-raising (12 percent). Conservative groups, led by the Capital Research Center, have kept up a drumbeat of criticism of the major corporations that donate to NOW LDEF.

PUBLICATIONS AND SERVICES: NOW LDEF publishes a variety of booklets and pamphlets on such topics as divorce, child support, access to health care, sexual harassment, and reproductive rights. The most comprehensive is *The State-by-State Guide to Women's Legal Rights* (1986). □

WOMEN'S LEGAL DEFENSE FUND

WOMEN'S LEGAL DEFENSE FUND

1875 CONNECTICUT AVENUE, NW, SUITE 710

WASHINGTON, DC 20009

(202) 986-2600

FOUNDED: 1971   CONTRIBUTORS: 1,500
BUBGET: $1.4 million   STAFF: 25
TAX STATUS: 501(c)(3)

PURPOSE: "To protect and advance the rights of women through litigation, counseling, public education programs, community services, and monitoring of local and national agencies responsible for enforcing the laws that prohibit sex discrimination."

BACKGROUND: For the first ten years after its founding in 1971, The Women's Legal Defense Fund (WLDF) relied on volunteer, *pro bono* services of feminist attorneys for more than 350 cases. With the start of its Litigation Project in 1983, WLDF has added staff to provide in-house cocounsel to work with *pro bono* lawyers.

WLDF uses its location in Washington to monitor the Department of Labor's Office of Federal Contract Compliance Programs and the Equal Employment Opportunity Commission. The Employment Rights Project for Women of Color was begun in 1983. The public education program of WLDF prepares public service advertising to raise awareness of legal and public policy decisions that affect women.

Local work in the District of Columbia includes an emergency domestic relations project, counseling on employment and credit discrimination, and advocacy on name change and retention rights. WLDF established My Sister's Place, a shelter in the District of Columbia for battered women and their children; in 1983 the shelter was spun off as an independent agency.

WLDF helped win the Child Support Enforcement Amendments of 1984, and worked with a national network of advocate organizations to assure that strong guidelines were issued at the state level by 1987, as required by the new law. WLDF continues to evaluate state guidelines and pressure child support agencies to enforce the law.

CURRENT PRIORITIES: WLDF activities include its Equal Employment Opportunity Monitoring Project; the Family Employment Security Advocacy Project; monitoring federal and state legislation and regulations; litigation; media outreach and public education programs. In the 1990s, WLDF will build a network of advocates in Women, Work, and Family Action Councils in all 435 congressional districts to have a political impact on women's issues. The project will begin with model councils in twelve major cities.

STRUCTURE: WLDF has a seventeen-member, self-recruiting board of directors, chaired by Ellen Malcolm. Judith Lichtman has served as president and chief executive since 1974.

RESOURCES: WLDF's revenue of $1.4 million in 1991 came from private grants (65 percent), individual contributions (27 percent), special events (5 percent), and other sources (3 percent). Expenditures went for program services (86 percent), and administration and fund-raising (14 percent).

PUBLICATIONS AND SERVICES: Contributors receive *WLDF News* quarterly. WLDF also publishes policy papers and handbooks on child custody and sex discrimination in the workplace. □

WOMEN'S PACS

The political action committees of such women's organizations as National Organization for Women (NOW PAC and NOW Equity PAC) and National Women's Political Caucus (NWPC Campaign Support Committee) make support for the ERA, abortion rights, and federally funded child care necessary criteria for endorsing candidates, as does the unaffiliated PAC, Women's Campaign Fund. EMILY'S List, another unaffiliated PAC, supports feminist Democratic women running for Congress. Affiliated PACs can accept contributions only from members of the parent organization; unaffiliated PACs can accept contributions from the general public.

WOMEN'S CAMPAIGN FUND

WOMEN'S CAMPAIGN FUND

1601 CONNECTICUT AVENUE, NW, SUITE 800

WASHINGTON, DC 20009

(202) 234-3700

FOUNDED: 1974   CONTRIBUTORS: 12,000
BUDGET: $1.2 million   STAFF: 5
TAX STATUS: PAC

PURPOSE: "A bi-partisan, national political committee devoted to helping women achieve elected office."

The Women's Campaign Fund (WCF) is an independent PAC that contributes only to women candidates. Women must satisfy three criteria to gain WCF support: favor ratification of the ERA, support freedom of choice on abortion, and support federal funding for abortions for poor women. WCF supports candidates at all levels of government —federal, state, and local—and in all regions of the country.

BACKGROUND: WCF provides candidates with direct financial support as well as expert advice on planning and organizing political campaigns. In 1981 WCF began a campaign training school to develop the expertise of women candidates, and provide an opportunity to meet fund-raising and media consultants, party officials, and PAC staff.

STRUCTURE: WCF has a thirty-three-member, self-recruiting board of directors. As a bipartisan committee, WCF's board of directors has Republican and Democratic cochairs. The executive director is Jane Danowitz.

RESOURCES: From $60,000 in 1976, WCF's support to candidates increased to some $500,000 by 1984, a level that has remained roughly steady. WCF raised just under $1.1 million in the 1986 campaign cycle, $1.1 million in the 1988 cycle, and nearly $1.2 million in the 1990 cycle. In addition to the usual direct-mail appeals, WCF also organizes gala dinners and parties in such cities as Washington, New York, and Los Angeles. □

EMILY'S LIST

1112 16TH STREET, NW

WASHINGTON, DC 20036

(202) 887-1957

FOUNDED: 1985   MEMBERS: 11,000
BUDGET: $1.5 million   STAFF: 7
TAX STATUS: PAC

EMILY's List is a donor network supporting pro-choice and pro-ERA Democratic women candidates for governorships and for seats in the U.S. Senate and House of Representatives.

BACKGROUND: EMILY is an acronym for a slogan: "Early Money Is Like Yeast" (it makes the dough rise). EMILY's List is the creation of IBM heir Ellen Malcolm, a Washington political activist who brought together a group of fundraisers in 1985 to launch what has become the country's leading financial resource for women candidates. For its first election cycle in 1986, EMILY's List raised $350,000, the largest commitment going to help elect Barbara Mikulski, the first Democratic woman elected to the Senate in her own right. In the next 1988 cycle, $600,000 was raised for nine congressional candidates, two of whom were elected—Nita Lowey of New York and Jolene Unsoeld of Washington. By 1990, EMILY's List raised $1.5 million for fourteen women, helping elect two governors—Ann Richards of Texas and Barbara Roberts of Oregon—and increase the number of Democratic women in the House to a record high of twenty.

MEMBERS: Members give a minimum contribution of $100 to the organization, and agree to make at least two additional gifts of at least $100 to two or more recommended candidates per election cycle. Members of the "Majority Council" give $1,000 or more annually. After Anita Hill's testimony was disregarded in the Senate hearings on Clarence Thomas's Supreme Court appointment, EMILY's membership more than tripled over the following year, reaching 11,000 in 1992.

STRUCTURE: An advisory committee of twenty-five women reviews and recommends candidates for support. Ellen Malcolm is president, and Wendy Sherman is executive director.

RESOURCES: EMILY expected to raise $3 million in the 1992 campaign cycle.

PUBLICATIONS AND SERVICES: Members receive a quarterly newsletter, *Notes from EMILY. Thinking of Running for Congress? A Guide for Democratic Women* is a recently published booklet. □

REPRODUCTIVE RIGHTS

Under English and American common law, abortion was legal until "quickening," when the fetus first moves. Connecticut became the first state to regulate abortion by law in 1821, prohibiting postquickening abortions induced by poisons, in an effort to protect women. The Roman Catholic church had traditionally held that the fetus gained a soul and became "animated" at forty days after conception for males and at eighty days for females; abortion before animation was condemned, but not considered homicide. Only in 1869 did Pope Pius IX establish the position that all abortion is homicide. Over the nineteenth century physicians gained control of abortions by supporting state laws allowing abortion only when a pregnancy threatened the life of the woman, in the opinion of her physician. Although "therapeutic abortions" were widely available in the first half of the twentieth century, advances in medicine meant they became harder to justify in terms of medical necessity. A movement to legalize abortion developed within the medical and legal professions, and the American Law Institute included with its Model Penal Code in 1959 provisions for legal abortion for three reasons: the physical or psychological health of the mother, a child likely to be born with grave physical or mental defects, or a pregnancy resulting from rape or incest.

Two well-publicized incidents taking place around this time created greater public receptivity to legal abortion. In 1962 Sherri Finkbine discovered in her fifth month of pregnancy that she had taken the tranquilizer thalidomide, which had caused serious birth defects in Europe. Unable to get a legal abortion in the United States, she went to Sweden to terminate her pregnancy. Second, from 1962 to 1965 an epidemic of rubella (German measles) caused some 15,000 children to be born with birth defects, mobilizing many physicians to support an easing of abortion laws. Colorado and California passed abortion reform bills in 1967 (Governor Ronald Reagan signed California's, albeit reluctantly). Hawaii and New York repealed their abortion laws in 1970, although repeal was strongly contested in New York.

Dr. Alan Guttmacher of Planned Parenthood Federation of America (PPFA) had founded the Association for the Study of Abortion (ASA) in 1964. Although it took a very cautious approach to abortion reform, ASA brought together activists who would launch the more militant National Association for Repeal of Abortion Laws (NARAL) in 1969. New York writer Lawrence Lader, the biographer of birth control advocate Margaret Sanger, founded NARAL together with ASA contacts Ruth Proskauer Smith and Dr. Lonny Myers of Illinois. The abortion legalization movement also drew support from population groups like the Association for Voluntary Sterilization (AVS) and Zero Population Growth (ZPG). NOW had endorsed legalization of abortion at its second national convention in 1967. A gradual process of change was taking place on the state level, with nineteen states reforming their abortion laws between 1967 and 1973—and a countermovement was beginning to stir as well, with Cincinnati physician John Willke writing and lobbying against legal abortion, helping defeat a referendum in Michigan in 1972.

With the Supreme Court's 1973 decision in *Roe* v. *Wade*,

legally regulating abortion by trimester, predominant activism on reproductive rights shifted from the "pro-choice" to the "pro-life" position. Although public opinion polls showed a majority supporting the right to abortion, at least in certain circumstances, pro-choice activists found it difficult to mobilize these supporters; younger women began to take abortion rights for granted. After Faye Wattleton was hired as executive director in 1978, Planned Parenthood Federation began to take a stronger advocacy position for abortion rights. The Religious Coalition for Abortion Rights (formed in 1973) assembled the mainstream Protestant and Jewish denominations to defend freedom of choice on abortion and counter the pro-life position.

Opposition to abortion clustered in a curious alliance of the Catholic church (liberal on many social issues since Vatican II, but doctrinally opposed to contraception as well as abortion) with conservative Protestant fundamentalists and New Right political activists. The National Right to Life Committee (1973) mobilized state networks of Catholics and conservative Protestants around the single issue of abortion, avoiding the contraception question and other social issues. Judie Brown's American Life League (1979) appealed to a right-wing constituency, with a "no compromises" approach to banning abortion. Joseph Scheidler's Pro-Life Action League (1986) in Chicago emphasized a direct-action approach to shutting down clinics, as did Randall Terry of Operation Rescue. Terry had been hit by several civil damages lawsuits, and his group had to reorganize as Operation Rescue National in 1991. After mounting blockades at clinics conducting abortions in Wichita, Kansas, in the summer of 1991—resulting in over 2,500 arrests —Operation Rescue National staged a similar event in Buffalo, New York, in 1992, but the protests faded after a week in the face of arrests and counterdemonstrations.

The abortion issue seems to crystallize two opposing worldviews. Religious, ethnic, and class differences combine with conflicting definitions of gender roles, motherhood, family, and life-style to form persistent and opposed social movements. In the research of sociologist Kristin Luker, pro-choice women activists tend to be college educated, work outside the home at above-average incomes, and are more secular in orientation. Pro-life women activists, in contrast, tend to be less educated and more religious, are less likely to work outside the home, and tend to work for lower wages if they do; the idea of motherhood has a far more central meaning to their lives.

After the Court's *Webster* v. *Reproductive Health Services* decision in 1989, allowing states greater power to regulate abortion, momentum began to swing back to the pro-choice side. NARAL and the pro-choice movement support the Freedom of Choice Act, introduced in Congress in 1989, to write the protection of *Roe* into federal statutory law. In May 1991 the Supreme Court held in *Rust* v. *Sullivan* that administrative regulations for Title X of the Public Health Service Act can prohibit clinics receiving funds under the act from mentioning abortion when counseling patients (the so-called "gag rule"). In July 1992 the Supreme Court in *Planned Parenthood* v. *Casey* in effect upheld *Roe*, but stated that states may restrict abortion as long as they do not place an "undue burden" on a woman. Pro-choice advocates fear that one more conservative Supreme Court appointment would create a majority to reverse *Roe* v. *Wade* and return full control over abortion to the states. Beyond the *Roe* battles, pro-choice activists support testing and research on the French abortion pill, RU 486, which may have additional medical uses. According to statistics from the federal Centers for Disease Control, 1.39 million abortions were performed in the United States in 1989, a rate of 24 per 1,000 women ages fifteen to forty-four.

PLANNED PARENTHOOD FEDERATION OF AMERICA, INC.

810 SEVENTH AVENUE

NEW YORK, NY 10019

(212) 541-7800

FOUNDED: 1916   CONTRIBUTORS: 480,000
AFFILIATES: 171   BUDGET: $44.6 million
STAFF: 190   TAX STATUS: 501(c)(3): Planned
Parenthood Federation of America; 501(c)(4):
Planned Parenthood Action Fund

PURPOSE: "To assure that all individuals have the freedom to make reproductive decisions. . . . There should be access to information and services related to sexuality, reproduction, methods of contraception, fertility management and enhancement, and parenthood."

The Planned Parenthood Federation of America (PPFA) is the national federation of 171 local Planned Parenthood organizations providing birth control services and information. Since the 1970s, PPFA has been increasingly visible as an advocate for keeping abortion legal and pushing for international population control policies. As the voice of the largest network of birth control service providers and volunteers, PPFA has enormous clout, and has been a primary target of New Right conservatives and Catholic opponents of abortion and contraception.

BACKGROUND: Margaret Sanger (1879–1966) opened the nation's first birth control clinic in 1916 in Brooklyn; the clinic was promptly raided and shut down by the police under New York's 1873 "Comstock Law" forbidding the discussion and dissemination of birth control. In 1923, Sanger opened the Birth Control Clinical Research Bureau in New York for dispensing and studying the effectiveness of contraceptives under the supervision of a licensed physician.

The American Medical Association unanimously recognized birth control as an integral part of medical practice in 1937. Two years later the Birth Control League and Clinical Research Bureau merged to become the Birth Control Federation of America, Inc. The name was changed in 1942 to Planned Parenthood Federation of America. In 1972 the group established an international division, Family Planning International Assistance, which became the largest U.S. nongovernmental provider of family planning services in developing countries.

In 1973 the Supreme Court ruled on the constitutional right to abortion in *Roe* v. *Wade*. That same year the National Right to Life Committee formed with the goal of overturning *Roe*, creating fierce opposition to the work of Planned Parenthood. Faye Wattleton

was named president of PPFA in 1978, becoming the first woman since Margaret Sanger to head the organization— and the most prominent black woman executive in the nonprofit sector. Only thirty-four years old at the time, she was something of a controversial choice. Wattleton led PPFA into the fight to keep abortion legal, greatly expanding its advocacy stance. Not everyone agreed with this new focus, and in the restructuring following Wattleton's appointment, 60 percent of the staff quit or were replaced. Wattleton resigned as PPFA president in 1992, after fourteen years in the job, to become host of a television talk show dealing with women's issues.

One tactic in the New Right's fight against Planned Parenthood was a campaign to cut off corporate funding of PPFA's educational work. While prolifers led by the National Right to Life Committee, the American Life League, and the Christian Action Council succeeded in changing the funding patterns of some corporations such as J.C. Penney, some of their efforts backfired and overall the campaign was not greatly successful.

In 1989 PPFA joined hundreds of other groups in sponsoring the April 9 March for Women's Equality/Women's Lives, which drew 200,000 participants just before the Supreme Court was to hear the *Webster* case. After the Court's *Webster* decision giving states the right to limit abortions, PPFA launched its Campaign to Keep Abortion Safe and Legal, collecting 1.2 million signatures to present to Congress. For this campaign, the organization recruited more than 200 nationally recognized individuals from the arts, science, politics, entertainment, and religion for a National Leadership Committee. Members included Katherine Hepburn, Rosa Parks, and Julian Bond. In addition, PPFA collaborated with congressional leaders who introduced the Freedom of Choice Act, codifying the rights cited by the Supreme Court in *Roe* and prohibiting state restrictions on abortion before fetal viability.

In 1989 PPFA began efforts to educate the public to provide a supportive climate for the introduction of the French drug RU 486 to the American market. The pill, which is legal in France, shows potential to provide an effective alternative to surgical abortion during early pregnancy. U.S. drug companies are dragging their feet about marketing it in the United States due to the vocal New Right constituency which has threatened boycotts. PPFA has advocated comprehensive, age-appropriate sexuality education for all grades, with a special emphasis on educating young people to lower the high rate of adolescent pregnancy in this country. This program has drawn wide attack from groups on the right who criticize the dispersal to teens of Valentines with condoms enclosed.

CURRENT PRIORITIES: PPFA's 1989–93 Five Year Plan includes the following goals: to reduce teen pregnancy by increasing access to family planning education and services, to increase public understanding and comfort with sexuality, to ensure the widest possible choice of safe and effective methods of fertility management, to keep abortion safe and legal, and to promote reproductive freedom in developing countries.

PPFA recently brought two impor-

tant cases before the Supreme Court. The first was a case against the Reagan administration's 1987 gag rule, prohibiting Title X–funded clinics from counseling patients about the option of abortion and mandating that abortion clinics be housed in entirely separate buildings than those providing any other health services. The second was an appeal for a hearing of a case against the Reagan administration's 1985 "Mexico City policy" to bar nongovernmental foreign recipients of U.S. governmental aid from providing or counseling on abortion. PPFA's international affiliate has refused to abide by this rule, causing it to be stripped of grants from the U.S. Agency for International Development (AID).

STRUCTURE: In addition to the national office in New York, PPFA has a legislative and public information office in Washington, D.C., and regional offices in Atlanta, San Francisco, and Chicago. There are 171 Planned Parenthood affiliates, employing 26,000 volunteers and staff. The PPFA board of directors, 36 people in 1991, is elected by affiliate presidents and board members. Nominations are solicited for specific expertise, such as finance, communication, or education. The national nominating committee selects the final slate, consisting of representatives from all four regions. The election takes place at the annual membership meeting in October.

The 501(c)(4) Planned Parenthood Action Fund (PPAF) was established in 1989 to advocate public policies that guarantee individual choice and full access to reproductive health care; 25 local (c)(4)s are affiliated with PPAF.

PPFA has a close relationship with the Alan Guttmacher Institute, an independent 501(c)(3) organization originally affiliated with PPFA, for research, policy analysis, and public education on reproductive health issues. PPFA's international division, Family Planning International Assistance, has three international regional offices and two country offices. PPFA is a founding member of the International Planned Parenthood Federation, with affiliates in 125 countries.

RESOURCES: PPFA national office revenue was $44.6 million in 1990, and revenue of the 171 affiliates totaled $339.1 million. The total combined revenue of $383.7 million derived from government grants (36 percent), clinic income (35 percent), private contributions (23 percent), and other sources (6 percent). Total expenses of $368.4 million include patient services (57 percent), international programs (5 percent), other community and program services (15 percent), administration (14 percent), fund-raising (5 percent), and other payments (4 percent).

PUBLICATIONS AND SERVICES: PPFA publishes educational pamphlets and books. Planned Parenthood affiliates provide medical services to more than 2.7 million women, men, and teens at 911 clinic sites in forty-nine states and D.C. Services include contraception, pregnancy diagnosis, infertility diagnosis and treatment, prenatal care, voluntary sterilization, screening for cervical and breast cancers, abortion, and HIV testing and counseling. For the definitive biography of PPFA's founder, see Ellen Chesler, *Woman of Valor: Margaret Sanger and the Birth Control Movement in America* (Simon & Schuster, 1992). □

NATIONAL ABORTION RIGHTS ACTION LEAGUE

1101 14TH STREET, NW, 5TH FLOOR

WASHINGTON, DC 20005

(202) 408-4600

FOUNDED: 1969   MEMBERS: 300,000
STATE AFFILIATES: 40   BUDGET: $11.5 million
STAFF: 47   TAX STATUS: 501(c)(4): National
Abortion Rights Action League; 501(c)(3):
NARAL Foundation; PAC: NARAL PAC

PURPOSE: "Preserving a woman's right to legal abortion."

The political arm of the pro-choice movement, the National Abortion Rights Action League (NARAL) is the largest U.S. organization working exclusively for the right to legal abortion.

BACKGROUND: Founded in 1969 by Lawrence Lader and other abortion reformers as the National Association for the Repeal of Abortion Laws, NARAL changed its name after the Supreme Court's *Roe v. Wade* decision in 1973 overturned state antiabortion laws. NARAL moved its headquarters from New York to Washington in 1976, under the direction of Karen Mulhauser, to lobby against a legislative backlash as the opponents of abortion took the initiative. Congress and state legis- latures immediately began chipping away at the right to abortion, as regu- lated by trimester under the *Roe* deci- sion, by passing laws to eliminate government funding for abortions, im- pacting primarily poor women. Henry Hyde (R–New York) introduced his Hyde Amendment to federal legislation each year after 1976, cutting all federal support for abortions.

In 1980 Ronald Reagan swept into the presidency, aided by his appeal to the New Right's cultural agenda, which included strong opposition to abortion. NARAL and other pro-choice groups grew rapidly as supporters finally sensed the danger to abortion rights. Reagan gave lip service to a constitu- tional amendment outlawing abortion, but never made a serious effort to get it enacted.

Drawing a lesson from the Equal Rights Amendment campaign, which was defeated by conservatives at the state level, NARAL adopted a strategy to build affiliated organizations on the state level. In 1982 Nanette Falkenberg became executive director of NARAL and spearheaded the program to de- velop state affiliates and impact state legislatures. "I'm pro-choice and I vote" proclaimed a popular bumper sticker, part of the campaign to dem- onstrate the extensive political clout wielded by pro-choice voters.

In 1989 the Supreme Court, shifted to the right by Reagan appointees, up- held a Missouri case (*Webster* v. *Repro- ductive Health Services*) in which the state had sought to limit abortions. On April 9, a half-million women and men converged on Washington for a pro- choice rally. The Court sided with Mis-

souri in its *Webster* decision, and states were handed greater freedom to restrict abortions. Guam and Pennsylvania en- acted stiffer limitations. In 1990, 350 anti-choice bills were introduced in state legislatures, although most failed.

CURRENT PRIORITIES: NARAL's top priority is working in the states to pre- vent the loss of abortion rights and to elect pro-choice legislators. In the Con- gress, it continues efforts to restore and expand public funding for abortions. Facing a Supreme Court only one jus- tice away from overturning *Roe v. Wade*, NARAL supports the Freedom of Choice Act to protect *Roe* rights. A new struggle rests on efforts to make the drug RU 486 available to women in the United States. The French pill of- fers a medical alternative to surgical abortion and can be used outside the public eye after prescription by a doc- tor. The drug is available in other coun- tries, including France and China, but as of 1991, its manufacturer refused to export the drug to the United States due to threats by the Right of massive boy- cotts and liability lawsuits.

MEMBERS: NARAL membership has steadily increased, from 90,000 in 1980, to 150,000 in 1983 following the election of President Reagan, to 300,000 mem- bers of the national organization and another 200,000 members of state affil- iates by 1990, a year after the *Webster* decision. Volunteers in NARAL's state affiliates are trained in speaking skills, lobbying techniques, and the basics of electoral work at the local level. Lead- ership workshops are conducted for members taking positions in political campaigns.

STRUCTURE: The NARAL board is composed of twenty-four people who serve three-year terms, for a maximum of six years. Any member can seek nomination by petition or by nomination by another member. The Nominating Committee chooses a slate of candidates from these nominations for members to ratify by mail ballot. The NARAL Foundation, formed in 1977, has a seven-member board of directors. NARAL PAC was formed in 1976. Kate Michelman has served as executive director since 1986. The forty-eight affiliates (usually statewide) in thirty-nine states are independent nonprofit organizations with their own boards, budgets, and memberships.

RESOURCES: Following the *Webster* decision, revenue to the three NARAL entities nearly tripled, from $4.3 million in 1988 to $11.5 million in 1991. Most of NARAL's support—$8.6 million in 1991—comes from member contributions, with 63 percent spent for programs and 37 percent for administration and fund-raising. The NARAL Foundation received $2.1 million in revenue in 1991, from individuals and foundations; expenditures of $2 million were divided 77 percent for program services and 23 percent for administration and fund-raising. NARAL PAC raised $626,000 during the 1986 campaign cycle, $582,000 during the 1988 cycle, just over $1 million in the 1990 cycle, and anticipated raising $2 million in the 1992 campaign cycle.

PUBLICATIONS AND SERVICES: Membership begins at $20 and includes *NARAL News* (circulation 300,000) two to four times a year. The NARAL Foundation prints a variety of materials on the abortion issue. *Who Decides? A Reproductive Rights Issues Manual* outlines NARAL's position on several abortion-related issues from teenagers' access to fetal tissue research. *Who Decides? A State-by-State Review of Abortion Rights in America* catalogs the status of abortion rights in each state. *Who Decides? We Do, with Our Votes* is a candidate's campaign guide to abortion issues. NARAL's founding is described in Lawrence Lader, *Abortion II: Making the Revolution* (Beacon, 1973), chapter 7. □

NATIONAL RIGHT TO LIFE COMMITTEE

419 7TH STREET, NW, SUITE 500

WASHINGTON, DC 20004-2293

(202) 626-8800

FOUNDED: 1973   MEMBERS: 1.6 million in state affiliates   STATE AFFILIATES: 50 plus D.C. LOCAL CHAPTERS: 3,000   BUDGET: $11 million   STAFF: 40   TAX STATUS: 501(c)(4): National Right to Life Committee; 501(c)(3): National Right to Life Educational Trust Fund; PAC: National Right to Life PAC

PURPOSE: "To protect all innocent human life threatened by abortion, infanticide, and euthanasia."

The National Right to Life Committee (NRLC) opposes abortion, infanticide, and euthanasia, and is committed to building a broad coalition around these issues. NRLC speaks with a moderate voice, deploring violence toward abortion clinics and opposing the civil disobedience tactics used by groups like Operation Rescue to prevent women from entering clinics. NRLC seeks to change the legality of abortion by working within the law, restricting its activities to education, lobbying, and supporting candidates for elective office.

BACKGROUND: The National Right to Life Committee was founded in June 1973, five months after the Supreme Court decision legalizing abortion. Activists who had been working on the issue in various states came together in Detroit to charter a nonsectarian, nonpartisan group with a board of representatives elected from every state. The first board included members from the fields of medicine, constitutional law, religion, medical ethics, and science.

Proposals for a constitutional amendment to give rights to the unborn died in Congress in the early 1980s, due in part to the disunity of the right-to-life movement. NRLC has had some success on the national level in limiting abortions, including the Hyde Amendment, successfully reapproved every year since 1977, to cut off Medicaid funds for abortions. They have also won a federal "conscience clause" guaranteeing medical personnel the right to refuse to participate in abortion procedures and banning nontherapeutic experimentation on live aborted fetuses. NRLC opposed the Equal Rights Amendment, but stated they would not object if ERA were modified so that it would not secure or expand any right to abortion or abortion funding.

In 1985 NRLC brought out the highly emotional video of an abortion, *The Silent Scream,* which reached a large audience. The movie was created by Dr. Bernard Nathanson, a former abortionist who changed his views. Also in 1985, the group premiered its nationally syndicated five-minute radio program *Pro-Life Perspective,* a daily broadcast aired by over 300 stations. In April 1990, following the Supreme Court's *Webster* decision giving states the right to limit abortion rights, the right-to-life movement brought together over 200,000 marchers to Washington for an anti-abortion rally.

Controversy over the acceptable degree of political compromise has centered on the NRLC president and chief executive—initially Dr. Mildred Jefferson, a black Boston obstetrician. She was followed by Dr. John Willke, a physician active in the pro-life campaign from the early 1970s. Willke resigned in 1991 when faced with a coup by executive director David O'Steen and his associate Darla St. Martin, who won a board vote on appointing members to Phyllis Schlafly's National Republican Pro-Life Committee. Dr. Wanda Franz, NRLC vice president, was elected president.

CURRENT PRIORITIES: Priorities for the organization continue to be pro-life education, political action, and legislation. While abortion is the primary interest of NRLC, it also opposes euthanasia, genetic engineering (including in vitro fertilization), and infanticide. Due to the widely divergent views of its members, NRLC takes no stand on such related issues as nuclear weapons, capital punishment, and birth control. In 1992 NRL PAC endorsed the reelection campaign of Republican President George Bush.

MEMBERS: NRLC serves as an umbrella organization for its 51 affiliates and nearly 4,000 associated chapters in the United States. NRLC estimates total affiliates' membership to be 1.6 million.

STRUCTURE: Local chapters send representatives to the board of directors of the state affiliates. The NRLC board of directors consists of one director from each state, elected by the state affiliate. Three at-large directors are elected annually by the membership. The executive committee consists of the officers and nine members selected by the board. David O'Steen is executive director.

RESOURCES: NRLC has an annual budget of $11 million, with a majority of revenue received from individual donors. NRLC receives contributions from direct mail and through the Combined Federal Campaign. Once heavily dependent on contributions from Catholics and the Catholic church, NRLC now has a wider base of support. NRL PAC raised $1.8 million in the 1986 campaign cycle, $1.9 million in the 1988 cycle, and $1.5 million in the 1990 cycle.

PUBLICATIONS AND SERVICES: NRLC publishes a biweekly newspaper, *The National Right to Life News*, which has 220,000 subscribers at $16 a year; books and materials are available for purchase. NRLC maintains a legislative update recording: (202) 393-LIFE. □

GAY AND LESBIAN RIGHTS

Although a Chicago Society for Human Rights was founded in 1924 to support homosexual rights, the United States had nothing comparable to the organized homosexual movement that developed in Germany in the 1920s. A social base for the gay movement developed after World War II, when many returning gay soldiers and sailors stayed on in large coastal cities like New York, Los Angeles, and San Francisco. The contemporary gay rights movement dates from the founding of the Mattachine Society in 1951 by Harry Hay (a Communist party member who was promptly expelled), who developed the theory that gays are an oppressed cultural minority. *ONE Magazine* was started by associates of Hay's in Los Angeles in 1952, and the first lesbian organization, Daughters of Bilitis, was founded in San Francisco in 1955.

The development of a political gay movement was influenced by the growing militancy of the black civil rights movement, the peace movement, and the women's liberation movement in the late 1960s. The June 1969 "Stonewall riot" in New York's Greenwich Village marked the public emergence of a militant gay rights movement. A Gay Liberation Front was active in New York in the early 1970s. In the liberal political mainstream, gays and lesbians organized the Alice B. Toklas Memorial Democratic Club in San Francisco in 1971. As gays clustered in San Francisco's Castro district, Harvey Milk realized he had an electoral base, and was elected a county supervisor as the country's first openly gay elected official in 1977 —and became a martyr assassinated together with Mayor George Moscone in 1979 by fellow supervisor Dan White. San Francisco's Gay Freedom Day parades drew large numbers in the late 1970s, and the first National March on Washington for Lesbian and Gay Rights was held in October 1979—in part a response to the New Right campaign against gay rights led at that time by singer Anita Bryant, and against California's Briggs Initiative (defeated that fall).

The movement has developed a set of national lobbying and legal defense groups as well as a political action committee: A national lobby was organized in 1973 as the National Gay Task Force ("and Lesbian" was added in 1985, making NGLTF); and the Human Rights Campaign Fund (HRCF) began in 1980 as a PAC, but reorganized as a lobby with an associated PAC in 1989. These and other gay organizations have had substantial success in getting sodomy laws repealed in about half the states. The Lambda Legal Defense and Education Fund was established in New York in 1973 on the NAACP LDF model to litigate issues of gay rights. A West Coast counterpart, National Gay Rights Advocates (NGRA) in San Francisco, closed in 1990 because of financial debts.

As the AIDS epidemic spread during the 1980s, much activist energy was channeled into support structures—pioneered by New York's Gay Men's Health Crisis—for people infected with the HIV virus. ACT UP (AIDS Coalition to Unleash Power) was formed in New York by gay writer and activist Larry Kramer to make militant demands for medical research, rapid release of experimental drugs, and provision of services to people with HIV. Autonomous ACT UP groups sprang up around the country, inspiring a parallel Queer Nation movement flaunting the slogan, "We're here, we're queer, get used to it!"

N A T I O N A L

NGLTF

GAY & LESBIAN
TASK   FORCE

**NATIONAL GAY AND LESBIAN
TASK FORCE**

1734 14TH STREET, NW

WASHINGTON, DC 20009

(202) 332-6483

FOUNDED: 1973   MEMBERS: 18,000
BUDGET: $1.2 million   STAFF: 15
TAX STATUS: 501(c)(4): National Gay and
Lesbian Task Force; 501(c)(3): NGLTF Policy
Institute

PURPOSE: "To create a society where
lesbians and gay men can live openly,
free from violence, bigotry and discrimination."

The National Gay and Lesbian Task
Force (NGLTF) is the leading national
membership organization advocating
for the civil rights of gays and lesbians.
NGLTF uses lobbying, grassroots organizing, public education, and direct action.

BACKGROUND: The National Gay Task
Force was organized in November 1973
in New York by seven lesbian and gay
activists. Early victories included getting the American Psychiatric Association to revise its classification of
homosexuality as an illness; encouraging resolutions of support for gay rights
from such groups as the National Council of Churches, NOW, and the ACLU;
and obtaining a Civil Service Commission ruling that homosexuals can serve
as federal employees. Task Force staff
helped arrange the first meeting of

openly gay and lesbian leaders at the
White House with President Carter's
special assistant Midge Costanza in
1977. Later that year Task Force
women secured official endorsement of
lesbian and gay rights at the federally
sponsored National Women's Conference in Houston. The Task Force's
focus in its first years was visibility; its
message, "We are everywhere."

Under Virginia Apuzzo, executive director from 1982 to 1985, the Task
Force tackled antigay violence and
opened a Washington, D.C., lobbying
office, staffed initially by Mel Boozer
and later by Jeff Levi, who became executive director in 1985. The Task
Force began work on AIDs policy issues
in 1983. In 1985 the National Gay Task
Force added "and Lesbian" to its title,
to affirm its commitment to lesbian issues. The NGLTF headquarters moved
from New York to Washington in 1986.

CURRENT PRIORITIES: NGLTF activity
concentrates on five areas: (1) *the anti-
violence project*, to stop street violence
and other harassment against gays and
lesbians through police protection and
enforcement of laws against hate
crimes; (2) *the privacy/civil rights project*; (3) *the lesbian and gay families
project*, which seeks family rights and
benefits for gay and lesbian couples; (4)
the campus project, to support students
in colleges and universities; and (5) *the
military freedom initiative*, to secure
the rights of gays in the armed services.

MEMBERS: NGLTF has 18,000 members, about two-thirds of whom are
men. The annual "Creating Change
Conference," held in November over
the Veterans Day weekend, builds the

grassroots network and trains activists in organizing and advocacy skills.

STRUCTURE: NGLTF has a twenty-four-member board of directors, cochaired by Susan Allee and Curtis Shepard; members are elected for a three-year term by vote of the entire membership. Bylaws require gender parity on the board, and 20 percent representation of lesbians and gays of color. NGLTF is a member of the International Lesbian and Gay Association, an international human rights group headquartered in Brussels. After eight years with NGLTF, Urvashi Vaid resigned as executive director at the end of 1992. Torie Osborn, formerly director of a Los Angeles gay and lesbian service center, takes over as NGLTF executive director in March 1993.

RESOURCES: NGLTF's revenue of $1.2 million in 1991 was derived 35 percent from membership dues, 21 percent from individual donations, and 44 percent from grants, special events, conferences, and sales. Expenditures of $1.2 million included 66 percent for programs, 17 percent for fund-raising, and 17 percent for administration, In 1987 NGLTF retired a burden of long-term debt of $90,000.

PUBLICATIONS AND SERVICES: Membership begins at $35 and includes the quarterly newsletter, *Task Force Report*. NGLTF issues an annual report card on the votes of members of Congress. ☐

CAMPAIGN FUND

HUMAN RIGHTS CAMPAIGN FUND

1012 14TH STREET, NW, SUITE 607

WASHINGTON, DC 20005

(202) 628-4160

FOUNDED: 1980   MEMBERS: 37,000
BUDGET: $4.5 million   STAFF: 26
TAX STATUS: 501(c)(4): Human Rights
Campaign Fund; 501(c)(3): Triangle Institute;
PAC: Human Rights Campaign Fund PAC

SLOGAN: "Mobilizing power to make progress."

The Human Rights Campaign Fund (HRCF) is the largest political fund-raising organization for the gay and lesbian community. Launched as a political action committee, HRCF now includes a powerful lobbying and advocacy program as well.

BACKGROUND: HRCF was organized in 1980 as a political action committee, providing financial support for candidates for the U.S. Senate and House, Democrats and Republicans, who pledge to support gay civil rights legislation. In 1986 HRCF absorbed the Gay Rights National Lobby, which had been formed in 1976 for congressional advocacy. In 1989 HRCF became a 501(c)(4) advocacy organization, to complement its PAC contributions with an aggressive lobbying, education, and grassroots mobilization program. Crucial victories for gay and lesbian interests have included the Americans with Disabilities Act, language concerning the

National Endowment for the Arts, immigration law reform, and the Hate Crimes Statistics Act—all during the 101st Congress in 1990. In 1992 HRCF made its first presidential endorsement, supporting Democratic candidate Bill Clinton.

CURRENT PRIORITIES: HRCF has worked on four primary concerns: (1) legislation to protect gays and lesbians from discrimination in employment, housing, and public accommodations; (2) adequate federal funding for AIDS research and treatment; (3) reform of immigration laws that prohibit homosexuals from entering the country; and (4) ending the exclusion of gays and lesbians from military service.

MEMBERS: HRCF became a membership organization with its reorganization in 1989. Members can participate in the "Speak Out" program, which targets messages prepared by HRCF staff to key members of Congress on major legislative issues. More than 65,000 supporters have participated and over 350,000 letters have been sent since the beginning of the program in 1989. Total membership, at 37,000 in early 1992, is expected to grow substantially as most contributors and "Speak Out" participants are converted to members as they renew. Major donor groups, called "Federal Clubs," are established in a dozen large cities. Dinner galas in seventeen major cities are important fundraisers.

STRUCTURE: HRCF has a twenty-one-member board of directors, elected by the members to serve three-year terms. A board of governors, composed of two representatives from each of HRCF's major cities, serves as an advisory group. Tim McFeeley, an attorney and fund-raiser from Boston, has been executive director since 1989.

RESOURCES: HRCF's revenue of $4.5 million in 1991 was derived from special events, major donors, and direct-mail appeals. As a political action committee, HRCF raised $1.5 million over the 1986 campaign cycle, and $2.3 million over the 1990 cycle. In the 1990 campaign, HRCF PAC raised $561,000 and contributed to 121 House races (winning all but 16) and 12 Senate races (winning all but 2), with contributions going 18 percent to women, 16 percent to candidates of color, and 17 percent to Republicans. HRCF PAC's budget for the 1992 campaign cycle was $1 million.

PUBLICATIONS AND SERVICES: Membership begins at $13 and includes the quarterly newsletter *Momentum.* A computer bulletin board, HRCF NET, contains weekly legislative bulletins, updates on AIDS issues, and conferences at (202) 639-8735. □

LAMBDA LEGAL DEFENSE AND EDUCATION FUND, INC.

666 BROADWAY, 12TH FLOOR

NEW YORK, NY 10012

(212) 995-8585

FOUNDED: 1973   CONTRIBUTORS: 20,000
BUDGET: $1.8 million   STAFF: 22
TAX STATUS: 501(c)(3)

PURPOSE: "To advance the rights of lesbians and gay men through test-case litigation and to educate the public, the legal profession, and the government about discrimination based on sexual orientation."

Lambda Legal Defense and Education Fund is the oldest and largest public interest law firm dedicated to defending the civil rights of lesbians and gay men, and is active in cases across the country.

BACKGROUND: Depending largely on volunteered services for its first decade, Lambda scored a major victory in 1983 when it won the first AIDS discrimination case, representing a physician who treated people living with AIDS who was evicted from his building; the ruling applied disability law protection to people living with AIDS—a precedent that has been affirmed by thirty-four states. Lambda also represented Naval Academy midshipman Joe Steffan, who was forced to resign from the Academy six weeks before graduation because he stated he was gay.

CURRENT PRIORITIES: Although Lambda fights all forms of discrimination against lesbians and gay men, it has emphasized AIDS-related issues and discrimination against people with HIV. Other concerns include domestic partner benefits, family relationships, hate-motivated violence, sodomy statutes, and immigration rights. The annual Lambda Liberty Award is presented on the anniversary of the passage in 1986 of New York City's prohibiting discrimination on account of sexual orientation.

STRUCTURE: Lambda has a twenty-six-member, self-recruiting board of directors, with Carol Buell and David Hollander serving as cochairs. After six years as executive director, Thomas Stoddard resigned in 1992; Kevin Cathcart, former director of Gay and Lesbian Advocates and Defenders (GLAD) in Boston, was named Lambda's new executive director. In 1990 Lambda opened an office in Los Angeles, headed by attorney Mary Newcombe; since the closing of San Francisco's National Gay Rights Advocates in 1990, Lambda has had a larger role to play on the West Coast.

RESOURCES: From its founding in 1973 through 1985, Lambda was a shoestring operation, with an income in 1983 of $53,000, rising to $309,000 in 1985. But by 1987, income had risen to over $1.1 million, and the value of donated legal services has increased from $475,000 in 1989 to $700,000 in 1990. Lambda's income of $1.2 million in 1990 was received from individuals (34 percent), donated legal services (38 percent), foundations (9 percent), bequests (8 percent), and other revenue (11 percent). Expenses of $1.1 million went for program services (74 percent), administration (15 percent), and fund-raising (11 percent). Lambda's 1992 budget was $1.8 million. Some 200 contributors give $1,500 or more a year.

PUBLICATIONS AND SERVICES: Contributors of $30 or more receive the quarterly newsletter *Lambda Update*. *AIDS Update* is published bimonthly. An annual report is available. □

6.

AGE AND
ABILITY

Caring for the needs of elders, children, widows, and the disabled has long been a concern of churches, charities, and benevolent associations. Only with the massive poverty of the Depression in the 1930s did the federal government move beyond the patchwork of state, local, and private programs to establish a national system of income support for older people, children, and the disabled through the Social Security Act. The emphasis remained, however, on the administration of programs and the provision of services by social workers and related helping professions. The civil rights movement of the 1960s had an energizing effect beyond people of color, women, and gays. Citizen lobbies for elders, children, and people with disabilities took up the language of rights, encouraging constituencies to organize on their own behalf. We've been forced to rethink our assumptions about age and ability, revising our language in the process, to add concepts like ageism and ableism.

ELDERS

The first social movements oriented toward elders developed in the 1930s during the Depression. Although aimed at the general population, Upton Sinclair's End Poverty in California (EPIC) movement attracted many older people among its half-million members by its pension program proposal. After Sinclair's defeat in the 1934 gubernatorial election, many older EPIC followers joined Dr. Francis Townsend's movement. The Townsend Plan for a monthly pension of $200 funded by sales taxes built a national membership of 1.5 million by 1936—which melted away after the Social Security Act passed in 1935, establishing the Old Age and Survivors Insurance (OASI) and Old Age Assistance programs. George McClain led a rival McClain Movement, which started in California as an offshoot of Robert Noble's "Ham and Eggs" organization and its effort to pass a state referendum for elders' benefits in 1938. McClain developed a California and a National League of Senior Citizens, which faded away in the 1940s.

Concerned with their own schemes, neither the Townsend Plan nor the McClain Movement was a significant force behind the enactment of Social Security in 1935, which was designed by professional social insurance reformers as part of Roosevelt's New Deal response to massive unemployment and poverty during the Depression. The Social Security Act wrapped together legislation that established public assistance programs, unemployment insurance, and retirement insurance. Labor unions were busy with industrial organizing drives in the mid-1930s, and many union leaders still looked to win retirement and other benefits primarily through collective bargaining. Consequently labor was not a central force behind the enactment of Social Security in 1935. Labor quickly accepted Social Security Act provisions, and unions became a leading force behind subsequent amendments, particularly Medicare and Medicaid in 1965. The National Council of Senior Citizens was established in 1961 as the advocacy arm of retired union members, specifically with the campaign for Medicare in mind. The enactment of Medicare and Medicaid (Titles XVIII and XIX of the Social Security Act) was a big victory over the American Medical Association, which opposed the legislation.

The increasing longevity and relative wealth of older people have greatly augmented their political clout. From 4 million people over sixty-five in 1890 (4 percent of the population), their number has grown to 29 million in 1990 (12 percent of a population of nearly 250 million). With the baby boom in retirement by the year 2030, 1 in every 5 U.S. residents will be over sixty-five. The American Association of Retired Persons (AARP), now the largest of all nonprofit membership groups, grew from an association to get insurance for retired teachers to a lobbying powerhouse in just two decades. The Gray Panthers, although a much smaller organization, symbolizes the growing activism of elders. The National Committee to Preserve Social Security and Medicare, a creation of the direct-mail industry, joined the elders' lobby in 1983 and—in response to widespread criticism—recently hired a substantial lobbying staff.

The 1961 White House Conference on Aging highlighted the problems of adequate health care, social services, and nursing home care facing the elderly. The Older Americans Act of 1965 established the federal Administration on Aging and a nation-wide network of Area Agencies on Aging; nutrition amendments of 1972 added programs to feed older people. Civil rights of older people were also written into legislation: Age discrimination in employment was made illegal in 1967, and the age for mandatory retirement was raised to 70 in 1978 and eliminated for most workers in 1986. Catastrophic health insurance under Medicare passed in 1988, but ran into a fire storm of criticism for its extra tax bite on the more affluent elderly and was repealed.

Public programs for elders have worked: Older people in America are better off than ever before. Where one in three elderly Americans lived below the poverty line as recently as 1960, only one in nine did in 1990. But well-being is not equally distributed—rates of poverty among black and other minority elderly are much higher. Thus our media stereotypes of elders range from "greedy geezers" playing golf to impoverished widows eating dog food.

Health care for elders remains a major issue, particularly nursing care and catastrophic illness insurance. And at a time when more than thirty-seven million people in the United States lack any health care coverage—while we spend more per capita than in any other country on health care—dealing with health care becomes a problem to be solved for the whole population. While some groups like Americans for Generational Equity argue that the share of national income going to the elderly is too high, others like Families USA are trying to find an intergenerational compromise that provides for elders while lifting the burden of poverty from younger generations as well.

Computer-using elders can join SeniorNet (399 Arguello Boulevard, San Francisco, CA 94118; (415) 750-5030), a national electronic network with E-mail, bulletin boards, conferences, and other services.

AMERICAN ASSOCIATION OF RETIRED PERSONS

601 E STREET, NW

WASHINGTON, DC 20049

(202) 434-2277

FOUNDED: 1958   MEMBERS: 33 million
CHAPTERS: 4,000   BUDGET: $307 million
STAFF: 1,200   TAX STATUS: 501(c)(3)

PURPOSE: "To enhance the quality of life for older persons; to promote independence, dignity, and purpose for older persons; to lead in determining the role and place of older persons in society; and to improve the image of aging."

The American Association of Retired Persons (AARP) stands in a class by itself. Take its tremendous size: AARP has twice the membership of the AFL-CIO and has become the second largest organization in the United States, after the Catholic church. AARP has the political clout of the proverbial 800-pound gorilla, but advocacy is almost a sideline. AARP sells insurance, prescription drugs, and financial services to its members. Its membership journal, *Modern Maturity*, is the largest circulation magazine in the country.

BACKGROUND: Ethel Percy Andrus, a retired high school principal, was having difficulty obtaining health insurance, and realized other retired people suffered the same problems. She founded AARP in 1958 to assist older people and provide various services including health insurance. Persons over fifty-five could become members by paying only $5 and spouses could join for free (in 1983 the minimum age was reduced to fifty and in 1992 annual dues were increased to $8). Insurance agent Leonard Davis created the Colonial Penn Group in 1963 to take over the AARP insurance business. AARP survived Andrus's death in 1967, and by 1978 claimed ten million members and became the subject of a *60 Minutes* television exposé, which accused it of being little more than a front for the insurance company. Although AARP reorganized and put the insurance business up for bid in 1979 (Prudential won), controversy continued. Was it a business or a nonprofit agency? AARP insisted it started business activities only when the market was not filling a need. Business representatives continued to question its tax-exempt status.

AARP services expanded from the sale of health insurance to include the sale of home and auto insurance, prescription drugs, and mutual funds. The organization also operates a travel service and a motor club. To provide these services, AARP works in partnership with private enterprises, receiving royalty income. Prudential provides the health insurance, the Hartford Insurance Group the auto and home insurance, Retired Persons Services the pharmacy services, Amoco the motor club, Olson-Travelworld and RFD Travel the travel service, and Scudder Stevens and Clark the mutual funds.

By 1988 AARP had emerged as a formidable national lobbying force. Since 1900, the nation's population as a whole has tripled while the number of seniors has grown eightfold. Almost half belong to AARP. Seniors cast about 20 percent of all votes in presidential elections. During the 1988 presidential elections, AARP videotaped an hour discussion on long-term affordable health care with Democratic presidential hopefuls Richard Gephardt and Michael Dukakis, then paid to air it just before the "Super Tuesday" primary elections. AARP lobbied for the passage of the catastrophic health insurance bill approved by Congress in 1988 and later revoked in the face of massive protest. The bill would have provided catastrophic care for seniors, but not long-term care. It was to be financed completely by an increased Medicare tax on higher-income seniors—the issue most hotly criticized.

CURRENT PRIORITIES: AARP's number-one priority continues to be retirement income security. Health care reform is a second major concern. After the failure of the catastrophic health care bill,

the group put out tentative support for some type of national health care for all ages. In 1991 AARP was rethinking its position on the issue of national health insurance, holding forums on the issue and trying to feel out the opinions of its diverse membership.

MEMBERS: With dues of only $5 and free membership for spouses, AARP's numbers have grown phenomenally, from 1 million members in 1975 to over 33 million in 1991. Each day some 8,000 new members join. A 1985 survey showed 39 percent of the members to be between the ages of fifty and sixty-four, and 61 percent over sixty-five. Half the people in the United States age sixty-five and over are members. Some 400,000 members volunteer for the organization through the 4,000 chapters on the local and state levels.

STRUCTURE: AARP has a 21-person board of directors, made up of 15 members and 6 officers. Board members are elected by AARP members who attend the biennial conventions, in classes of five for six-year staggered terms. Officers are also elected at the conventions. Terms range from two years for secretary and treasurer to eight years for the vice president, who will follow a two-year term as vice president with two years as president-elect, two years as president, and two years as former president. Cyril Brickfield served as executive director from 1975 to 1987, during the period of AARP's great expansion. Jack Carlson, from the Chamber of Commerce of the United States lasted fifteen weeks in the job, and was replaced by Brickfield's assistant Horace Deets, executive director since 1988. AARP has a policy think tank, the Public Policy Institute, and a voter education arm, AARP/VOTE (not a PAC). There are 900 staff in AARP's Washington, D.C., headquarters, and another 300 employees in the publications office in Long Beach, California, 10 regional offices, and 2 state offices. On the local level there are some 3,600 chapters.

RESOURCES: AARP's $297 million revenue in 1991 included $100 million (34 percent) from membership dues, $82 million (27 percent) from group insurance administrative allowances, $41 million (14 percent) from publication advertising, $30 million (10 percent) in program income and royalties, and $44 million (15 percent) in interest. Expenditures of $307 million include $105 million (34 percent) for publications, $61 million (20 percent) for programs and field services, $22 million (7 percent) for legislation, research, and development, $60 million (20 percent) for member services and acquisition, $39 million (13 percent) for activities and facilities administration, and $20 million (6 percent) for headquarters operation. AARP had an operating surplus of $32 million in 1987, $34 million in 1988, and $14.5 million in 1990—but ran a loss of $9.5 million in 1991. AARP had a fund balance of $115 million in 1991.

PUBLICATIONS AND SERVICES: AARP members receive the magazine *Modern Maturity* six times a year. With 22.5 million copies mailed, it has the largest circulation of any magazine in the country, surpassing *Reader's Digest* in 1988 and *TV Guide* in 1989. *AARP Bulletin*, a newsletter, is published eleven times a year to inform members of political and topical developments; an annual financial report is included in the July/August issue. *Highlights* is a bimonthly newsletter with information on AARP programs and resources. AARP provides a wealth of services, including an investment program, a travel service, a pharmacy service, a motor club, as well as health, auto, and home insurance. AARP also administers two federal job training and placement programs. And yes, there is an AARP Visa card. □

NATIONAL COUNCIL OF SENIOR CITIZENS

1331 F STREET, NW

WASHINGTON, DC 20004

(202) 347-8800

FOUNDED: 1961   MEMBERS: 300,000
CLUBS: 5,000   BUDGET: $77.7 million
STAFF: 120   TAX STATUS: 501(c)(4): National Council of Senior Citizens; 501(c)(3)s: NCSC Housing Management Corporation; NCSC Education and Research Center;
PAC: NCSC PAC

PURPOSE: "Human dignity for people of all ages."

The National Council of Senior Citizens (NCSC) is the lobbying arm of retired members of a dozen AFL-CIO unions. A major force behind the enactment of Medicare, NCSC maintains a strong presence on Capitol Hill, and administers employment and housing programs for seniors.

BACKGROUND: NCSC was organized in Detroit in 1961, with leadership from the United Auto Workers and the United Steelworkers, as the labor movement geared up to fight for the Medicare amendments to Social Security, finally enacted in 1965. At the time, the American Association of Retired Persons did not have a strong commitment to lobby for legislation. In addition to Medicare, NCSC helped win regular Social Security cost-of-living adjustments (COLAs), the conversion of welfare programs for the elderly and disabled to the Supplemental Security Income program, Medicaid health benefits for the poor, and expansion of the Food Stamp program. Appropriately enough, NCSC staff work in a union shop, represented by the Office and Professional Employees International Union.

NCSC has administered the Senior AIDES program since 1968, with funds from the Department of Labor, training and employing people fifty-five or older with limited incomes for twenty hours a week in such community service jobs as day care or teacher aides and paralegal work. There are 150 Senior AIDES projects in twenty-seven states and D.C., employing an average of 10,300 people. NCSC's Senior Community Service Employment Program employs another 10,000 persons at or near the poverty level. The Environmental Protection Agency funds NCSC's Senior Environmental Employment Program, which hires older men and women to work at EPA offices throughout the country. The NCSC Housing Manage-

ment Corporation manages thirty low-income housing buildings, with over 3,300 units and more under construction.

CURRENT PRIORITIES: Health care has always been a leading concern for NCSC, and its top priority is a national health care program. Maintaining Medicare benefits and federal regulation of "Medigap" insurance policies are also primary concerns. Defending Social Security benefits, pension plan protection, and housing for the elderly remain perennial concerns.

MEMBERS: Membership is provided along with retirement benefits for members of the Auto Workers, Steelworkers, and certain other unions, although others may join as well for dues of $10. There are around 300,000 national dues-paying members, and an estimated 5 million members in the 5,000 local clubs. Key leaders and activists receive "Legislative Updates" and "Seniorgrams" to help promote the NCSC agenda.

STRUCTURE: NCSC has a board of directors of some 150 people, including at-large and regional representatives, elected at the national conference held every four years. A 20-person executive committee coordinates oversight between meetings of the board. Lawrence Smedley is executive director.

RESOURCES: NCSC had revenue of $79.6 million in 1991, of which $71.7 million (90 percent) was in government grants and contracts, $2.5 million (3 percent) was in dues and contributions, and $5.4 million was in other revenue (7 percent). Expenses of $77.6 million included $71.3 million (92 percent) in government contract expenditures, $1 million (1 percent) for membership development, and $4.2 million (5 percent) for administration, and the remainder for other expenses. NCSC PAC raised $600,000 in the 1986 campaign cycle, $473,000 in the 1988 cycle, and contributed $115,000 to candidates in the 1990 campaign cycle.

PUBLICATIONS AND SERVICES: Membership is $10 and includes *Senior Citizen News* (circulation 300,000) monthly, with information on programs and legislative issues; an annual *Congressional Voting Record* is published as a special supplement. The *Retirement Newsletter* is mailed by pension funds along with checks to 12,000 retirees. NCSC also offers supplemental health insurance, low-cost prescription drugs, and discounts on travel and car rentals. NCSC's Nursing Home Information Service provides a clearinghouse on long-term care facilities. NCSC's Legislative Hotline number is (202) 639-8513. □

GRAY PANTHERS PROJECT FUND

1424 16TH STREET, NW

WASHINGTON, DC 20036

(202) 387-3111

FOUNDED: 1970   MEMBERS: 30,000

LOCAL NETWORKS: 65   BUDGET: $325,000

STAFF: 3   TAX STATUS: 501(c)(3)

PURPOSE: "We work for economic justice for persons of all ages and oppose ageism, racism, and sexism, which stereotype and stigmatize."

"Age and youth in action" is the motto of the Gray Panthers, an intergenerational approach that embodies the organization's commitment to a society not defined by age. National convener Maggie Kuhn—the "wrinkled radical," as a biographical film called her—has captured media attention with her soft-spoken manner and persuasive oratory. Currently responding to a financial crisis, the Gray Panthers are attempting to frame a new partnership with the local networks.

BACKGROUND: When Maggie Kuhn turned sixty-five, she was forced to retire from the staff of the Presbyterian church. Angry, she and five friends wrote a manifesto announcing their determination to continue participating fully in society. After reading this call, seventy-five people came to a meeting at Columbia University, where they chose the Vietnam War as their first activist issue, calling themselves the Consultation of Older and Younger Adults. With the militant Black Panthers in mind, a television reporter coined the nickname "Gray Panthers." The press loved it, and the name stuck.

The Gray Panthers published *Nursing Homes: A Citizen's Action Guide* in 1977, detailing substandard conditions. Senate hearings that followed led to improved nursing home regulations. In 1978 they helped win the passage of a law changing the mandatory retirement age from sixty-five to seventy. They persuaded the National Association of

Broadcasters to amend its code of ethics, adding age to race and sex as areas of possible bias to guard against in TV programming. The Gray Panthers Media Watch Project cautions against stereotypical portrayals of elders or young people on TV.

During the 1980s, Gray Panthers fought for the maintenance of Social Security benefits, under attack by the Reagan administration. The campaign for a national health care system stayed at the top of the list of the Panthers' priorities into the 1990s. On the issue of catastrophic illness, the Gray Panthers opposed legislation supported by the American Association of Retired Persons as not comprehensive enough and not covering disabled people or the young.

By 1991 the Gray Panthers were in an organizational and financial crisis—income had dropped by half. In 1992 Jule Sugarman, a veteran advocate for children and human services, was asked to work as interim executive director and help devise new by-laws to formalize relationships with the local networks. The former board of directors resigned, and a national convention was held in November to ratify the new charter.

CURRENT PRIORITIES: The Gray Panthers organization has six priority issues: (1) a national health care system, (2) federal support for affordable housing, (3) reduced military spending, (4) a safe and clean environment, (5) economic and social justice, and (6) anti-discrimination (including the elimination of ageism, sexism, and racism).

MEMBERS: Membership grew from 1970 through the mid-1980s. Since 1988, local chapters have declined even as members-at-large increased. There are 30,000 national members. One-third of the members are under age thirty-five.

STRUCTURE: In 1992 the board of directors was reorganized to include twelve members nominated and elected from five regions. Four additional directors are elected by the board, and the national convener and the past chairperson also serve, for a total of eighteen directors. The Gray Panthers moved its headquarters from Kuhn's hometown of Philadelphia to Washington in 1990, to be closer to Congress and to other organizations with which it works in coalition. Maggie Kuhn continues to serve as national convener. Local networks are independent organizations and must apply for recognition as affiliated groups; they have a great deal of autonomy in choosing programs for action.

RESOURCES: The Gray Panthers' $325,000 revenue comes primarily from individual contributions and membership dues. The organization administers an endowment of $750,000 from the estate of Margaret Mahler, a child psychiatrist from New York, for grants to scholars over age seventy to work on issues addressed by the Gray Panthers.

PUBLICATIONS AND SERVICES: Membership is $20 and includes local network affiliation and the quarterly newspaper *Network* (circulation 30,000). For background see *No Stone Unturned: The Life and Times of Maggie Kuhn*, by Maggie Kuhn with Christina Long and Laura Quinn (Ballantine Books, 1991). □

CHILDREN

Since the establishment of the Children's Bureau in 1912, the federal government has played a role in the welfare of children. Children's Bureau director Julia Lathrop issued a report in 1917 calling for federal aid to the states for public health programs covering maternity and infancy. Jeannette Rankin, the first woman elected to Congress, introduced a maternal and child health bill in 1918, and a version passed in 1921 as the Sheppard-Towner Act. Attacked as a Communist plot against the family by extreme conservatives and opposed by the American Medical Association, the legislation lapsed in 1928, to be revived with the New Deal.

In an era when one-sixth of children over ten worked for wages, child labor became a central concern of social reformers. Many states enacted legislation to give some protection to children, such as limiting them to a ten-hour day. The National Child Labor Committee proposed a child labor amendment to the Constitution, which passed the Congress in 1914, but ratification by the states was blocked by an alliance between manufacturers and farmers spearheaded by the southern textile industry. During Roosevelt's New Deal, the Fair Labor Standards Act incorporated provisions regulating child labor, and the child labor amendment was not revived.

Social Security's Survivor's Insurance and Aid to Dependent Children (ADC) programs were designed to provide income support to widows with children. The ADC welfare component was expanded to describe families (AFDC) and include state options for unemployed parents. As the program expanded, more efforts were made to link participation with education and job training for mothers. During the 1960s the civil rights movement and the war on poverty brought a new focus on poor children, with such programs as Project Head Start, the Youth Corps, and neighborhood youth employment programs. The Women, Infants and Children (WIC) Program provided a national focus on maternal and child health and nutrition.

The dimensions of children in poverty are dismaying: Twelve million children (one child in five) in the United States live in poverty. Nearly one black child in two is poor—although the majority of poor children are white (one in seven white children is poor). One in five children has no health insurance coverage. More than half the children who live in female-headed families are poor, and families headed by women make up 53 percent of all poor families. The United States may be the first industrial society to take better care of its elders than its children.

Advocacy for children has long been the domain of professional organizations of social workers and child welfare workers, from the American Humane Association to the Child Welfare League of America. With roots in the civil rights movement, the Children's Defense Fund has emerged as the leading public interest advocate for children, with a citizen constituency beyond child welfare professionals. Child advocates are beginning to organize citizen lobbies on the state level, like California's Children Now. On the international level, the United Nations adopted the Convention on the Rights of the Child in 1989, a treaty document with roots in the 1924 World Child Welfare Charter of the League of Nations and the 1959 U.N. Declaration of the Rights of the Child.

CHILDREN'S DEFENSE FUND

25 E STREET, NW

WASHINGTON, DC 20001

(202) 628-8787

FOUNDED: 1973   CONTRIBUTORS: 10,000
BUDGET: $9 million   STAFF: 115
TAX STATUS: 501(c)(3)

PURPOSE: "To provide a strong and effective voice for the children of America, who cannot vote, lobby or speak out for themselves . . . (with) particular attention to the needs of poor, minority, and disabled children."

The Children's Defense Fund (CDF) is the nation's foremost advocate for children, promoting better child care, health services, Head Start, and family support systems. CDF says its leadership is based on four principles: hard work, careful homework and analysis, multiple strategies, and persistence.

BACKGROUND: Marian Wright Edelman founded and directs CDF; indeed to many people Edelman *is* CDF. The daughter of a Baptist minister from South Carolina, Edelman earned her law degree from Yale and became the first black woman admitted to the bar in Mississippi—where in the mid-1960s she directed the NAACP Legal Defense and Educational Fund office in Jackson. She began her advocacy for children by protecting Mississippi's fledgling Head Start program. In 1968 Edelman moved to Washington, D.C., as counsel for Martin Luther King, Jr.'s Poor People's March, and later founded the Washington Research Project, which became CDF in 1973. Its first report, "Children Out of School in America," helped catalyze legislation guaranteeing equal educational opportunity to disabled students.

When Ronald Reagan entered the White House in 1981 and began cutting the nation's welfare programs and promoting a deflationary recession, the number of children living in poverty jumped by more than a million a year for the first three years of his presidency. Intensive lobbying by CDF helped stem the flow of budget cuts, and contributed to major improvements in Medicaid health coverage for poor children between 1984 and 1989. CDF turned its attention to teenage pregnancy in 1983, forming a volunteer teen pregnancy prevention network and launching a hard-hitting media campaign. After years of lobbying by CDF, child advocacy professionals, and women's groups, Congress passed comprehensive child care policy legislation in 1990, providing funds for states to improve child care services and increasing the Earned Income Credit for low-income working families with children.

CURRENT PRIORITIES: The centerpiece of CDF's five-year plan is to identify, assist, train, and empower local leaders and networks to take effective action for children. The plan emphasizes seven activities: (1) a massive public education campaign about how poorly America cares for its children; (2) a visitation program to neonatal intensive care nurseries, homeless shelters, and drug-ridden schools and neighborhoods to create personal understanding of the conditions children face; (3) identifying

and demonstrating programs and policies that work for children; (4) establishing a new child research and information center and new leadership training institutes to empower local child advocates; (5) launching a new crusade for black children, involving black corporate, education, and religious leaders at all levels; (6) building a committed constituency for children that cuts across race, class, age, and political party; and (7) empowering parents and grandparents as protectors of children, promoting stable families, and preventing teenage pregnancy.

CONTRIBUTORS: Although CDF is not a membership organization, it expanded its base of individual contributors to some 10,000 during the 1980s. CDF's annual conference in Washington attracts educators, social workers, child welfare administrators, health care professionals, church leaders, and juvenile justice workers. In 1990 some 1,300 people from forty-two states attended.

STRUCTURE: CDF has a twenty-member, self-recruiting board of directors, chaired until 1992 by attorney Hillary Rodham Clinton (wife of Arkansas governor and 1992 Democratic Presidential nominee Bill Clinton) and including Julius Chambers, director of the NAACP LDF; Dorothy Height, president of the National Council of Negro Women; James Joseph, president of the Council on Foundations; Donna Shalala, chancellor of the University of Wisconsin; and Eddie Williams, president of the Joint Center for Political and Economic Studies. In addition to the Washington headquarters ("a house on the hill for children"), CDF has offices in Ohio, Minnesota, and Texas. The Prenatal Caring and Child Advocacy Project is housed in South Carolina.

RESOURCES: CDF's revenue of $9 million in 1990 came 65 percent from grants (mostly from foundations), 19 percent from contributions, 6 percent from sale of publications, and 10 percent from other sources. Expenses totaled $8.9 million, with 56 percent for programs, 23 percent for publications and public education, 11 percent for fund-raising, and 10 percent for administration.

PUBLICATIONS AND SERVICES: CDF publishes a monthly newsletter, *CDF Reports* (circulation 7,000), available by subscription for $29.95. CDF distributed nearly 200,000 copies of its book, *Children 1990: A Report Card, Briefing Book, and Action Primer*. Other publications, including the annual *Children's Defense Budget* and a series of advocate's guides, are for sale by mail order. Marian Wright Edelman writes a moral message to Americans in *The Measure of Our Success: A Letter to My Children and Yours* (Beacon Press, 1992). □

THE DISABLED

By the most inclusive count, forty-three million Americans (17 percent of the population) have some form of disability—a large potential constituency. But this constituency has long been fragmented by types of disabilities, which result in different impairments and needs—as is evident by comparing blindness, deafness, cerebral palsy, spinal injury, diabetes, cancer, heart disease, AIDS, mental illness, and mental retardation. Each disability has had its own advocacy group (the blind have two rival groups), often run *for* the group by professional social service administrators, not *by* the group members themselves.

As Edward Berkowitz shows in *Disabled Policy* (Cambridge University Press, 1987), the United States has taken two often contradictory approaches to people with disabilities—income maintenance programs (including workers' compensation and disability insurance) and corrective programs (including rehabilitation, independent living, and civil rights/accessibility laws). Workers' compensation programs, pioneered by the states of Wisconsin and New Jersey in 1911, were designed to move the control over the treatment of injured workers from the courts to state governments. By 1948 workers' compensation laws had been enacted in all states. As workers' compensation only covered people injured by accidents in the workplace, many people whose disabilities had other causes were left uncovered. The Social Security Act was amended in 1950 to create a new welfare category for the totally and permanently disabled, and again in 1956 to include the Disability Insurance program under Social Security (the "D" in OASDI) for total and permanent disabilities. The 1972 Social Security amendments created the Supplemental Security Income program to replace the state-run welfare programs for the blind, elderly, and totally and permanently disabled (leaving only Aid to Families with Dependent Children—AFDC—as a federal "welfare" program). In contrast to the income maintenance programs, corrective programs are designed to enable people with disabilities to work in the regular economy and live independently. The federal vocational rehabilitation program has operated since 1920 to provide services and training to return disabled people to work.

Disability rights as a concept cuts across the fragmented field of associations covering single mental and physical disabilities. The idea of a "cross-disability coalition" began to take form with the independent living movement, led by the Center for Independent Living (CIL) in Berkeley, incorporated in 1972 by Ed Roberts and other students at the University of California who had lived together in a residence program at the university's Cowell Hospital. Joined by New York teacher Judy Heumann, who like Roberts is postpolio, CIL established an off-campus service center and movement headquarters. Roberts later became California's director of rehabilitation services under Governor Jerry Brown. The movement was sparked primarily by people with mobility problems who used wheelchairs—as a result of polio, spinal injuries, or cerebral palsy. There has been relatively less joint work with organizations of or for the blind, deaf, and mentally retarded. Nevertheless, equal access to education, employment, transportation, health care, and attendant services has been a unifying theme. And victories for one group are celebrated by all; disability activists everywhere cheered as deaf students at Gallaudet University in Washington, D.C., received national attention for their successful "Deaf President Now" campaign in 1988.

The civil rights revolution for the disabled began with the 1973 amendments to the Vocational Rehabilitation Act. Although similar language was included in the 1964 Civil Rights Act and the 1972 Education Amendments Act, the new wave of disability activism began with efforts to implement Section 504 of the 1973 amendments, which banned discrimination against any qualified handicapped individual in any program receiving federal financial assistance. As federal officials delayed issuing regulations, a lobbying umbrella called the American Coalition of Citizens with Disabilities pushed for a strong compliance and enforcement program, setting a deadline in April 1977 for action. The Berkeley CIL organized a "504 coalition" in the San Francisco Bay Area, and 300 disabled people demonstrated in Washington at the office of Health, Education and Welfare (HEW) secretary Joseph Califano. Demonstrators in Washington, Denver, San Francisco, and Los Angeles held sit-ins at HEW offices. Califano issued the Section 504 regulations, and the next year the 1978 amendments to the Vocational Rehabilitation Act provided funds for centers for independent living throughout the country. The Education of the Handicapped Act of 1975 required the "free appropriate public education of all handicapped children."

The most recent significant victory for the movement is the Americans with Disabilities Act of 1990, which extends the protections of Title V of the Vocational Rehabilitation Act of 1973 to the private sector, requiring access and forbidding discrimination in public accommodations. Employers of fifteen or more workers cannot discriminate against the disabled, and must make "reasonable accommodation" to their disabilities.

The NAACP Legal Defense and Educational Fund provided a model for the Disability Rights Education and Defense Fund (DREDF) organized in Berkeley in 1979 to secure enforcement of laws and regulations on the books. The movement has a think tank, World Institute on Disabilities, founded by Ed Roberts and Judy Heumann in 1983. ADAPT, organized in 1982 by an informal group of independent living centers, has been the direct-action arm of the movement, conducting numerous demonstrations, blockades, and sit-ins to secure enforcement of civil rights. The National Council on Independent Living (NCIL) represents independent living centers. The spirit of the movement has impacted such traditional organizations as the United Cerebral Palsy Association, which has become an important center of policy analysis and advocacy for the disability movement. The World Institute on Disabilities operates WIDNet, an electronic information and database service; for information call (510) 763-4100.

DREDF

DISABILITY RIGHTS EDUCATION AND DEFENSE FUND, INC.

2212 6TH STREET

BERKELEY, CA 94710

(415) 644-2555

FOUNDED: 1979   BUDGET: $705,000
STAFF: 17   TAX STATUS: 501(c)(3)

PURPOSE: "Dedicated to the independent living movement and the civil rights of persons with disabilities."

The Disability Rights Education and Defense Fund (DREDF) is a national law and public policy advocate for people with disabilities.

BACKGROUND: DREDF provides information, technical assistance, referrals, and legal representation to adults and children with disabilities, in both individual and class-action cases involving rights to employment, education, transportation, housing, and access to public accommodations. DREDF played a major role in drafting and passing the landmark Americans with Disabilities Act (ADA) of 1990 and other significant legislation.

CURRENT PRIORITIES: Under a grant from the Equal Opportunity Employment Commission, DREDF is providing training and technical assistance on compliance with the ADA to municipalities, states, and private businesses.

STRUCTURE: DREDF is governed by a nine-member, self-recruiting board of directors, and is assisted by a fifteen-member national policy council of civil rights attorneys and leaders. DREDF's headquarters is in Berkeley, California, and it maintains a governmental affairs office in Washington, DC. Jim Gleich has been executive director since 1991.

RESOURCES: DREDF's revenue of $705,000 in 1991 is derived from foundation grants, attorney's fees, and the State Bar of California Trust Fund.

PUBLICATIONS AND SERVICES: DREDF has a new hotline for matters pertaining to the Americans with Disabilities Act, (800) 466-4ADA. □

ADAPT

12 BROADWAY

DENVER, CO 80203

(303) 733-9324

FOUNDED: 1983   BUDGET: $60,000
STAFF: 3 volunteers
TAX STATUS: unincorporated,
informal association

PURPOSE: "To train, develop, and empower disabled activists."

ADAPT is the disability rights counterpart of Earth First!, ACT UP, and Operation Rescue, committed to militant demonstrations and civil disobedience to make its point for full access to public transit and facilities and for attendant services for independent living.

BACKGROUND: ADAPT was started in 1983 by staff and volunteers of the Atlantis Community, an independent living center founded in Denver in 1975, the second in the country after Berkeley. Originally ADAPT was an acronym for American Disabled for Action on Public Transit, activists seeking full access to buses, airplanes, and trains nationwide. The central demand was a federal mandate that all buses bought with public funds be equipped with wheelchair lifts. President Jimmy Carter issued such a rule, but the American Public Transit Association (APTA) sued to void the requirement. ADAPT initiated a series of demonstrations at every APTA national convention—protesting, picketing, blocking doors, demanding to be heard. Arrests of dozens of disabled activists generated national publicity, and resulted in many cities opting for access in public transit. Passage of the Americans with Disabilities Act in 1990 finally made access for all a requirement of federal law.

After this victory ADAPT changed its name to American Disabled for Attendant Programs Today, seeking Medicaid funding for consumer-controlled, home-based, personal assistance services. ADAPT opposes the "warehousing" of the disabled in nursing homes, and demands the secretary of the Department of Health and Human Services (DHHS) establish a national attendant services program, so disabled people could live at home with greater dignity and freedom—and at less cost. ADAPT proposes paying for attendant care by diverting one-quarter (approximately $5.5 billion) of the Medicaid funding that now goes to nursing homes. Besides DHHS secretary Dr. Louis Sullivan, ADAPT's favorite target for demonstrations is the American Health Care Association, the lobby for the major nursing home chains. Some disabled activists suggest ADAPT has too narrow a focus on people using wheelchairs, and argue for including interpreters for deaf people and readers for blind people within the definition of attendant services.

STRUCTURE: Operating without a formal organizational structure or paid staff, ADAPT relies on volunteers Mike Auberger, Wade Blank, and Robin Stephens from the staff of Atlantis Community to coordinate national activities.

RESOURCES: Fund-raising for the $60,000 budget is done locally with fun runs, bell-ringing, and other solicitations.

PUBLICATIONS AND SERVICES: ADAPT's quarterly newsletter *Incitement* is available for a $10 subscription; contact ADAPT/*Incitement*, 1339 Lamar Square Drive #B, Austin, TX 78704; (512) 442-0252. □

7.

FOOD, SHELTER, AND SUSTAINABLE DEVELOPMENT

Food, shelter, and improving living conditions are human rights. Article 25 of the Universal Declaration of Human Rights states, "Everyone has the right to a standard of living adequate for the health and well-being of himself and his family, including food, clothing, housing, and medical care and necessary social services." The point is echoed in Article 11 of the International Covenant on Economic, Social, and Cultural Rights, which acknowledges the "right of everyone to . . . adequate food, clothing and housing, and to the continuous improvement of living conditions." How well are we doing meeting these fundamental human rights?

DOMESTIC PROGRAMS

Everyone agrees the United States has the wealth to meet the basic food needs of its people. Yet despite cash payments through Supplemental Security Income, Aid to Families with Dependent Children, and other public assistance programs, some 32 million Americans lived below the poverty line in 1990 ($13,400 for a family of 4), with 12.5 million living on incomes less than half of the poverty line. The U.S. Department of

Agriculture spent $24 billion on domestic food assistance programs in 1990, including Food Stamps to 20 million people a month ($15.5 billion), the school lunch program feeding 24 million students a day ($4 billion), school breakfasts feeding 3.8 million poor children ($600 million), child and adult care center food programs, serving 1.6 million meals a day to children and 19,000 a day to adults ($800 million), the special supplemental food program for Women, Infants and Children (WIC), providing food coupons for 1.4 million infants and 2.1 million children "at nutritional risk" ($2.1 billion), and several smaller programs that distribute milk and surplus commodities. By 1992, a record number of 25 million people (nearly one in ten Americans) were Food Stamp recipients.

In addition to government feeding programs, private food banks collect and distribute donated food that might otherwise be wasted. Second Harvest, a national network of 180 food banks, distributed over 475 million pounds of food in 1990, worth some $755 million, to over 42,000 agencies including food pantries, soup kitchens, homeless shelters, and senior citizen and child care centers. A declining base of jobs has pushed more people into poverty, and federal food programs have operated under the threat of cutbacks since the Reagan administration began trimming the domestic budget in 1981. Advocacy for food has been essential to preserve existing programs and develop more adequate provisions for people who fall through the social safety net. Among the leaders in food advocacy are two national grassroots lobbies, Results and the church-based Bread for the World, and the Washington advocacy think tank Food Research and Action Center (FRAC). Two multiissue organizations also focus on food and hunger legislation: the lobby Interfaith Impact for Justice and Peace, and the think tank Center for Budget and Policy Priorities. The Children's Defense Fund is another important advocate for food programs for mothers and children.

Homelessness and adequate housing for all are even greater challenges, but one organization, Habitat for Humanity, has accepted the idea of housing as a fundamental human right and has set about demonstrating how that right might be realized. Rock stars attracted a younger generation with music telethons, and spectacular events—USA for Africa, Hands Across America, Farm Aid—raised large amounts of money but lacked a mechanism for continuing involvement in hunger, housing, and development issues. The HandsNet computer network (an outcome of Hands Across America) now links food banks, advocates for the homeless, self-help housing promoters, and legal service activists (20195 Stevens Creek Boulevard, Suite 120, Cupertino, CA 95014; (408) 257-4500).

INTERNATIONAL PROGRAMS

The World Bank estimates that over 1 billion people (a fifth of the world's population) in the developing countries are poor, living on less than $370 a year (of those, some 675 million live in extreme poverty on less than $275 a year). People living at this level are very vulnerable to hunger with a single crop failure or illness of a wage earner, and experience high levels of infant and child mortality. The majority of the world's poor presently live in south and east Asia, but these areas—particularly east Asia—are making substantial progress in economic development. In sub-Saharan Africa the situation is getting worse, and poverty is expected to increase in absolute terms and relative to the world as a whole—going from 16 percent of the world's poor in 1985 to 30 percent in 2000.

Hunger is not caused by too many people or not enough food. The world produces enough food to feed all its people. When a country's economic growth is consistent and basic needs are met, people have greater security and fewer children (what population analysts call the "demographic transition"). Efforts to limit population growth through family planning programs are important, but success follows development and social security.

Two circumstances of hunger need to be distinguished: famine and chronic undernourishment. Famine is caused by war, drought, flood, or crop failure, and can be alleviated by emergency assistance. Civil war, for example, was at the heart of the hunger crises in Ethiopia, Sudan, Angola, and Mozambique during the 1980s and Somalia in the 1990s. Except in refugee camps, the direct provision of food may not be the best solution even in the case of famine. Public project employment for cash and aid for the unemployable sustains existing food markets and supports local farmers. Dealing with chronic undernourishment requires sustainable economic development and redirection of resources to basic programs of health care, sanitation, and clean drinking water—and elementary education to make these work. Basic services must involve women and girls, who are disproportionately victims of poverty. UNICEF is emphasizing four simple programs to make a substantial improvement in child mortality in developing countries: universal child immunization against six deadly diseases (measles, polio, diphtheria, whooping cough, tetanus, and tuberculosis), oral rehydration therapy for diarrhea, breast feeding, and child growth monitoring with simple charts to detect hidden malnutrition. The U.N.–sponsored World Summit for Children in 1990 set goals to reduce infant mortality by one-third and malnutrition by one-half and to eliminate polio by the year 2000.

Some fundamental lessons are clear from three decades of international development efforts. Military spending by developing countries has diverted resources from meeting basic human needs. Women must be educated and involved in development programs. Economic growth must be accompanied by redistribution of resources to provide basic security for the poor. Solutions to hunger, environmental destruction, and rapid population growth must be developed in concert. The developed countries' policies on trade, debt, and international assistance impact poverty and hunger.

Assistance to regions or countries suffering from disaster, famine, or war has been conducted since the nineteenth century by such organizations as the Red Cross and various religious organizations as an adjunct to missionary work, as charitable "relief," or more recently as professionalized human service. After World War II the U.S. Agency for International Development (USAID) and various United Nations specialized agencies became important providers of development assistance. A new generation of "private voluntary organizations" (PVOs) or "nongovernmental organizations" (NGOs) stepped into the development arena. The Oxford Committee for Famine Relief (now Oxfam) was founded in England in 1942, and CARE (originally the Cooperative for American Remittances to Europe) was formed in the United States in 1945. Oxfam evolved toward participatory forms of education and fund-raising in the United Kingdom, the United States, and other countries; CARE moved in the direction of a professionalized service agency, obtaining a substantial portion of its budget from USAID. Activists on the left set up a think tank, the Institute for Food and Development Policy, with its Food First program of educational materials designed to dispel the myths of hunger. Werner Erhardt, founder of est, helped organize The Hunger Project to publicize the idea that an end to hunger by the year 2000 is possible. Bread for the World and Results lobby for international food and development programs as well as for domestic programs. Habitat for Humanity has housing construction programs abroad as well as in the United States. In 1991 InterAction, a coalition of 132 international relief and development organizations, adopted a code of ethics for its members covering governance, finances, fund-raising, and organizational integrity.

OXFAM AMERICA

115 BROADWAY

BOSTON, MA 02116

(617) 482-1211

FOUNDED: 1970   CONTRIBUTORS: 100,000
BUDGET: $12.7 million   STAFF: 60
TAX STATUS: 501(c)(3)

PURPOSE: "Oxfam America is an international agency that funds self-help and disaster relief in poor countries in Africa, Asia, Latin America, and the Caribbean and also prepares and distributes educational materials for people in the United States on issues of development and hunger."

Oxfam promotes sustainable development by working in partnership with local people who understand local problems and conditions. Local participation and empowerment are the keys to Oxfam's success. Although its work is similar to the overseas programs of the American Friends Service Committee, Oxfam has no religious affiliation. Oxfam takes no money from the U.S. government, and speaks with an independent voice against programs and policies that hurt people in the Third World.

BACKGROUND: The name "Oxfam" comes from the Oxford Committee for Famine Relief, founded in England in 1942. Oxfam America is one of seven autonomous Oxfams worldwide (along with Australia, Belgium, Canada, Quebec, Hong Kong, and the United Kingdom and Ireland). Oxfam America was started in Washington, D.C., in 1970, at the time of the Bangladesh crisis. In 1972-73, the group reorganized in Boston.

Oxfam does not shy away from the world's trouble spots. Oxfam began delivering emergency assistance to Cambodia in 1979, and was soon recognized as a credible source of news on circumstances there. In 1986 Oxfam was involved in a dispute with the State Department over the U.S. trade embargo of Nicaragua. They prevented Oxfam from sending a shipment of agricultural supplies to Nicaragua as part of a "Tools for Peace and Justice" program. Eventually the shipment got through, but in following years Oxfam changed its strategy to collect only money instead of secondhand tools to assist Nicaraguan farm groups.

Too much money can be disruptive in many circumstances, so Oxfam prefers to sponsor labor-intensive projects—providing seeds, tools, or building materials. The typical Oxfam grant is small, averaging $23,000. Similarly, Oxfam often chooses not to give out food. Food aid can have a negative impact on the local economy and the small farmers who depend on selling crops to survive. When disaster relief is the appropriate response, Oxfam administers aid only where it is already involved and understands the local situation.

Like most development organizations, Oxfam is nonpartisan and will not assist groups involved in armed conflict. Nevertheless, Oxfam does aid civilians in combat areas, such as the campesino victims of El Salvador's civil war—running the risk of controversy. Oxfam speaks out about the roots of hunger in systemic injustice: "Hunger is not accidental. Nor are hungry people the victims of forces beyond anyone's control. . . . Real hunger is the result of *systematic impoverishment.*"

CURRENT PRIORITIES: Once again in 1990–91, famine relief for Ethiopia and Sudan topped the priority list. In Latin America, Oxfam America continues to emphasize its work with indigenous peoples. In the Amazon it has increased its work with local people trying to save the rain forest. It funds projects in the Central American countries of Nicaragua, El Salvador, and Guatemala. Oxfam America does not work in the Middle East, but Oxfam U.K. and Ireland does. After the Persian Gulf War, Oxfam America served as a fiscal agent for people wanting to donate to refugee programs sponsored by its sister organization.

Women are targeted by many Oxfam projects, which promote the organizing abilities of women and provide training in income-generating skills, literacy, and nutrition. Many projects help women establish cooperatives and provide small no-interest loans to start businesses. In India, Oxfam is increasing its successful program funding women's organizations.

Each November since 1973 Oxfam has sponsored a "Fast for a World Harvest," its major fund-raising and educational event of the year, one week before Thanksgiving. Individuals fast for one day and send the money they would have spent on food to Oxfam. The greatest support comes from dining programs in schools and colleges.

CONTRIBUTORS: Regular contributors have increased steadily to the current 80,000. A 1986 survey found the average Oxfam donor to be between thirty-five and fifty in age, with an even number of males and females, to be highly educated, and likely to volunteer for another organization as well.

STRUCTURE: Oxfam America has a twenty-one-member, self-recruiting board of directors. Executive directors have included Joseph Short from 1977 to 1984, and John Hammock from 1984 to date. Oxfam maintains a headquarters in Boston, a small office in Oakland, California, and seven overseas field offices opened in 1988 serving southern Africa, South America, Central America, south Asia, Cambodia, Sudan, and the Horn of Africa (previously, program directors traveled to their regions several times a year from the Boston headquarters). Oxfam America collaborates with Oxfam Canada in southern Africa and with Oxfam Belgium in Nicaragua and Cambodia. Staff attend world Oxfam conferences every other year to improve communication and collaboration. Oxfam America is the second largest group, after Oxfam U.K. and Ireland, which maintains over 700 used goods and clothing stores, much like Goodwill Industries in the United States.

RESOURCES: Fund-raising success fluctuates with press attention to world hunger—widespread publicity in 1985 to the famine in Ethiopia brought a huge upsurge in donations to Oxfam from $6 million to $16 million in less than a year. After the surge of income, contributions dropped back to 1984 levels and have risen gradually. Oxfam received $13.8 million in revenue in 1990, mostly from families and individuals (84 percent), with smaller amounts from schools, colleges, churches, foundations, and corporations. Expenditures of $12.7 million went for overseas programs (65 percent), education programs (11 percent), fund-raising (18 percent),

and administration (6 percent). In 1991 Oxfam funded 268 projects in twenty-eight countries, for a total of $6.6 million in grants for projects in Latin America, Africa, Asia, and the Caribbean.

PUBLICATIONS AND SERVICES: *Oxfam America News* (circulation 100,000) is sent to contributors three times a year. Oxfam America produces a "Facts for Action" pamphlet series, and a catalog of literature and audiovisual materials available by mail order. □

HABITAT FOR HUMANITY INTERNATIONAL

HABITAT AND CHURCH STREETS

AMERICUS, GA 31709-3498

(912) 924-6935

FOUNDED: 1976   CONTRIBUTORS: 400,000
VOLUNTEERS: 108,000   AFFILIATES: 700
BUDGET: $21.3 million   STAFF: 250
TAX STATUS: 501(c)(3)

GOAL: "To eliminate poverty housing and homelessness from the world and to make decent shelter a matter of conscience and action."

Habitat for Humanity International is an ecumenical Christian ministry, founded by Alabama businessman Millard Fuller, which uses volunteer labor and donated money and materials to construct housing for low-income people who contribute "sweat equity" and typically receive twenty-year, no-interest mortgages. Payments from mortgages go back into a revolving fund to build more houses. Habitat expanded rapidly over the last five years as former president Jimmy Carter volunteered his labor and his name for fund-raising. Habitat built its 10,000th house in 1991 during its fifteenth-anniversary year, and expects to be building 7,500 a year by 1994.

BACKGROUND: Millard Fuller was a law student at the University of Alabama at Tuscaloosa and a budding entrepreneur when he joined Morris Dees in a partnership, investing in real estate and selling specialty items to fellow college students. After graduation they set up law and business partnerships in Montgomery in 1960, establishing several mail-order enterprises. Fuller was a millionaire by age 30. In late 1965 Fuller's wife, Linda, experiencing a crisis in their marriage, decided to leave with their two children; Millard followed her to New York and they reconciled, renewing their Christian faith. Deciding to lead new lives, the Fullers drove through the South and stopped in to visit an old friend who had moved to Koinonia Farm in Georgia. There they met Clarence Jordan, who set the Fullers on a path that would lead to the founding of Habitat for Humanity. After a month talking with Jordan at Koinonia, Fuller sold his business share to partner Morris Dees and began giving his money away to charities (in 1971 Dees would sell his business and found the Southern Poverty Law Center).

Koinonia Farm was a visionary communal experiment launched by Jordan in 1942. After completing doctoral studies in 1936 at Southern Baptist Theological Seminary in Louisville, Kentucky, Jordan pastored a black church in Louisville's West End—developing his ideas of pacifism, racial equality, and radical sharing, which he summarized with the Greek word *koinonia*, or "fellowship." During the war Jordan and his wife Florence looked for a farm near Jordan's home in the South to establish the Koinonia community, finally settling on 440 acres in Sumpter County, Georgia, eight miles southwest of Americus. As the civil rights movement developed in the mid-1950s, Jordan's radical views on interracial fellowship drew attacks from the Ku Klux Klan and a boycott by the local community. Koinonia survived the next decade, but the struggle to hold the farm together with its ever-shifting constellation of members took a toll on Jordan, who was also engaged in writing his vernacular "Cotton Patch" translations of Scriptures. The Fullers came upon Koinonia Farm in 1965 just as Jordan realized the communal experiment was close to an end. But first Millard Fuller would spend two years working for his denominational headquarters, the United Church of Christ, raising money for Tougaloo College, a black college in Mississippi.

By 1968 only the Jordans and one other family remained at Koinonia Farm. Fuller wrapped up his fund-raising work for Tougaloo College and planned a meeting to discuss with Jordan his new vision of a Fund for Humanity, a vehicle to buy and hold land in trust for poor people to farm in partnership. The interracial group assembled at Koinonia from around the country decided to keep the farm, reconstituted as Koinonia Partners, maintaining the mail-order business selling pecans and fruitcakes and beginning to build low-cost housing on the north side of the farm. A letter from Jordan in October 1968 announcing Koinonia Partners to his mailing list of 12,000 friends of Koinonia produced enough contributions for housing construction to begin. Jordan died suddenly in 1969, but his new vision was on the road to reality.

For the next four and a half years, the Fullers worked for Koinonia Partners; Millard focused on building houses with volunteer labor while Linda helped with food and cookbook orders, craft and sewing industries, and a day-care facility. By 1972 Koinonia Village with twenty-seven new homes was complete, and plans were under way for a second development nearby. The Fullers began to wonder if their approach to building houses would work in the shantytowns of Zaire, which they had visited on a mission tour six years before.

Sponsored by the Christian Church (Disciples of Christ), the Fullers went to Mbandaka, Zaire, to revive a cement block project and begin to build houses. Eventually they obtained a permit to build 114 homes in a strip of vacant land that had separated European settlers from blacks in colonial times—known as Bokotola ("man who does not care for others"), its name was changed to Losanganya ("reconciler, everyone together") at the dedication of the housing project. Financing was patched together one house at a time with gifts from churches and individuals across the United States. Returning home in 1976, the Fullers convened a meeting of twenty-seven people from nine states at Koinonia to found a new organization committed to building low-cost housing wherever needed in the world. They established Habitat for Humanity, which would draw up its constitution and by-laws and elect its first board of directors in March 1977 in Stony Brook, New York.

An inspirational evangelist for the cause, Millard Fuller spread Habitat's message of "love in the mortar joints" as he spoke to church conferences around the country. New projects got under way in San Antonio, Texas, and in the Appalachian mountains of Morgan and Scott counties in eastern Tennessee. Fuller's books expounded Habitat's "theology of the hammer," and the organization began more projects in Africa, Central America (Habitat worked in Nicaragua throughout the contra war), and across the United States. Habitat was given a big publicity boost when former president Jimmy Carter, whose home in Plains is not far from Koinonia and Americus, joined the board of directors in 1984 and he and Rosalynn volunteered for work projects. By 1990 Habitat had projects in over 500 U.S. cities and towns, and in 80 locations in 29 other countries.

Habitat's rapid expansion during the 1980s forced the board to confront the problem of managing growth while keeping the vision. Although public pronouncements remained upbeat and inspirational, Habitat projects were beginning to outrun the organization's capacity to administer and finance (a highly publicized week-long Jimmy Carter Work Project in Tijuana in 1990 ran considerably behind schedule, and had to be finished—not inappropriately —by local residents). In 1991 the board of directors precipitated a crisis by asking Fuller to relinquish his administrative responsibilities and concentrate on "raising money and making speeches." Fuller replied he was not interested in a ceremonial role and offered to resign. Jimmy Carter expressed his continuing support for Habitat, but urged a reconciliation between Fuller and the board. In a compromise facilitated by board chairman Geoff Van Loucks, Atlanta home builder John Weiland, and former Ohio governor Richard Celeste, Fuller retains the title of president and Jeff Snider will continue as executive vice president and chief operations officer. Habitat's fifteenth-anniversary celebration in Columbus, Ohio, in September 1991 brought together volunteers for a celebration of organizational survival, success, and reconciliation.

CURRENT PRIORITIES: Habitat built over 3,700 houses in 1990 (with the headquarters responsible for 2,566 and affiliates for 1,181). By 1994, Habitat plans to build 7,500 houses annually. New areas of emphasis include renovating or constructing emergency shelters for the homeless and developing financing for poor rural and inner city areas that can't raise their own money for housing. A new emphasis on minority partnership development will actively recruit increased minority participation on the International board of directors and on local affiliate boards. The Vision/Habitat program—begun when the Fullers were in Africa—collects used eyeglasses, which are shipped to projects overseas; proceeds from the sale of one barrel of glasses can often finance a whole house in a developing nation.

Habitat welcomes fresh approaches to generate enthusiasm and involve new constituencies. In Charlotte, North Carolina, an all-women's project raised a house during two days in March 1991 with the help of local women contractors and Rosalynn Carter. A Habitat affiliate in Milledgeville, Georgia, began a project of technical assistance to projects building and renovating housing for the disabled. The headquarters office has adopted the program as Habitat for Humanity with Disabilities, with a goal of making all Habitat housing barrier-free and accessible to persons with disabilities. A new "Fund for Humanity with Disabilities" will make loans to affiliates for minimally accessible housing; fourteen affiliates are committed to building all housing using accessibility guidelines.

CONTRIBUTORS AND VOLUNTEERS: Financial contributors to Habitat's headquarters have grown to 400,000. Volunteers from across the country provide half the staff of 250 in Habitat's Americus office, with the average volunteer staying ten months. An estimated 108,000 volunteers worked with affiliated projects worldwide. Over 10,000 volunteers serve on the boards of directors of local affiliates in the United States. Through the Global Village Work Camp Program in 1990, 315 volunteers from the United States paid their own way to participate in one of fifteen work camps.

STRUCTURE: Habitat has a twenty-eight-member, self-recruiting board of directors, chaired by Geoff Van Loucks. Some 700 local affiliates in all 50 states maintain their own organizations and revolving funds for housing. Affiliated national organizations have been started in Canada and Australia. Over

400 covenant churches support the International office, and another 600 assist local affiliates; there are also 152 campus chapters that raise money and recruit volunteers. International projects are organized by region: east and southern Africa, west and central Africa, Asia, Pacific, Central America/Mexico, South America/Caribbean. A project in Armenia is Habitat's first housing venture in the former Soviet Union.

RESOURCES: Habitat's revenue leaped from $7 million in 1987 to $10 million in 1988, $15 million in 1989, and $20.7 million in 1990. Habitat's revenue in 1990 included $19.8 million in contributions, $522,000 in donated assets, and $406,000 in other income. Expenses included $14.1 million for program services (66 percent) and $7.1 million for administration and fund-raising (34 percent). An estimated $37 million was also raised by local affiliates in 1990. Habitat receives foundation grants, both money and in-kind support from corporations, and support from the National Association of Home Builders and the National Association of Realtors.

PUBLICATIONS AND SERVICES: Contributors receive the quarterly newspaper, *Habitat World* (circulation 570,000). The story of Clarence Jordan and his communal experiment at Koinonia Farm is told in Dallas Lee, *The Cotton Patch Evidence* (1971). Millard Fuller's several books trace Habitat's development: *Bokotola* (1977); *Love in the Mortar Joints* (1980) and *No More Shacks!* (1986), both coauthored with Diane Scott; and *The Excitement Is Building*

(1990), coauthored with Linda Fuller. The books, videotapes, and other materials are available from Habitat. □

BREAD FOR THE WORLD

802 RHODE ISLAND AVENUE, NE

WASHINGTON, DC 20018

(202) 269-0200

FOUNDED: 1974   MEMBERS: 43,000
CHAPTERS: 250   BUDGET: $3.4 million
STAFF: 52   TAX STATUS: 501(c)(4): Bread for the World; 501(c)(3): BFW Institute on Hunger and Development

PURPOSE: "A nationwide Christian movement that seeks justice for the world's hungry people by lobbying our nation's decision makers."

Bread for the World (BFW), an interdenominational Christian citizens movement, is the most effective lobby in Washington on domestic and world hunger legislation. BFW does not distribute food or provide direct relief, focusing instead on influencing national policy and government spending. The BFW Institute conducts policy research and prepares educational materials.

BACKGROUND: BFW began with a discussion in New York in 1972 among Christians concerned about world hunger. Arthur Simon (a Lutheran minister and brother of Senator Paul Simon of Illinois) was one of the conveners. Recognizing that churches had a good record with direct assistance, they were concerned that churches were failing to mobilize citizens to influence policy decisions on hunger issues. During 1973 an organizing committee—7 Protestants and 7 Catholics—began a pilot project in New York City, enlisting 500 advocates for the hungry. In 1974 BFW assembled a board of directors, and recruited Eugene Carson Blake, recently retired as general secretary of the World Council of Churches, as president, and Thomas J. Gumbelton, Catholic Auxiliary Bishop of Detroit, as vice president. Art Simon became the first executive director, a post he filled until 1991. Organized on state and congressional district lines, BFW's network has an impact on committee and subcommittee actions as well as final votes on legislation.

In 1980 BFW was instrumental in securing U.S. funding for famine relief in Cambodia, Somalia, and Ethiopia. The early 1980s occupied BFW with fending off cuts proposed by the Reagan administration for domestic food programs and for UNICEF support. In 1984 BFW successfully lobbied Congress to establish the Child Survival Fund, and tripled its support with the Universal Child Immunization Act of 1986. Responding to the African crisis in 1985, BFW promoted passage of $800 million in emergency famine assistance. Since 1988, BFW has pushed for increased funding for the Women, Infants and Children (WIC) program, which expanded services to an additional 500,000 women and children.

CURRENT PRIORITIES: Each year when the defense budget is under review, BFW pushes the Harvest of Peace Resolution, which calls for the nations of the world to reduce military spending in half by the year 2000 and redirect resources to developing nations to end poverty and hunger. BFW's leading priority for 1991 was the Horn of Africa Recovery and Food Security Act, which calls for timely and fair distribution of relief aid directly to poor people through nongovernmental organizations seeking to improve food production and social and environmental conditions. In 1992 BFW launched the "Every Fifth Child" campaign to alleviate poverty by increasing congressional appropriations for WIC, Head Start, and the Job Corps, and joined a coalition calling for the end of hunger in America.

MEMBERS: BFW members can work either as members of a local group or as individuals in a congressional district network. Over 2,500 volunteer leaders in 250 local chapters mobilize members to write letters on specific legislation, meet with members of Congress in their home districts and in Washington, respond with telephone calls to legislative alerts, and speak to church and community groups. Some 1,000 covenant churches help support the organization and receive monthly packets of materials on hunger issues. In 1979 Simon set a goal of 200,000 members by or during the 1990s, but BFW remained at a plateau of around 43,000 members through the 1980s.

STRUCTURE: BFW has a forty-member board of directors, of which thirteen are elected each year for three-year terms by ballot of the membership. Regional offices are located in Chicago, Minneapolis, and Pasadena. Art Simon stepped down as BFW president after fifteen years; David Beckmann, a senior adviser on nongovernmental organizations for the World Bank, was hired to succeed Simon in 1991.

RESOURCES: BFW received income of $2.8 million in 1991, including $2.3 million from members, $220,000 from covenant churches, and $226,000 from grants. Expenses of $2.5 million were divided 68 percent for program services and 32 percent for administration and fund-raising. The BFW Institute received income of $635,000 in 1990, and spent $578,000, divided 77 percent for program services and 23 percent for administration and fund-raising.

PUBLICATIONS AND SERVICES: Membership is $25 and includes the *BFW Newsletter* (circulation 42,000) ten times a year; each newsletter contains an action for the month. An annual report is available. The BFW Institute publishes a catalog of educational materials, and features a detailed survey, *Hunger 1992: Second Annual Report on the State of World Hunger*, and a collection of information and action tips, *Hunger 1992: Ideas that Work.* For the analysis of world hunger underlying BFW's work, see Arthur Simon, *Bread for the World* (Paulist Press, 1975; rev. ed., 1984). Simon's latest book, *Harvesting Peace: The Arms Race and Human Need* (Sheed & Ward, 1990), argues that cuts in military spending can provide support for development in the Second and Third Worlds. BFW message checks are available. □

Results

Generating Political Will to End Hunger

RESULTS
236 MASSACHUSETTS AVENUE NE, SUITE 300
WASHINGTON, DC 20002
(202) 543-9340

FOUNDED: 1980   SPONSORS: 2,000
GROUPS: 107   BUDGET: $620,000   STAFF: 9
TAX STATUS: 501(c)(4): Results; 501(c)(3): Results Education Fund

PURPOSE: "Creating the political will to end hunger and dedicated to the knowledge that each one of us makes a difference."

Results is a secular lobby on hunger issues, organized around a network of local groups.

BACKGROUND: Results is the creation of Sam Harris, who became involved in the world hunger issue in the late 1970s through The Hunger Project while he was a music teacher in Miami. After moving to Los Angeles in 1980, Harris initiated a group that experimented with ways for citizens to be effective in creating the necessary "political will to end hunger." For over four years Results ran as an all-volunteer organization, with Harris flying around the country on special twenty-one-day unlimited-flight airline tickets, helping start new groups of letter writers.

CURRENT PRIORITIES: Results has lobbied to increase funding for UNICEF's Child Survival Fund, and backed the

Self Sufficiency for the Poor Act in 1988, a $50 million set-aside of Agency for International Development (AID) funds for "micro-enterprise lending," small loans for poor people in the Third World to start family businesses. Results emphasizes the "World Summit for Children Implementation Act," a follow-up to the meeting of seventy-one heads of state at the U.N. in September 1990. On the first anniversary, Results held a nationwide program of candlelight vigils in September 1991 with a theme of "Keeping the Promise" of the Summit. Results will also focus attention on follow-up activities of the 1992 U.N. Conference on Environment and Development in Brazil.

MEMBERS: Individuals can participate at three levels: "Partners" agree to attend at least three of the four monthly meetings of the local Results group (generally there are four partners per group). "Participants" attend one monthly meeting, take part in actions, and learn to speak about the issues in public. "Monthly sponsors" agree to contribute $10 a month to the organiza-tion. Partners and participants get training in issues, writing for the media, and public speaking at regional meetings and an annual conference. In addition to the 107 groups in the United States, in 1992 there were 14 groups in the United Kingdom, 4 in Australia, 3 in Canada, 3 in Germany, 2 in Japan, and 1 each in Russia, Ukraine, and El Salvador.

STRUCTURE: Results has a fifteen-member board of directors, with four members nominated and elected by the "partners" involved with local groups. Two seats are reserved for Democratic and Republican members of Congress, and two to increase racial and gender diversity.

RESOURCES: All of Results' $620,000 budget for 1992 come from individual contributors.

PUBLICATIONS AND SERVICES: Sponsors and subscribers for $25 receive Results' quarterly newsletter, *Entry Point* (circulation 3,000). □

8.

FROM ANIMAL
WELFARE TO
ANIMAL RIGHTS

Prevention of cruelty to animals became an important movement in early nineteenth-century England, where it grew alongside the humanitarian current that advanced human rights, including the antislavery movement and later the movement for woman suffrage. The first anticruelty bill, intended to stop bull-baiting, was introduced in Parliament in 1800. In 1822 Colonel Richard Martin succeeded in passing an act in the House of Commons preventing cruelty to such larger domestic animals as horses and cattle; two years later he organized the Society for the Prevention of Cruelty to Animals (SPCA) to help enforce the law. Queen Victoria commanded the addition of the prefix "Royal" to the Society in 1840. Following the British model, Henry Bergh organized the American SPCA in New York in 1866 after returning from his post in St. Petersburg as secretary to the American legation in Russia; he hoped it would become national in scope, but the ASPCA remained primarily an animal shelter program for New York City.

Other SPCAs and Humane Societies were founded in the United States beginning in the late 1860s (often with support from abolitionists) with groups in Pennsylvania, Massachusetts, and San Francisco among the first. Originally concerned with enforcing anticruelty laws, they soon began running animal shelters along the lines of a model developed in Philadelphia. The American Humane Association (AHA), with divisions for children and animals, was founded in 1877, and emerged as the leading national advocate for animal-protection and child-protection services. As the scientific approach to medicine expanded, opposition grew to the use of animals in medical laboratory research—particularly in the era before anesthetics and painkillers became widely available. The antivivisection movement was strong in England and the United States in the 1890s (the American Anti-Vivisection Society was formed in Philadelphia in 1883), but was overwhelmed by the prestige of scientific medicine by the early twentieth century. The humane movement focused more on dogs and cats as the use of horses as beasts of burden declined and the keeping of pets increased. The center of action shifted to protection of wild animals and birds, as undertaken by the Audubon Societies founded in the late 1890s.

In the period following World War II, the decline of agriculture as a way of life, the growth of affluent suburbia, and the increasing number of older people living independently combined to increase appreciation of dogs and cats as companion animals (43 percent of U.S. households have a pet; there are an estimated 51 million to 58 million dogs, and the number of cats has grown rapidly to an estimated 49 million to 60 million). Humane groups flourished on this expanding base of pet lovers. Growth of humane organizations led to conflicts among leaders over the extent to which principles of animal protection should be carried, and whether controversy would erode public support.

Around the time David Brower and the Young Turks of the World War II generation were shaking up the Sierra Club, a group of younger members were agitating to expand the advocacy mission of the American Humane Association. The Humane Society of the United States (HSUS) split from the AHA in 1954, and then suffered its own splits in the 1960s. The Society for Animal Protective Legislation (SAPL) was established in 1955 to lobby for the first federal Humane Slaughter Act (passed in 1958); together with the Animal Welfare Institute also under the direction of Christine Stevens, SAPL has lobbied for every important piece of animal legislation since, including the Laboratory Animal Welfare Act (1966), the Endangered Species Act (1969), the Horse Protection Act (1970), the Marine Mammal Protection Act (1972), and their various subsequent extensions and strengthening amendments. Helen Jones incorporated a group in 1959 that would become the International Society for Animal Rights; Cleveland Amory set up his Fund for Animals in 1967; and Belton Muras left HSUS in 1968 to form the Animal Protection Institute. Following the growing interest in primates stimulated by the highly publicized work of Jane Goodall with chimpanzees and Dian Fossey with gorillas, Shirley McGreal formed the International Primate Protection League in 1973. Despite the AHA's relative decline, its Hollywood office still holds the franchise on approving the use of animals in motion pictures.

The humane movement had been grounded primarily in benevolent sentiments (some would say sentimentality) toward animals. Eighteenth-century English philosopher Jeremy Bentham had placed animals within his utilitarian moral calculus of pleasure and pain, stating, "The question is not, Can they *reason*? nor, Can they *talk*? but, Can they *suffer*?" But this philosophical grounding for human relations with animals was left undeveloped. In the 1970s the humane movement began to find its first respectable intellectual and ethical underpinning in the work of philosophers Peter Singer and Tom Regan. Singer revived utilitarian thinking where Bentham left off, popularizing the concept of "speciesism" as a parallel to racism and sexism. Regan moved beyond the idea of animal welfare to argue the case for animal rights, not from utilitarianism, but in the natural rights tradition.

Philosophy aside, the civil rights and women's liberation movements directed fresh attention to human rights, and an extension of rights principles by analogy to animals proved an easier step than many would have anticipated. That step did not look so big when environmentalists were winning rights-like protection for endangered species, and attorneys were asking, "Do trees have standing?" Feminist biologist Caroline Merchant extended the question to ecosystems by asking, "Do rocks have rights?" Women make up some 75 percent of activists for animals, and it's not surprising that they've carried over language and lessons from the women's movement. Animal rights activists borrowed direct-action tactics popularized by other movements, and applied them to oppose laboratory experimentation on animals, wearing fur, factory farming (particularly confinement-raising of veal), and hunting. Environmental groups like Greenpeace and the Sea Shepherd Society showed how to draw attention to marine mammals and other endangered species. People for the Ethical Treatment of Animals (PETA) emerged in 1980 as the most visible representative of the new militancy, with its demonstrations at the National Institutes of Health and as spokesperson for the underground activities of the Animal Liberation Front. And taking a lesson from the NAACP Legal Defense and Educational Fund, and with help from the Sierra Club Legal Defense Fund staff, Joyce Tischler organized the Animal Legal Defense Fund in 1981.

Several important animal protection victories in the 1970s and 1980s were the product of coalitions, not single organizations. Led by one-time Maritime Union reformer and left journalist Henry Spira, 400 groups in the Coalition to Stop the Draize Rabbit Blinding Test got cosmetics companies like Avon and Revlon to develop alternatives to the infamous Draize Eye Irritancy Test. Spira was drawn to the animals' cause by taking a class on animal liberation with philosopher Peter Singer. Applying his activist background, Spira organized his first campaign of demonstrations against animal experimentation at the American Museum of Natural History in New York in 1976; the labs were closed in 1977. Spira's coalition then went on to obtain a repeal of New York State's pound seizure law. The Draize test was the target in 1980. Next the coalition took on the LD 50 test (the lethal dose of a toxic substance that will kill half or more of a group of test animals), getting the Food and Drug Administration to review its policy and acknowledge the test could be replaced by experiments using cell biology and other techniques. Spira's work helped introduce a new level of tactical and political sophistication to animal welfare advocacy.

The revived animal rights movement is still in an early stage of development. Many of the groups begun since the 1950s are in their first generation of leadership, and manifest "founder's syndrome" to one extent or another. Competition is still heavy for available issue niches on animal experimentation, farm animals, hunting, zoos and circuses, fur, and animal testing.

Questions of "purity" divide animal activists, particularly over whether animal welfare and animal rights are complementary or contradictory. Must a true friend of animals be a vegetarian, or further, a vegan who eats no animal products? Can animal rights groups make alliances with mainstream conservation organizations who condone hunting (or at least do not officially oppose it)? Tom Regan upholds animal rights fundamentalism, a program of nothing less than a compete abolition of all exploitation of animals for human purposes. Others, including PETA's Ingrid Newkirk, argue that cooperation with all allies issue by issue is the only path to victories for animals. However impractical, utopian, or just plain wrongheaded many of their goals may appear to the general public—and to many participants in other movements—animal rights advocates have come a long way in the past decade, and are no longer out beyond the fringe.

THE HUMANE SOCIETY OF THE UNITED STATES

2100 L STREET, NW

WASHINGTON, DC 20037

(202) 452-1100

FOUNDED: 1954 MEMBERS: 400,000
BUDGET: $21.1 million STAFF: 123
TAX STATUS: 501(c)(3)

PURPOSE: "The protection of all animals —pets, wildlife, farm and entertainment animals—through educational, legislative, investigative and legal means."

The Humane Society of the United States (HSUS) is the leading national organization of the animal welfare and protection movement. Often at pains to distinguish itself from animal rights militants, HSUS adopts a generally moderate tone and is willing to make compromises to achieve gains through legislation or regulation.

BACKGROUND: HSUS was founded as the National Humane Society at the end of 1954 as a result of stormy disputes within the seventy-five-year-old American Humane Association (AHA). The AHA board represented animal shelter programs, and resisted the young insurgents who wanted to take a strong advocacy position on laboratory animals, livestock transport and slaughter, and humane education in the schools. A reform slate was elected to the board in 1954, and the board majority retaliated by firing or forcing the resignations of several key staff, including Fred Myers (editor of AHA's *National Humane Review*), Helen Jones (AHA education director), Larry Andrews (AHA field services director), and Marcia Glaser.

These four became the staff of the National Humane Society. AHA took the new group to court and forced the name change to HSUS in 1956, and rumors about Myers's "communist tendencies" were circulated in an attempt to discredit and destroy the fledgling organization.

Over the next decade HSUS suffered its own acrimonious splits on issues of militancy. Several prominent HSUS figures left to form their own organizations, including Helen Jones, who founded the Society for Animal Rights. When the Animal Protection Institute was founded in the late 1960s by Belton Muras, executive director of California's HSUS branch, that new organization was plagued by lawsuits and rumormongering from HSUS, much as HSUS had suffered fifteen years previously.

HSUS first planned to organize self-supporting branches in every state, but this effort was abandoned in favor of a centralized structure with regional offices around the country. In the early 1960s HSUS amended its bylaws to allow local humane societies to affiliate with the national organization; annual inspections proved too expensive, and this plan was dropped in favor of a program to accredit local animal control groups. Fred Myers remained executive director until 1963. After a period of interim directors, John Hoyt (a minister from Ft. Wayne, Indiana) was hired as chief executive in 1970, and he began a period of rapid expansion. HSUS established the National Association for Humane and Environmental Education (NAHEE) as its youth education arm, staffed a legal department, and began to lobby for such legislation as the En-

dangered Species Act, the Humane Methods of Slaughter Act, the Animal Welfare Act, the Marine Mammal Protection Act, and the Horse Protection Act.

As laboratory break-ins and occasional acts of vandalism and arson by animal rights militants received widespread attention in the 1980s, HSUS found its position as the responsible spokesman for animal protection being undermined by a backlash against all animal advocacy. Together with the American SPCA and the Massachusetts SPCA, HSUS published a statement in *The New York Times* in 1991 clearly stating their opposition to violence and the destruction of property, and outlining their programs to reduce the suffering of animals through nonviolent means.

If HSUS's steps to distance itself from militant animal liberationists were controversial in animal rights circles, questions concerning salaries and perks for top staff troubled its wider constituency. Syndicated columnists Jack Anderson and Dale Van Atta revealed that HSUS board members required an internal audit of issues including the purchase of a house for president Hoyt and a loan to vice president Paul Irwin. The board chairman reported a review of top staff salaries (over $100,000) determined they were not excessive, but that policies and procedures governing compensation and benefits would be tightened. A new controller was hired, and expanded board committees will oversee financial administration.

CURRENT PRIORITIES: The 1991 joint resolution includes the following priorities:

(1) *laboratory animals:* eliminating the LD 50 and Draize tests for product testing, strong enforcement of the Animal Welfare Act by the U.S. Department of Agriculture, and use of alternatives to dissection and experimentation on animals for students and more generally in biomedical research; (2) *farm animals:* establishing adequate standards for the care and transportation of farm animals, including extending the protection of state anticruelty legislation to livestock, and the elimination of confinement and intensive-rearing methods; (3) *wild animals:* prohibiting such cruel practices as steel-jaw traps, eliminating sport hunting on national wildlife refuges, and opposing the wearing of fur; (4) *companion animals:* combating overpopulation by promoting the spaying and neutering of dogs and cats, increasing humane education, and working to ban pound seizure (the practice of using animals from shelters for research experimentation); and (5) *exhibition and work animals:* prohibiting abusive training practices and the capture of animals in the wild for exhibition or work purposes. HSUS's public education programs include "The Beautiful Choice" campaign, which encourages consumers to buy personal care products certified as produced without animal testing, and the "Shame of Fur" campaign to end the wearing of fur.

MEMBERS: Membership was up to 400,000 in 1990. Members who pledge to write letters, send telegrams, or make phone calls are invited to join the Action Alert Team and receive *The Animal Activist Alert* newsletter four times a year.

STRUCTURE: HSUS is governed by a twenty-four-member board of directors, elected at-large by the membership. The membership votes to amend society bylaws. There are eleven vice presidents on the staff, including senior vice president Patricia Forkan, John Grandy for wildlife and habitat protection, and Michael Fox for farm animals and bioethics. HSUS has headquarters in Washington, D.C., ten regional offices serving forty-three states, and two other major sites—the Animal Control Academy in Alabama, providing training for shelter workers; and the National Humane Education Center, headquarters for NAHEE in Connecticut, providing educational materials and training for teachers and students. The regional offices provide support for local humane organizations, animal-control agencies, officials, educators, the media, and the general public. HSUS also runs the Center for Respect of Life and Environment (CRLE), concerned with curricula and animal issues at universities. In 1991 the board approved the establishment of two new related organizations—Humane Society International (the international arm of HSUS), and EarthKind (to address the well-being of animals negatively affected by environmental changes). The board also created the new position of chief executive (Paul Irwin), directly responsible for the related organizations and with final responsibility for the HSUS. The duties of the president (John Hoyt) were redefined to primary responsibility for HSUS.

RESOURCES: HSUS's 1991 revenue of $21.1 million was derived from dues and contributions (36 percent), gifts and grants (24 percent), bequests (30 percent); investment income (7 percent); and sale of literature and other income (3 percent). Expenditures of $17.5 million included public education (34 percent), animal protection programs (35 percent), membership development and fund-raising (22 percent), administration (8 percent) and annuities (1 percent).

PUBLICATIONS AND SERVICES: Membership starts at $10 and includes a quarterly magazine, *The HSUS News* (circulation 300,000); an annual report is printed in the summer issue. *Close-Up Reports* are issued periodically to solicit member participation in specific campaigns. *Shelter Sense* is designed for professionals in animal work. NAHEE publishes *KIND Teacher* for elementary school educators and *Kind News* for children in the elementary grades. HSUS has a catalog of posters, bumper stickers, books, filmstrips, fact sheets, and reprints. □

The Fund for Animals, Inc.

THE FUND FOR ANIMALS INC.

200 W. 57TH STREET

NEW YORK, NY 10019

(212) 246-2632

FOUNDED: 1967 CONTRIBUTORS: 200,000
BUDGET: $1.8 million STAFF: 21
TAX STATUS: 501(c)(3)

PURPOSE: "To eliminate cruelty to animals wherever, however, whenever it occurs."

The Fund for Animals was founded by writer, humorist, lecturer, and television personality Cleveland Amory, to protect wildlife, combat hunting, and "put cleats on the little old ladies in tennis shoes," as he enjoys saying. The Fund is noted for its dramatic campaigns to protect seals and whales, its rescue of wild burros and horses scheduled for destruction, and its opposition to hunting and other blood sports (Amory coined the slogan, "Support your right to arm bears"). The Fund maintains three sanctuaries for rescued animals.

BACKGROUND: Amory dates his concern for animal protection to a bullfight he watched in Mexico in the mid-1950s. He joined several humane organizations, and finally decided to form his own in 1967. Amory was acclaimed for his popular books on high society, *The Proper Bostonians* (Dutton, 1947) and *Who Killed Society?* (Harper, 1960), and reached a wide audience with his magazine articles. Recently he was back on the best-seller lists with *The Cat Who Came for Christmas* (Penguin, 1988) and *The Cat and the Curmudgeon* (Little, Brown, 1990). Amory's leadership style has always been to hire talented people with a flair for publicity and give them free rein. Marian Probst, who serves as Amory's assistant, has been the administrative mainstay of the organization.

When Paul Watson was fired by Greenpeace for using force in seal hunt disruption, Amory bankrolled his ship the *Sea Shepherd*, which rammed a pirate whaler off the coast of Portugal (Watson went on to form the Sea Shepherd Conservation Society). The Fund has made a special project of rescuing herds of wild burros and horses from public lands in the West, where they often compete for sparse vegetation with cattle and sheep. The Fund went to court to prevent the federal government from shooting burros and horses to thin herds in the Grand Canyon, China Lake Naval Weapons Center, and Death Valley. In its quest to save animals, The Fund uses a variety of tactics, including "legislation, litigation, education, confrontation."

Its successful rescue programs have provided The Fund with a multitude of animals to adopt out, and it maintains the 600-acre Black Beauty Ranch near Ben Wheeler, Texas, as a haven for the thousands of burros, San Clemente goats, and horses it has saved. The most famous permanent resident at the Ranch is Nim Chimpsky, the chimpanzee who was taught sign language and later was slated for a drug experiment. In 1991 *Animals' Voice* magazine charged that Black Beauty Ranch manager Billy Saxon ran his own livestock business on the side, and that animals on the ranch had been neglected. The Fund had hired a new manager to replace Saxon in 1990, and other investigators found no evidence of neglect or mistreatment of animals at the ranch. The Fund also supports the Animal Trust Sanctuary in Ramona, California, for goats, burros, and smaller animals, and a rabbit sanctuary in Simpsonville, South Carolina.

STRUCTURE: The Fund has six staff in its New York City headquarters, another six in Washington, D.C., and twelve field agents in eight states and Mexico. Amory serves as president and chairman of a ten-member, self-recruiting board of directors, drawing no salary. Marian Probst is secretary/treasurer. Writer Lewis Regenstein, who opened The Fund's Washington office in 1972, worked on staff until 1982. Wayne Pacelle, former associate editor of *The Animals' Agenda*, was hired as national director in 1988 and has added a fresh dimension of youthful leadership to The Fund. In 1991 Pacelle announced The Fund would campaign to end hunting nationally, and work to democratize state fish and game agencies by adding directors interested in wildlife preservation and opposed to hunting.

RESOURCES: The Fund runs on a relatively low overhead, paying modest salaries and avoiding direct-mail solicitations. Amory's articles, books, and public appearances attract most of the new supporters.

PUBLICATIONS AND SERVICES: Contributors receive a quarterly bulletin, *The Fund for Animals*. Amory's major work on animal issues is *Man Kind: Our Incredible War on Wildlife* (Harper & Row, 1974), an attack on hunting and the fur trade. The Fund sells an "Animal Rights Resources Catalog" listing literature, films, and lesson plans available from over 120 organizations. □

PEOPLE FOR THE ETHICAL TREATMENT OF ANIMALS

P.O. BOX 42516

WASHINGTON, DC 20015

(301) 770-7444

FOUNDED: 1980   MEMBERS: 350,000
BUDGET: $10.7 million   STAFF: 90
TAX STATUS: 501(c)(3)

PURPOSE: "Establishing and defending the rights of all sentient animals . . . through public education, research and investigations, legislation, special events, direct action and grassroots organizing."

People for the Ethical Treatment of Animals (PETA) represents the abolitionists of the animal rights movement. Inspired by the writing of philosophers Peter Singer and Tom Regan, PETA would do away with animal experimentation, factory farming, hunting and trapping, products made of fur and leather, and the exploitation of animals for entertainment—including circuses and zoos. PETA has gained the esteem of animal rights activists by its bold exposés of animal abuse in research labs and by serving as the public voice of the underground Animal Liberation Front.

BACKGROUND: Alex Pacheco served a dramatic apprenticeship in activism: He shipped out with Paul Watson on the *Sea Shepherd* in 1979 on its search for the pirate whaler *Sierra*, which Wat-

son finally rammed off Lisbon, Portugal. Fleeing to England, Pacheco met activists from well-established movements opposing vivisection and fox hunting. Back in the United States and enrolled in George Washington University, Pacheco volunteered at the animal shelter in Washington, D.C., where Ingrid Newkirk worked as a humane officer. The two teamed up to form People for the Ethical Treatment of Animals (PETA) in 1980, to educate the public on animal rights and to investigate abuses in animal experimentation—the issue that has brought PETA its most dramatic publicity.

Pacheco got a job at Dr. Edward Taub's Institute for Behavioral Research in Silver Spring, Maryland, and quickly decided to expose the conditions suffered by animals there. After PETA filed a complaint under anti-cruelty laws, police raided the lab and rescued seventeen surgically mutilated primates. Taub was prosecuted, his $221,000 grant from the National Institutes of Health (NIH) was canceled, and NIH ended up with the surviving primates. (PETA has spent several years battling NIH to free the surviving "Silver Spring monkeys.") A year later a Defense Department wound lab was closed after PETA exposed plans to shoot animals with high-velocity bullets to examine tissue damage. The public outcry resulted in a permanent ban on the shooting of dogs and cats in experiments.

In 1985 PETA publicized seventy hours of graphic videotapes documenting mistreatment of primates at the Head Injury Laboratory at the University of Pennsylvania, arousing members of Congress and leading to a suspension of funding for the lab. In the same year, PETA distributed videotapes taken by the Animal Liberation Front from the University of California, Riverside, behavior research lab and from an animal facility at the City of Hope Hospital in Duarte near Los Angeles. NIH suspended all funds for animal experiments at City of Hope and the lab was closed.

PETA joined the campaigns against the use of animals in product testing by cosmetic companies and manufacturers of other household products. The Draize Eye Irritancy Test and the LD 50 test (the lethal dose that kills 50 percent of animal subjects) earned the most notorious reputations. By 1990 animal testing had been abandoned by many major companies, including Amway, Avon, Revlon, and Mary Kay. PETA has also been active in campaigns against fur, hunting, and animals in entertainment.

CURRENT PRIORITIES: PETA suggests three criteria in deciding which areas to target for action: Large numbers of animals are involved, their suffering is severe, and their suffering is imposed over a long period of time. These criteria highlight first, factory farming and the slaughter of animals for human consumption; and second, the capture and confinement of animals for scientific experimentation.

PETA's research and cruelty investigations unit continues its well-publicized work on the abuse of animals in scientific research. As a long-range goal, PETA supports legislation to abolish the use of animals in research—drawing strong opposition from the medical research community in universities and industry. As a short-range program, PETA supports alternative teaching techniques that avoid animal dissection in high school biology classes, and attacks abuses in the animal supply industry. The current campaign against the use of animals in product testing is directed at L'Oreal, the world's largest cosmetics company, and Gillette.

However, it's easier to arouse sympathy for animals in research labs than to convince people to stop eating meat —although the latter accounts for a much larger number of animals exploited. PETA's "Meat Stinks" campaign promotes vegetarianism, and many staff are vegans (who avoid all animal food-products—eggs, milk, cheese, and the like). PETA lines up celebrities and rock bands for pro-vegetarian ads and public service announcements, drawing support from singer k.d. lang, rock band The B-52's, and Paul and Linda McCartney. PETA's "Fur Is Dead" campaign has been highlighted by musicians and stars, including a "Rock Against Fur" concert in New York, coinciding with the fur industry convention.

PETA cosponsors the Caring Consumer Campaign, with a product logo and a shopping guide to assist in ethical purchasing. Companies whose products carry the logo guarantee that neither they nor their suppliers conduct any testing on animals. PETA continues to offer its popular workshop "Animal Rights 101" across the country, teaching activists how to organize around animal rights issues.

MEMBERS: Direct-mail campaigns have sharply increased PETA's contributors, from 84,000 in 1987 to 350,000 in 1990. Members have no role in governance.

STRUCTURE: PETA is tightly controlled by Pacheco and Newkirk, who serve as president and vice president respectively of the board of directors; Betsy Swart is secretary/treasurer. The board has only the legal minimum of three directors, offering the freedom to act in accordance with an uncompromising vision, but providing little independent oversight for the organization. Kim Stallwood, who was hired from England in 1987, served as executive director until 1992. PETA began and then disbanded a chapter structure, fearing legal responsibility for the actions of far-flung groups.

RESOURCES: PETA's 1991 revenue of $10.5 million was derived 86 percent from contributions and donations, 12 percent from merchandise sales, and 2 percent from other sources. Expenditures of $10.7 million included 13 percent for campaigns and educational programs; 20 percent for research and cruelty investigations; 30 percent for public outreach, grassroots training, and organizing; 14 percent for membership development; 12 percent for operating expenses; and 11 percent for merchandise. Staff has increased along with revenue from thirty in 1987 to ninety in 1990.

PUBLICATIONS AND SERVICES: Members who contribute $20 or more receive *PETA News* six times a year, periodic action alerts, and an annual report. Recognizing that its supporters lead typically busy lives, PETA produces well-designed guides with simple and specific actions anyone can take to make the world better for animals. Handbooks available by mail order include *The PETA Guide to Becoming an Activist*, and *The PETA Guide to Compassionate Living*, *The PETA Guide to Action for Animals*, and *Facts for Activists* (a loose-leaf notebook of fact sheets). PETA has a mail-order catalog of publications, videos, buttons, bumper stickers, clothing, and cruelty-free products. PETA message checks are available. Ingrid Newkirk has written a practical action guide, *Save the Animals! 101 Easy Things You Can Do* (Warner Books, 1990), and *Free the Animals! The Untold Story of the U.S. Animal Liberation Front and Its Founder, "Valerie"* (Noble Press, 1992). □

ANIMAL LEGAL DEFENSE FUND

ANIMAL LEGAL DEFENSE FUND
1363 LINCOLN AVENUE
SAN RAFAEL, CA 94901
(415) 459-0885

FOUNDED: 1981   CONTRIBUTORS: 50,000
BUDGET: $300,000   STAFF: 4
TAX STATUS: 501(c)(3)

Animal Legal Defense Fund (ALDF) is the legal arm of the animal rights movement. From a discussion group of attorneys interested in animal law (calling themselves Attorneys For Animal Rights, or AFAR) started in 1979 by Joyce Tischler and Laurence Kessenick, ALDF has grown to a national network of 350 attorneys and law students who apply a litigation model inspired by the Sierra Club LDF to animal issues. ALDF's strategy is to seek major impact litigation, cases that establish new kinds of protection for animals or broader application of existing law.

BACKGROUND: AFAR's first legal battle in 1981 stopped a plan by the U.S. Navy to shoot wild burros at its China Lake weapons testing center. With a small grant from the Animal Protection Institute, Tischler became the first full-time employee of AFAR later that year. Incorporated as ALDF in 1983, the group sued in 1984 to halt the export of primates from Bangladesh to a research laboratory in the United States; and in 1986 ALDF attorneys obtained an injunction to block the U.S. Department of Agriculture (USDA) plan to brand dairy cows on the face during its herd reduction program. ALDF has helped block hunting for bears and mountain lions in California, and has begun an international animal law project focused on CITES, the Convention on International Trade in Endangered Species.

The major problem in the law facing animal advocates is "standing to sue." Animals are not recognized as persons and thus have no rights; an animal protection organization has no standing to sue on animals' behalf unless it can show injury to its members. In the celebrated case of *Sierra Club* v. *Morton*, the Supreme Court held that an organization has standing to sue on behalf of the environment if it shows that its members use the natural site and their aesthetic interest will be injured by some act or failure to act. Suing veal producer Provimi, Inc., under consumer protection laws, ALDF was denied standing in 1985, but in 1990 ALDF was granted standing to sue the USDA for failure to issue regulations under the Animal Welfare Act to protect animals used in research, including rats, mice, and birds; in 1992 the court ruled for ALDF. Recently ALDF sued the U.S. Patent Office to challenge its rule allowing the patenting of genetically altered animals. ALDF's ultimate goal is to change animals' legal status from property to person.

STRUCTURE: ALDF has a twelve-member, self-recruiting board of directors. Joyce Tischler is executive director.

PUBLICATIONS AND SERVICES: Contributors receive the quarterly newsletter *The Animals' Advocate* (circulation 60,000). ALDF maintains a dissection hotline offering suggestions to high school and college students who object to dissection: (800) 922-FROG. Booklets on "Objecting to Dissection" are available. ☐

MULTIISSUE ORGANIZATIONS

9.

PROGRESSIVES

Just as the end of the Cold War opened up divisions among conservatives, it should serve to heal them among progressives. The post–Cold War world offers the prospect of a new coalition of liberalism and the Left, which have had little fruitful collaboration since the Progressive party movement of 1948 drove a wedge between them. William F. Buckley used anticommunism to hold together a "fusionist" coalition among the conflicting branches of conservativism in the 1950s, but the demise of communism (which has split conservatism into feuding factions again) now offers the opportunity for a progressive "fusion" at the junction of liberalism and the Left—reviving the grand tradition of populism, progressivism, social democracy, and New Deal reforms. The components of this progressive fusion remain to be formulated, but would likely include a full employment economy that competes with Japan and Europe in the world market, a defense of social justice and human rights in the fullest sense, a new system of global security based on international institutions for conflict resolution, and global environmental protection with sustainable economic growth for developing countries.

In the 1930s President Franklin D. Roosevelt knitted together the New Deal coalition of labor, liberals, big city machines that mobilized working-class white ethnic groups, urban blacks in the North, and lower- and middle-income southern whites. Without explicitly saying so, the New Deal incorporated much of the reform spirit and program of earlier populist, progressive, and socialist movements. The coalition held together through Harry Truman's Fair Deal and eight years of Dwight Eisenhower's "Modern Republicanism" (which accepted the New Deal reforms as a given) to John F. Kennnedy's New Frontier and Lyndon Johnson's Great Society. The Friends Committee on National Legislation is a Quaker lobby in the progressive spirit of this tradition, informed by a pacifist vision.

Cold War liberalism was a response to Stalin's consolidation of control over Eastern Europe in 1947. President Truman announced his "containment" doctrine, supporting Greece and Turkey against Communist insurgents, and proposed the Marshall Plan of economic aid to revive Europe. Americans for Democratic Action (ADA) formed in 1948, specifically excluding Communists, who helped organize Henry Wallace's Progressive party campaign against Truman. The Progressive party fiasco marked the end of Communist influence in the labor movement and set the stage for Senator Joseph McCarthy's demagogic attack against the Left in the early 1950s. The National Committee for an Effective Congress (NCEC), founded in 1948, was a pioneer liberal political action committee in tune with the ADA but taking a looser, more pragmatic approach to electing liberals to Congress. Both the ADA and NCEC were on the defensive during the anticommunist assaults of Senator Joseph McCarthy and Dwight Eisenhower's presidency, only to revive with John F. Kennedy's election in 1960.

Lyndon Johnson defeated conservative Barry Goldwater in a landslide victory in 1964, but just four years later he declined to run again—virtually forced from office—and the New Deal coalition fell apart. Since 1968 Republicans held the White House for twenty of the next twenty-four years. What happened? The mid-1960s produced a political divide that split the Democrats along new fault lines. The Vietnam War divided Democrats into a Cold War liberal wing headed by Senator Henry Jackson and Vice President Hubert Humphrey, who would hold the line against communism at all costs, and a new liberal wing led first by Senators Eugene McCarthy and Robert Kennedy and later George McGovern, who would reassess America's Cold War foreign policy. A backlash to the civil rights movement and urban riots in the black inner cities pulled away the "George Wallace Democrats," southern whites and northern urban white ethnics who gravitated toward the Republicans, at least when voting for president. The countercultural radicalism of the late 1960s seemed to blend into the feminist, gay liberation, and environmental movements of the 1970s, further alienating the culturally conservative working-class base of the Democrats.

The New Left that emerged in the early 1960s took little guidance from either liberals or the Old Left (although some of its early leaders were "red diaper babies," children of Old Leftists). When Students for a Democratic Society (SDS) developed its platform for participatory democracy (the Port Huron Statement) in 1962, it established a "nonexclusionary" principle that ignored as irrelevant the anticommunism of the Cold War liberals. The SDS found a student civil rights counterpart in the Student Nonviolent Coordinating Committee (SNCC), which produced a new generation of black leaders. Both the SDS and SNCC disintegrated by the end of the 1960s, with some poststudent SDSers regrouping in a democratic socialist organization, the New American Movement (NAM) in 1971. One wing of the SDS began the Economic Research and Action Project (ERAP) in the mid-1960s. Out of the ERAP community organizing experience came several people who helped start new community organizing projects in the 1970s —which became the Citizen Action network in the 1980s. Another outgrowth of the civil rights, antipoverty, and antiwar movements of the 1960s and early 1970s was the liberal ecumenical religious lobby in Washington, D.C.; Interfaith Impact for Justice and Peace (founded in 1990) was formed by a merger of two such groups, National Impact (1968) and Interfaith Action for Economic Justice (1974).

The old Socialist party was also pulled apart in 1972 by the Vietnam War and the question of backing George McGovern's Democratic campaign to unseat Richard Nixon as president. One faction, led by ex-Trotskyist Max Schactman, supported the war and formed the Social Democrats USA (SDUSA), drawing closer to its allies in the AFL-CIO leadership and the

Democrats' Henry Jackson wing. Another faction led by Michael Harrington opposed the war and formed the Democratic Socialist Organizing Committee (DSOC). In 1982 the NAM and DSOC merged to form the Democratic Socialists of America (DSA), which has worked to support social movements and build a left wing in the Democratic party. The SDUSA became part of the neoconservative movement that supported Ronald Reagan in the 1980s.

Reforms in the Democratic party primary process initiated by McGovern opened the party to new activist constituencies —including white-collar teacher and public employee unions, blacks, women, gays, environmentalists, and peace movement advocates. Republicans portrayed the Democrats as captured by the "special interests," attentive only to the concerns of upper-middle-class "limousine liberals." Democrats could not find the language and programs to mediate these new constituencies, defend the economic and cultural concerns of its working-class and lower-middle-class base, and articulate a vision of the public interest and the common good. Conservatives captured the "values" issues—portraying themselves as the defenders of family, work, neighborhood, and patriotism.

The progressive center gained the most ground during the 1970s. John Gardner launched Common Cause in the "good government" tradition, attracting "procedural liberals" working for campaign finance reform and ethics in government. Common Cause supports a moderate progressive reform agenda similar to the League of Women Voters, but finds its constituency of men and women primarily through direct mail. Seeing that Gardner could do it, Ralph Nader in 1971 started his first direct-mail membership organization—Public Citizen —building on his consumer protection record to promote corporate accountability and responsive government. Nader's Public Interest Research Groups (PIRGs) developed a constituency on college campuses in some twenty states.

The Greens emerged in the late 1980s out of the environmental movement, the counterculture, and New Age thinking. Inspired by European Green parties, The Greens took several years to wade through its participatory, consensual process and formulate a program and strategy. Divided into grassroots movement and political party wings, The Greens split the difference by trying to be both simultaneously. Other "third" or minority party movements under way include the 21st Century party initiated by the National Organization for Women; the Labor Party Advocates initiated by Anthony Mazzocchi of the Oil, Chemical and Atomic Workers; the New party, initiated by academic Joel Rogers and activists Danny Cantor and Sandy Pope; and the independent presidential candidacy of Ron Daniels, former director of the National Rainbow Coalition. After the "death of communism" and the break-up of the Soviet Union in 1991, remnants of the Marxist "vanguard" parties and other independent Marxists began an agonizing reappraisal of their experience—and drifted either toward DSA, minor party activity, or the Left Greens.

NATIONAL ADVOCATES

FRIENDS COMMITTEE ON NATIONAL LEGISLATION

FRIENDS COMMITTEE ON NATIONAL LEGISLATION

245 SECOND STREET, NE

WASHINGTON, DC 20002

(202) 547-6000

FOUNDED: 1943   CONTRIBUTORS: 9,000
BUDGET: $900,000   STAFF: 16
TAX STATUS: 501(c)(4): Friends Committee on National Legislation; 501(c)(3): FCNL Education Fund

PURPOSE: "A world free of war and the threat of war; a society with equity and justice for all; a community where every person's potential may be fulfilled; an earth restored."

Friends Committee on National Legislation (FCNL) is a Quaker lobby, focused on peace and social justice, which provides one of the most respected and up-to-date legislative information services on Capitol Hill.

BACKGROUND: FCNL was founded in 1943 by leaders of the American Friends Service Committee, who wanted a lobbying arm in Washington to work on issues relating to conscription, conscientious objection, and alternatives to military service. FCNL has consistently opposed militarism and foreign intervention, and supported international institutions and efforts toward disarmament. During the 1960s FCNL gave strong support to civil rights legislation, and became involved in such social justice issues as jobs, poverty, welfare reform, housing, and health care. Following another Quaker tradition, FCNL is one of the few groups giving close attention to American Indian issues.

CURRENT PRIORITIES: In 1992 FCNL was working for campaign finance reform, the Religious Freedom Restoration Act, a ban on U.S. nuclear weapons tests, a moratorium on arms transfers to the Middle East, lifting nonmilitary sanctions against Iraq, support for the peace agreement in El Salvador, and legislation to prevent proliferation of nuclear weapons.

STRUCTURE: FCNL is governed by a general committee of 250 Quakers, mostly appointed by twenty-six Friends Yearly Meetings and eight other Friends organizations, with some chosen at-large. The general committee holds an annual meeting, and an executive committee meets regularly to oversee programs and staff. FCNL's founding executive secretary was E. Raymond Wilson. Ed Snyder joined FCNL's staff in 1955, becoming executive secretary following Wilson's retirement in 1962 and serving through 1989. Joe Volk was hired as executive secretary in 1990.

RESOURCES: FCNL had revenues of $621,000 in 1990 and expenses of $665,000, spent for programs (62 percent) and administration and fund-raising (38 percent). The FCNL Education Fund had revenue of $377,000 and expenses of $450,000, including programs (62 percent), and administration, annuity, and fund-raising (38 percent). In response to prior year deficits, FCNL's budgets were reduced to a combined total of approximately $900,000 for 1991.

PUBLICATIONS AND SERVICES: Contributors of $25 or more receive the *FCNL Washington Newsletter* (circulation 9,000) monthly. Members of the Legislative Action Program, including a core of 650 Friends meetings contacts and the 250 members of the governing general committee, receive action alerts about specific legislation. The newsletter *Indian Report* (circulation 4,000) is available by subscription; the bulletin *FCNL Housing Hook-Up* is sent on request. The FCNL update/action message, with information on legislation before Congress and suggested actions to take, is revised weekly and available by telephone at (202) 547-4343; it is also posted on CompuServe and PeaceNet. Ed Snyder's reflections on FCNL, *On the Occasion of 35 Years as a Quaker Lobbyist in Washington*, is available as a pamphlet. □

ADA

AMERICANS FOR DEMOCRATIC ACTION

1625 K STREET, NW, SUITE 1150

WASHINGTON, DC 20006

(202) 785-5980

FOUNDED: 1948   MEMBERS: 35,000
CHAPTERS: 25   BUDGET: $1 million   STAFF: 7
TAX STATUS: 501(c)(4): Americans for Democratic Action; 501(c)(3): ADA Education Fund; PACs: ADA PAC, ADA Campaign Committee

PURPOSE: "Promoting a liberal agenda that is progressive, socially conscious and economically just."

Americans for Democratic Action (ADA) was launched in early 1947 to defend and extend New Deal programs, and counter Henry Wallace's Progressive Citizens of America (PCA). ADA supported the Truman Doctrine and the Marshall Plan, and stood against Wallace's 1948 presidential campaign with the Communist-dominated Progressive party. Initial success during the Truman administration was rolled back under right-wing attacks during Eisenhower's presidency. ADA's fortunes revived under President Kennedy as ADAers were appointed to influential government positions, only to split over the Vietnam War in 1968. Labor leaders began to return to ADA as unions ran into hard times in the Carter and Reagan years. Today ADA is one of the few public interest groups that lobbies a progressive economic agenda—full employment, tax policy, national health insurance. ADA's annual convention serves as a meeting ground for liberal legislators, union officials, and civil rights leaders.

BACKGROUND: ADA's story begins with the Union for Democratic Action (UDA), a group that split off in 1941 from Norman Thomas's isolationist Socialist party at the onset of World War II. UDA, based primarily in New York, was headed by James Loeb, Jr., and supported a war that would conclude in a democratic peace. After Republican victories in the 1946 congressional elections, Loeb and other liberal leaders were convinced they needed to reorganize and free themselves from charges of Communist influence. ADA's charter, excluding Communists and Fascists from membership, thus marked the end of the popular front era, in which liberals, progressives, and Communists had cooperated to build New Deal institutions and fight fascism. Communists and Communist-led unions joined Henry Wallace's PCA, which claimed 50,000 members and which became the Progressive party for his presidential campaign in 1948. Liberal Democrats, CIO union leaders, and social democrats abandoning the Socialist party joined ADA, which gathered 25,000

members. Labor had been convinced to stick with Truman by his veto of the hated Taft-Hartley Act in 1947 (which the Republican congress passed over Truman's veto). ADA received strong membership and financial assistance from the CIO unions, including the Textile Workers, Steelworkers, Auto Workers, and Communications Workers. ADA founders included liberals Chester Bowles, Hubert Humphrey, Joseph Rauh, Jr., Eleanor Roosevelt, and Wilson Wyatt; labor leaders David Dubinsky and Walter Reuther; theologian Reinhold Niebuhr; academics John Kenneth Galbraith and Arthur Schlesinger, Jr.; NAACP president Walter White; and ACLU attorney Morris Ernst.

Two Cold War foreign policy issues separated Wallace's Progressives and ADA in 1947: the "containment" policy embodied in the Truman Doctrine, granting military assistance to Greece and Turkey to resist Communist insurgencies, and the Marshall Plan for the economic rehabilitation of Europe, initially offered to include Eastern Europe and the Soviet Union as well. Wallace initially endorsed the Marshall Plan, but withdrew his support after participation was rejected by the Communist parties of Eastern Europe. The Marshall Plan was then opposed by PCA and ten Communist-led unions within the fifty-one-member CIO board.

A successful fight for a strong civil rights plank in the 1948 Democratic convention was led by ADA member Hubert Humphrey, who won election in Minnesota that year to the U.S. Senate, along with liberals Paul Douglas of Illinois and Henry Jackson of Washington. Conservative southerners walked out of the Democratic convention and nominated Strom Thurmond as their presidential candidate on the Dixiecrat ticket. Despite defections of the Progressives to the left and the Dixiecrats to the right, Truman defeated Dewey in the 1948 election.

Although the picture looked bright for ADA in 1948, the tenor of the times quickly shifted. China fell to the Communists in 1949; Whittaker Chambers charged that diplomat Alger Hiss had been a secret Communist and member of an espionage ring, leading to Hiss's two trials in 1949 and 1950; and the Korean War broke out in 1951. Following the abrupt decline of the Progressive party after its 1948 fiasco, ADA was the most visible organization on the left and became the favorite whipping boy of the right. ADA enthusiastically backed Adlai Stevenson in his campaign, and two ADA founders, Wilson Wyatt and Arthur Schlesinger, Jr., took key posts in his campaign. The right wing campaigned to identify the Democrats with ADA, and ADA with socialists and Communists. With Stevenson's loss to Eisenhower, ADA became marginalized on the Democrats' left. As Senator Joseph McCarthy made his wild charges of Communist infiltration throughout government, ADA ironically began to be branded as a Communist front because of its opposition to the House Un-American Activities Committee and its criticism of FBI investigations.

ADA's fortunes revived with the election of John Kennedy as president in 1960. Under Kennedy numerous ADA officials and members were appointed to important posts: Former executive secretary James Loeb and John Kenneth Galbraith were named ambassadors; Arthur Schlesinger, Jr., became a presidential adviser and speech writer. Over thirty prominent ADA leaders held government appointments. But ADA's chances for continued influence died with Kennedy in 1963. Never sympathetic with Lyndon Johnson's style, ADA supported his domestic antipoverty and civil rights programs, but came to oppose him over the Vietnam War. When Johnson declined to run for reelection, he threw his support to his loyal vice president, former ADA stalwart Hubert Humphrey. Labor supported the war and Humphrey. When the ADA national board by vote of 65 to 47 endorsed challenger Senator Eugene McCarthy for the Democratic nomination, most union leaders walked out. Presidents of the Steelworkers, Garment Workers, and Communications Workers unions resigned from the ADA board, and cut off financial contributions.

ADA struggled during the 1970s, bereft of its erstwhile labor allies and overshadowed by the flourishing environmental, women's, and civil rights groups, which gained ground during the Nixon and Ford administrations. But with hopes for labor law reform dashed during the Carter years, union leaders drifted back to their remaining allies in ADA. And as liberalism became the not-to-be-spoken "L-word" during the 1980s, under constant attack during the Reagan and Bush administrations, ADA became more of a rallying spot for liberals. By 1991 ADA was experiencing a modest revival.

CURRENT PRIORITIES: ADA's legislative agenda includes both domestic and foreign policy objectives. On the domestic side, ADA supports a spectrum of liberal Democratic economic and social legislation: progressive equitable taxation and adequate funding for social programs; campaign finance reform; an energy policy emphasizing conservation, recycling, alternative energy sources, and reduced toxic emissions; the Family and Medical Leave Act; the Freedom of Choice Act, which would codify the right to abortion specified in *Roe* v. *Wade;* the Striker Replacement Act, which safeguards the jobs of striking workers; and a universal national health insurance plan. ADA supports a 50 percent cut in the defense budget over five years, and opposes funding for SDI, B1-B and B-2 bombers, chemical weapons, and arms sales. ADA supports foreign relations based on assessment of a country's human rights record, and assistance to emerging democracies in Eastern Europe, Latin America, and Africa.

MEMBERS: Membership peaked around 55,000 in 1968, declined through the 1970s, and has revived to include 35,000 households at present.

STRUCTURE: ADA has a large board of directors, some 336 at present, elected to represent twenty-five active chapters in proportion to membership, plus directors elected at-large, and the officers. The board convenes quarterly, and an executive committee meets monthly. ADA presidents are typically leading congressional liberals—the current president is Senator Paul Wellstone (D-Minnesota), and recent presidents include Reps. Charles Rangel (D-New York), the late Ted Weiss (D-New York), Barney Frank (D-Massa-chusetts), Don Edwards (D-California), and former Reps. Robert Drinan (D-Massachusetts) and Patsy Mink (D-Hawaii). Youth for Democratic Action has active chapters at six campuses. The annual convention in June in Washington, D.C., adopts policy resolutions and brings the membership together for a political revival of the liberal–labor–civil rights coalition. Past national directors have included Leon Shull, from 1963 through 1984, and Ann Lewis, Democratic political consultant (and sister of Rep. Barney Frank), from 1985 to 1987. Amy Isaacs, who worked with ADA for most of the last twenty years, was hired back from Planned Parenthood as national director in 1989. ADA PAC supports congressional candidates, and the ADA Campaign Committee supports presidential candidates.

RESOURCES: ADA operates on a budget of $1 million. ADA/PAC, which spent over $100,000 in the 1984 presidential campaign cycle, raised $40,000 in the 1990 cycle.

PUBLICATIONS AND SERVICES: Membership is $40 and includes the quarterly newsletter *ADA Today* (circulation 35,000); the annual ADA congressional voting record is presented in the February issue. *ADAction News and Notes* (circulation 1,800), available by subscription, sends ADA's grassroots action network weekly legislative updates while Congress is in session. For the early history of ADA, see Clifton Brock, *Americans for Democratic Action* (Public Affairs Press, 1962). □

NATIONAL COMMITTEE FOR AN EFFECTIVE CONGRESS

10 E. 39TH STREET

NEW YORK, NY 10016

(212) 686-4905

FOUNDED: 1948   CONTRIBUTORS: 40,000
BUDGET: $1 million   STAFF: 22
TAX STATUS: PAC

The National Committee for an Effective Congress (NCEC) is the leading political action committee supporting liberal candidates, primarily Democrats, for the U.S. Congress. With an extensive computerized data base, NCEC brings a capacity for sophisticated electoral analysis and strategy to the candidates it supports.

BACKGROUND: NCEC was founded in New York by liberal Democrats concerned about the sharp tilt to the right in the Congress after the 1946 elections. Although drawing on much the same crowd (except for labor leaders) as founded the Americans for Democratic Action (ADA), NCEC was spared most of ADA's disputes and upheavals. Unlike ADA, NCEC is not a membership organization, has no chapters, and does not take stands on a wide range of issues. NCEC simply appeals to a liberal constituency for money to help liberal candidates for Congress.

With the endorsement of Eleanor Roosevelt, and led by Maurice Rosenblatt, Harry Louis Selden, and Sidney Scheuer, NCEC helped the Democrats recapture the Senate in 1948, bringing in liberal freshman senators Hubert Humphrey of Minnesota, Paul Douglas of Illinois, and Estes Kefauver of Tennessee. NCEC bills itself as independent and nonpartisan, and its support has not been limited to Democrats, although liberal Republicans are hard to come by these days. In an earlier era, NCEC backed Republican moderate senators Hugh Scott of Pennsylvania, Jacob Javits of New York, John Sherman Cooper of Kentucky, and Thomas Kuckel of California. Over the years NCEC has supported a variety of liberal issues, leading the call for the censure of Senator Joseph McCarthy of Wisconsin, endorsing civil rights legislation, criticizing the Vietnam War, and calling for the impeachment of President Richard Nixon. Arms control became a major issue in the 1980s.

CURRENT PRIORITIES: When the Federal Election Campaign Act limited the amount groups could contribute to any one candidate's campaign, NCEC explored other avenues of assistance. NCEC pioneered the computer analysis of electoral data to highlight areas where campaign efforts should be directed, and now has the most sophisticated electoral data base available to liberal candidates. NCEC helps candidates with demographic targeting at the precinct level, media market targeting, polling, and consulting (NCEC does for Democrats what the Republican National Committee does for Republicans).

STRUCTURE: NCEC has a thirty-nine-member, self-recruiting board of directors, and a fourteen-person executive committee. Distinguished former members of the board have included political scientist Hans Morganthau and historian Barbara Tuchman. Founder Sidney Scheuer served as chairman from 1956 until his death in 1987; his son Thomas Scheuer was elected chairman in 1989. Current notable board members include Steve Allen, Henry Steele Commager, Frances Lear, James Michener, Stewart Mott, Telford Taylor, Helen Vanderbilt, and George Wald. Russell Hemenway has been executive director since 1966.

RESOURCES: NCEC raised $2.6 million in the 1986 campaign cycle, $2.2 million in the 1988 cycle, and $2 million in the 1990 cycle, with $2.5 million projected for the 1992 cycle.

PUBLICATIONS AND SERVICES: Contributors receive the newsletter *Election Update* six times a year. For an early academic analysis of NCEC, see Harry M. Scoble, *Ideology and Electoral Action: A Comparative Case Study of NCEC* (Chandler, 1967). □

COMMON CAUSE

2030 M STREET, NW

WASHINGTON, DC 20036

(202) 833-1200

FOUNDED: 1970   MEMBERS: 275,000
STATE GROUPS: 48 plus D.C.
BUDGET: $12.2 million   STAFF: 115
TAX STATUS: 501(c)(4)

PURPOSE: "A citizens' lobbying group focusing on ethics and accountability issues at the national, state, and local levels."

Common Cause (CC) is the contemporary embodiment of the good government reform tradition, seeking to enhance citizen participation in politics. Founded by liberal Republican John Gardner, CC lobbies for ethics in government and campaign finance reform on behalf of a middle-class constituency of moderate progressives. Embracing a variety of issues as secondary objectives, CC also lobbies for arms control, environmental protection, and civil rights.

BACKGROUND: John Gardner launched Common Cause in 1970, after a distinguished career as president of the Carnegie Corporation (1955–1965), Lyndon Johnson's secretary of health, education and welfare (1965–1968), and president of the National Urban Coalition (1968–1970). Washington insiders scoffed at his goal of a citizens lobby to give voice to the public interest and reduce the impact of special interest money on government officials, but Gardner convinced several wealthy backers (including David Rockefeller) to put up $700,000 in seed money for an initial direct-mail appeal. To most people's surprise, it drew an enthusiastic response. In less than ten years, CC became one of the leading lobbies on Capitol Hill and in state legislatures around the country.

The timing was perfect: Common Cause was up and running when the Watergate scandal hit the Nixon administration in 1972, and its lawsuit against

CREEP (the Committee to Re-Elect the President) disclosed the massive contributions to the Nixon campaign, which provided the cash to support the Watergate burglars. CC had quickly established credibility as a grassroots lobby in 1971 with its campaign to defeat a proposed federal subsidy to the SST (supersonic transport airliner). Again mobilizing its membership, CC became a leading force behind the Federal Election Campaign Amendments of 1974, which created the Federal Election Commission, limited individual donations to a federal candidate to $1,000 per election, and established public financing of presidential campaigns. Over the years CC has also had a major impact on ethics and accountability reforms at the state level, including financial disclosure requirements. CC was a prominent member of the coalition that got the oil-depletion allowance repealed in 1975, ending an important tax loophole for the petroleum industry.

Common Cause has never been stuck in Gardner's shadow; the organization has been able to recruit an array of skilled leaders from the start. Jack Conway (a former United Auto Workers officer, War on Poverty staffer, and founder of the Center for Community Change) led CC as president and chief executive through its early rapid growth to 1975. David Cohen (an associate of Conway's and experienced lobbyist— currently president of the Professionals' Coalition for Nuclear Arms Control) followed as president, honing the lobbying operation, serving until 1981. Fred Wertheimer, who had been CC's chief lobbyist, has been president since. Gardner resigned as chairman of the board in 1977 to start Independent Sector, a national forum for the nonprofit sector, remaining on the CC board—indeed, setting up his new office in the same building. Nan Waterman served as chairwoman until 1980. Archibald Cox, the first Watergate special prosecutor (fired by President Nixon in his infamous "Saturday night massacre" in October 1973), was enlisted as board chairman and continued through 1991, while remaining a full-time Harvard law professor. Edward "Ned" Cabot, a business executive who heads the nonprofit organization Housing All Americans, stepped into the chairman position in 1992.

Common Cause established an early record on peace and arms control issues. As the Vietnam War was contested in Congress in 1971, CC lobbied to bring the conflict to an end. With fear of nuclear conflict with the Soviet Union growing in the early Reagan years, CC gave a high priority to nuclear arms control, hiring lobbyist Michael Mawby from SANE. Liberal issues backed by CC include stricter environmental laws, energy conservation measures, tougher auto emissions standards, solar bank legislation, arms control, District of Columbia voting representation, ratification of the Equal Rights Amendment (ERA), and opposition to the B-1 bomber, the MX missile, and aid to the Nicaraguan contras. Positions more pleasing to conservatives include a balanced budget, trucking and airline deregulation, and a sunset law requiring federal programs to end after ten years unless reauthorized by Congress. CC supported a 51 percent congressional pay raise to $135,000 per year, at the same time calling for an end to all honoraria received by members of

Congress (Public Citizen opposed the raise, arguing that lower government salaries would keep representatives closer to the average person). Among CC's successes at congressional reform stands its part in the House Ethics Committee's investigation of Speaker Jim Wright, leading to his 1989 resignation and that of majority whip Tony Coelho. CC also called for investigation of the Keating Five, five senators implicated in the savings and loan scandal of the late 1980s.

CURRENT PRIORITIES: Common Cause's congressional campaign finance reform package calls for (1) a limit on campaign spending, (2) a dramatic reduction in the role of special interest PACs, (3) alternative campaign funds, and (4) shutting down the "soft" money system that brings huge contributions back into federal campaigns. CC's ethics in government program would eliminate such abuses as vacations and personal travel paid by special interests, and personal use of leftover campaign funds.

MEMBERS: Membership expanded rapidly in the early years, peaking at 325,000 in 1975 during the Watergate scandal. Once President Nixon left office, and the Carter administration projected a more responsive and responsible government, members dropped off to 205,000 by 1981. The Reagan administration spurred growth again in the early 1980s as CC climbed on the arms control bandwagon. Between 1985 and 1991 membership leveled off, fluctuating from 250,000 to 290,000. Along with the annual board election, members are polled on policy priorities for the organization. In a 1985

membership poll, 67 percent described themselves as Democrats, 19 percent as Republicans; 53 percent called themselves liberal, 7 percent conservative. Members can sign up for the activist network and respond to action alerts on legislative issues.

STRUCTURE: The governing board of Common Cause consists of sixty members, twenty elected by the membership each year to serve three-year terms. CC conducts an issues poll of the membership to guide the governing board in establishing policy positions and priorities.

RESOURCES: Common Cause received $12.2 million in revenue in 1990, 90 percent in dues and contributions of $100 or less. CC does not solicit funds from corporations, foundations, or government. Expenditures of $12.2 million included $7.7 million for program services (63 percent) and $4.5 million for administration, membership development, and fund-raising (37 percent).

PUBLICATIONS AND SERVICES: Membership costs $30 and includes *Common Cause Magazine* (circulation 280,000) quarterly. An annual financial statement is available on request. Books and pamphlets may be ordered from a publications catalog. John Gardner set out his vision and rationale for the organization in a brief book, *In Common Cause* (1972; rev. ed., Norton, 1973). Andrew S. McFarland analyzes the organization's first decade in *Common Cause: Lobbying in the Public Interest* (Chatham House, 1984). □

PUBLIC CITIZEN

2000 P STREET, NW

WASHINGTON, DC 20036

(202) 833-3000

FOUNDED: 1971   MEMBERS: 100,000
BUDGET: $7.6 million   STAFF: 70
TAX STATUS: 501(c)(4): Public Citizen;
501(c)(3): Public Citizen Foundation
PAC: Public Citizen Fund for a Clean Congress

PURPOSE: "To enhance such areas as governmental responsiveness, consumer protection, corporate responsibility, protection of the environment, civil liberties, and civil rights."

The consumer movement blossomed in the late 1960s thanks to Ralph Nader, who is one tough customer. Public Citizen is the visible vanguard of the many organizations he has created—and the only one dependent on broad public support. If Public Citizen had a mantra, it would be "regulation." The organization has left its mark on public policy governing health, energy and environment, campaign finance reform, and taxation.

BACKGROUND: Ralph Nader achieved fame with his 1965 book *Unsafe at Any Speed*, which highlighted the faults of General Motors' Corvair. Public reaction led to legislation creating the National Highway Traffic Safety Administration in 1966. A folk hero at age thirty-one, Nader's reputation was enhanced when it was learned that GM had hired a private detective to discredit him. He received a $480,000 settlement from GM for invasion of privacy, and fed the money back into his consumer advocacy organizations. Nader's ascetic life-style became part of his legend (St. Ralph, *The New Republic* called him)—he doesn't own a car and lives alone. Beginning in 1969, Nader recruited young law students and attorneys willing to work for subsistence salaries—"Nader's Raiders" —and poured out reports on subjects from clean air and water to nursing homes and corporate regulation. Nader doubted that mass support could be attracted for consumer advocacy until John Gardner used direct mail to generate a substantial membership for Common Cause in 1970. Two mail appeals from Nader in 1971 brought in 62,000 contributions and several hundred thousand dollars to start Public Citizen.

Public Citizen is organized into five working groups: *Congress Watch* monitors legislation on Capitol Hill, documents campaign financing abuses, tracks House and Senate voting records, and lobbies for the Public Citizen agenda; directors have included Mark Green (later director of the Democracy Project and a Democratic candidate for U.S. Senator in New York) and Joan Claybrook, current president and chief executive of Public Citizen. The *Litigation Group* brings precedent-setting class-action lawsuits against government agencies and corporations. The *Health Research Group*, under the direction of Dr. Sidney Wolfe, fights for protection against unsafe foods, drugs, and workplaces, and for greater consumer control over personal health decisions; staff spends about half their time dealing with the Food and Drug Administration. Wolfe has authored two surprising best-sellers published and distributed by Public Citizen, *Pills that Don't Work* (1980) and *Worst Pills, Best Pills* (1988), which have earned millions for the organization. Widely acknowledged as a determined champion of the health consumer, Wolfe was awarded a prestigious MacArthur Foundation fellowship in 1990. The *Critical Mass Energy Project* lobbies for stronger nuclear safety regulations and works for safe and affordable energy, emphasizing renewable sources. *Buyers Up* is a fuel buying cooperative that helps consumers in the Middle Atlantic region exercise economic leverage in the marketplace. A *Tax Reform Research Group*, active for fourteen years through passage of the Tax Reform Act of 1986, was discontinued in 1987; the work is continued by former director Robert McIntyre, who now heads the labor-backed Citizens for Tax Justice. A field organizing project coordinates lobbying by activists on state and national legislation.

In the late 1970s Nader combined victories and defeats. On the one hand, Nader staff were being incorporated in government during the Jimmy Carter administration. Joan Claybrook, for example, was appointed administrator of the National Highway Traffic Safety Administration. But Nader lost his campaign to create a Consumer Protection Agency. And often during the Reagan years he seemed to be fighting a holding action. Conservative critics denounce Nader for his cozy relationship with attorneys in the plaintiff bar, the "fat cat lawyers" who litigate personal injury and product liability cases. Nevertheless Nader remains, in the words of a *Washington Post Magazine* feature, "the only universally recognized symbol of pure honesty and clean energy left in a culture . . . shot through with greed, cynicism and weariness."

CURRENT PRIORITIES: Key priorities for Public Citizen include a national health insurance program similar to the Canadian system, public financing of all House and Senate campaigns, a rapid phaseout of nuclear energy production, and the development of renewable energy technologies.

MEMBERS: Public Citizen's base of 60,000 initial supporters grew to 100,000, then eroded slowly during the late 1970s after the Watergate scandal passed and it appeared that many of Nader's reforms were being incorporated by the Carter administration. Public Citizen did not grow substantially during the Reagan years, when potential supporters were more concerned with threats to peace and the environment. However, following two years of congressional scandals (Speaker Wright, the Keating Five) and the $200 billion savings and loan industry bailout, contributors increased sharply from 40,000 in 1988 back up to 100,000 in 1990 as Public Citizen called for "cleaning up the mess in Congress." Members have no role in governance.

STRUCTURE: Nader's operations have always been staff directed, and Public Citizen is no exception. The board of directors of Public Citizen has three members. The new, expanded Public Citizen Foundation board has seven members, including Morris Dees, Jr., founder of the Southern Poverty Law Center, Texas populist Jim Hightower, and union executive and Labor party advocate Anthony Mazzochi. Both boards select their own new members. Joan Claybrook, president and chief executive of Public Citizen since 1982, sits on both boards. In 1992 Public Citizen organized a PAC, the Fund for a Clean Congress, to defeat the "five worst Congressional incumbents"— dubbed the "Get-Newt PAC" by *The Wall Street Journal* for its TV ads opposing Newt Gingrich (R-GA), the House Minority Whip.

RESOURCES: Public Citizen accepts no money from corporations or government. Revenue of $7.3 million in 1991 came from subscriptions and publication sales, contributions, grants, court awards, and royalties. Expenditures of $7.6 million were divided 52 percent for programs, 21 percent for publications, 15 percent for development, and 12 percent for administration.

PUBLICATIONS AND SERVICES: Contributors receive *Public Citizen* (circulation 100,000) six times a year; an annual report is published in the March/April issue. For an additional contribution, the monthly *Health Letter* (circulation 80,000) is available. *Critical Mass Energy Bulletin* is available by subscription. Books and reports are offered for sale through a publications catalog. David Bollier and Joan Claybrook present Public Citizen's history and defense of federal regulation of health, safety, and the environment in *Freedom*

from Harm (1986). For the house history of Nader's activities, see David Bollier, *Citizen Action and Other Big Ideas: A History of Ralph Nader and the Modern Consumer Movement* (1989), available from Nader's headquarters organization, Center for Study of Responsive Law, P.O. Box 19367, Washington, DC 20036. Public Interest Research Group (PIRG) activity is described in Kelley Griffin, *More Action for a Change* (Dembner Books, 1987). □

DEMOCRATIC SOCIALISTS OF AMERICA

15 DUTCH STREET

NEW YORK, NY 10038

(212) 962-0390

FOUNDED: 1982   MEMBERS: 10,000
LOCALS: 40   BUDGET: $450,000   STAFF: 5
TAX STATUS: 501(c)(4): Democratic Socialists of America; 501(c)(3): Institute for Democratic Socialism; PAC: DSA National PAC

PURPOSE: "A humane social order based on popular control of resources and production, economic planning, equitable distribution, feminism, racial equality and non-oppressive relationships."

The Democratic Socialists of America (DSA) is the country's leading advocate of democratic socialism. A merger of Old and New Left organizations and traditions, DSA combines work in unions and social movements with electoral activity, mostly in the Democratic party. Led by writer and activist Michael Harrington until his death in 1989, DSA positions itself as "the left wing of the possible." Since the demise of the Soviet empire and the discrediting of Marxism-Leninism in all its forms, the democratic socialist tradition that DSA shares is, for all practical organizational purposes, "the only left left."

BACKGROUND: DSA has benefited greatly from its popular association with Michael Harrington, the best-known American socialist since Eugene Debs and Norman Thomas. Harrington's book on the persistence of poverty, *The Other America*, was a surprise best-seller in 1962. Coming to the attention of President Kennedy via a laudatory review by Dwight MacDonald in *The New Yorker*, Harrington's book is credited with inspiring the "War on Poverty" in the mid-1960s. Harrington was well known in the Socialist International (SI), the predominantly European association of Labor, Socialist, and Social Democratic parties. His skill as a writer and his friendship with its leaders—Willy Brandt of West Germany, Olof Palme of Sweden, François Mitterrand of France, and Felipe Gonzalez of Spain—allowed DSA to play a role in the SI well out of proportion to its modest influence in American politics. Harrington's commentaries on National Public Radio in the 1980s reached a wide audience.

Harrington's roots were in the Socialist party of Debs and Thomas. Although his introduction to social action was through Dorothy Day's Catholic Worker group in New York, Harrington was recruited into socialist youth activity in

1952, lean years for American radicals. He lined up with a faction led by Max Schactman, a one-time aide to Leon Trotsky, who had split with Trotsky in 1938 over the nature of the Soviet Union (Trotsky held it to be a "degenerated workers' state" deserving critical support, while Schactman analyzed the USSR as a new form of class society, "bureaucratic collectivism"). After Schactman led his small faction into the Socialist party in 1958, Harrington rapidly emerged as a leader in the Young Peoples Socialist League (YPSL). Schactman promoted the "realignment" strategy, working within the Democratic party to push out racist southerners and recast Democrats as consistently progressive and Republicans as conservatives. To everyone's surprise, Schactman drifted steadily toward the right, defining the interests of the working class with the positions articulated by the AFL-CIO leadership, and coming to support the Johnson administration during the Vietnam War.

Conflict within the Socialist party over the war and electoral strategy came to a head in 1972 on whether to endorse George McGovern's candidacy for president—a dispute that ended with the organization split into three splinters. The left wing, led by David McReynolds, opposed any endorsement and held on to the name Socialist party, and still runs occasional minor party campaigns. The right-wing Schactmanite faction, which gave only a lukewarm endorsement to McGovern, renamed themselves Social Democrats USA (SDUSA) and in the 1980s provided the Reagan administration with several neoconservatives. And the center fraction led by Harrington, which gave strong support to McGovern, formed the Democratic Socialist Organizing Committee (DSOC) in 1973.

Harrington argued a majority progressive movement could be built within the Democratic party by uniting the constituencies of the "three Georges"—George McGovern (middle-class liberals), George Meany (blue-collar, predominantly northern and urban unionists), and George Wallace (blue-collar, predominantly southern and nonunion populists). DSOC had a strong national profile, with a number of local elected officials, Democratic party activists, middle-echelon union officials, and a few labor leaders—including Victor Reuther of the Auto Workers and William Wimpisinger of the Machinists.

The New American Movement (NAM) was organized in 1971 by New Left activists in the wake of the disintegration of Students for a Democratic Society (SDS) in 1968; conveners of NAM's first national conference included Michael Lerner, Harry Boyte, and Roberta Lynch. NAM emphasized rank-and-file unionism, workplace democracy, community organizing, socialist feminism, and gay liberation. If DSOC identified with Irving Howe's *Dissent* magazine, NAM read James Weinstein's journal *Socialist Revolution* (founded in 1970: toned down to *Socialist Review* in 1978) and his weekly newspaper, *In These Times*, launched in 1975. NAM attracted a variety of radicals beyond the young post-SDS activists—Richard Healey recruited his mother, former southern California Communist party leader Dorothy Healey, who brought along a couple dozen former Communists who had left

the party after 1968, adding a distinctive Old Left generation to the ranks of NAM and later DSA. Others emerging from NAM included Barbara Ehrenreich and Stanley Aronowitz.

Initially DSOC and NAM were separated by their differences over labor (rank and file versus leadership), feminism (socialist versus traditional feminism or none at all), locus of political work (community organization versus electoral activity), the Middle East (support for Palestinians versus support for Israel), and international perspective (Third World revolution versus the Socialist International reform). These differences faded by the late 1970s with the rising conservative tide, and seemed of minor importance. NAM was strong at grassroots, while DSOC had a substantial national presence. Merger talks smoothed over most of the sharp points of disagreement, and led to consolidation of locals and members, and then full merger. Only a small group (which formed the socialist organization Solidarity) opposed to electoral work in the Democratic party left from NAM, and only a few strong partisans of Israel left from DSOC. DSOC had around 3,000 members at the time of the merger, NAM around 1,000. With merger publicity, DSA had 5,000 members at the end of 1982.

Little of the old NAM/DSOC split is recognizable in DSA today. Modest polarizations ("greens" versus "reds") were harmonized by the "pistachio caucus." Harrington was able to retain from DSOC or bring into DSA a number of labor leaders and elected officials—including Congressmen Ron Dellums (D-California) and Major Owens (D-New York); David Dinkins, now mayor of New York City; Ruth Messinger, now Manhattan borough president; D.C. council member Hilda Mason; and a number of state and local officials. DSA worked to create a broad democratic left within the Democratic party, supporting the Progressive Alliance in the early 1970s and the Democratic Agenda conferences in the late 1970s. DSA members split support in the 1984 Democratic primaries between Walter Mondale and Jesse Jackson, and worked for Mondale against Reagan in the general election. DSA NPAC supported Jesse Jackson throughout the primaries in 1988, with Harrington writing some of his speeches; in the presidential race the DSA National PAC endorsed Michael Dukakis's unsuccessful campaign against George Bush. Although younger members brought concerns for feminism, gay liberation, and ecology that went beyond Harrington's usual analysis, DSA assimilated his "visionary gradualism" as the only feasible strategy of transition to democratic socialism.

CURRENT PRIORITIES: DSA's priorities include health care, reproductive rights, labor support, and developing a progressive agenda within the Democratic party. During 1991 DSA emphasized universal health care, organizing a tour of Canadian health care workers in cooperation with its socialist sister, the New Democratic Party of Canada. In its reproductive rights work, DSA emphasizes not only the legal right to choose abortion, but equal access to abortion and other reproductive health services. DSA sponsors the American Solidarity Campaign, an organizational vehicle for community support of the labor movement. Over the past decade DSA has led several programs to develop a progressive agenda in the Democratic party, including the Democratic Agenda and New Directions conferences; DSA chapters support progressive candidates in Democratic primary campaigns and nonpartisan races for local offices. DSA is the leading sponsor of the annual Socialist Scholars Conference in New York City.

MEMBERS: Starting out with some 5,000 members, DSA dropped to 4,000 in 1985, and subsequently revived to a new peak of 10,000 in 1991 with a successful direct-mail campaign. As the Marxist left was collapsing along with the Soviet Union, DSA seemed to be the only national socialist organization with any influence and promise. Standing commissions organized around interests and constituencies may be joined by any member; currently active are the Feminist, Labor, Environmental, Religion and Socialism, African American, Hispanic, Anti-Racism, and Gay/Lesbian/Bisexual commissions, each with its own newsletter. DSA's Youth Section, with 2,000 members in thirty campus chapters, is the country's largest socialist youth organization.

STRUCTURE: A delegated national convention, open to all members, is held every two years. The convention elects a National Political Committee of twenty-five members, which selects a National Interim Committee of eight members. Honorary chairs include feminists Barbara Ehrenreich and Gloria Steinem, *Dissent* editor Irving Howe, Delores Huerta of the United Farm Workers, black theologian Cornel

West, and former Machinists president William Wimpisinger. Vice-chairs include Rep. Ron Dellums, former CORE director James Farmer, Citizen Action leader Steve Max, and theologian Rosemary Reuther. DSA bylaws provide that half of all governing board members be women, and one-third be people of color. DSA's 501(c)(3), the Institute for Democratic Socialism, has a twenty-four-member board. Michael Lighty is national director.

PUBLICATIONS AND SERVICES: Membership is $40 and includes the magazine *Democratic Left* (circulation 8,000) six times a year. An occasional discussion bulletin, *Socialist Forum*, is available for a $10 subscription. The larger locals have occasional newsletters. Newsletters are also published by the Labor, Feminist, Ecosocialist, and Religion and Socialism caucuses. Michael Harrington described the founding of DSOC and DSA, and his relationship with the Socialist International, in *The Long-Distance Runner: An Autobiography* (Henry Holt, 1988). Harrington's early career, including his disorienting sudden rise to fame, is related in his first autobiographical volume, *Fragments of the Century* (Touchstone, 1973). □

THE GREENS (USA)

P.O. BOX 30208
KANSAS CITY, MO 64112
(816) 931-9366

FOUNDED: 1984   MEMBERS: 3,000
LOCALS: 135   BUDGET: $60,000   STAFF: 2
TAX STATUS: political party: The Greens (USA); 501(c)(3): Green Education Fund

PURPOSE: "A society based on ten key values: ecological wisdom, social justice, grassroots democracy, nonviolence, decentralization, community-based economics, post-patriarchal values, respect for diversity, personal and global responsibility, and future focus."

Although inspired by the activity of European greens, the U.S. green movement has struggled to create a uniquely American blend of environmental, feminist, decentralist, New Age spiritual, bioregional, and post-Marxist left perspectives. After several years deliberating strategy and program, in 1991 The Greens arrived at a structure that combined advocacy organization and political party, but in 1992 the structure was simplified to a political party.

BACKGROUND: The founding meeting of U.S. Greens was held in the summer of 1984 at Macalaster College in St. Paul, Minnesota, where sixty-two activists gathered at the invitation of spiritual feminist Charlene Spretnak and former New Left organizer and theorist Harry Boyte. The group named itself the

Committees of Correspondence (after the early American revolutionaries), and set up a temporary office in the city. The meeting also endorsed the "ten key values" statement, the centerpiece of The Greens' vision and the fundamental points of agreement. The first four key values were borrowed from "the four pillars" of the German Greens: ecological wisdom, grassroots democracy, social responsibility, and nonviolence. To these, U.S. Greens added six more: decentralization, community-based economics, postpatriarchal values, respect for diversity, global responsibility, and sustainable future focus.

The office was moved to St. Louis in 1985, and the membership dithered for three years trying to agree on how to build the organization, renamed Green Committees of Correspondence. Mark Satin, a sympathetic participant in the first four national meetings, described the period in his *New Options* newsletter: "Quarterly meetings were marked by endless turmoil, by an almost religious devotion to the process of full-consensus decision making, and by failure to carry out even such basic tasks as fund raising, organizer training and membership building."

The first national gathering, held in Amherst, Massachusetts, as an educational forum in 1987, highlighted the conflicting perspectives among the Greens. Followers of ecoanarchist Murray Bookchin led a "political" (leftist) challenge to Charlene Spretnak's "spiritual" (holistic New Age) wing. Bookchin's "anthropocentric" social ecology opposed "biocentric" deep ecology. Ynestra King argued a left ecofeminism against Spretnak's spiritual feminism.

A division emerged between grassroots activists, emphasizing direct action and the patient building of alternative institutions, and electoral activists pushing to organize a Green party as quickly as possible. The Left Green Caucus was organized as a forum for various left perspectives including democratic socialism, anarchism, and ecofeminism.

The second national Greens gathering in Eugene, Oregon, in 1989 was intended to begin defining the Greens' political program. Interregional Committee member John Rensenbrink had initiated the Strategic Policies and Actions in Key Areas (SPAKA) process, through which statements would be drafted on dozens of topics. Consensus was not reached on most positions, and the topical drafts were sent back to the discussion groups for revision. At the third national gathering in Estes Park, Colorado, in 1990 the SPAKA process brought statements for ratification. Coordinators of the SPAKA process had difficulty getting the volunteers on dispersed committees to complete work on time. After considerable emotional turmoil, the gathering approved some twenty position statements ranging from racism to Native Americans to economic policy. A Rainbow Caucus of minority Greens was organized and played an active part. Questions of structure, and the relationship of movement to party, were left to the fourth national gathering in Elkins, West Virginia, in 1991, which changed the organization's name to The Greens (USA), and adopted a structure which accommodated the interests of both electoral and nonelectoral activists.

CURRENT PRIORITIES: Green parties are working to get on the ballot in several states. By early 1992 Greens had achieved ballot status in Alaska and California (which requires 80,000 voters to register with a new party), and were well along in Hawaii and Arizona. The Greens has a statement covering various issues, but no real strategy for having an impact on national politics. A national action plan adopted at the 1991 gathering includes three themes: (1) solar power through community power; (2) a Detroit Summer project in 1992 to work on "just and sustainable urban transformation"; and (3) "Goodbye Columbus: 500 years of dignity and resistance." Distrusting leadership, hierarchy, and power (and short of money), Amy Belanger coordinates The Greens from Kansas City. In reality, the organization remains a loose alliance of local and state groups. Tied to a minor party strategy, it may elect occasional local figures, but wider success is likely to remain elusive. The Greens remains an example of prefigurative, expressive politics.

MEMBERS: There are some 2,000 national members; another 9,000 may be members of local and state Green groups.

STRUCTURE: Autonomous locals constitute the grassroots base of The Greens. The membership is invited to the Annual Gathering, at which a decision-making congress, consisting of delegates elected by proportional representation from locals, sets policy goals for the organization. The congress elects a seven-member Coordinating Committee to carry out campaigns, supervise staff, and serve as media spokespeople between congresses. Locals also each elect two delegates to a regional council. A national Green Council is composed of two representatives elected from each of the eleven regional councils. The national Green Council oversees the Coordinating Committee, and interprets policy between meetings of the annual congress. The Green Education Fund serves as a 501(c)(3) charitable organization for tax-deductible contributions for local projects related to nonelectoral activities of The Greens.

PUBLICATIONS AND SERVICES: Membership is $25 and includes the quarterly newsletter *GroundWork* and the occasional journal *Regeneration*. *The Greens Bulletin* is a monthly internal forum available for a $35 subscription. Many larger locals have their own newsletters. Many early Green advocates in the United States were influenced by Frijof Capra and Charlene Spretnak, *Green Politics: The Global Promise* (Dutton, 1984). For the visions of current Green activists, see Brian Tokar, *The Green Alternative*, rev. ed. (1987; R & E Miles, 1992), and John Rensenbrink, *The Greens and the Politics of Transformation* (R & E Miles, 1992). □

INTERFAITH IMPACT FOR JUSTICE AND PEACE

110 MARYLAND AVENUE, NE

WASHINGTON, DC 20002

(202) 543-2800

FOUNDED: 1990   MEMBERS: 10,000
BUDGET: $600,000   STAFF: 7
TAX STATUS: 501(c)(4): Interfaith Impact for
Justice and Peace; 501(c)(3): Interfaith Impact
Foundation

PURPOSE: "The progressive religious community's united voice in Washington."

Interfaith Impact for Justice and Peace coordinates a national lobbying effort for social justice, formed in 1990 in a merger of National Impact (founded 1968) and Interfaith Action for Economic Justice (founded 1974). Interfaith Impact is the leading grassroots social action lobby of the mainstream Protestant denominations. Issue networks engage individuals directly and mobilize regional, state, and local affiliates.

BACKGROUND: In response to the assassination of the Reverend Martin Luther King, Jr., in 1968, the Washington Interreligious Staff Council (WISC) formed National Impact (NI) to pressure Congress on issues of peace and social justice. NI started setting up state Impacts in 1975, and had twenty state affiliates organized by congressional district in 1990. For the first fifteen years, all members received

legislative alerts, monthly reports, and background papers on all the topics addressed. In 1983 NI began targeting people with specialized agendas through issue networks, covering such subjects as peace, civil rights and liberties, women, energy and ecology, and domestic human needs. NI also began the tradition of an annual legislative briefing in Washington for religious denominational leadership and activists from around the country.

Interfaith Action for Economic Justice, the second partner to the merger, started as the Inter-Religious Taskforce on U.S. Food Policy, stimulated by the 1974 World Food Conference. Again the Washington Interreligious Staff Council played a leading role in founding the organization, which was conceived as a coalition of the member denominations. Staff prepared reports on food and hunger issues for distribution through the member churches and the NI network, testified before Congressional committees, and developed a reputation for expertise on world hunger issues. As the Taskforce got involved with the problems of food on a global scale, assessing policies of the International Monetary Fund and the World Bank, its wider focus prompted the name change to Interfaith Action for Economic Justice. Programs were organized around working groups on domestic human needs, farm and food policy, and international development and economic policy.

During the Reagan administration in the 1980s, Interfaith Action worked to defend the food stamp, maternal health, and child nutrition programs, but most of all raised issues of social justice as poor people, including farming families, were hurt by cutbacks in social programs. A voter registration project was begun in 1983, and in 1989, at the urging of the Commission on Religion in Appalachia, Interfaith Action actively supported the United Mine Workers in their strike against the Pittston company in southwest Virginia, West Virginia, and Kentucky (successfully settled in 1990)—opening new contacts between the liberal religious community and organized labor.

By 1989 the decline in membership and contributions to the mainstream Protestant denominations began to hit Interfaith Action, cutting its half-million-dollar budget by $90,000. The Washington liberal religious community began to look at the areas of overlap in issue work and committee memberships between National Impact and Interfaith Action, and to look for ways to consolidate the two organizations. Leaders of both groups settled on forming a new organization, and Interfaith Impact was founded in 1990. During a transition period Gretchen Eick and Arthur Keys, executive directors of National Impact and Interfaith Action respectively, served as codirectors. The Reverend James Bell, formerly director of Interfaith Ministries in Wichita, Kansas, was hired as the new executive director in 1991.

CURRENT PRIORITIES: Members can sign up for any of six issue networks: (1) Civil, Human and Voting Rights; (2) Domestic Poverty and Human Needs; (3) Economic Policy and Sustainable Development; (4) Energy, Environment and Agriculture; (5) International Peace; and (6) Justice for Women and Families. Interfaith Impact continues the tradition of an annual briefing in Washington for its membership on issues before Congress.

STRUCTURE: Interfaith Impact has a board of directors of sixty members, most representing the national affiliated denominations, the state affiliates, and other regional and local affiliates. A budget of $600,000 in 1991 was slated to expand to $700,000 in 1992.

PUBLICATIONS AND SERVICES: Members receive the quarterly magazine *Interfaith Impact* and the *Action* newsletter (both circulation 10,000) with ideas for lobbying on key issues. Legislative updates are posted weekly on HandsNet and are also available through a toll-free hotline; (800) 424-7290. A brief history of National Impact and Interfaith Action was compiled by Martin McLaughlin in the report *Advocates for Justice* (August 1991). □

COMMUNITY ORGANIZING

The community organizing movement is a contemporary expression of progressive populism. At its best, community organizing revives the civic republican tradition, with its vision of a commonwealth of active citizens. Community organizing as practiced today has no single wellspring, but draws on several sources including labor organizing, the civil rights movement, the New Left, and the social work tradition.

Chicago has been a critical center for three of the four major community organization networks: Saul Alinsky's Industrial Areas Foundation (IAF), the Midwest Academy and its associated Citizen Action network, and National Training and Information Center (NTIC) and its associated National People's Action. Only the Association of Community Organizations for Reform Now (ACORN), founded in Arkansas, had its origins outside Chicago. IAF builds communitywide organizations by assembling representatives of existing community groups, primarily religious congregations. IAF doesn't enter a community until local volunteers have assembled the preliminary coalition and obtained a commitment of money to support IAF's professional organizer for a year. ACORN, in contrast, avoids existing community leaders and uses crews of young staff to comb neighborhoods to identify and enlist people outside the current structure of neighborhood influence to build its own unitary organization. National People's Action coordinates a limited set of national activities on behalf of neighborhood or citywide organizations that work with its National Training and Information Center. Similarly, Citizen Action coordinates national programs for a network of statewide organizations linked by training and conferences provided by Midwest Academy.

IAF sticks to pressuring local governmental agencies and corporations, for the most part avoiding direct involvement in electoral politics—a "keep them honest" approach. Citizen Action, in contrast, has moved to elect its members to city councils and state legislatures, and to work within the Democratic party to support candidates for the U.S. Congress and Senate, and to endorse presidential primary candidates. ACORN has also gotten involved at a more local level—school councils and boards, municipal commissions and the like—as well as ventured into Democratic presidential primary endorsements. National People's Action conducts demonstrations and lobbying at the national level, but avoids political endorsements. The constituency of IAF, Citizen Action, and National People's Action is the working class with some lower-middle-class members; ACORN works more with poor, welfare, moderate-income, below-union-wage workers.

Beyond the four community organization networks, a variety

of independent training centers have emerged during the last twenty years, influenced by various movement traditions: Mike Miller's Organize Training Center in San Francisco builds on his work with the civil rights movement and IAF; Oakland's Center for Third World Organizing was founded by ACORN veteran Gary Delgado; Si Kahn's Grassroots Leadership in North Carolina draws on his background in civil rights and community action. A few are rooted in older traditions: The Highlander Center in Tennessee, founded by Myles Horton, has provided grassroots leadership development for social movements throughout the South since the 1930s. Although conservatives have recently set up training programs for young activists, they have nothing comparable to the progressives' community organizing networks.

IAF

INDUSTRIAL AREAS FOUNDATION

36 NEW HYDE PARK ROAD

FRANKLIN SQUARE, NY 11010

(516) 354-1076

FOUNDED: 1940   AFFILIATE MEMBERS: 1.5 million families   AFFILIATES: 28
BUDGET: $1 million   STAFF: 9 professional organizers   TAX STATUS: 501(c)(3)

SLOGAN: "Power, action, justice."

IAF "IRON" RULE: "Never do for others what they can do for themselves."

Drawing on the spirit and experience of the CIO unions in the 1930s, Saul Alinsky developed a model for grassroots organizing based on a federation of religious parishes and congregations, a style that is both confrontational and pragmatic, and a training center, In-

dustrial Areas Foundation (IAF), that continues to refine his strategy and tactics with a network of influential organizations. Alinsky trained many important figures in community organizing—Ed Chambers, Tom Gaudette, Dick Harmon, Mike Miller—and, directly or indirectly, influenced many more, including Fred Ross and Cesar Chavez. IAF's second generation of Alinsky-style organizations is having a particularly significant influence in Texas.

BACKGROUND: Saul Alinsky was a young criminologist in 1939 when he was sent by the Chicago Area Project to start an antidelinquency program in Chicago's Back of the Yards area—Upton Sinclair's "Jungle"—just as the CIO's Packing Workers Organizing Committee was negotiating for recognition by the meat-packing industry. The success of the Back of the Yards Neighborhood Council, described in his book *Reveille for Radicals* in 1945, made Alinsky the theorist of the "People's Organization," a new type of community organization displacing the settlement house tradition with a federation of religious congregations and neighborhood associations that looked more like a central labor council. Alinsky resigned from the Chicago Area Project and set up his Industrial Areas Foundation in 1940, with a board of directors that included Catholic bishop Bernard Sheil, Kathryn Lewis (John L.'s daughter), and patrician philanthropist Marshall Field III, who provided the initial financing.

After the Second World War, Alinsky's work seemed to stall. Back of the Yards was succeeding, but ventures in Kansas City and St. Paul petered out. In 1949 Alinsky met Fred Ross in California, and agreed that IAF would back his plan to organize Mexican Americans into a Community Service Organization (CSO). Ross introduced an innovative house-meeting organizing program, registered enough new voters to elect Ed Roybal (later an influential congressman) to the Los Angeles City Council, and over the next decade developed a network of thirty CSOs in California with the help of talented young organizers Cesar Chavez and Dolores Huerta.

Back in Chicago, Alinsky developed a team of organizers who would make their mark on the Second City. Journalist Nick von Hoffman got his start with Alinsky, researching Chicago neighborhoods. Ex-seminarian Ed Chambers returned from an assignment in Lackawanna, New York, to join von Hoffman and Alinsky in helping Catholic and Protestant clergy develop the Organization for the Southwest Community in 1959, and The Woodlawn Organization

(TWO) in 1961. Tom Gaudette was hired by Alinsky to start the Northwest Community Organization in 1962. Alinsky's fame grew from TWO's confrontation with the University of Chicago's South Campus urban renewal program. After a long campaign resulting in Mayor Daley's intervention, TWO won a voice in modifying the final plan. Alinsky's work drew national attention through *Fortune* magazine writer Charles Silberman's 1964 book, *Crisis in Black and White* (Vintage), which featured TWO as a new model for black empowerment. The publicity led religious leaders in Rochester, New York, to invite Alinsky to set up an organization in the black community. FIGHT, the resulting group, led an acrimonious and partially successful campaign to get more jobs for blacks at Eastman Kodak, at one point mobilizing church shareholders to vote stock proxies against management at the corporation's annual meeting.

In 1969 a substantial grant from Gordon Sherman of Midas Muffler company allowed Alinsky to set up an IAF organizer training program in Chicago, run by Ed Chambers and Dick Harmon. Since Alinsky's death in 1972, Chambers has directed the "modern IAF" into a successful era of less flamboyant and more methodical organizing. Abandoning Alinsky's "three years and out," principle, IAF maintains an ongoing relationship with the groups it sets up. Currently IAF has twenty-eight affiliated organizations in seven states: New York, New Jersey, Maryland, Texas, Tennessee, Arizona, and California (ironically, the Chicago groups that continue are no longer affiliated).

One of IAF's great success stories is

Communities Organized for Public Service (COPS) in San Antonio. The fundamental redistribution of power COPS accomplished helped elect Henry Cisneros as the first Hispanic mayor of a major American city, and spawned IAF affiliates in Houston, El Paso, Fort Worth, Austin, and the Rio Grande Valley. Together known as Texas Interfaith, led by IAF state director Ernesto Cortes, the six affiliates claim 300 churches and 300,000 families as members. In Brooklyn's depressed Brownsville area, IAF's East Brooklyn Congregations established Nehemiah Homes, which built 2,100 homes priced under $50,000 for low-income people. Drawing national attention, the program will be expanded to other communities with federal assistance under the National Nehemiah Housing Opportunity Act of 1988. IAF affiliate Baltimoreans United In Leadership Development (BUILD) organized the Commonwealth Project to guarantee scholarships to students accepted into college and jobs to other high school graduates, and is beginning a housing program on the Nehemiah model. Three IAF affiliates in southern California are developing joint programs, after lobbying successfully to raise the state's minimum wage in 1987.

CURRENT PRIORITIES: IAF continues to strengthen communities and the democratic process by building organizations that develop indigenous leaders and give poor and working-class people power in the public sphere. IAF works with broad-based organizations that reflect religious diversity, a strong racial and ethnic mix, multiple goals and interests, and independence of political parties and ideologies. All community leaders attend at least one of IAF's three annual intensive ten-day National Training Conferences.

STRUCTURE: IAF is governed by a six-member board of trustees, including Archbishop Patrick Flores of San Antonio, Barry Menuez of the Episcopal Church, Msgr. Jack Egan of Chicago, Bishop John Adams of the A.M.E. Church in Atlanta, and attorney Sidney Perlstadt of Chicago; Marvin Wurth of Fidelity Software Development is president. Ed Chambers remains IAF director, and works closely with his "cabinet" of seven national organizers and field supervisors.

RESOURCES: IAF is supported by foundation and corporate contributions; it accepts no government funding. Local IAF affiliates raise most of their own money through contributions from member organizations; the Catholic Church's Campaign for Human Development has provided significant support to affiliates over the years. Affiliate budgets total some $5 million, supporting 45 organizers. IAF affiliates claim over 1.5 million families in affiliates' 1,200 member congregations.

PUBLICATIONS AND SERVICES: For a brief recap of IAF history and a review of current activities and personalities, see the booklet *IAF 50 Years Organizing for Change* (IAF, 1990). Sanford D. Horwitt writes Alinsky's definitive biography and a history of IAF projects in *Let Them Call Me Rebel: Saul Alinsky—His Life and Legacy* (Knopf, 1989). Alinsky's books include *John L. Lewis: An Unauthorized Biography* (University of Chicago Press, 1946; Vintage, 1970) and *Rules for Radicals* (Random House, 1971). See also Marion K. Sanders, *The Professional Radical: Conversations with Saul Alinsky* (Harper & Row, 1970). □

ASSOCIATION OF COMMUNITY ORGANIZATIONS FOR REFORM NOW

739 8TH STREET, SE

WASHINGTON, DC 20003

(202) 547-9292

FOUNDED: 1970   MEMBERS: 75,000 families
STATE GROUPS: 26 plus D.C.
LOCAL CHAPTERS: 400   BUDGET: $3 million
STAFF: 200   TAX STATUS: 501(c)(4): ACORN;
501(c)(3): Institute for Social Justice; PAC:
ACORN PAC

PURPOSE: "To advocate a stronger local neighborhood voice in and power over the economic, political, and social institutions that dominate the lives of families of low and moderate income."

ACORN is heir to the welfare rights organizing of the 1960s, and has devised a replicable model of developing new organizations and leaders from low- and moderate-income communities. Expanding from a base established in Arkansas in the early 1970s, by 1980 ACORN was active in twenty states. ACORN has ventured into electoral politics, and recently has become a major force in the squatters movement that matured into urban homesteading

in abandoned and HUD-owned housing. Avoiding the "bracket creep" common to other community organizing networks, ACORN has stuck with its low-income and increasingly minority constituency.

BACKGROUND: ACORN emerged from the National Welfare Rights Organization (NWRO), founded in 1966 by Syracuse Congress of Racial Equality (CORE) chairman George Wiley. Inspired by a 1965 "Strategy to End Poverty" paper by Columbia University professors Richard Cloward and Frances Fox Piven, Wiley enlisted a group of civil rights workers who had gone through the Community Action Training Center at Syracuse University. Wiley's model developed a local organization of welfare recipients, with indigenous leadership, which worked to obtain additional "special need" benefits for which members were qualified but not receiving. NWRO rapidly developed a national structure of chapters, but their very success soon led to serious financial and organizational problems. State welfare agencies undercut NWRO's membership appeal by shifting to flat grants, and by 1969 Wiley was looking for new models to expand NWRO's constituency beyond welfare recipients.

Wiley dispatched twenty-two-year-old Wade Rathke in 1970 to Arkansas, former home of NWRO president Johnnie Tillman and a relatively small population state with a substantial proportion of low-income people, both black and white. Beginning with a local welfare rights group and a small staff including Gary Delgado, a seasoned organizer with NWRO in Providence and

New York, Rathke conducted an initial successful campaign in Little Rock that defined ACORN (then the Arkansas Community Organizations for Reform Now) as an independent organization with a broad appeal to low-income people. ACORN emphasized its local democratic roots by adopting Arkansas's 1836 motto, "The People Shall Rule." During the first two years, Rathke defined the ACORN model as a multi-issue, multitactic, mass organization with member participation in policy, financing, and achievement of group and community goals. By 1972 ACORN was strong enough to declare its independence and cut its ties to NWRO, which was on the wane as Wiley set up the Movement for Economic Justice to reach a wider constituency.

Over the next three years ACORN organized communities across Arkansas, set up a statewide council, and showed it could train new organizers to replicate the ACORN model. ACORN conducted statewide campaigns over generic drug pricing, lifeline electric utility rates, and property taxes—generating attention beyond Arkansas. Organizers were invited to set up projects in South Dakota and Texas, and by the end of 1975 the "A" in ACORN was changed from "Arkansas" to "Association" to reflect its new three-state operations. ACORN set up ACORN Associates, Inc., to offer consultation and technical assistance for fees, and the Arkansas Institute for Social Justice as its 501(c)(3) training arm (known as the Institute for Social Justice after 1978).

ACORN began its expansion to neighboring southern states in 1976, launching organizing projects in Ten-nessee, Louisiana, and Missouri, and also leaping on to Florida, Colorado, Pennsylvania, Nevada, and Iowa—eleven states and twenty-five cities by late 1977. ACORN set up groups in Michigan, Oklahoma, and Arizona in 1978, and explored absorbing existing projects—Carolina Action, Georgia Action, and California's Citizens' Action League affiliated with ACORN in 1979. Expansion led to conflicts where existing community organizing projects wanted to keep their independence; by moving to Boston ACORN triggered a battle over turf with Massachusetts Fair Share, a group that later joined the Citizen Action network.

Expansion was also accompanied by innovation: With financial help from the Movement for Economic Justice, led by Wiley associate Bert DeLeeuw, in 1979 ACORN founded the United Labor Unions (ULU), aimed at the low-income workers in hotel, fast-food, home health care, and other service jobs in Louisiana, Massachusetts, Michigan, Illinois, and Arkansas (ULU is now affiliated with the Service Employees International Union). ACORN also pioneered ventures into progressive media controlled by community organizations, and currently has two FM stations on the air in Dallas and Little Rock, and TV licenses approved for Atlanta and Watsonville, California.

When the Carter administration named activist Marge Tabankin as VISTA director, she was eager to send volunteers to work with ACORN. Although they were a welcome source of paid staff, ACORN was soon charged by local officials that the VISTAs were being used illegally to lobby and to organize unions. (The VISTAs also created an unanticipated resentment: Regular salaries for ACORN staff organizers were so low that the VISTAs' "subsistence" wages were higher!) ACORN ended its use of VISTA volunteers, and increased its staff salaries.

Rathke saw expansion to twenty states as a way for ACORN to exercise political influence on a national scale through the Democratic party, specifically at its 1980 convention. To clarify its own program and summarize the disparate experience of state programs from Florida to South Dakota, ACORN developed The People's Platform, which was ratified—with conflict over planks on guaranteed income, union rights, and opposition to nuclear power —by the 2,000 delegates attending its annual convention in St. Louis in 1979. ACORN groups mobilized to elect uncommitted delegates to the Democratic National Convention, to push The People's Platform, and to work with allies in labor, church, and other progressive groups—although it limited its coalition-building clout by avoiding direct endorsement of any candidates. ACORN did get the Democrats to set up a commission on the participation of low- and moderate-income people in the Democratic party. Two years later in 1982, however, the recommendations of the commission were rejected by the Democratic National Committee.

Ronald Reagan's election in 1980 brought a changed political climate that left low-income community groups struggling to retain programs and services. ACORN mobilized a "Dump Reagan" campaign that provided the only visible evidence of opposition to Reagan at the Republican's 1984 Dallas convention. Although the campaign obviously fell short of its goal, the Reagan era pushed ACORN into voter registration, candidate endorsement, and coalition-building.

Friendly critics point to several shortcomings of ACORN's practice. First, the differences in backgrounds exacerbate unavoidable power differences between staff and indigenous leadership: Although ACORN members are increasingly minority and female, ACORN staff organizers, half of whom are women, are predominantly young, white, college educated, and from upper-middle-class backgrounds (and poorly paid). Second, although ACORN understands the importance of nurturing allies, many groups continue to experience a sectarian attitude in ACORN's hard-nosed tactics of building its own organization. Finally, ACORN's failure to take stronger positions on issues of race and gender may have kept away possible allies among women's and civil rights organizations; however, this approach has the benefit of preserving solidarity based on class within the organization.

CURRENT PRIORITIES: ACORN took the lead in allying with the squatters movement occupying abandoned inner city housing. Following the concern for housing in poor urban communities, ACORN has mobilized support for the Community Reinvestment Act—resisting weakening amendments in 1991 by bringing busloads of members who camped out in front of the Capitol, attended hearings, and lobbied to keep the law intact. ACORN supported provisions in the savings and loan bailout bill, the Financial Institutions Reform, Recovery and Enforcement Act

(FIRREA) of 1989, which established boards and commissions to monitor affordable housing. ACORN works with the affordable Housing Advisory Councils of the regional Home Loan Bank Boards, and in 1991 got commitments from thirty banks in twelve cities to invest $500 million in home mortgages and home improvement loans in low-income neighborhoods. Recently ACORN held its first conference of local elected officials for a group of forty members.

For its twentieth anniversary in 1990 ACORN revised The People's Platform, which it first passed in 1979, to include the following planks: (1) *Energy:* low-cost energy, protection from giant utilities and energy companies; (2) *Health care:* medical care for all without regard to ability to pay; (3) *Housing:* decent, affordable housing for low- and moderate-income people; (4) *Work:* summer jobs for youth, guaranteed jobs or training leading to jobs for low- and moderate-income people; the right to organize, to have a safe workplace, and to child care; (5) *Rural issues:* preserve the family farm, break monopoly control of the food industry, guarantee a fair share for rural America; (6) *Community development:* community-based economic development, control private development, provide basic public services; (7) *Banking:* ban redlining, strengthen the Community Reinvestment Act (CRA) and the Home Mortgage Disclosure Act (HMDA); (8) *Taxes:* tax wealth; close loopholes; exempt food, medicine, and clothing from sales tax; base taxes on ability to pay; (9) *Environment:* protect communities from hazardous wastes, expand the public's "right to know"; (10) *Neighborhood se-curity:* keep neighborhoods safe from rape and other violence against women, and from drug abuse and drug trade violence; (11) *Civil rights:* strong federal and state enforcement of civil rights laws against discrimination in employment, housing, education, health care, and law enforcement; (12) *Communications:* greater control over the media by low- and moderate-income people; (13) *Education:* make parents an integral part of local schools, equalize funding, open facilities to the community; (14) *Representation:* more democracy in neighborhoods, in elections, in government, in business.

MEMBERS: ACORN's 75,000 families are approximately 70 percent black and Latino, and 70 percent female, mostly from working-class or poverty backgrounds. ACORN holds a delegated annual conference.

STRUCTURE: ACORN's board of directors includes two directors from each state affiliate, plus the president (currently Maude Hurd). The state delegates to the board are selected by the executive committee of each state affiliate, and serve two-year terms. The chief organizer, Wade Rathke, serves at the pleasure of the board. The chief organizer appoints the head organizer for each state or region, subject to the approval of the state or regional executive committee. The Institute for Social Justice continues ACORN's two-week training programs. By the mid-1980s ACORN established a national office in Washington, D.C., giving it better access to lobbying and national media.

The nonprofit ACORN Community Land Association (ACLA) preserves land for low- and moderate-income housing, working with ACORN housing corporations in five cities (Chicago, Philadelphia, Little Rock, Phoenix, and New York). The local housing corporations acquire and rehabilitate houses, passing the house title to the homesteader and the land title to ACLA.

RESOURCES: ACORN's revenue is 80 percent generated by the organization itself, through membership dues, grassroots fund-raising (bake sales, raffles, dinner and dances), and door-to-door canvassing in better-off neighborhoods. Foundations and church-related groups like the Campaign for Human Development provide the remaining 20 percent.

PUBLICATIONS AND SERVICES: Contributors receive the occasional newspaper *USA* (United States of ACORN). *Homesteader* is the quarterly newsletter of the Acorn Community Land Association. An *ACORN Members Handbook* is revised annually. For a history, see Gary Delgado, *Organizing the Movement: The Roots and Growth of ACORN* (Temple University Press, 1986). ACORN organizers Madeleine Adamson and Seth Borgos won a National Endowment for the Humanities grant for a traveling exhibit on the American protest tradition; research provided material for their informative illustrated book, *This Mighty Dream: Social Protest Movements in the United States* (Routledge & Kegan Paul, 1984). □

NTIC

NATIONAL TRAINING AND INFORMATION CENTER/NATIONAL PEOPLE'S ACTION

810 N. MILWAUKEE AVENUE

CHICAGO, IL 60622

(312) 243-3094

FOUNDED: 1972   AFFILIATES: 300 community groups in 120 cities   BUDGET: $700,000
STAFF: 14   TAX STATUS: 501(c)(3): National Training and Information Center; 501(c)(4): National People's Action

PURPOSE: "To organize neighborhood groups nationwide into a vocal and powerful lobbying and pressure group."

The National Training and Information Center (NTIC) and its related National People's Action (NPA) coordinate a loose association of neighborhood, church, union, farm, and seniors' organizations that focuses on housing programs for low- and moderate-income communities.

BACKGROUND: Gale Cincotta began her organizing career on Chicago's West Side in the early 1960s as a PTA leader, working to bring more resources to her six sons' schools. In the mid-1960s she joined the Organization for a Better Austin (OBA), where she met Tom Gaudette, the IAF organizer who developed the Northwest Community Organization and OBA, and Shel Trapp, who served as director of the organizations. Cincotta became president of OBA, and began a partnership with Trapp that continues in NTIC.

As Cincotta became active in changing the Austin area, banks and insurance companies were "redlining" the community, refusing to loan to new homeowners and businesses. Cincotta and Trapp brought together a coalition of neighborhood organizations, churches, unions, and senior citizen groups in Chicago to obtain adequate investment to revitalize their neighborhoods. Seeing the need for action on a national scale, Cincotta and Trapp convened a national grassroots housing conference in Chicago in 1972, at which National People's Action was founded. NPA moved its annual meetings to Washington, D.C., to push for congressional action; NPA helped write and gain passage of the Home Mortgage Disclosure Act of 1975 and the Community Reinvestment Act of 1977. With the laws in place, Cincotta led raucous confrontational demonstrations in the Alinsky style against federal agencies and local lending institutions, eventually winning agreements with several Chicago banks for $185 million in loans to lower-income neighborhoods. NTIC's training for groups from other cities in the often tedious details and techniques of organizing, researching, and negotiating with financial institutions has resulted in reinvestment agreements worth over $3 billion. In the words of the *Wall Street Journal*, Cincotta has become "the leading advocate of forcing banks to lend to the poor."

CURRENT PRIORITIES: NTIC/NPA continues work on housing issues, where it has had great success—winning community reinvestment agreements from local banks, ending lending and insurance redlining, and obtaining afford-able homeowners insurance in lower-income neighborhoods. NTIC monitors the savings and loan bailout bills, looking for ways to benefit low-income renters and potential buyers. NPA supported the National Affordable Housing Act of 1990, which provides $2 billion in new funds for affordable housing programs; Cincotta was invited to the White House for the signing of the law. NTIC has developed a close relationship with housing and urban development secretary Jack Kemp, and has consulted on regulations for low-interest loan provisions. New concerns include community anticrime and drug efforts like Project CLEAN in Chicago, utility rate issues, and health care. NTIC's newspaper *Disclosure* publicizes achievements of affiliated organizations, including the activities of ADAPT, the organization of disabled activists whose confrontational demonstrations match NPA's style.

AFFILIATES: NPA claims 300 community affiliates in 120 cities. NTIC trains primarily in the midwestern states, conducting workshops in Illinois, Iowa, Indiana, Kansas, Kentucky, Minnesota, New York, Oklahoma, Ohio, Texas, and Wisconsin.

STRUCTURE: NTIC has an eight-member board of directors, and NPA has a six-member board. Cincotta is president of both. Cincotta is also executive director of NTIC and chairperson of NPA. Four regional conferences now precede the annual NPA national conference in April in Washington, D.C.

RESOURCES: NTIC has a budget of $700,000, derived from corporations (42 percent), foundations (35 percent), program activities (10 percent), government contracts (9 percent), and churches (4 percent). The NPA budget is under $25,000 and supports the annual conference.

PUBLICATIONS AND SERVICES: For $15 individuals can subscribe to the NTIC newspaper *Disclosure*, published six times a year. The quarterly *NTIC Reports* newsletter is sent to funders and affiliate organization leaders. NTIC publications include *Community Reinvestment Act (CRA) Handbook* (1979), *Insurance Redlining: Profits vs. Policyholders* (1978), and two booklets on organizing by Shel Trapp, *Dynamics of Organizing* (1976) and *A Challenge for Change* (1976). For a sketch on Cincotta, see chapter 3 in Anne Witte Garland, *Women Activists: Challenging the Abuse of Power* (The Feminist Press at CUNY, 1988). □

* · ;**CITIZENACTION**

CITIZEN ACTION

1406 W. 6TH STREET, SUITE 200

CLEVELAND, OH 44113

(216) 861-5200

FOUNDED: 1979; reorganized 1989
MEMBERS: 3 million   STATE AFFILIATES: 32
BUDGET: $5 million   STAFF: 40
TAX STATUS: 501(c)(4): Citizen Action Fund;
501(c)(3): Citizens Fund

PURPOSE: "To promote effective citizen participation in the economic, environmental, and political decisions that affect their lives."

Citizen Action coordinates a network of statewide organizations that mobilize a working-class and lower-middle-class constituency on issues including national health insurance, utility rates, toxic waste, and energy efficiency. Through the independent but closely associated Midwest Academy, Citizen Action affiliates share organizer training programs and an annual conference that knits groups together. With tight links to labor and senior citizens groups, Citizen Action has the ability to lobby and engage in electoral politics with considerable impact. Citizen Action has combined the idealism of the New Left with the pragmatic orientation of Saul Alinsky to become the vanguard of "progressive populism."

BACKGROUND: Heather Booth got her start as an activist in the Mississippi Summer civil rights project in 1964, helping register voters and run freedom schools. Returning to Chicago, she organized an early women's group in 1967 and explored ways to transplant the spirit of the freedom schools to the new social movements in northern cities. Booth founded the Midwest Academy in 1973 to provide training for organizers in neighborhood organizations, religious groups, unions, and women's and peace organizations. Her husband, Paul Booth, a founding leader of Students for a Democratic Society (SDS) in the early 1960s, was president of Chicago's Citizen Action Program (CAP), formed in 1969 by organizer trainees from Saul Alinsky's Industrial Areas Foundation. The Midwest Academy and IAF worked together on CAP's campaigns against air pollution, residential "redlining" by banks, and a crosstown expressway.

Out of this mix the Midwest Academy developed its model of direct-action organizing, combining the idealism of student activists of the 1960s with the pragmatic discipline of IAF to build multiissue organizations that represent a potential majority coalition— uniting often antagonistic groups including whites, blacks, and Hispanics; the poor, the working class, and the middle class; labor, environmentalists, and women. Groups training with the Midwest Academy developed two models of organization: the unitary statewide membership organization with local chapters, typified by Massachusetts Fair Share and Oregon Fair Share; and the statewide coalition of organizations, exemplified by the Illinois Public Action Council and the Ohio Public Interest Campaign, both founded in 1975.

At the heart of the Midwest Academy's coalition strategy is an alliance with organized labor. In 1977 Heather Booth got together with William Winpisinger, president of the International Association of Machinists, and William Hutton of the National Council of Senior Citizens (composed primarily of retired union members) to discuss a grassroots movement to curb the power of the energy industry. The next spring the leaders of some 70 labor, citizen, senior, and farm organizations met in Washington, D.C., to found the Citizen/Labor Energy Coalition (CLEC), which set up its office at the Machinists' headquarters. CLEC worked to stop natural gas decontrol and end the oil depletion allowance that gives a special tax break to energy companies, to foster solar energy alternatives, and to fund low-income energy assistance and weatherization programs. By 1983 CLEC had 300 member organizations in thirty-five states, and had developed a door-to-door canvass program to raise funds and take its message to the public.

The success of CLEC taught Midwest Academy leaders the potential of addressing issues beyond energy through a national structure uniting state citizens groups. In 1979 five state groups met in Chicago to form a national federation, Citizen Action. The founding organizations were Oregon Fair Share, Massachusetts Fair Share, Illinois Public Action Council, Connecticut Citizen Action Coalition, and Ohio Public Interest Campaign. They were soon joined by New Hampshire People's Alliance, Indiana Citizen Action Coalition, Pennsylvania Public Interest Campaign, and Minnesota COACT. Statewide organizations that began as CLEC projects evolved into multiissue groups in New Jersey, Wisconsin, and Pennsylvania. By 1985 Citizen Action had twenty state organizations representing 2 million people, a combined budget of $12 million, and a total staff of 1,500 organizers, door-to-door canvassers, and researchers.

Although most affiliates started with an Alinsky-style direct-action approach of pressuring local agencies and corporations, the electoral success of conservatives in the 1980s pushed Citizen Action toward the political arena. Doreen Del Bianco and Miles Rappaport, leaders of Connecticut Citizen Action Group, won election to the state legislature in 1982 and 1984 respectively. Citizen Action affiliates in Iowa and Illinois played a major role in electing Democratic U.S. senators Tom Harkin and Paul Simon in 1984. Citizen Action's growing clout was apparent when six of the eight Democratic presidential primary contenders showed up to speak at the Midwest Academy conference in 1987. Since 1973 Midwest Academy claims to have trained more than 20,000 people from over 1,500 organizations.

In 1990 Heather Booth became director of the Coalition for Democratic Values, an organization of leading progressive Democrats, formed as a counterweight to the centrist Democratic Leadership Council. Jackie Kendall, a veteran organizer with the Illinois Public Action Council, became director of the Midwest Academy in 1982. Ira Arlook, of the Ohio Public Interest Campaign and codirector of Citizen Action with Booth from 1979 to 1988, is now director.

CURRENT PRIORITIES: A national health insurance program has been Citizen Action's top priority for several years, currently supporting legislation proposed by Rep. Marty Russo (D-Illinois). Citizen Action also supports parental and medical leave for employees, strict enforcement of toxic waste laws, and various steps to lower utility bills and support solar and alternative energy sources. Citizen Action stays close to progressive Democrats, and has little enthusiasm for third parties.

MEMBERS: Citizen Action's total claimed membership of 3 million includes members of groups within state coalition organizations, organizational members in the unitary state organizations, and individual members reached in the door-to-door canvass (who tend to be "new-collar" types—younger, lower income, and more suburban than direct-mail contributors—and not on the mailing lists of liberal groups). These "new collar" members tend to be swing voters, weakly affiliated with political parties—a key constituency for Democrats. Citizen Action's telephone and door-to-door canvass operations reach up to 300,000 households a week, contacting some 15 million people a year.

STRUCTURE: In 1989 Citizen Action consolidated its various nonprofit structures as Citizen Action Fund, with a 32-member board of directors representing affiliate organizations. Independent affiliates are active in twenty-two states; ten states in the process of organization have staff paid by the national office. The annual Midwest Academy conference draws over 1,200 Citizen Action leaders, organizers, and canvass staff. Ira Arlook has been executive director of both Citizen Action and the Ohio Public Interest Campaign from the start. Headquarters of the Midwest Academy is 225 West Ohio Street, Suite 250, Chicago, IL 60610; (312) 645-6010.

RESOURCES: Citizen Action's $3.5 million revenue is derived primarily from membership contributions (70 percent) and foundation and major donors (20 percent). Affiliates claim total combined budgets of $20 million.

PUBLICATIONS AND SERVICES: Members receive copies of their state organization newsletter. The quarterly *Citizen Action News* (circulation 200,000) is sent to subscribers and direct contributors. For background see Harry C. Boyte, Heather Booth, and Steve Max, *Citizen Action and the New American Populism* (Temple University Press, 1986). □

PROGRESSIVE PUBLIC FOUNDATIONS

During the 1970s activists on the left devised a new structure—the progressive public foundation—to channel money and support to a variety of local organizing projects. Initially established by young people with inherited wealth, the local groups that formed the Funding Exchange have expanded their donor networks to include other interested contributors. Most groups restrict funding to a limited geographic area— Vanguard Public Foundation in San Francisco, Bread and Roses Community Fund in Philadelphia, North Star Fund in New York City. Some cover several states, like Haymarket People's Fund in New England, the Appalachian Community Fund, and the Fund for Southern Communities. A Territory Resource is an independent public foundation serving the Pacific Northwest, and Resist is a smaller-scale foundation that covers the entire country. The Peace Development Fund has applied the model to national funding of local peace projects. A National Network of Women's Funds (NNWF) shares information among some 60 women's foundations in cities across the country; for information contact NNWF, 1821 University Avenue, Suite 409 North, St. Paul, MN 55104; (612) 641-0742.

FUNDING EXCHANGE

666 BROADWAY, 5TH FLOOR

NEW YORK, NY 10012

(212) 529-5300

FOUNDED: 1979   REGION: throughout the U.S.
MEMBER FUNDS: 15   GRANTS: $4 million;
total network: $7.3 million   STAFF: 11
TAX STATUS: 501(c)(3)

SLOGAN: "Change, not charity."

United Ways for progressive change— that's one way to look at the Funding Exchange network. Established by young people with inherited wealth, the 15 member public foundations of the Funding Exchange solicit contributions and make small grants to grassroots groups working for social and economic justice, peace, human rights, and community organization. Community boards and representatives share responsibility with donor boards for the funding decisions. The common denominator is an orientation to social change, not social services.

BACKGROUND: Alternative or Left philanthropy dates back at least as far as the Garland Fund, established in the 1920s, which played an important role launching the litigation program of the NAACP. A couple dozen smaller progressive foundations were active by the 1960s, supporting the civil rights and peace movements of that decade— most of these established from individual fortunes. What is novel in the new alternative philanthropy is the progressive public foundation (which receives more than 35 percent of its support from more than one source), funded not primarily from an endowment but from annual gifts by a core of committed members. The national movement got rolling when Sally Pillsbury (of the Minnesota milling family) met Obie Benz at a meeting of the Council on Foundations in Minneapolis in 1973; Benz described the Vanguard Public Foundation he had started the year before in San Francisco with other young people with inherited wealth. Sally relayed the story to her son George, who was living in Cambridge, Massachusetts. After contacting Benz, George Pillsbury and friends decided to create the Haymarket People's Fund in Boston.

With George Pillsbury's help, the six original progressive public foundations got together in 1978 to form the Funding Exchange, which opened its New York City office in 1979. By 1991 the network had expanded to include fifteen member, associate, and affiliate funds. Staff provide technical assistance to member funds in fund-raising strategies and skills, donor outreach, legal support, publicity and promotion. The Funding Exchange also helps start new community-based funds and works to expand the network of individual donors committed to social change philanthropy. Funding Exchange affiliates have conducted conferences on socially responsible investing, and workshops helping people with inherited wealth overcome "affluenza," the guilt and confusion that can accompany the possession of unearned wealth by people with progressive politics. Since 1979 the total of all grants from all member funds comes to over $40 million. Grants made by the whole network now total about $7.3 million per year.

STRUCTURE: In 1979 the Funding Exchange established National Community Funds (NCF) as a means of operating donor-advised funds and making grants to geographic areas not served by member funds as well as grants to national and international organizations and activities. NCF was designed to work with the donor who plans to give $20,000 or more to social change activity. In 1990 NCF administered over seventy donor-advised funds and distributed $3.5 million in grants. As of 1992 NCF was renamed the Donor-Advised Program.

The Funding Exchange also manages three smaller funds: the Paul Robeson Fund for Film, Video, and Radio, which awards $300,000 a year to independent productions on social issues; OUT: a Fund for Gay and Lesbian Liberation, which awards $100,000 a year; and the Saguaro Fund, which awards $100,000 a year to multiracial organizations and projects by and for people of color. The Funding Exchange has raised over $9.5 million toward its endowment campaign goal of $15 million. Cecilia Rodriguez, founder and former director of *La Mujer Obrera* in El Paso, Texas, became executive director in 1991.

PUBLICATIONS AND SERVICES: The Funding Exchange distributes four useful publications: *Gift Giving Guide: Methods and Tax Implications of Giving Away Money*, rev. ed. (1987), on the nuts and bolts of tax law and the mechanisms for tax-advantaged giving; *Robin Hood Was Right: A Guide to Giv-*

ing Your Money for Social Change (Vanguard Public Foundation, 1977), which contains more on the reasons for giving to support social change; *Inherited Wealth: Your Money and Your Life*, rev. ed. (1987); and the *Directory of Socially Responsible Investments*, rev. ed. (1986). □

M E M B E R   F U N D S

APPALACHIAN COMMUNITY FUND

517 UNION AVENUE, SUITE 206

KNOXVILLE, TN 37902

(615) 523-5783

FOUNDED: 1986   REGION: West Virginia and the Appalachian counties of Kentucky, Tennessee, and Virginia   GRANTS: $230,000

BREAD AND ROSES COMMUNITY FUND

924 CHERRY STREET

PHILADELPHIA, PA 19107

(215) 928-1880

FOUNDED: 1971   REGION: greater Philadelphia area; Camden, NJ GRANTS: $100,000

CHINOOK FUND

2413 W. 32ND AVENUE

Denver, CO 80211

(303) 455-6905

FOUNDED: 1987   REGION: Colorado GRANTS: $66,000

CROSSROADS FUND

3411 W. DIVERSEY AVENUE, SUITE 20

CHICAGO, IL 60647

(312) 227-7676

FOUNDED: 1980

REGION: metropolitan Chicago

GRANTS: $100,000

FUND FOR SOUTHERN COMMUNITIES

552 HILL STREET SE

ATLANTA, GA 30312

(404) 577-3178

FOUNDED: 1981   REGION: Georgia, North Carolina, and South Carolina GRANTS: $239,000

HAYMARKET PEOPLE'S FUND

42 SEAVERNS AVENUE

BOSTON, MA 02130

(617) 522-7676

FOUNDED: 1974   REGION: New England GRANTS: $607,000

HEADWATERS FUND

122 W. FRANKLIN AVENUE, ROOM 110

MINNEAPOLIS, MN 55404

(612) 879-0602

FOUNDED: 1984

REGION: Minneapolis–St. Paul metropolitan area   GRANTS: $143,000

LIBERTY HILL FOUNDATION

1316 THIRD STREET PROMENADE, B-4

SANTA MONICA, CA 90401

(310) 458-1450

FOUNDED: 1976   REGION: Los Angeles and San Diego counties   GRANTS: $258,000

THE LIVE OAK FUND FOR CHANGE

P.O. BOX 4601

AUSTIN, TX 78705

(512) 476-5714

FOUNDED: 1981   REGION: Texas
GRANTS: $180,000

MCKENZIE RIVER GATHERING FOUNDATION

3558 SE HAWTHORNE

PORTLAND, OR 97214

(503) 233-0271

454 WILLAMETTE STREET

EUGENE, OR 97401

(503) 485-2790

FOUNDED: 1976   REGION: Oregon
GRANTS: $319,000

NORTH STAR FUND

666 BROADWAY, 5TH FLOOR

NEW YORK, NY 10012

(212) 460-5511

FOUNDED: 1978   REGION: New York City
GRANTS: $396,000

THE PEOPLE'S FUND

1325 NUUANU AVENUE

HONOLULU, HI 96817

(808) 526-2441

FOUNDED: 1972   REGION: Hawaii
GRANTS: $60,000

PEOPLE'S RESOURCE OF SOUTHWEST OHIO

P.O. BOX 6366

CINCINNATI, OH 45206

FOUNDED: 1980   REGION: southwestern Ohio, including Cincinnati and Dayton
GRANTS: $35,000

VANGUARD PUBLIC FOUNDATION

14 PRECITA AVENUE

SAN FRANCISCO, CA 94110

(415) 285-2005

FOUNDED: 1972   REGION: San Francisco Bay Area, northern California, Fresno
GRANTS: $519,000

WISCONSIN COMMUNITY FUND

122 STATE STREET, SUITE 508

MADISON, WI 53703

(608) 251-6834

FOUNDED: 1982   REGION: Wisconsin
GRANTS: $70,000

RESIST

ONE SUMMER STREET

SOMERVILLE, MA 02143

(617) 623-5110

FOUNDED: 1967   CONTRIBUTORS: 4,500
GRANTS: $95,000   STAFF: 3
TAX STATUS: 501(c)(3)

SLOGAN: "A call to resist illegitimate authority."

Founded in the period of resistance to the Vietnam War, Resist has evolved into an organization that works like a public foundation, raising money from individuals and making small grants to grassroots groups or local chapters of national organizations involved in antiracist, peace, feminist, and pro-working-class organizing.

BACKGROUND: Resist was launched in 1967 to oppose the Vietnam War and the draft. In its early years, Resist declared itself in opposition to imperialism abroad and repression at home. Over the last two decades the organization has evolved to a democratic socialist–feminist perspective. Resist has made over 2,500 grants since 1967; presently the typical grant is in the $200 to $800 range.

CURRENT PRIORITIES: Resist supports groups working on (1) Central and Latin America, (2) community and antiracism organizing, (3) peace and antimilitarism, (4) women's rights, abortion and reproductive rights, (5) gay and lesbian rights, (6) prisoners and criminal justice, (7) environment, (8) Native Americans, (9) AIDS, and (10) peace and justice in the Middle East.

CONTRIBUTORS: Resist's fund-raising is built around a core of 700 donors who pledge a regular amount of money each month—providing some 27 percent of Resist's income. Another 4,000 people make annual or one-time contributions. Over the last few years, Resist has reached out geographically to fund projects beyond its original New England base, and to build a national base of donors. Three states (Massachusetts, New York, and California) provide 57 percent of Resist's donors. Small contributions are typical and welcome—83 percent of the donors give $100 or less. Resist also handles donor-advised gifts.

STRUCTURE: Resist has a thirty-two-member, self-recruiting board of directors representing a variety of positions on the left. Half the board are women. Among the board members are Noam Chomsky, Mitchell Goodman, Grace Paley, and George Vickers. The board meets ten times a year, to give timely support to groups responding to emergencies.

RESOURCES: In 1991 Resist gave a total of $95,000 to 195 organizations, up from $64,000 to 153 groups in 1989.

PUBLICATIONS AND SERVICES: Contributors and grantees receive an eight-page newsletter, *Resist* (circulation 5,200), ten times a year. □

A TERRITORY RESOURCE

603 STEWART, SUITE 221

SEATTLE, WA 98101

(206) 624-4081

FOUNDED: 1978   CONTRIBUTORS: 175
GRANTS: $200,000   STAFF: 3
TAX STATUS: 501(c)(3)

PURPOSE: "To be a resource for organizations attempting to establish a society that is politically and economically democratic, equitable and environmentally sound."

A Territory Resource (ATR) is a public foundation providing support to citizens groups working for economic and social justice in the five states of Idaho, Montana, Oregon, Washington, and Wyoming.

BACKGROUND: ATR began in 1978 with four members and an initial $40,000 in awards. Although similar in intention to the Funding Exchange groups, ATR did not begin with grant recipient constituencies represented on its board. ATR subsequently moved to include both donor and advisory members on its board, but remains an independent progressive foundation.

MEMBERS: ATR has 43 contributors at the full membership level ($3,500 per year or more), 30 associate members (giving between $1,500 and $3,500), and 100 additional donors giving less than $1,000.

STRUCTURE: ATR has a twelve-member board of directors, with seven elected by the full members and five selected to represent the activist community receiving grants. Valerie Reuther is executive director.

RESOURCES: In 1990 ATR awarded seventy grants to fifty-five organizations in the Pacific Northwest and northern Rockies. Program grants (twenty to twenty-five per year) average $3,000 to $10,000. ATR also awards twenty-five technical assistance grants and twenty cultural grants (all under $1,000 each) to grassroots groups.

PUBLICATIONS AND SERVICES: Contributors receive the quarterly newsletter, *A Territory Report* (circulation 1,700). □

PEACE DEVELOPMENT FUND

PEACE DEVELOPMENT FUND

44 NORTH PROSPECT STREET

P.O. BOX 270

AMHERST, MA 01004

(413) 256-8306

FOUNDED: 1981   CONTRIBUTORS: 1,400
GRANTS: $1 million   STAFF: 15
TAX STATUS: 501(c)(3)

PURPOSE: "Building a grassroots peace and social justice movement nationwide."

The Peace Development Fund (PDF) is a public foundation, supported by individual contributors, that makes grants to community-based peace and justice projects that educate the public about the economic and social costs of military spending, the effects of U.S. foreign policy, and the effects of racism on national well-being, including the "environmental racism" of toxic waste dumping in communities of color. PDF supports global demilitarization and nonviolent conflict resolution.

BACKGROUND: PDF was founded in 1981, in the early days of the Nuclear

Weapons Freeze Campaign, by members of the Traprock Peace Center, including Bob Mazer and Meg Gage, who served as executive director until 1992. After meeting Gage, Pat Close of Seattle founded a west coast counterpart, the Pacific Peace Fund, in 1983.

PDF funds peace activists at the grassroots, making small grants (averaging around $3,600) to such groups as the Snake River Alliance in Idaho, the Piedmont Peace Project in rural North Carolina, and the Southern Association of Black Educators. PDF also supports local chapters of such national organizations as Educators for Social Responsibility, Jobs with Peace, and SANE/FREEZE. During the past decade, PDF has awarded over 1,000 grants totaling some $6.2 million.

CURRENT PRIORITIES: In addition to grants to 122 organizations, in 1990 PDF made thirty-four Teaching Peace grants to programs for youth from kindergarten through twelfth grade, made technical assistance grants to fifteen organizations, and provided training to fifty-five organizations through its Exchange Project. PDF also makes donor-advised grants. Normally awarding grants in three cycles per year, PDF made $150,000 in emergency grants in 1990–91 during the sudden Middle East crisis to groups rallying opposition to the Gulf War.

STRUCTURE: The Pacific Peace Fund (PPF) operated as an affiliated group with an interlocking board of directors for several years. PPF merged into PDF in 1988, and now serves as the western regional office handling all grant applications from groups west of the Mississippi (PDF, 5516 Roosevelt Way NE, Seattle, WA 98105; (206) 525-0025). Ravi Khanna is the executive director, and Dan Petegorsky directs the western regional office.

RESOURCES: PDF revenue in 1990 totaled $1.6 million; grants awarded have risen from $106,000 in 1982 to just over $1 million in 1989 and 1990.

PUBLICATIONS AND SERVICES: Contributors receive the newsletter *Peace Developments* (circulation 6,000) three times a year. An annual report is available. □

10.

CONSERVATIVES

How did the conservative movement, routed in Barry Goldwater's catastrophic defeat to Lyndon Johnson in the 1964 presidential campaign, return to elect its champion Ronald Reagan just sixteen years later? What at first looks like the political comeback of the century becomes, on closer examination, the product of a particular political moment that united an unstable coalition. In the liberal press, conservatives are often portrayed as a monolithic right wing. Close up, conservatives are as varied as their counterparts on the left.

Indeed, the circumstances of the late 1980s—the demise of the Soviet Union, Reagan's legacy, the Bush administration—have frayed the coalition of traditional conservatives, libertarian advocates of laissez-faire economics, and Cold War anticommunists first knitted together in the 1950s by William F. Buckley, Jr., and the staff of the *National Review*. The Reagan coalition added to the conservative mix two rather incongruous groups: the religious Right, primarily provincial white Protestant fundamentalists and evangelicals from the Sunbelt (defecting from the Democrats since George Wallace's 1968 presidential campaign); and the neoconservatives, centered in New York and led predominantly by cosmopolitan, secular Jewish intellectuals.

Goldwater's campaign in 1964 brought conservatives together for their first national electoral effort since Taft lost the Republican nomination to Eisenhower in 1952. Conservatives shared a distaste for Eisenhower's "modern Republicanism" that largely accepted the welfare state developed by Roosevelt's New Deal and Truman's Fair Deal. Undeterred by Goldwater's defeat, conservative activists regrouped and began developing institutions for the long haul. Many of the New Right leaders—Phyllis Schlafly, Richard Viguerie, Paul Weyrich, Ed Feulner—got their start in politics with the Goldwater campaign. And surprise! so did a few people not widely identified with the Right—including Dave Foreman, founder of Earth First!, and San Francisco's Harvey Milk, the country's first openly gay elected public official.

The conservative comeback got momentum in 1966 when a group of conservative businessmen, remembering Reagan's effective endorsement of Goldwater, convinced him to run for governor of California. Building on backlash to the 1960s campus turmoil (particularly at Berkeley) during the anti–Vietnam War movement and civil disorders (in Watts and other cities), Reagan's victory over Pat Brown highlighted the vulnerability of the Democratic coalition. Kevin Phillips's "southern strategy" pointed the way for Richard Nixon to take advantage of the backlash to civil rights and pull away "George Wallace Democrats" from Hubert Humphrey, resulting in Nixon's 1968 presidential victory. Although conservatives were unhappy with Henry Kissinger's detente with the Soviet Union, Nixon's vice president Spiro Agnew, with his virulent attacks on student activists and war protesters, appeased the Right. Labor's defection from McGovern in 1972 made Nixon's reelection easier. Nixon's second-term crisis over Watergate, however, slowed the shift of southern whites and northern ethnics from Democrats to Republicans. By running Jimmy Carter, an evangelical southerner, against Gerald Ford in 1976, Democrats further postponed an electoral realignment.

THE REVOLUTION THAT WASN'T

The Reagan victory in 1980 was partly a result of Carter's failures—rampant inflation and the Iranian hostage crisis foremost among them. It was also the product of a smoothly orchestrated campaign to emphasize the Soviet threat, and a well-mobilized religious Right. The Reagan administration accomplishments from the conservative agenda were, in retrospect, remarkably few: a tax cut that strongly benefited the wealthy, a Pentagon buildup that left huge deficits, and the appointment of a conservative federal judiciary. Taxes have since been made more progressive again, and the military budget is set for reductions, leaving only the conservative federal judiciary and Supreme Court and a vast national debt (which some conservatives call "Reagan's third term," blocking any expansion of social programs by the Democrats). Reagan's military Keynesianism buoyed the economy for several years, but the impact of years of budget and trade deficits led to a recession by 1991. Deregulation of the banking and savings industries led to catastrophic bailout programs that have further crippled the economy during George Bush's presidency. Divided over domestic and foreign policy, conservatives are having difficulty designing a positive program for governance.

Conservatives are not only divided ideologically, they have sharp personal rivalries and organizational weaknesses that get less public airing than those of progressives. "The Left has an advantage," Paul Weyrich said in an interview, "they're more collectivistic, while the Right is more individualistic. They just don't cooperate as well." "The conservative mindset" requires someone to guide and inspire, Weyrich told *New Republic* editor Fred Barnes. "Liberals, I'm sorry to say, are more attracted to ideas and ideology. They're willing to work together without an authority figure."

Many national conservative organizations have been structured around charismatic individuals and may not survive their departures. The established think tanks—American Enterprise Institute, Hoover Institution, Hudson Institute—are the most stable, but most of them are tilting pragmatically toward the center under neoconservative administrators. Of the newer groups, the Heritage Foundation is best institutionalized (even though Ed Feulner has been its only chief executive, it thrives on his entrepreneurial and administrative skills, not his charisma). Weyrich's Free Congress Foundation is less so, but it could survive him. The American Conservative Union (ACU), a membership organization, is stable if weak, and dependent on David Keene. On the other hand, it's hard to imagine Eagle Forum without Phyllis Schlafly, the American Family Association without Don Wildmon, or Concerned Women for America without Beverly LaHaye, despite its chapter structure. When Rev. Jerry Falwell's mind turned to other matters, his Moral Majority and Liberty Federation were disbanded in 1989. The National Conservative Political Action Committee (NCPAC), the nemesis of Democratic senators in the 1980 campaign, collapsed after its founder Terry Dolan died of AIDS in 1986. Howard Phillips set aside his personal project, The Conservative Caucus, to develop the U.S. Taxpayers party, from which he launched a minor party presidential campaign in 1992.

Despite gains in the Reagan years, some conservative leaders worry about the Right's failure to develop structures at the grassroots. "Many conservatives are monarchists at heart," Weyrich writes in *Policy Review*. "They *love* the Presidency. They think that if you own the Presidency, that is all that really counts." Quoting Chicago's late Mayor Daley that "in the final analysis, all politics is local," Weyrich reminds conservatives that to have power means "holding territory" at the local and state levels. Conservative and libertarian policy think tanks are up and running in dozens of states and associated through The Madison Group, and the American Legislative Exchange Council (ALEC) connects conservative state legislators.

Yet the Right has few structures that can mobilize individuals on the local level—with the exceptions of fundamentalist church networks, and issues like antiabortion campaigns. The Right has nothing to compare with the liberals' ability to call upon the leaders of labor unions and black and Hispanic organizations to mobilize their members as campaign workers. Conservatives have nothing comparable to the progressives' community organizing networks, door-to-door canvass campaigns, or public foundations that fund grassroots groups. The John Birch Society still has its local groups and American Opinion bookstores, but they are viewed by many conservatives and most of the general public as beyond the pale of the "respectable Right."

Conservative leaders often have been more adept at making money for themselves and their mailing houses than at getting money they raise into practical politics. As young conservative Amy Moritz writes in Heritage Foundation's *Policy Review*, "Conservatives claim seven of the top 14 money-raising political action committees but only two of the top 14 PAC campaign contributors." According to Moritz, the conservative movement suffers from a "Jim and Tammy Bakker Syndrome—an unwillingness and/or ability to police itself in the matter of ethical fund-raising practices." But maybe conservatives have more organizational leverage than Weyrich suggests. Conservatives have achieved strong grassroots influence in the Republican party (which raised $207 million over the 1989–90 campaign cycle, compared to the Democrats' $87 million). And as former ACU director Dan Casey notes, the conservatives' unofficial national magazine is *Readers' Digest* (circulation 16 million). Not to be technologically outflanked by progressives, Accuracy in Media recently set up a computer network for conservatives: Contact AIM NET (1275 K Street, NW, Suite 1150, Washington, DC 20005; (202) 371-6710).

VARIETIES OF CONSERVATISM

Sociologist Peter Berger (who half-jokingly refers to himself as the last Hapsburgian monarchist) made a playful suggestion in *Commentary* that since most conservatives view history as a decline from a better time in the past, one might classify types of conservatism by the periods they identify as the golden age and the onset of decline. For the traditional conservatives the golden age is the Middle Ages—thirteenth century for Roman Catholics, seventeenth century for the Anglican version. Southern agrarian paleoconservatives obviously look to the antebellum South. Libertarians would choose the nineteenth century of the robber barons, while the New Right populists prefer the nineteenth century of small-town America. And neoconservatives date decline only from the mid-1960s—clearly a different vision from the traditionalists. Dan Himmelfarb, writing in

Commentary on "Conservative Splits," identifies the differing philosophic grounding of neoconservatives in liberal-democratic modernity (valuing liberty, self-government, and equality of opportunity) and paleoconservatives in medieval Christian theology (valuing belief, hierarchy, and prescription). On anticommunism, the glue in the fusionist formula, Himmelfarb writes, "Neoconservatives are anti-Communist because Communism is the enemy of freedom and democracy, paleoconservatives because it is the enemy of religion, tradition, and hierarchy."

Traditional conservatives: Before William F. Buckley, Jr., ideological conservatives seemed to be a cranky crowd saying "No!" to the twentieth century. Russell Kirk, author of *The Conservative Mind* (Henry Regnery 1953), was one of its few respected representatives. Buckley and his circle at *National Review*, founded in 1955, developed a contemporary conservatism through the "fusion" of three streams of thought: Burkean traditionalism, free-market libertarian economics, and anticommunism. Several former Communists, including Whittaker Chambers, were close to the magazine—and the editorial board included ex-Communist Frank Meyer and former Trotskyists James Burnham and Willmore Kendall. Buckley and the *National Review* circle made conservatism intellectually respectable, and brought it into the political mainstream.

Buckley hosted the founding meeting of the Young Americans for Freedom (YAF) in 1960 at his home in Sharon, Connecticut, helping Stanton Evans author YAF's declaration of principles known as the Sharon Statement. Buckley also joined in founding The American Conservative Union in 1964 following Goldwater's defeat. Buckley worked with ACU long enough to insist that John Birch Society members be kept off the board, and then withdrew—preferring to play, as his biographer, John Judis, writes, "a catalytic but not an organizational role." Buckley continued to insist during the 1960s that the Birch Society be rejected as outside the "respectable Right," as he also did with Willis Carto's Liberty Lobby in the early 1980s, suing its newspaper *Spotlight* for libel and winning a modest judgment.

ACU continues as the membership and lobbying vehicle of

traditional conservatives, and its annual Conservative Political Action Conference (CPAC), cosponsored with YAF, remains an important get-together—although the New Right groups set up the rival Conservative Leadership Conference in 1990. YAF has always been a loose cannon; governed by a shifting board elected at each convention, it tends to be the personal machine of whoever gets control of the organization. *Human Events*, the weekly newspaper owned and edited by Thomas Winter and Allan Ryskind, has taken a more populist direction, supporting the social issues of the New Right and enjoying Pat Buchanan's challenge to George Bush. Despite Buckley's efforts for an ecumenical respectable conservatism, the *National Review* retains a flavor distinctly Roman and Anglo-Catholic, Ivy League, and Manhattan upper class. In recent years Buckley has settled into Tory libertarianism, refusing Far Right ventures into minor party campaigns, favoring some degree of drug legalization, and chastising Pat Buchanan for making anti-Semitic statements. Traditional conservatives of the old school, tiring of Buckley's fusionist cocktail, are reclaiming their territory as paleoconservatives.

Libertarians: To progressive critics like *In These Times*, it's "anarchy with mutual funds and hot tubs," but to its advocates, laissez-faire as an economic and social philosophy is the true path to freedom. Libertarianism is built around the work of such economists in the classical liberal tradition as Friedrich von Hayek, Ludwig von Mises, and their noted followers like Nobel laureate Milton Friedman. Libertarians celebrate free markets and condemn all forms of state control, regulation, or intervention. As anarcho-libertarian Murray Rothbard put it, "Simply think of the State as a criminal band, and all of the Libertarian attitudes will logically fall into place." Rothbard labels three types of libertarians: "hippies" (who favor decriminalization of drugs and victimless crimes), "rednecks" (who hate taxes, love guns, and want to ride motorcycles without wearing helmets), and "preppies" (who are think tank policy mavens).

Ayn Rand inspired many young libertarians with her novels *The Fountainhead* (Bobbs-Merrill, 1943) and *Atlas Shrugged* (Random House, 1957). Rand developed a philosophy of economic individualism called "objectivism," which celebrated selfishness (her heroine's symbol is the dollar sign). Among her circle of youthful followers, led by psychologist Nathaniel Brandon, was economist Alan Greenspan, presently chairman of the Federal Reserve Board. Rand's atheism put her beyond Buckley's boundary of respectable conservatism. Libertarianism gained a more respectable grounding in social philosophy in Robert Nozick's *Anarchy, State, and Utopia* (Basic Books, 1974), a response to John Rawls's utilitarian defense of the liberal welfare state in *A Theory of Justice* (Harvard University Press, 1971).

The Libertarian party grew out of a 1969 split in the Young Americans for Freedom, when the Libertarian Caucus pushed a plank on drug legalization. YAF traditionalists denounced the libertarians as "lazy-fairies," and following a near riot, purged them from the organization. The Libertarian Caucus regrouped, gathering in some disaffected anarchists from SDS and one-time followers of Ayn Rand to form the party in 1971. The party ran John Hospers as its first presidential candidate in 1972; he received 6,000 votes and one electoral vote from a renegade Republican elector. That elector, Roger MacBride, became so celebrated in libertarian circles that he was nominated as the Libertarian candidate in 1976. The best showing came in 1980, when ARCO attorney Ed Clark and David Koch ran on the Libertarian ticket, receiving 920,000 votes (1.1 percent of the ballots cast). The Libertarian ticket was headed by David Bergland in 1984, and former Texas Republican congressman Ron Paul in 1988. Andre Marrou was the presidential nominee in 1992. Libertarians have drawn a substantial minority of votes for state and local offices here and there, and have elected an occasional local official and state legislator. Although they are in truth the "third" party, they are too far behind the Republicans and Democrats to encourage many libertarians.

By 1976 Ed Crane was disillusioned with the Libertarian party, and more impressed with the power of think tanks to influence policymakers. From a start in San Francisco in 1977, Crane's Cato Institute moved to Washington with the backing of entrepreneur Charles Koch. Bob Poole's Reason Foundation stayed on the West Coast, and has developed *Reason* magazine as the most popular vehicle of libertarian thinking. Manhattan Institute in New York City has provided a home to several noted libertarian writers, including Charles Murray and George Gilder. Although they have differences, the think tanks have succeeded in popularizing their ideas on free-market economics, social tolerance, and a military designed for self-defense and nonintervention abroad. Libertarian gadfly and godfather Murray Rothbard has long abandoned his quest for allies on the left, and is now courting a new alliance with paleo-conservatives.

The New Right: The New Right was constructed by young veterans of the Goldwater campaign—Richard Viguerie, Paul Weyrich, Howard Phillips—who wanted a populist approach to rally a majority conservative coalition, constructed around social issues, not free-market economics. They wanted to engage the George Wallace voters—not only the low- and moderate-income southern whites, but also the northern middle class who had followed Senator Joseph McCarthy, and the blue-collar ethnic Democrats, the Catholics whose parents had listened to the radio broadcasts of Father Charles Coughlin in the 1930s and were not permanently won to the Democrats by John Kennedy. The New Right faulted traditional conservatives for their elitism and their failure to get their hands dirty in practical politics. Kevin Phillips, who coined the term "New Right" in 1975, mocked Buckley and his circle as "Squire Willy and his companions of the Oxford Unabridged Dictionary" and denounced the *National Review* as primed with "cast-off Hapsburg royalty, Englishmen who part their names in the middle, and others calculated to put real lace on Buckley's Celtic curtains."

The Richard A. Viguerie Company (RAVCO) pioneered direct-mail fund-raising for the Right with the Goldwater campaign mailing list, which helped build several organizations (and nearly destroyed several as well, by overmailing when responses declined). Viguerie tried to buy the weekly newspaper *Human Events* from the traditional conservatives; rebuffed, he set up a rival magazine, *Conservative Digest*, in 1975. Losing money, Viguerie sold *Conservative Digest* in 1985; after going through two more owners and two new formats (including an effort by Paul Weyrich and former Birch Society editors), the magazine went out of business in 1989. By 1987 Viguerie was so far in debt he sold his office building for a reported $10 million to Reverend Sun Myung Moon's Unification Church, whose American Freedom Coalition has become one of Viguerie's leading direct-mail clients. Weyrich helped found Heritage Foundation as a new variety of activist think tank, and went on to form his Committee for the Survival of a Free Congress. Howard Phillips set up The Conservative Caucus, and in the mid-1980s was touting a "Freedom Fighters International" consisting of leaders of Nicaragua's contras, Angola's UNITA, Mozambique's Renamo, and Afghanistan's mujahedin. Nothing more was heard of this by 1991, when Phillips set The Conservative Caucus aside in a quixotic effort to build a new minor party, the U.S. Taxpayers Party. Since the demise of the National Conservative PAC, Senator Jesse Helms's National Congressional Club remains the strongest PAC of the New Right.

The Religious Right: The Christian Right was active in politics long before the late 1970s—recall from the 1950s and 1960s Dr. Fred Schwarz's Christian Anti-Communism Crusade, Billy James Hargis's Christian Crusade, and Reverend Carl McIntire's 20th-Century Reformation Hour radio network. The New Right televangelists all played on conservative themes to some extent, but Reverend Jerry Falwell and Reverend Pat Robertson took their viewers furthest into politics, Falwell creating the Moral Majority and Robertson using his *700 Club* audience as a base for a Republican presidential primary bid against George Bush in 1988. Each was pulled out of politics by the wake of the PTL scandal involving Jim and Tammy Faye Bakker, and later Reverend Jimmy Swaggert's sex scandal and, to a lesser degree, the flap over Reverend Oral Roberts. Beverly LaHaye, wife of Reverend Tim LaHaye, has managed to keep her Concerned Women for America network intact and relatively unscathed by the scandals.

Reverend Sun Myung Moon's Unification Church has numerous front groups on the fringe of right-wing activity, including the American Freedom Coalition, but his greatest impact has been through his triumvirate of conservative publications —the daily newspaper *The Washington Times*, the weekly magazine *Insight*, and the monthly intellectual catalog *World and I*. During the early 1980s, Moon's anticommunism seemed in tune with Reagan's conservative program; recently Moon's authoritarian religious agenda has been more in the open, particularly since he declared himself to be the Messiah at a San Francisco conference in August 1990. Recently he seems more interested in setting up factories in Russia, China, and North Korea—giving pause to his old anticommunist allies. Conservative leaders are beginning to back away from Moon, and how much longer he will continue to absorb the huge losses of his Washington publications is anybody's guess.

Neoconservatives: At times, neoconservatism has seemed to be two New York families: neocon godfather Irving Kristol, his wife, historian Gertrude Himmelfarb, and son Dan; and *Commentary* editor Norman Podhoretz, his wife, writer and editor Midge Decter, and son-in-law Elliot Abrams. Kristol's *The Public Interest* is the definitive neoconservative source on domestic social policy, and *The National Interest* fills a comparable niche for foreign policy. Of course there are many others. Jeane Kirkpatrick won her job as Reagan's U.N. ambassador for an article distinguishing between authoritarian and totalitarian societies, making the point that the former could be changed in a democratic direction while the latter could not (a theory that failed to anticipate the collapse of communism by the end of the decade, to say the least). Former Social Democrats USA (SDUSA) executive director Carl Gershman became an assistant to Kirkpatrick at the U.N. and is now director of the National Endowment for Democracy. Other SDUSA members are positioned in the AFL-CIO hierarchy. Prominent neocons include Catholic theologian Michael Novak and Lutheran-turned-Catholic Richard John Neuhaus. Some intellectuals and politicians who were offered the tag declined the honor, most notably sociologist Daniel Bell and New York Democratic senator Patrick Moynihan. Neoconservatives dominate Freedom House, the human rights monitor, and the International Rescue Committee, a relief organization. And—what most annoys the paleoconservatives—neocon administrators direct several of the leading foundations that fund conservative causes.

Paleoconservatives: Paleocons have a focus in Allan Carlson's Rockford Institute and its publication, *Chronicles: A*

Magazine of American Culture, edited by Thomas Fleming, a New Left dropout who draws inspiration from the southern agrarian conservatives—and recruit columnists like southern regionalist John Shelton Reed. Patrick Buchanan, with his "America First" campaign, represents another aspect of this tradition, its ethnic Catholic isolationist, nativist wing.

The Radical Right: Out on the conspiracy fringe, the John Birch Society survived founder Robert Welch's death in 1985, but is reduced from 100,000 members in its heyday around 1964 to some 20,000 members today. After a series of factional disputes and splits, in 1989 G. Allen Bubolz moved the headquarters from Belmont, Massachusetts, to Appleton, Wisconsin, hometown of Senator Joe McCarthy; veteran Birch writer and editor John McManus took over as chairman in 1991. Out on the racist right, the Liberty Lobby led by Willis Carto has become what the Anti-Defamation League calls "the most active anti-Semitic organization in the country." Its newspaper *The Spotlight* has a circulation of over 100,000. Several Liberty Lobby staff and associates started the Populist party in 1982, and ran David Duke for president in 1984; the party split in 1986 ejecting Carto's faction. By 1987 Duke was running as a Republican in Louisiana. The Liberty Lobby is associated with the Institute for Historical Review, which tries to disprove the Holocaust.

THE AMERICAN CONSERVATIVE UNION

38 IVY STREET, SE

WASHINGTON, DC 20003

(202) 546-6555

FOUNDED: 1964   MEMBERS: 55,000

BUDGET: $2 million   STAFF: 6

TAX STATUS: 501(c)(4): The American

Conservative Union; 501(c)(3): ACU Foundation

PURPOSE: "Communicating the goals and principles of conservatism."

The American Conservative Union (ACU) is the leading organization of traditional conservatives. ACU was founded to support free-market capitalism and oppose communism and Soviet expansion; it backs the "original intent" doctrine of constitutional interpretation against liberal judicial activism, traditional moral values, and a strong national defense. ACU hit a peak of support and influence during its unsuccessful opposition to the Panama

Canal Treaty in the late 1970s, and declined sharply following the election of President Reagan, an internal scandal and controversy involving its chairman, and the rise of more aggressive New Right organizations. Recent efforts have revived ACU to a modest presence on the Washington scene, where it issues the definitive conservative ratings of congressional voting records, and is the leading sponsor of the annual Conservative Political Action Conference (CPAC), the foremost gathering of conservative activists.

BACKGROUND: ACU was founded at the very nadir of conservative fortunes in the post–World War II era, in the wake of Barry Goldwater's resounding defeat in the presidential election of November 1964. Among the 100 activists present at the founding meeting at Washington's Mayflower Hotel were conservative leaders Rep. John Ashbrook, William F. Buckley, Jr., William Rusher, and Goldwater campaign finance director J. William Middendorf. ACU, it was hoped, would hold together the dispirited troops from the Goldwater campaign.

Over the next decade ACU established itself as the premier organization of the Right, beginning its annual "rating of Congress" in 1971, providing the conservative standard by which the voting record of members of Congress could be assessed. Congressmen Phil Crane, Mickey Edwards, and John Ashbrook served as chairmen, as did columnist M. Stanton Evans. John Lofton and Jeffrey Bell worked as editors of the ACU newsletter. In 1974 ACU convened the first annual Conservative Political Action Conference in Washington, D.C., cosponsored with Young Americans for Freedom and the conservative publications *Human Events* and *National Review*. ACU supported Ronald Reagan's unsuccessful primary battle against Gerald Ford in the 1976 Republican presidential primary. Reaching its peak of influence in 1977–78 during the unsuccessful fight against President Carter's Panama Canal Treaty, ACU had thirty staff organizing state affiliates, placing radio and TV ads, and dispatching "truth squads" to debate Canal Treaty supporters. Congressman Phil Crane (R-Illinois) attempted to use his position as ACU chairman in 1977–78 as a springboard for a run at the Republican presidential nomination; opposing factions of the board replaced him with Congressman Robert Bauman (R-Maryland).

Although it thrived in adversity, ACU went into sharp decline with the conservative movement's success. Following the victory of Ronald Reagan in the presidential election in 1980, contributions to ACU dropped by 50 percent. Panama Canal Treaty opponents couldn't be converted into regular organizational supporters, and donors not "fatigued" or complacent were shifting to such aggressive New Right operations as the Heritage Foundation, the Free Congress Foundation, the National Conservative PAC, or the Republican party itself. And then, to top it off, in 1980 ACU chairman Robert Bauman lost his bid for reelection to the House after news broke that he had solicited sex from a sixteen-year-old boy. Bauman refused to resign from the board after his term as chairman ended in 1981, and was ousted by vote of the directors in 1983.

Conservatives

Direct mail appeals fell flat, and ACU was soon nearly $800,000 in debt, reduced to a staff of one. ACU was saved by attorney and political consultant David Keene, *Human Events* editor Thomas Winter, Senator Jesse Helms, and other conservative stalwarts who worked to rebuild the organization. During the 1980s ACU supported the Reagan military buildup, lobbying for the MX missile, the B-1 bomber, and SDI, and supported military aid to Jonas Savimbi's UNITA forces in Angola and the Nicaraguan contras. During the Reagan administration, ACU also got involved with Senate confirmation hearings, particularly for Attorney General Ed Meese and Supreme Court nominees William Rehnquist and Antonin Scalia.

CURRENT PRIORITIES: ACU continues its popular rating of Congress and cosponsors the Conservative Political Action Conference, which features such conservative favorites as Oliver North and Dan Quayle. On the Hill, ACU lobbies Congress for the SDI program, and continues its strong support for conservative judicial nominees, including Clarence Thomas's Supreme Court appointment in 1991.

STRUCTURE: ACU has a thirty-two-member, self-recruiting board of directors, chaired by David Keene, with Thomas Winter as first vice-chairman. Senators Jesse Helms (R-North Carolina), James McClure (R-Idaho), and Steve Symms (R-Idaho) serve on the board, as do James Abrahamson, Jeffrey Bell, Morton Blackwell, M. Stanton Evans, Alan Gottlieb, Alan Keyes, Richard Viguerie, and Reps. Vin Weber (R-Minnesota) and Duncan Hunter (R-California). Angela "Bay" Buchanan (Pat's sister) and novelist Tom Clancy recently joined the board. Robert Billings is executive director. ACU started the Conservative Victory Fund as a related political action committee, but spun it off in 1977; ACU PAC took its place but has not been active recently.

PUBLICATIONS AND SERVICES: Members receive the ACU newsletter *Capitol Review* and the annual *ACU's Rating of Congress* pamphlet. □

THE HERITAGE FOUNDATION

214 MASSACHUSETTS AVENUE, NE

WASHINGTON, DC 20002

(202) 546-4400

FOUNDED: 1973   CONTRIBUTORS: 175,000
BUDGET: $19.3 million   STAFF: 162
TAX STATUS: 501(c)(3)

PURPOSE: "Dedicated to the principles of free competitive enterprise, limited government, individual liberty, and a strong national defense."

Founded with financing from brewer Joseph Coors, The Heritage Foundation has developed a new model of the think tank as activist policy advocate. As *The Economist* noted, "Heritage's ideology is red-blooded, celebratory capitalism," and Heritage "wears its views not just on its sleeve, but tattooed on its forehead." Ideological in vision, Heritage is pragmatic in tactics. Heritage not only conducts policy research, it markets its conclusions in short, timely briefing papers that impact current debates on Capitol Hill and in the White House. Known for its "bombs and bucks" agenda—concentrated on defense, foreign policy, and economic policy—Heritage has recently moved to tackle issues of cultural values.

BACKGROUND: In 1971 Joseph Coors, grandson of German immigrant brewer Adolph Coors, sent his aide Jack Wilson to Washington to scout out organizations to bankroll on the political right. Coors connected with Paul Weyrich, then press secretary to Colorado senator Gordon Allott, and began to support Analysis Research Corporation, which had been set up to do research for Republican conservatives. Needing a vehicle suited to their emerging brand of activist research, Coors and Weyrich decided to form their own organization. Coors contributed the $250,000 to support The Heritage Foundation in its first year, with Weyrich as president.

Weyrich was eager to get more directly involved in political campaigns and lobbying Congress. Heritage trustees decided against setting up a 501(c)4 lobbying arm or a related PAC, resolving to work within the educational framework of a 501(c)3 organization qualifying for tax-deductible contributions. Weyrich went on to form his Free Congress groups, and Edwin J. Feulner, Jr., former staffer for Republican representatives Melvin Laird and Philip Crane and director of the Republican Study Committee, became the president and chief executive at Heritage in

1977. Feulner has fostered Heritage's distinctive style of marketing policy research, recruited and retained a talented staff, built a broad base of support, and raised an endowment to sustain activities over the long haul. Heritage has attracted a skilled and stable management team—"pragmatic ideologues," they like to say—including Burton Yale Pines as senior vice president for research from 1981 to 1992, Phillip Trulock as executive vice president since 1977, Stuart Butler as director of domestic and economic policy studies, and Charles Heatherly as vice president for academic relations. As Feulner affirmed in a 1991 interview, "My overriding managerial objective has been to make sure that Heritage is a permanent part of the Washington policy-making apparatus."

The Heritage approach is to issue policy proposals as brief papers in its *Backgrounder, Issue Bulletin*, or *Executive Memorandum* series, sent to all congressional staff, to key government agencies, and to some 3,500 journalists. Staff summarize research in op-ed articles for newspapers and soundbites for television. Heritage's *Mandate for Leadership* books, first published in 1980, laid out a full legislative and regulatory agenda, agency by agency, for the new Reagan administration—supporting a military buildup, tax cuts, reductions in social programs, and deregulation of economic institutions. *Mandate II* in 1984 highlighted social cutbacks and called for "low-intensity conflict" to battle communism in nine countries, including Central America, Afghanistan, Ethiopia, and Angola. *Mandate III* in 1989 continued this tradition in its program for the new Bush administration. Washington correspondent David Broder comments, "It is the readiness to get in and mix it up in the real-world political and policy debates in Congress, rather than remain in ivory-tower purity, that has made Heritage's Capitol Hill headquarters a respected force in Washington."

Feulner has been acutely aware of the shortage of conservatives interested in government careers. Heritage has pushed to develop the ranks of conservative cadres who can move into the federal bureaucracy with the next truly conservative president (this conservative infrastructure was never cultivated during the Nixon administration, in Heritage's view, with the result that Reagan had to rely on moderates for experienced government appointees). Willa Johnson started the Resource Bank, now directed by former Nixon research assistant Robert Huberty, which links up over 1,600 individual scholars and 400 research centers. The "Third Generation" project brings together young conservatives from Washington congressional and think tank staffs for a fortnightly lecture and social gathering at the Heritage headquarters.

In 1982 Heritage set up an Asian Studies Center, supported by Korean and Taiwanese companies, including the Federation of Korean Industries, which contributed $2.2 million (at the urging of the Korean CIA, it was rumored). Addressing the entire Asian-Pacific region, the Center has focused on the Philippines, U.S.-Japan relations, and problems of Korean reunification. The Center produces an annual *US-Asia Statistical Handbook*. An Institute for Hemispheric Development has been promoting a free trade between the United States and Mexico, and the United Nations Assessment Project has been critical of the World Health Organization (WHO), the U.N. Conference on Trade and Development (UNCTAD), the U.N. Conference on Women, and Soviet use of the U.N. for espionage. The U.S. Congress Assessment Project produced a book, *The Imperial Congress: Crisis in the Separation of Powers* (1989), which decries the increasing power of the (Democratic) Congress to thwart the will of (Republican) presidents, reversing the conservative complaint under the Kennedy and Johnson administrations of the "imperial presidency."

CURRENT PRIORITIES: Heritage continues to put a strong emphasis on development and deployment of an SDI system, a free-trade zone spanning the Americas, a reduction in marginal tax rates, educational choice plans, and empowerment for the poor. Recognizing that a solution will be found for the health insurance crisis, Heritage is pushing a plan that would minimize government's role by offering everyone a choice among various private health insurers and health maintenance organizations. And in a new venture into cultural issues, Heritage has hired William Bennett to be the Heritage "culture czar," exploring how government policy affects the family, religion and the churches, education and the universities, and the media. Heritage maintains a resident scholar program with support from the Bradley Foundation, and a "new majority" program to recruit conservative African Americans, Hispanic Americans, and Asian Americans.

CONTRIBUTORS: In 1991 Heritage had over 175,000 individual, corporate, and foundation supporters, nearly double the number in 1985. Heritage also has big-time donors: 22 "Founders" give $100,000 or more; 95 "Associates" give at least $10,000. Contributors who make major provisions through wills or charitable trusts are members of Heritage's Windsor Society, which meets annually at Windsor Castle near London (25 members were hosted by Katheryn and Shelby Cullom Davis in 1989). The President's Club, a special program for donors of $1,000 or more, has over 1,300 members; an executive committee for donors of $2,500 or more has 200 members. Heritage hosts two meetings a year in Washington for President's Club members.

STRUCTURE: Heritage has a fifteen-member, self-recruiting board of trustees, chaired by Shelby Cullom Davis (former U.S. ambassador to Switzerland), and including vice-chairman Robert Krieble, Joseph Coors, neoconservative Midge Decter, Republican activist Lewis Lehrman, conservative philanthropist Richard Mellon Scaife, and former treasury secretary William Simon.

RESOURCES: Heritage's income of $19.3 million in 1991 came from individuals (50 percent), foundations (25 percent), corporations (13 percent), investment income (7 percent), and publication sales and other (5 percent). Expenditures went for research (45 percent), marketing (39 percent), fund-raising (12 percent), and management (4 percent). Major foundation funding sources have included the Bradley Foundation,

Coors Foundation, Shelby Cullom Davis Foundation, J.M. Foundation, Olin Foundation, and Scaife Foundation.

PUBLICATIONS AND SERVICES: Heritage's flagship magazine is the quarterly *Policy Review* (circulation 14,000), available for a $16 subscription. Other periodicals include *Business/Education Insider, SDI Report, Federal Budget Reporter, Mexico Watch,* and *Former U.S.S.R. Monitor.* Heritage *Bulletins* and *Backgrounders* are brief papers aimed at Congress and the press. Publications are listed in an annual catalog, and an annual report is available. □

FREE CONGRESS FOUNDATION

717 SECOND STREET, NE

WASHINGTON, DC 20002

(202) 546-3000

FOUNDED: 1974   BUDGET: $4.2 million
STAFF: 34   TAX STATUS: 501(c)(3): Free
Congress Research and Education Foundation;
501(c)(4): Coalitions for America; PAC: Free
Congress PAC

Paul Weyrich, one of the most savvy Washington political operatives to emerge from the New Right, has built a complex structure of conservative projects with support from Colorado brewer Joseph Coors. A founder of The Heritage Foundation, Weyrich began the Committee for the Survival of a Free Congress in 1974 to back conservative candidates for Congress with money and technical assistance. Augmenting his organizational base in 1977 to include a think tank and a lobbying arm, Weyrich promotes a New Right populism under the rubric of "cultural conservatism."

BACKGROUND: Weyrich came to Washington from a Colorado radio station after the 1966 election as the press aide to Colorado Republican senator Gordon Allott, and worked on the Senate staff for eleven years. The Colorado connection led Weyrich to Joseph Coors, whom he involved in new organizations challenging traditional conservatives for dominance of the emerging New Right. Weyrich's Free Congress cluster began in 1974 with a political action committee, the Committee for the Survival of a Free Congress (countering organized labor's plan to elect a "veto-proof" Congress). In 1977 Weyrich started the Free Congress Foundation as a think tank and Coalitions for America as a lobbying network. A Roman Catholic by upbringing who switched to the more conservative Greek (Eastern Rite) Catholic church, Weyrich cultivated close ties to the Protestant religious Right—in 1979 he encouraged Reverend Jerry Falwell to get into politics, and suggested the name "Moral Majority" for his organization. Robert Billings, a director of the Free Congress Foundation, became executive director of Falwell's Moral Majority.

Weyrich is consistent in applying his standards of morality to conservatives as well. He angered many allies when he single-handedly undid President Bush's nomination of John Tower as secretary of defense in 1981, reporting to a Senate committee that many times he had seen Tower "intoxicated and in the company of a woman not his wife." The episode seems not to have damaged Weyrich's effectiveness in Washington.

Weyrich worries that liberals have a positive policy agenda, while conservatives typically act as an oppositional movement, speaking in negative terms —opposing communism, big government, and egalitarianism. Weyrich is developing a positive social policy agenda, which he terms "cultural conservatism," promoting tax policies that reward work (expanded earned-income tax credits, child care tax credits, rebates on Social Security taxes for workers supporting dependent children), expanding parental choice in education to include private schools, defending the right to life, deterring crime through strengthening neighborhood policing, and combating drug abuse with widespread testing of employees, prisoners, and parolees. Weyrich also believes liberals have a strong advantage over conservatives in organizing at the grassroots among a variety of mobilizable constituencies; the Free Congress Foundation helps train conservative activists at the state and local levels across the United States—and recently ventured into Eastern Europe to train free-market advocates.

William F. Buckley, Jr., drew the line around the "respectable Right" to exclude the John Birch Society, but Weyrich draws it further out. In 1985 he joined the editorial board of *Conservative Digest*, a monthly started by direct-mail virtuoso Richard A. Viguerie in 1975 after he lost a bid to take over the weekly *Human Events*. Running out of money, Viguerie sold *Conservative Digest* in 1985 to Colorado entrepreneur William Kennedy, who changed its format to look like *Reader's Digest* (which promptly threatened a lawsuit), convinced he could build up circulation to 200,000 by attracting blue-collar populists and evangelicals. Kennedy brought in a team of disgruntled John Birch Society writers, including editor Scott Stanley, Bill Hoar, and Robert Lee. After losing his shirt in precious metals, Kennedy sold the magazine in 1988 to Weyrich backer Robert Krieble and Larry Abraham. After two years of revamping, *Conservative Digest* was still hemorrhaging over $500,000 a year, and the magazine was shut down. Weyrich abandoned his dream of a flagship publication for the populist New Right.

CURRENT PRIORITIES: The work of the Free Congress Foundation is organized in a slowly shifting constellation of semi-autonomous projects, presently organized around eight centers, all housed in the headquarters brownstones near the Capitol: (1) the Center for Conservative Governance, directed by John Exnicios, conducts seminars on impacting government policy for conservatives ranging from grassroots activists to new members of Congress; (2) the Center for State Policy, directed by Matthew Miller, focuses on policy at the state and local levels and publishes the monthly newsletter *Empowerment!* (circulation 3,000); (3) the Krieble Institute, directed by John Exnicios, takes the message of democratic political pluralism, private property rights, market economics, and legal institutions to the countries of Eastern Europe and the former Soviet Union; (4) the Center for

Social Policy, directed by Michael Schwartz, addresses issues of education, family, and welfare dependency; (5) the Center for Law and Democracy, directed by Tom Jipping, which addresses issues at the intersection of law, culture, and politics—including arts and music, abortion, child care, pornography, religious liberty, juvenile justice, and civil rights; (6) the Center for Cultural Conservatism, directed by William Lind, promotes the Free Congress Foundation's hallmark application of traditional values to social policy; (7) the Center for Transportation and Urban Studies publishes *The New Electric Railway Journal* (circulation 10,000); and (8) the Center for Fiscal Responsibility, directed by former congressman Joseph DioGuardi, works for integrity and honest accounting in federal budgeting.

Coalitions for America, the 501(c)4 lobbying unit, functions as conservative counterpart to the liberal Leadership Conference on Civil Rights, drawing together 110 business, defense, and family groups from throughout the country to work on legislative and regulative issues. Coalitions for America operates through six issues groups: (1) the Kingston Group, which focuses on domestic economic policy for free enterprise and limited government, including legislation on deficit reduction and tax reform; (2) the Stanton Group, which works on defense and foreign policy, supporting SDI and combating communism in Central America; (3) the Library Court Group, which promotes domestic social policy supporting traditional values, including family policy, the right to life, and educational reform; (4) the "721 Group" (named after the address), which concentrates on criminal justice and judicial reform, and supports conservative judicial nominees; (5) the Jewish/Conservative Alliance, identifying areas of agreement between Jewish and conservative organizations; and (6) The Carroll Group, conservative lay Catholics who meet monthly on issues affecting the Catholic church and society in America.

STRUCTURE: The Free Congress Foundation has a sixteen-member, self-recruiting board of directors. Jeffrey Coors (son of beer baron Joseph Coors) is chairman, Robert Krieble (former chairman of Loctite Corporation, and inventor of an industrial "superglue") is vice-chairman, and other board members include Rep. Ralph Hill (D-Texas), Senator William Armstrong (R-Colorado), and Clifford Heinz. Paul Weyrich is president and chief executive of the Free Congress Foundation and Coalitions for America; Tom Exnicios is director of the Free Congress PAC. Long-time Weyrich associates Connie Marshner and Pat McGuigan recently left the Free Congress Foundation to direct their own projects.

RESOURCES: Revenue of $4.2 million in 1991 was derived from foundations (62 percent), individuals (7 percent), corporations (19 percent), and publication sales and other (12 percent). Expenditures were allocated to program research and education (67 percent), fund-raising (15 percent), marketing (6 percent), and administration (12 percent). Over the years, the Free Congress Foundation has received several million dollars in grants from right-wing philanthropist Richard Mellon Scaife's

Carthage and Scaife foundations. Other major contributors have included J.M. Foundation, Bradley Foundation, Coors Foundation, Olin Foundation, and the Krieble family. The Free Congress PAC raised $533,000 in the 1986 campaign cycle, $450,000 in the 1988 cycle, and $235,000 in the 1990 cycle.

PUBLICATIONS AND SERVICES: An annual report is available. Various newsletters are available by subscription. The first Free Congress programmatic manifesto was *Cultural Conservatism: Toward a New National Agenda* (Institute for Cultural Conservatism, 1987). The domestic policy agenda is developed further in *Cultural Conservatism: Theory and Practice* (1991). □

THE CATO INSTITUTE
224 SECOND STREET, SE
WASHINGTON, DC 20003
(202) 546-0200

FOUNDED: 1977   BUDGET: $3.8 million
STAFF: 30   TAX STATUS: 501(c)3

PURPOSE: "To develop policy options consistent with the traditional American values of peace, free enterprise, and individual rights."

The Cato Institute is the foremost libertarian think tank and policy advocate in Washington, D.C., developing proposals based on the principles of individualism, free markets, pluralism, and limited government.

BACKGROUND: Cato founder Ed Crane, who prefers to call himself a classical liberal rather than a libertarian, started as an activist with the Libertarian party in California. While running the Libertarian party's 1976 presidential campaign from a Washington, D.C., office, Crane was impressed with the influence of think tanks like the Brookings Institution and the American Enterprise Institute. Returning to San Francisco in 1977, Crane founded The Cato Institute with financing from Charles Koch (pronounced "Coke"), who had formed a diversified Sunbelt conglomerate from the Kansas oil company he inherited.

Crane and Koch grew disillusioned with minor party politics after the 1980 presidential race, when Libertarian candidates ARCO lawyer Ed Clark and David Koch (Charles's younger brother and president of Koch Engineering) received 920,000 votes (1.1 percent of the total) but were overshadowed by John Anderson's independent candidacy, which attracted 5.7 million votes. Crane and Koch decided they could have a greater impact as maverick policy advocates within the system, and moved Cato to Washington in 1981, occupying Capitol Hill's historic Watterson House (built by the first Librarian of Congress). The Institute is named for "Cato's Letters," pamphlets on parliamentary reform by two anonymous British essayists who were widely read in England and the American colonies in the early 1700s and helped provide a philosophical foundation for the American Revolution (the pseudonym refers to Roman statesman and writer Cato the Elder).

CURRENT PRIORITIES: Cato's military and foreign policy program, directed by Ted Galen Carpenter, leans sharply toward isolationism: Well before the end of the Cold War Cato argued for reducing the U.S. role in NATO and cutting back Pentagon expenditures. Cato sees the military's mission as defending the country, not policing the world. As Crane commented, "The problem with conservatives is they look at someone in a uniform and they see a patriot instead of a bureaucrat." Holding little regard for current programs of aid to developing countries, Cato would privatize the World Bank.

On the domestic policy front, Cato has developed numerous innovative ideas emphasizing limited government. As part of a program to eliminate entitlement programs, Cato proposes to allow young people to opt out of Social Security by establishing private pension plans. Cato would legalize drugs, arguing that drug prohibition doesn't work and has created one of the world's largest criminal enterprises. Cato favors increasing immigration to the United States, following cornucopian economist Julian Simon in maintaining that immigrants make jobs, not take jobs. And Cato would end agricultural subsidies, which, they argue, primarily benefit a small number of politically well-connected landowners.

Cato also emphasizes regulatory studies, designed to reduce government oversight and planning. In 1989 Cato took over publication of the quarterly journal *Regulation* (circulation 5,000) from the American Enterprise Institute; it is now edited by Cato chairman William Niskanen. With Nobel laureate economist James Buchanan as a distinguished senior fellow, Cato emphasizes monetary policy and the need for stable money as the foundation of a smoothly functioning market economy.

Cato's Center for Constitutional Studies, directed by former Justice Department official Roger Pilon, supports principled judicial activism, rejecting the conservatives' popular nostrum "judicial restraint." Judicial deference, in Cato's view, gives too much power to the legislative and executive branches in the name of self-government. Cato's judicial activism puts individual liberty first, self-government second.

STRUCTURE: Cato has a fifteen-member, self-recruiting board of directors, chaired by William Niskanen and including Charles and David Koch, Georgetown University professor Earl Ravenal, Howard Rich (chairman of Laissez Faire Books), and Fredrick Smith (chairman of Federal Express).

RESOURCES: Cato's revenue of $3.8 million in 1990 derived primarily from contributions (84 percent). Expenditures of $3.6 million supported programs (79 percent), fund-raising (7 percent), and administration (14 percent). In 1989 Cato launched a $10 million capital campaign to build a new headquarters at 1000 Massachusetts Avenue, NW, and to start a program endowment.

PUBLICATIONS AND SERVICES: Contributors receive *Cato Policy Report* six times a year; the *Cato Review*, a public policy journal published three times a year, is available by subscription. Ca-

to's policy agenda is spelled out in *An American Vision: Policies for the '90s*, edited by Edward H. Crane and David Boaz (Cato Institute, 1989). An annual report is available on request, as is a catalog of publications. □

LEGAL EAGLES

By the early 1970s, the impact of progressive public interest law firms was clear. The NAACP Legal Defense and Educational Fund and the American Civil Liberties Union had a long record of advancing civil rights and civil liberties with an activist approach to establishing and enforcing rights through the courts. With help from the Ford Foundation, a new set of public interest law firms were set up in the 1960s, including the Mexican American Legal Defense and Education Fund, the Native American Rights Fund, the Natural Resources Defense Council, and the NOW Legal Defense and Education Fund, among others. Ralph Nader had independently set up his network of litigation projects in the name of public interest law and a consumers' movement. Conservatives experienced a new feeling of being shellacked in court, from all sides.

The establishment of Pacific Legal Foundation in California in 1973 offered conservatives a new alternative. Beginning in 1975 with the founding of the National Legal Center for the Public Interest with financing from Colorado beer baron Joseph Coors, conservatives began a counterattack. The National Center helped set up a network of conservative public interest law firms, including Mid-America Legal Foundation (1975), Landmark Legal Foundation

(1976) in Kansas City, Southeastern Legal Foundation (1976) in Atlanta, Washington Legal Foundation (1976) in D.C., Atlantic Legal Foundation (1977) in New York, and Mountain States Legal Foundation (1977) in Denver. Of these, Pacific Legal Foundation and Washington Legal Foundation have had the greatest impact on public interest litigation.

PACIFIC LEGAL FOUNDATION

2700 GATEWAY OAKS DRIVE

SACRAMENTO, CA 95833-3501

(916) 641-8888

FOUNDED: 1973   CONTRIBUTORS: 20,000
BUDGET: $4 million   STAFF: 51
TAX STATUS: 501(c)(3)

PURPOSE: "To defend competitive free enterprise, a strong economy, private property rights, freedom from excessive government regulation, balance in pursuing environmental goals, and productive and fiscally sound government."

Pacific Legal Foundation (PLF) specializes in environmental, property rights, and land use cases, balancing protection of the environment against the need for jobs, energy, and food production.

BACKGROUND: Ronald A. Zumbrun founded PLF in 1973, with assistance from the California Chamber of Commerce, to argue the conservative position on the public interest in the courts. Zumbrun had helped design Governor Ronald Reagan's welfare reform program in California, and served as an attorney for the California Department of Social Welfare. Since its beginning, PLF has been a party to over 600 cases, as the attorney of record in one-third of the cases and filing friend of the court briefs in the others. Currently PLF has around 120 active cases.

In 1987 PLF won a landmark decision for property owners with the Supreme Court ruling in *Nollan* v. *California Coastal Commission*, a case that took five years from administrative hearings to the Supreme Court. The Court held that the Coastal Commission could not require the Nollans to grant public access to their beach in exchange for a building permit without paying just compensation. The decision limits governmental powers to regulate land use without compensation to property owners and expands the scope of the Fifth Amendment's "taking clause." PLF is using the precedent of *Nollan* to oppose popular growth limitation ordinances and initiatives in California on behalf of developers. And in 1992 The Supreme Court held in *Lucas* v. *South Carolina Coastal Council* that governments cannot deprive property owners of all economically viable use of their property without compensation.

PLF recently won two significant cases involving compelled contributions or "agency shop" fees used for political purposes. The California Supreme Court in 1989 in *Cumero* v. *Public Employment Relations Board* ruled that compelled teachers association dues could only be used for purposes of bargaining with local school districts. And in *Keller* v. *State Bar of California*, the U.S. Supreme Court ruled in

1990 that compelled membership fees could be used only for regulation of the legal profession; use of fees for political purposes violates a dissenting individual's rights of freedom of speech and association.

PLF lives up to its reputation as the "anti-Nader's Raiders" by taking on a variety of liberal causes. PLF has challenged rent control in New York, Santa Monica, and Berkeley. Confronting the peace movement, PLF won a ruling that Oakland's Nuclear Free Zone ordinance was too broadly drafted. And PLF prevailed in its claim in federal district court in *Associated Builders and Contractors* v. *Baca* that local governments may not require contractors to pay "prevailing wages" or union scale on private construction projects.

In 1991 PLF won an important victory for the national movement to limit legislators' terms in office when the California Supreme Court in *Legislature of the State of California* v. *Eu* upheld a voter-approved term-limitation initiative, Proposition 140. PLF argued an amicus brief defending California's 1978 property-tax-cutting initiative, Proposition 13, before the U.S. Supreme Court in *Nordlinger* v. *Hahn*, in which The Court ruled in 1992 that the law did not violate the Constitution.

By 1991 the economic recession was cutting into contributions from PLF's business supporters, and Zumbrun devised an innovative response: He, litigation director John Findley, and former PLF attorney Robert Best organized a private law firm, Zumbrun, Best and Findley, to take fee-generating cases related to PLF's expertise. Zumbrun and Findley will become contract employees of PLF.

STRUCTURE: PLF has a twenty-one-member, self-recruiting board of trustees, primarily corporate executives from the West, but also including actor Fess Parker, former *National Review* publisher William Rusher, and George Mason University economist Walter Williams. Wendy Borcherdt has been the only woman on the board in recent years. PLF has field offices in Anchorage and Seattle.

RESOURCES: For its 1990–91 fiscal year, PLF had revenue of $3.8 million, 41 percent from contributions, 46 percent from grants, and 13 percent from other income. Expenditures of $4 million went 72 percent for program services, 14 percent for administration, and 14 percent for fund-raising.

PUBLICATIONS AND SERVICES: Contributors receive the quarterly bulletin *In Perspective* and the newsletter *At Issue*, reporting on current cases ten times a year. An annual report is available. □

WASHINGTON
LEGAL FOUNDATION

WASHINGTON LEGAL FOUNDATION

1705 N STREET, NW

WASHINGTON, DC 20036

(202) 857-0240

FOUNDED: 1977   BUDGET: $2.1 million
STAFF: 15   TAX STATUS: 501(c)(3)

PURPOSE: "An unabashedly pro-free enterprise public interest litigation and policy center . . . promoting economic and individual rights, civil liberties for business, due process for the victims of violent crime, judicial restraint, and limited and accountable government."

Washington Legal Foundation (WLF) is a fervent advocate for business rights and a conservative judiciary. WLF bills itself as a legal counterweight to the ACLU, the NAACP LDF, the Natural Resources Defense Council, Ralph Nader's Public Citizen, and other anti-business public interest litigators. Keeping a close eye on public relations, WLF fights as many battles in the media as in the courtroom.

BACKGROUND: WLF was founded in 1977 by attorney Daniel Popeo, who worked on the White House legal staff under Presidents Nixon and Ford and as an Interior Department lawyer enforcing health and safety regulations. In WLF's first case, representing fifty-five congressmen, Popeo sued to block the Carter administration's transfer of the Panama Canal. Although the suit was lost on appeal, WLF was in the news. Popeo won a case against the Carter administration to uphold the mutual defense pact with Taiwan.

Beginning an attack on crime, WLF petitioned the Transportation Department to initiate random drug testing, and developed a model crime victim impact statement used in many states in criminal sentencing. WLF sued John Hinckley, who attempted to assassinate President Reagan, on behalf of wounded Secret Service agent Timothy McCarthy, seeking a judgment that would seize any future movie and book income. In a highly publicized environmental case, WLF defended self-employed truck mechanic John Pozsgai, of Morrisville, Pennsylvania, who was fined $200,000 and sentenced to three years in prison for placing topsoil on a dump site classified as a wetland before he bought it. Despite warnings from the EPA, Pozsgai did not obtain a permit from the Army Corps of Engineers. In 1990 the Supreme Court declined to hear WLF's appeal of Pozsgai's conviction, and WLF has petitioned President Bush to commute his sentence and remit his fine.

CURRENT PRIORITIES: WLF's Litigation Division supports a national program of representing businesses, conservative congressmen, and state attorneys general on such issues as environmental regulation, product liability, rights of crime victims, First Amendment rights for business, and sentencing guidelines for white-collar crime. The Legal Studies Division conducts research and writes a variety of publications for government, business, academic, and media audiences. Challenging much of contemporary legal education, WLF attacks the critical legal studies movement and protests progressive public interest work done by law students. WLF maintains that a leftist trend in law schools has accelerated, ironically enough, as conservative legal scholars have been appointed to the federal judiciary by Presidents Reagan and Bush. WLF supports the Lawyers' Pro Bono Project, a nationwide network of practicing attorneys committed to free enterprise and judicial restraint. WLF's public relations effort includes a "working luncheons" series for business, media, government, and judiciary leaders.

WLF continues to watchdog the American Bar Association's role in judicial confirmation hearings. In 1987 it sued the ABA for meeting with liberal groups to get information on judicial nominees, but the Supreme Court ruled the ABA's activities were legal. In an attack on the plaintiffs' bar, in 1991 WLF initiated its SCALES (Stop the Collapse of America's Legal Ethics) project, aimed at curbing the "litigation explosion" and deterring "frivolous" lawsuits by requiring plaintiffs' attorneys to advise clients of the possible adverse costs of litigation and alternative approaches available. WLF is working with state bar associations to implement a "statement of client's rights and lawyer's responsibilities."

STRUCTURE: WLF has a 90-member National Board of Advisors, primarily conservative congressmen and a few corporate executives; members include Senators Jesse Helms, Orrin Hatch, and Gordon Humphrey, Rep. Henry Hyde, and brewer Joseph Coors. A Legal Policy Advisory Board of 58 legal scholars and practitioners helps make the intellectual case for pro-business legal policy. Of the 148 advisers on these two boards, only 5 are women. Daniel Popeo is general counsel and Paul Kamenar is executive legal director.

RESOURCES: WLF claims support from 120,000 individuals and small businesses and 450 corporations and foundations. WLF revenue in 1990 came from individuals (37 percent), foundations (30 percent), corporations (20 percent), and investment earnings (13 percent). Expenditures went for legal

programs (52 percent), legal education and public information (20 percent), and administration (28 percent).

PUBLICATIONS AND SERVICES: WLF distributes five levels of reports: *Legal Backgrounders*, *Legal Opinion Letters*, *Working Papers*, *Monographs*, and *Contemporary Legal Notes*. One recent monograph is David T. Hardy's *America's New Extremists: What You Need to Know About the Animal Rights Movement* (1990). A publications catalog and an annual report are available. □

WOMEN AND FAMILY ON THE RIGHT

The backlash to the women's movement, abortion rights, gay rights, and the civil liberties movement against censorship has produced some of the strongest organizations on the right—most closely identified with a charismatic individual. Phyllis Schlafly, a noted anticommunist conservative Catholic activist since the Goldwater campaign, shifted to social issues with her Stop ERA organization in 1972. Building from her base among conservative Republican women in Illinois, Schlafly transformed her group to the multiissue Eagle Forum in 1975 and began work on a variety of issues including family policy, education, taxation, and the arts. Beverly LaHaye developed Concerned Women for America (1979), one of the largest grassroots networks on the right, from a network of fundamentalist Protestants cultivated by her husband, evangelist Reverend Tim LaHaye. Reverend Don Wildmon, "the Jerry Falwell of the '90s," has taken on television programming with his American Family Association. In 1988 Dr. James Dobson's Focus on the Family (which produces a widely carried radio program of the same name) took over the Family Research Center, now headed by Gary Bauer, former director of the Office of Policy Development in Reagan's White House and presently the vice president of Focus on the Family.

EAGLE FORUM

BOX 618

ALTON, IL 62002

(202) 544-0353

FOUNDED: 1972   CONTRIBUTORS: 80,000
BUDGET: $800,000   STAFF: 15
TAX STATUS: 501(c)(4): Eagle Forum;
501(c)(3): Eagle Forum Education and Legal
Defense Fund; PAC: Eagle Forum PAC

Phyllis Schlafly, an anticommunist stalwart on the Republican right during the 1950s and 1960s, founded Eagle Forum to fight against ratification of the Equal Rights Amendment (ERA). Schlafly and her "Eagles" succeeded in blocking the ERA in Illinois and other key states, and Eagle Forum has continued to advocate for "pro-family values" on such issues as abortion, education, and child care.

BACKGROUND: Phyllis Schlafly, the country's foremost antagonist of contemporary feminism, is a model of the liberated woman who manages to have it all: She earned a masters degree from Radcliffe. She managed a successful congressional campaign for a conservative Republican challenger at age twenty-four, and ran her first unsuccessful race for the U.S. House of Representatives as a young mother four years later in 1952. She wrote nine books while raising six children. She entered law school at age fifty-two and graduated three years later. By her opponents' admission, she is an eloquent and imperturbable public debater. As former NOW president Karen DeCrow noted with irony, "She's everything you should raise your daughter to be."

Schlafly burst onto the national political stage with *A Choice Not an Echo*, her book attacking the Republican establishment and supporting Barry Goldwater for the Republican presidential nomination in 1964. Long identified with the Catholic Right, she married Fred Schlafly, a Hard Right Cold Warrior who lectured for Fred Schwartz's Christian Anti-Communist Crusade and headed the World Anti-Communist League. Her base of power is conservative women in Illinois, where she was president of the Illinois Federation of Republican Women from 1960 to 1964. She ran for president of the National Federation of Republican Women in 1967 and lost, then ran a second unsuccessful race for Congress in 1970. During the 1960s and 1970s she authored six more books, including two coauthored with Hard Right admiral Chester Ward, and seven were self-published in paperback through her Père Marquette Press. Although Robert Welch claimed her as a member of the John Birch Society, Schlafly denies ever having been a member. Her books reflect a quasi-conspiratorial view that the Council on

Foreign Relations and the State Department—the *Gravediggers*, as the title of one of her books put it—intended to turn the United States over to the Soviet Union. Henry Kissinger and the SALT treaties are the central targets of her wrath in *Kissinger on the Couch* (Arlington House, 1975) and *Ambush at Vladivostok* (1976).

The campaign against the ERA enabled Schlafly to break out of the right-wing fringe and become a player in mainstream conservatism. As the ERA gained early momentum toward ratification, Schlafly formed the organization Stop ERA in 1972, which incorporated as Eagle Forum in 1975. (As with much of her politics, Schlafly's "Eagle" has a religious as well as a patriotic grounding—she cites Isaiah 40:31: "They that wait upon the Lord shall renew their strength; they shall mount up with wings as eagles, they shall run, and not be weary; and they shall walk and not faint.") Illinois proved a strategic base, as the state constitution requires a two-thirds majority for ratification of an amendment to the U.S. Constitution—requiring only one-third plus one to defeat.

CURRENT PRIORITIES: Eagle Forum supports women's exemption from the military draft and combat duty; backs strengthening parental rights in education; and opposes classroom discussion of religion in a comparative perspective, values clarification programs, and sex education. Any use of relaxation or guided imagery techniques in education is attacked as a variety of mysticism. The Forum's pet project is phonics in the first grade. Schlafly regularly attacks the National Education Associa-

tion's influence over schools, and opposes federal assistance for child care. Eagle Forum honored Betsy North, wife of Oliver North of Iran-Contra fame, with the National Full-time Homemaker of the Year Award in 1987. In 1990 Eagle Forum joined the conservative campaign to cut off support for the National Endowment for the Arts, seen as funding obscene and sacrilegious art.

STRUCTURE: Long run from the Schlafly household in Alton, Illinois (across the Mississippi from St. Louis), Eagle Forum opened a Washington office in 1981. The *Phyllis Schlafly Report* is published by the separate Eagle Trust Fund. The organization has a seven-member board of directors, whose members replace vacancies at the annual board meeting. In 1991 Schlafly formed an independent political action committee, the Republican National Coalition for Life PAC.

RESOURCES: Eagle Forum's $800,000 revenue comes 75 percent from individual donors, 10 percent from members, and the remainder from foundation grants and publication sales. Eagle Forum PAC raised $39,000 in the 1986 campaign cycle, $101,000 in the 1988 cycle, and $102,000 in the 1990 cycle.

PUBLICATIONS AND SERVICES: Contributors receive the monthly *Phyllis Schlafly Report* (circulation 30,000), started in 1967. *Education Reporter* (circulation 10,000) is a monthly newsletter available by subscription. The organization offers a selection of articles and books by Schlafly. For background see Carol Felsenthal, *The Sweetheart of* *the Silent Majority: The Biography of Phyllis Schlafly* (Doubleday, 1981; Regnery Gateway, 1982). □

CONCERNED WOMEN FOR AMERICA

370 L'ENFANT PROMENADE, SW, SUITE 800

WASHINGTON, DC 20024

(202) 488-7000

FOUNDED: 1979   MEMBERS: 200,000
CHAPTERS: 2,000 prayer/action chapters in 50 states   BUDGET: $9.3 million   STAFF: 25
TAX STATUS: 501(c)(3): Concerned Women for America; 501(c)(4): CWA Legislative Action Committee

PURPOSE: "To preserve, protect, and promote traditional and Judeo-Christian values through education, legal defense, legislative programs, humanitarian aid, and related activities which represent the concerns of men and women who believe in these values."

Concerned Women for America (CWA), led by founder Beverly LaHaye, promotes traditional family values, supports a right to life, and opposes the feminist and gay and lesbian rights movements. LaHaye described CWA as "A pro-family, pro-life organization dedicated to protecting the rights of the family through prayer and action."

BACKGROUND: Beverly LaHaye, wife of televangelist Reverend Tim LaHaye, brought together nine women in San Diego to form CWA in 1979 to employ traditional Christian values to counter the feminist movement. CWA's first focus was opposition to the Equal Rights Amendment (ERA). Within a year, women had started forty CWA prayer/action chapters in fourteen states. CWA opened a Washington office in 1983, and moved its headquarters there from San Diego in 1985. During the contra war, CWA solicited donations to aid Nicaraguans fleeing the war and living in Costa Rica or coming to Florida. In both 1985 and 1986, CWA hosted a speech by Oliver North at its annual conference.

CWA has litigated more than twenty lawsuits, winning the right of Christian youth groups to meet in public school rooms, and appealing a case that attempted to protect the right of a public school teacher to keep his personal bible on his desk during class and to have two religious books in his class library. CWA represented seven fundamentalist families in a Tennessee lawsuit claiming their children's rights were violated by having to read passages from the *Diary of Anne Frank* (containing assertions that all religions are equal) and *The Wizard of Oz* (which portrays some witches as good). People for the American Way represented the school board. In 1987 an appeals court ruled against CWA. Recently CWA rallied support against Ted Kennedy's bill to require schools receiving federal money to present sex education. CWA convinced the sponsor of a 1990 crime bill to alter the contents so that spanking would not be considered child abuse. They also fought against government testing of the French abortion pill, RU 486.

CURRENT PRIORITIES: The right to life and fetal rights continue as priorities. CWA opposes the "homosexual agenda," including legislation that would penalize persons for crimes against others based on their sexual orientation. CWA opposes federally subsidized day care and calls for a restructuring of the tax code so that married mothers can afford to stay at home. Key targets of CWA ire are Planned Parenthood Federation of America, the National Education Association, and the National Organization for Women.

MEMBERS: CWA has built a strong grassroots organization, with some 2,000 prayer/action chapters whose members meet to pray for political leaders and to write letters on issues. CWA holds an annual Leadership Conference to train area representatives who promote the organization and recruit new members. CWA claims 700,000 members, but only some 200,000 of these have given at least $15 within the past fifteen months.

STRUCTURE: CWA has a thirteen-person, self-recruiting board of directors; members serve three-year terms.

RESOURCES: Most of CWA's $9.3 million in revenue in 1991 was contributions from individuals. Expenditures of $9.2 million included public information (58 percent), legal defense (2 percent), administration (9 percent), and fund-raising (30 percent). The balance helped retire all but $113,000 of a $300,000 deficit run up in 1989.

PUBLICATIONS AND SERVICES: Members who contribute at least $15 a year receive the magazine *Family Voice* (circulation 170,000) eleven times a year. Beverly LaHaye hosts a national radio program, *Beverly LaHaye Live.* She discusses the spiritual groundings and history of CWA in *Prayer: God's Comfort for Today's Family* (Thomas Nelson, 1990). Books and videotapes may be ordered and the CWA legal staff contacted via a toll-free number: (800) 458-8797. □

BIBLIOGRAPHICAL NOTES

The references that follow emphasize books that are widely available (preferably in paperback), either in bookstores or general libraries, and not excessively academic, esoteric, or obscure. These books have informed the overview and introductory sections in *The Activist's Almanac*, and they provide resources for activists who want perspective and context for movements and their organizations.

INTRODUCTION: MAKING CHANGE

Activism and democracy: Richard Flacks reflects on social movements as people making history, and the relationship between the activist and the ordinary person, in *Making History: The American Left and the American Mind* (Columbia University Press, 1988). Sara M. Evans and Harry C. Boyte argue for the importance of grassroots movements to a vital democracy in *Free Spaces: The Sources of Democratic Change in America* (Harper & Row, 1986), which Boyte elaborates in *CommonWealth: A Return to Citizen Politics* (Free Press, 1989). From a neoconservative standpoint, see Peter L. Berger and Richard John Neuhaus, *To Empower People: The Role of Mediating Structures in Public Policy* (American Enterprise Institute, 1977).

Trends and typologies: The demographic underpinnings of contemporary social movements were described first in Landon Y. Jones, *Great Expectations: America and the Baby Boom Generation* (1980). Arnold

Mitchell's report on the VALS study, *The Nine American Lifestyles* (Warner Books, 1983), is suggestive on class and cultural differences. A similar typology of eleven groups developed for Times Mirror by Norman Ornstein, Andrew Kohut, and Larry McCarthy, *The People, the Press, and Politics* (Addison-Wesley, 1988), is also provocative.

Cycles and generations: The cyclical theory of movements is argued by Arthur Schlesinger, Jr., in *The Cycles of American History* (Houghton Mifflin, 1986). A more elaborate and speculative typology of four alternating generations—idealist, reactive, civic, and adaptive—is developed in William Strauss and Neil Howe, *Generations: The History of America's Future, 1548–2069* (Morrow, 1991). Bill Moyer's model of activist roles and stages within social movement cycles is circulated in tabloid form as *The Movement Action Plan: The Eight Stages of Successful Social Movements* (1987) and *The Practical Strategist: MAP Strategic Theories for Evaluating, Planning, and Conducting Social Movements* (1990), available from Social Movement Empowerment Project, 721 Shrader Street, San Francisco, CA 94117; (415) 387-3361.

Social movements: For an illustrated overview and introduction to social movements, see Madeline Adamson and Seth Burgos, *This Mighty Dream: Social Protest Movements in the United States* (Routledge & Kegan Paul, 1984), and *The Power of the People: Active Nonviolence in the United States*, edited by Robert Cooney and Helen Michalowski (New Society Publishers, 1987). Recent activism is reviewed in *Social Movements of the Sixties and Seventies*, edited by Jo Freeman (Longman, 1983).

Classic sociological articles from the "resource mobilization" school are compiled in *Social Movements in an Organizational Society: Collected Essays*, edited by Mayer N. Zald and John D. McCarthy (Transaction Books, 1987). The field is reviewed by Doug McAdam, McCarthy, and Zald in "Social Movements," chapter 21 in *Handbook of Sociology*, edited by Neil J. Smelser (Sage, 1988); and by J. Craig Jenkins in "Resource Mobilization Theory and the Study of Social Movements," in *Annual Review of Sociology* (1983), and in "Nonprofit Organizations and Policy Advocacy," in *The Nonprofit Sector: A Research Handbook*, edited by Walter W. Powell (Yale University Press, 1987). Another helpful summary and synthesis is provided by Sidney Tarrow, *Struggle, Politics, and Reform: Collective Action, Social Movements, and Cycles of Protest* (Center for International Studies, Cornell University, 1991). Barbara Epstein skillfully summarizes "new social movement theory" in chapter 7 of her study of the nonviolent direct-action movement, *Political Protest and Cultural Revolution* (University of California Press, 1991).

Parties, advocacy organizations, and interest groups: Political scientists typically treat social reform organizations as interest groups. For generally sympathetic views, see Andrew S. McFarland, *Public Interest Lobbies: Decision Making on Energy* (American Enterprise Institute for Public Policy Research, 1977); Jeffrey M. Berry, *Lobbying for the People: The Political Behavior of Public Interest Groups* (Princeton University Press, 1977), and *The Interest Group Society*, 2nd ed. (Scott, Foresman, 1989); Michael W. McCann, *Taking Reform Seriously: Perspectives on Public Interest Liberalism* (Cornell University Press, 1986); and *Interest Group Politics*, edited by Allan J. Cigler and Burdett A. Loomis, 2nd ed. (Congressional Quarterly, 1986). The emergence of think tanks is traced by James Allen Smith, *The Idea Brokers: Think Tanks and the Rise of the New Policy Elite* (Free Press, 1991).

Nonprofit law and organizational structure: The definitive text on nonprofit law is Bruce R. Hopkins, *The Law of Tax-Exempt Organizations*, 6th ed. (John Wiley & Sons, 1992). For the complex rules governing lobbying by 501(c)(3)s and (c)(4)s including the 1976 lobby law and 1990 IRS regulations, see the Independent Sector publication by Bob Smucker, *The Nonprofit Lobbying Guide: Advocating Your Cause—and Getting Results* (Jossey Bass, 1991); and *Being a Player: A Guide to the IRS Lobbying Regulations for Advocacy Charities*, by Harmon, Curran, Gallagher and Spielberg (January 1991), available from Alliance for Justice, 1601 Connecticut Avenue, NW, Suite 600, Washington, DC 20009; (202) 332-3224.

Working for change: To find work with public interest organizations, see *Community Jobs: The Employment Newspaper for the Non-Profit Sector*, now published by ACCESS: Networking in the Public Interest, 96 Mt. Auburn Street, Cambridge, MA 02138; (617) 495-2178. Ralph Nader and associates describe some 600 public interest organizations in *Good Works: A Guide to Careers in Social Change*, edited by Jessica Cowan, 4th ed. (Barricade Books, 1991).

Social investing: A good introduction to socially responsible investing is Amy L. Domini with Peter D. Kinder, *Ethical Investing* (Addison-Wesley, 1984). For current guides, see Ritchie P. Lowry, *Good Money: A Guide to Profitable Social Investing in the '90s* (Norton, 1991), and John Harrington, *Investing with Your Conscience* (John Wiley, 1992). See also Susan Meeker-Lowry, *Economics as if the World Really Mattered* (New Society Publishers, 1988).

Social consuming: For background on consumer protection, see Robert N. Meyer, *The Consumer Movement: Guardians of the Marketplace* (Twayne, 1989). The Council on Economic Priorities (30 Irving Place, New York, NY 10003) revises *Shopping for a Better World* annually. You can check out social policies of 100 major companies in *The Better World In-*

vestment Guide, by The Council on Economic Priorities and Myra Alperson, Alice Tepper Marlin, Jonathan Schorsch, and Rosalyn Will (Prentice Hall, 1991). Environmental consciousness informs John Elkington, Julia Hailes, and Joel Makower, *The Green Consumer* (Penguin Books, 1990).

Citizen activism: One of the best guides for citizen lobbying is George Alderson and Everett Sentman, *How You Can Influence Congress: The Complete Handbook for the Citizen Lobbyist* (Dutton, 1979). From an associate of Ralph Nader, see Marc Caplan, *A Citizens' Guide to Lobbying* (Dembner Books, 1983). For a brief outline, see Nancy Amidei, *So You Want to Make a Difference* (1991), available from OMB Watch, 1731 Connecticut Avenue, NW, Washington, DC 20009; (202) 234-8494. For youth, see Barbara A. Lewis, *The Kid's Guide to Social Action* (Free Spirit Publishing, 1991).

Keeping a local organization or chapter financially solvent is another essential task for activists. Three excellent guides to fund-raising are Kim Klein, *Fund-raising for Social Change,* 2nd ed. (Chardon Press, 1988); Joan Flanagan, *The Grassroots Fundraising Book* (Contemporary Books, 1982); and Michael Seltzer, *Securing Your Organization's Future* (The Foundation Center, 1987). For an analysis of how media work and how activists can get their message out, see Charlotte Ryan, *Prime Time Activism: Media Strategies for Grassroots Organizing* (South End Press, 1991).

Directories: Check your library for the annual multivolume *Encyclopedia of Associations* (Gale) or *Public Interest Profiles* from the Foundation for Public Affairs (Congressional Quarterly, 1991), an expensive reference work updated every three years or so.

1. FROM CONSERVATION TO ENVIRONMENTALISM

The conservation movement: The outstanding volume on the origins of traditional conservation organizations is Stephen Fox, *John Muir and His Legacy: The American Conservation Movement* (Little, Brown, 1981); reissued in paperback as *The American Conservation Movement: John Muir and His Legacy* (University of Wisconsin Press, 1986). For portraits of twelve significant figures, see Douglas H. Strong, *Dreamers and Defenders: American Conservationists* (1971; University of Nebraska Press, 1988). Stewart L. Udall's classic *The Quiet Crisis* reviews the history of the American conservation movement, and has been reissued with a supplement on the environmental movement in *The Quiet Crisis and the Next Generation* (Peregrine Smith, 1988). A strong case for the importance of hunters and anglers in the conservation movement is argued by John F. Reiger, *American Sportsmen and the Origins of Conservation* (Winchester Press, 1975). Roderick Nash takes a scholarly approach to the theme of wilderness in *Wil-*

derness and the American Mind, 3rd ed. (1967; Yale University Press, 1982), which includes extensive bibliographic notes.

Conservation policy: Current thinking on policy initiatives is presented in three instructive collections. The "Group of Ten" leaders of major environmental organizations published *An Environmental Agenda for the Future* (Island Press, 1985). For opportunities in the post-Reagan period, see the reflective *Crossroads: Environmental Priorities for the Future*, edited by Peter Borelli (Island Press, 1988), and in a more detailed schematic style, *Blueprint for the Environment: A Plan for Federal Action*, edited by T Allan Comp.

The new environmentalism: For insights on the emergence of the environmental movement from the conservation tradition, see Jim O'Brien, "Environmentalism as a Mass Movement: Historical Notes," *Radical America*, Vol. 17, Nos. 2–3 (1983), pp. 7–27; and Samuel P. Hays, "From Conservation to Environment: Environmental Politics in the United States Since World War Two," *Environmental Review* (Fall 1982), pp. 14–41, elaborated in his book *Beauty, Health and Permanence: Environmental Politics in the United States, 1955–1985* (Cambridge University Press, 1987). Roderick Nash explores the extension of moral principles to animals and the natural world in *The Rights of Nature: A History of Environmental Ethics* (University of Wisconsin Press, 1989). On the new activists, see Rik Scarce, *Eco-Warriors: Understanding the Radical Environmental Movement* (Noble Press, 1990), and Christopher Manes's polemic, *Green Rage: Radical Environmentalism and the Unmaking of Civilization* (Little, Brown, 1990). On deep ecology, see Bill Devall and George Sessions, *Deep Ecology: Living as if Nature Mattered* (Peregrine Smith, 1985), and Devall, *Simple in Means, Rich in Ends: Practicing Deep Ecology* (Peregrine Smith, 1988). Social ecologist Murray Bookchin and deep ecologist Dave Foreman turn a vituperative debate into an informative dialogue in *Defending the Earth* (South End Press, 1991). Another new current is described in Kirkpatrick Sale, *Dwellers in the Land: The Bioregional Vision* (Sierra Club Books, 1985). *E Magazine* (circulation 75,000) offers independent coverage and commentary on the environmental movement (P.O. Box 5098, Westport, CT 06881; (203) 854-5559).

Conservative reaction: For a critique of environmentalism as an elitist preoccupation, see William Tucker, *Progress and Privilege* (Anchor Press/ Doubleday, 1982). Former Atomic Energy Commission director Dixy Lee Ray attacks environmentalism in *Trashing the Planet* (Regnery Gateway, 1990). From the populist right, see Ron Arnold, *Ecology Wars: Environmentalism as if People Mattered* (Free Enterprise Press, 1987), and *The Wise*

Use Agenda, edited by Alan M. Gottlieb (Free Enterprise Press, 1989). Libertarians gathered around the Political Economy Research Center (PERC) have a distinctive approach, developed in Terry L. Anderson and Donald R. Leal, *Free Market Environmentalism* (Pacific Institute for Public Policy, 1991).

Data and directories: *The Green Index* (Island Press, 1991), is a state-by-state ranking of environmental health, drawing on 256 indicators, compiled by the Institute for Southern Studies, P.O. Box 531, Durham, NC 27702 (publishers of *Southern Exposure,* a journal of politics and culture). The twentieth anniversary of Earth Day in 1990 provoked an outpouring of "save it yourself" guides, the most comprehensive of which is *The Global Ecology Handbook: What You Can Do About the Environmental Crisis,* edited by Walter H. Corson, published for The Global Tomorrow Coalition by Beacon Press. For a full-color graphic overview of global environmental issues, see Geoffrey Lean, Don Hinrichsen, and Adam Markham, *Atlas of the Environment* (Prentice Hall, 1990), produced in collaboration with the World Wildlife Fund. See also *Gaia: An Atlas of Planet Management,* edited by Norman Myers (Doubleday, 1984); in the same Gaia series is *State of the Ark: An Atlas of Conservation in Action,* by Lee Durrell (Doubleday, 1986), an illustrated survey of threats to plant and animal species. From the Pluto Project, see *The State of the Earth Atlas,* edited by Joni Seager (Simon & Schuster, 1990). The World Resources Institute compiled a global statistical survey, *The 1992 Information Please Environmental Almanac* (Houghton Mifflin, 1991). Since 1984 the cutting edge of the global environmental debate has been the annual *State of the World* volumes edited by Lester Brown of the Worldwatch Institute. Pressure from environmentalists finally caught the attention of the World Bank, which in 1990 began an annual survey, *The World Bank and the Environment,* available from World Bank Publications, P.O. Box 7247–8619, Philadelphia, PA 19170-8619; (201) 225-2165. For the most comprehensive listing of agencies and organizations, see the annual *Conservation Directory* from the National Wildlife Federation. More details are available in *Your Resource Guide to Environmental Organizations,* edited by John Seredich (Smiling Dolphins Press, 1991), which covers 150 groups. Environmental computer networks and databases are described by Don Rittner, *EcoLinking: Everyone's Guide to Online Environmental Information* (Peachpit Press, 1992).

2. PEACE AND FOREIGN POLICY

Overview of peace movements: For historical surveys of peace activity, see Charles Chatfield with Robert Kleidman, *The American Peace Movement: Ideals and Activism* (Twayne, 1992), and *Peace Movements in Amer-*

ica, edited by Charles Chatfield (Schocken, 1973). Lawrence S. Wittner covers the mid-century in *Rebels Against War: The American Peace Movement, 1933–1983* (Temple University Press, 1984). For the Vietnam War period, see Nancy Zaroulis and Gerald Sullivan, *Who Spoke Up? American Protest Against the War in Vietnam, 1963–1975* (Holt, Rinehart and Winston, 1984). Events of the 1980s are reviewed in Roger C. Peace III, *A Just and Lasting Peace: The U.S. Peace Movement from the Cold War to Desert Storm* (Noble Press, 1991), including campaigns on nuclear disarmament, Central America, South Africa, federal budget priorities, and new visions of common security. Current information can be found in *The Bulletin of the Atomic Scientists.*

Owls: Our typology is borrowed from the study *Hawks, Doves and Owls: An Agenda for Avoiding Nuclear War*, edited by Graham T. Allison, Albert Carnesale, and Joseph S. Nye, Jr. (Norton, 1985). How the establishment shaped American foreign policy after World War II is illuminated by Walter Isaacson and Evan Thomas, *The Wise Men: Six Friends and the World They Made* (Simon & Schuster, 1986). Fragmentation of the foreign policy establishment into professional elites and rival think tanks is traced in I. M. Destler, Leslie H. Gelb, and Anthony Lake, *Our Own Worst Enemy: The Unmaking of American Foreign Policy* (Simon & Schuster, 1984). For a history of nuclear arms control efforts in the context of the Cold War, see John Newhouse, *War and Peace in the Nuclear Age* (Knopf, 1988; Vintage, 1990), the companion book to the PBS television series.

Hawks: For a left critique of hawkish influence on foreign policy since World War II, see Thomas Bodenheimer and Robert Gould, *Rollback! Right-Wing Power in U.S. Foreign Policy* (South End Press, 1989). Position papers of the Committee on the Present Danger are collected in *Alerting America*, edited by Charles Tyroler II (Pergamon-Brassey's, 1984). The unsavory collection of racists, Fascists, and death squad leaders assembled in the World Anti-Communist League (recently renamed the World League for Freedom and Democracy) is described in Scott Anderson and Jon Lee Anderson, *Inside the League* (Dodd, Mead & Co., 1986); its American affiliate is the U.S. Council for World Freedom, headed by Gen. John Singlaub, U.S. Army (Ret.), who tells his side of the story in *Hazardous Duty: An American Soldier in the Twentieth Century* (Summit Books, 1991).

Doves: On Quakers as pioneers of social change, see Margaret Hope Bacon, *The Quiet Rebels: The Story of the Quakers in America* (New Society Press, 1985). For the debate over the four pacifist organizations founded in the Progressive era, see Guenter Lewy, *Peace and Revolution: The Moral Crisis of American Pacifism* (Eerdmans Publishing, 1988), and *Peace Be-*

trayed? Essays on Pacifism and Politics, edited by Michael Cromartie (Ethics and Public Policy Center, 1990).

Armaments and organizations: A concise and inexpensive guide to military data is Ruth Leger Sivard's annual *World Military and Social Expenditures* (fondly known as WMSE, pronounced "whimsy"), available from World Priorities, Box 25140, Washington, DC 20007. The Stockholm International Peace Research Institute compiles a comprehensive reference in its annual *SIPRI Yearbook: World Armaments and Disarmament* (Oxford University Press). If you like maps, you'll appreciate the graphic approach in *The War Atlas: Armed Conflict—Armed Peace*, by Michael Kidron and Dan Smith (Simon & Schuster, 1983), from the Pluto Project. For a useful brief guide to organizations and resources, see *Working for Peace: An Annotated Resource Guide* (1989), published by The Fund for Peace, 345 East 46th Street, New York, NY 10017. For a comprehensive listing of organizations and educational materials, see the Institute for Defense and Disarmament Studies' reference, *Peace Resource Book: A Comprehensive Guide to Issues, Groups, and Literature, 1988/89*, edited by Carl Connetta (Ballinger, 1988), which updates earlier directories compiled in 1984 and 1986.

Information and alternatives: ACCESS: A Security Information Service (1511 K Street, NW, Suite 643, Washington, DC 20005; (202) 783-6050) compiles a comprehensive guide to information and organizations, *The ACCESS Resource Guide: An International Directory of Information on War, Peace and Security*, edited by William H. Kincade and Priscilla B. Hayner (Ballinger, 1988), and *Search for Security: A Guide to Grantmaking in International Security and the Prevention of Nuclear War* (ACCESS, 1989). ACCESS also maintains an extensive computerized data base, and provides inquiry and speaker referral services.

The Center for Defense Information (1500 Massachusetts Avenue, NW, Washington, DC 20005; (202) 862-0700) publishes *The Defense Monitor*, which presents a detailed analysis of a single defense issue or system in each issue.

The Arms Control Association, 11 Dupont Circle, NW, Washington, DC 20036; (202) 797-6450, publishes the monthly journal *Arms Control Today* (circulation 3,700); *Arms Control and National Security: An Introduction* (1989), the best single source on arms control negotiations and agreements from 1945 through 1989; and Matthew Bunn, *Foundation for the Future: The ABM Treaty and National Security* (1990), a critique of SDI in all its latest variations.

3. RIGHTS AND LIBERTIES

Civil liberties: For the historical development of rights, see James MacGregor Burns and Stewart Burns, *A People's Charter: The Pursuit of Rights in America* (Knopf, 1991). David Kairys provides historical perspective in "Freedom of Speech," chapter 7 in the *Politics of Law: A Progressive Critique* (Pantheon, 1982), edited by Kairys. For the 100th anniversary of Roger Baldwin's birth the ACLU commissioned a collection on current civil liberties issues in *Our Endangered Rights: The ACLU Report on Civil Liberties Today*, edited by Norman Dorsen (Pantheon, 1984); on the bicentennial of the Bill of Rights, ACLU director Ira Glasser wrote *Visions of Liberty: The Bill of Rights for All Americans* (Arcade, 1991). Recent cases are reviewed by Ellen Alderman and Caroline Kennedy, *In Our Defense: The Bill of Rights in Action* (Morrow, 1991). The libertarian perspective is presented in *The Rights Retained by the People: The History and Meaning of the Ninth Amendment*, edited by Randy E. Barnett (George Mason University Press, 1990). For a directory of various human rights, civil liberties, and civil rights groups, see the *Human Rights Organizations and Periodicals Directory*, edited by David Christiano and Lisa Young, 6th ed. (1990), published by the Meiklejohn Civil Liberties Institute, P.O. Box 673, Berkeley, CA 94701.

Human rights: For an overview of international agreements on human rights, see Robert F. Drinan, S.J., *Cry of the Oppressed: The History and Hope of the Human Rights Revolution* (Harper & Row, 1987), and David P. Forsythe, *Human Rights and World Politics*, 2nd ed. (1983; University of Nebraska Press, 1989). For text and commentary, see *The Human Rights Reader*, edited by Walter Laqueur and Barry Rubin, rev. ed. (1979; Meridian Books, 1989), and *The Universal Declaration of Human Rights, 1948–1988: Human Rights, the United Nations and Amnesty International* (Amnesty International USA Legal Support Network, 1988). On indigenous peoples, see Julian Berger, *The Gaia Atlas of First Peoples* (Anchor Books, 1990). For country by country surveys, see the annual *Freedom in the World* from Freedom House (120 Wall Street, New York, NY 10005; (212) 514-8040); and the periodic *World Human Rights Guide*, compiled by Charles Humana, 3rd ed. (1983; Oxford University Press, 1992).

Labor: For a mainstream historical overview, see Thomas R. Brooks, *Toil and Trouble: A History of American Labor*, rev. ed. (1964; Dell, 1971). Melvyn Dubofsky and Warren Van Tine tell the story of the United Mine Workers' militant leader and CIO founder in *John L. Lewis: A Biography* (Quadrangle, 1977; abridged ed., University of Illinois Press, 1986). Labor lawyer Thomas Geoghegan brings his experience with the rank-and-file movements of the 1970s and 1980s to *Which Side Are You On? Trying to Be* *for Labor When It's Flat on Its Back* (Farrar, Straus & Giroux, 1991). For a concise review of workers' rights under collective bargaining, see the ACLU handbook, *The Rights of Union Members*, by Clyde W. Summers and Robert J. Rabin (Avon, 1979). The Labor-Management Reporting and Disclosure Act of 1959 is reviewed and evaluated in Doris McLaughlin and Anita L. W. Schoomaker, *The Landrum-Griffin Act and Union Democracy* (University of Michigan Press, 1979). An activist approach to revitalizing the labor movement is embodied in the journal *Labor Research Review*, published by the independent Midwest Center for Labor Research, 3411 W. Diversey, Suite 10, Chicago, IL 60647; (312) 278-5418.

Guns and rights: Lee Kennett and James Anderson present a balanced historical analysis in *The Gun in America: The Origins of an American Dilemma* (Greenwood Press, 1975). Background supporting gun control legislation was assembled in *Firearms and Violence in American Life* (1969), a staff report to the National Commission on the Causes and Prevention of Violence, prepared by George D. Newton and Franklin E. Zimring. For an analysis skeptical of gun control's usefulness in preventing violence, see James D. Wright, Peter H. Rossi, and Kathleen Daly, *Under the Gun: Weapons, Crime and Violence in America* (Aldine, 1983), and Gary Kleck, *Point Blank: Guns and Violence in America* (Aldine, 1990). The case for restricting access to firearms is updated in Zimring and Gordon Hawkins, *The Citizen's Guide to Gun Control* (Macmillan, 1987). For a collection of classic articles and arguments pro and con, see *The Gun Control Debate: You Decide*, edited by Lee Nisbet (Prometheus, 1990).

4. RACE AND ETHNICITY

Perspectives on race and ethnicity: Michael Omi and Howard Winant offer a new synthesis of racial and ethnic theories in *Racial Formation in the United States* (Routledge, 1986). For the ethnicity paradigm, see Nathan Glazer and Daniel P. Moynihan, *Ethnicity: Theory and Experience* (Harvard University Press, 1975), and the thematic essays in *Harvard Encyclopedia of American Ethnic Groups* (Harvard University Press, 1980). For the recent focus on class, see William Julius Wilson, *The Declining Significance of Race* (University of Chicago Press, 1978), and *The Truly Disadvantaged: The Inner City, the Underclass, and Public Policy* (University of Chicago Press, 1987), For an historical survey of racial and ethnic groups, see Leonard Dinnerstein, Roger L. Nichols, and David M. Reimers, *Natives and Strangers: Blacks, Indians, and Immigrants in America*, 2nd ed. (Oxford University Press, 1990).

African Americans: For an overview of the African American freedom movement, see Vincent Harding, *There Is a River: The Black Struggle for*

Freedom in America (Harcourt Brace Jovanovich, 1981). Eric Foner, *Reconstruction: America's Unfinished Revolution, 1863–1877* (Harper & Row, 1988), is the definitive study to date on this crucial period. The gradual introduction of segregation following the Compromise of 1877 is traced by C. Vann Woodward in *The Strange Career of Jim Crow* (Oxford University Press, 1955). On the often strained relations between blacks and movements for change, see Robert L. Allen, *Reluctant Reformers: Racism and Social Reform Movements in the United States* (Howard University Press, 1974; Anchor Books, 1975). For background on black separatism and nationalism, see Edmund David Cronon, *Black Moses: The Story of Marcus Garvey and the Universal Negro Improvement Association* (University of Wisconsin Press, 1955).

The central role of Martin Luther King, Jr., in the civil rights movement of the 1950s and 1960s is developed in David J. Garrow, *Bearing the Cross: Martin Luther King, Jr., and the Southern Christian Leadership Conference* (William Morrow, 1986; Vintage, 1988), and Taylor Branch, *Parting the Waters: America in the King Years, 1954–1963* (Simon & Schuster, 1988). The best sociological perspectives are found in Aldon D. Morris, *The Origins of the Civil Rights Movement: Black Communities Organizing for Change* (Free Press, 1984), and Doug McAdam, *Political Process and the Development of Black Insurgency* (University of Chicago Press, 1982). Robert Weisbrot recounts the period in *Freedom Bound: A History of America's Civil Rights Movement* (Norton, 1989). The history of CORE in its vital period is analyzed by August Meier and Elliott Rudwick in *CORE: A Study in the Civil Rights Movement, 1942–1968* (University of Illinois Press, 1973). An important assessment of the Student Nonviolent Organizing Committee is Clayborne Carson, *In Struggle: SNCC and the Black Awakening of the 1960s* (Harvard University Press, 1981). Hubert H. Haines, *Black Radicals and the Civil Rights Movement, 1954–1970* (University of Tennessee Press, 1988), assesses the "radical flank effects" on support for "moderate" movement organizations.

The Public Broadcasting System's award-winning television series *Eyes on the Prize* is a stunning visual documentary; the accompanying book is Juan Williams, *Eyes on the Prize: America's Civil Rights Years, 1954–1965* (Penguin Books, 1984). From his research for the series, producer Henry Hampton and Steve Fayer with Sarah Flynn compiled *Voices of Freedom: An Oral History of the Civil Rights Movement* (Bantam Books, 1990), in which the leaders of the movements and countermovements discuss their roles.

American Jews: For an impressive depiction of the history, culture, and politics of Eastern European Jewish immigrants in America, emphasizing their roles in the labor movement and the Left, see Irving Howe, *World of Our Fathers* (Simon & Schuster, 1976). Arthur Liebman, *Jews and the Left*

(John Wiley & Sons, 1979), details Jewish involvement with socialist, Communist, and New Left organizations from the 1880s to the 1970s. Arthur Hertzberg presents a general history in *The Jews in America: Four Centuries of an Uneasy Encounter: A History* (Simon & Schuster, 1989); see also Howard M. Sachar, *A History of the Jews in America* (Knopf, 1992). An optimistic assessment of Jewish integration into the American mainstream is presented by Charles E. Silberman, *A Certain People: American Jews and Their Lives Today* (Summit, 1985). Jonathan Kaufman traces the stress fractures afflicting an old partnership in *Broken Alliance: The Turbulent Times Between Blacks and Jews in America* (Scribner's, 1988); a subject also treated in *Bridges and Boundaries: African Americans and American Jews*, edited by Jack Salzman with Adina Black and Gretchen Sullivan Sorin (George Braziller, 1992). Polar contrasts in American Jewish political currents are apparent in two magazines of political analysis, *Commentary* (circulation 28,000), edited by neoconservative Norman Podhoretz, and *Tikkun* (circulation 40,000), edited by former New Left activist Michael Lerner.

American Indians: For a concise review of Indian law's complex development, see Charles F. Wilkinson, *American Indians, Time, and the Law* (Yale University Press, 1987). Attorneys and professors Vine Deloria, Jr., and Clifford Lytle trace the development of Indian law in *American Indians, American Justice* (University of Texas Press, 1983), and tell the story of John Collier's New Deal reform effort in *The Nations Within: The Past and Future of American Indian Sovereignty* (Pantheon, 1984). On the destruction of the American Indian Movement (AIM) by the FBI, see the reissued edition of Peter Matthiessen's suppressed book *In the Spirit of Crazy Horse* (1983; Viking, 1991).

Hispanic Americans: A classic worth reading is Carey McWilliams, *North from Mexico: The Spanish-Speaking People of the United States* (1948; Greenwood Press, 1968). For a general survey, see Joan Moore and Harry Pachon, *Hispanics in the United States* (Prentice-Hall, 1985), or from the perspective of two Hoover Institution senior fellows, L. H. Gann and Peter J. Duignan, *The Hispanics in the United States: A History* (Westview Press, 1986). The development of Mexican American political organizations is traced by Mario T. Garcia, *Mexican Americans: Leadership, Ideology, and Identity, 1930–1960* (Yale University Press, 1989). The next generation of activists is covered in Carlos Munoz, Jr., *Youth, Identity, Power: The Chicano Movement* (Verso, 1989); Juan Gomez-Quinones, *Chicano Politics: Reality and Promise, 1940–1990* (University of New Mexico Press, 1990); and Part I of Mario Barrera, *Beyond Aztlan: Ethnic Autonomy in Comparative Perspective* (Praeger, 1988). For a neoconservative view, see Linda Chavez, *Out of the Barrio: Toward a New Politics of Hispanic Assimilation* (Basic Books, 1991). Following the example of the National Urban League,

The State of Hispanic America was begun as an annual publication by the National Council of La Raza, 810 First Street, NE, Suite 300, Washington, DC 20002.

Asian Americans: For a comprehensive survey see Ronald Takaki, *Strangers from a Different Shore: A History of Asian Americans* (Little, Brown, 1989). Ronald Daniels has written an excellent study with a narrower focus, *Asian America: Chinese and Japanese in the United States Since 1850* (University of Washington Press, 1989). For a history of the Japanese American Citizens League, see Bill Hosokawa, *JACL in Quest of Justice* (Morrow, 1982).

5. GENDER AND SEXUALITY

Woman suffrage and feminism: For perspective on the changing meanings of gender and sexuality, see John D'Emilio and Estelle B. Freedman, *Intimate Matters: A History of Sexuality in America* (Harper & Row, 1988). Eleanor Flexner, *Century of Struggle* (1959; Belknap, 1975) traces the movement for woman suffrage from the Seneca Falls meeting in 1848 through enactment of the Nineteenth Amendment in 1920. The disproportionate role of Quaker women is highlighted by Margaret Hope Bacon, *Mothers of Feminism: The Story of Quaker Women in America* (Harper & Row, 1986). For the 1910s and 1920s, see Nancy Cott, *The Grounding of Modern Feminism* (Yale University Press, 1987). The "second generation" of women Progressives who worked in the Franklin Roosevelt administration is described in Susan Ware, *Beyond Suffrage: Women in the New Deal* (Harvard University Press, 1981).

The new women's movement: For an account of the surprising progress made in that obscure period following World War II when women's issues seemed invisible, see Cynthia Harrison, *On Account of Sex: The Politics of Women's Issues, 1945–1968* (University of California Press, 1988), which emphasizes women appointees and activists in the Democratic and Republican parties and The President's Commission on the Status of Women; and Leila J. Rupp and Verta Taylor, *Survival in the Doldrums: The American Women's Rights Movement, 1945 to the 1960s* (Oxford University Press, 1987), which pays more attention to the National Women's Party of Alice Paul. On the emergence of the women's liberation movement, see Jo Freeman, *The Politics of Women's Liberation* (David McKay, 1975); Sara Evans, *Personal Politics: The Roots of Women's Liberation in the Civil Rights Movement and the New Left* (Knopf, 1979); Bernice Cummings and Victoria Schuck, *Women Organizing: An Anthology* (Scarecrow, 1979); Myra Marx

Ferree and Beth B. Hess, *Controversy and Coalition: The New Feminist Movement* (Twayne, 1985), Marcia Cohen, *The Sisterhood* (Fawcett Columbine, 1988); Alice Echols, *Daring to Be Bad: Radical Feminism in America, 1967–1975* (University of Minnesota Press, 1989); and Flora Davis, *Moving the Mountain: The Women's Movement Since 1960* (Simon & Schuster, 1991). Two books analyze the ERA battle: Jane Mansbridge, *Why We Lost the ERA* (University of Chicago Press, 1988), and Mary Frances Berry, *Why ERA Failed: Women's Rights and the Amending Process of the Constitution* (Indiana University Press, 1988). On the conservative reaction to the women's movement, see Susan Faludi, *Backlash: The Undeclared War on American Women* (Crown, 1991), particularly the interviews in parts 3 and 4. The revived no-advertising *Ms.* magazine (circulation 165,000) offers current coverage of the feminist movement.

Information: For a global perspective on women, see Joni Seager and Ann Olson, *Women in the World: An International Atlas* (Simon & Schuster, 1986), from the Pluto Project. Another concise data summary is Ruth Leger Sivard, *Women . . . A World Survey* (1985), available from World Priorities, Box 25140, Washington, DC 20007.

Reproductive rights: For historical background from a participant, see Lawrence Lader, *Abortion II: Making the Revolution* (Beacon Press, 1973). Suzanne Staggenborg applies social movement theory in *The Pro-Choice Movement: Organization and Activism in the Abortion Conflict* (Oxford University Press, 1991). Women's attraction to pro-life or pro-choice positions is explored by sociologist Kristin Luker, *Abortion and the Politics of Motherhood* (University of California Press, 1984). The legal history of abortion is analyzed by Laurence H. Tribe, *Abortion: The Clash of Absolutes* (Norton, 1990). Connections and conflicts between the political Right and right-to-life organizations are traced in Michele McKeegan's *Abortion Politics: Mutiny in the Ranks of the Right* (Free Press, 1992).

Gay and lesbian rights: The gay rights movement up to the Stonewall riot in 1969 is covered in John D'Emilio, *Sexual Politics, Sexual Communities: The Making of a Homosexual Minority in the United States, 1940–1970* (University of Chicago Press, 1983). Barry D Adam, *The Rise of a Gay and Lesbian Movement* (Twayne, 1987), brings an international perspective to a social history through 1985. See also the interviews in Eric Marcus's *Making History: The Struggle for Gay and Lesbian Equal Rights, 1945–1990: An Oral History* (HarperCollins, 1992). For a biography of the Mattachine Society's founder, see Stuart Timmons, *The Trouble with Harry Hay: Founder of the Modern Gay Movement* (Alyson Publications, 1990). San Francisco journalist Randy Shilts has written two books essential to understanding the contemporary gay movement: *The Mayor of Castro Street: The Life and*

Times of Harvey Milk (St. Martin's Press, 1982), about the nation's first openly gay elected city official; and *And the Band Played On: Politics, People, and the AIDS Epidemic* (St. Martin's Press, 1987; Penguin, 1988). Larry Kramer describes the founding of ACT-UP in *Reports from the Holocaust: The Making of an AIDS Activist* (St. Martin's Press, 1989). The movement has a quarterly theoretical journal with a left-postmodern slant from San Francisco, *Out/Look;* a monthly magazine from Los Angeles, *The Advocate;* and a weekly newspaper from Boston that offers national news coverage, *Gay Community News.*

6. AGE AND ABILITY

Elders: For a look at advocacy organizations, see Henry J. Pratt, *The Gray Lobby: Politics of Old Age* (University of Chicago Press, 1976). William W. Lammers, *Public Policy and the Aging* (Congressional Quarterly Press, 1983) reviews the development of laws and programs. Ken Dychtwald and Joe Flower predict consequences of demographic trends in *Age Wave* (Bantam Books, 1990).

Children: For background, see Joseph Hawes, *The Children's Rights Movement: A History of Advocacy and Protection* (Twayne, 1991). The Children's Defense Fund publishes *S.O.S. America! A Children's Defense Budget* (1990) with data about children in the United States and policy proposals. UNICEF publishes an annual report, *The State of the World's Children,* with data on nutrition, health, education, and other conditions relating to children—available from UNICEF Publications, Room 939, 3 United Nations Plaza, New York, NY 10017.

Disability rights: For a historical view, see Edward D. Berkowitz, *Disabled Policy: America's Programs for the Handicapped* (Cambridge University Press, 1987). Early activism is reviewed in Roberta Ann Johnson, "Mobilizing the Disabled," Chapter 5 in *Social Movements of the Sixties and Seventies,* edited by Jo Freeman (Longman, 1983). *The Disability Rag* is a lively and outspoken monthly newspaper for activists edited by Mary Johnson, available for a $12 subscription (Box 145, Louisville, Ky 40201).

7. FOOD, SHELTER, AND SUSTAINABLE DEVELOPMENT

Food and shelter: Bread for the World's *Hunger 1992: Second Annual Report on the State of World Hunger* (1991) is an excellent data source, to be revised annually. The neoconservative, optimistic, cornucopian view is collected in Dennis T. Avery, *Global Food Progress 1991* (Hudson Institute,

1991). An excellent analysis of development strategies is provided in Jean Dreze and Amartya Sen, *Hunger and Public Action* (Oxford University Press, 1991). The Hunger Project, *Ending Hunger: An Idea Whose Time Has Come* (Praeger, 1985) is an illustrated, coffee-table book featuring debates on the questions of population, food, foreign aid, military spending, and creation of a New International Economic Order. For discussion of food, hunger, and development issues, see *Why? Magazine*, available for an $18 subscription from World Hunger Year, 505 Eighth Avenue, 21st floor, New York, NY 10018–6582, a project initiated by the late folk singer Harry Chapin. *Seeds* magazine, a faith-based forum on domestic and world hunger issues available for a $20 subscription, has been revived at P.O. Box 6170, Waco, TX 76706-0170; they also distribute an excellent *Hunger Action Handbook* (1987) with helpful ideas for local work. For another compact action handbook, see *What You Can Do to Help the Homeless*, by The National Alliance to End Homelessness (Fireside, 1991).

Sustainable development: For a comprehensive data source, see the annual *World Development Report* from World Bank Publications, P.O. Box 7247-8619, Philadelphia, PA 19170-8619; (201) 225-2165. For international service and tourism from a left perspective, see Medea Benjamin and Andrea Freedman, *Bridging the Global Gap: A Handbook to Linking Citizens of the First and Third World* (Seven Locks Press, 1989), and Medea Benjamin, *The Peace Corps and More: 114 Ways to Work, Study and Travel in the Third World* (Global Exchange, 1991), available from Global Exchange, 2142 Mission Street, #202, San Francisco, CA 94110; (415) 255-7296. Thomas P. Fenton and Mary J. Heffron have compiled a valuable series of bibliographical resource guides on international development topics, with a liberal to left perspective, all published by the Maryknoll order's Orbis Press.

8. ANIMAL WELFARE TO ANIMAL RIGHTS

Animal welfare and animal rights: Although not the first book written on animal rights, Henry Salt's *Animals' Rights Considered in Relation to Human Progress* (1892; represented by Society for Animal Rights, 1980) is a remarkable classic that bears reading today; his full range of concerns are sampled in *The Savor of Salt: A Henry Salt Anthology*, edited by George Hendrick and Willene Hendrick (Centaur Press, 1989). The relationship of Victorian times to the rise of the humane, antivivisection and conservation movements are considered in James Turner, *Reckoning with the Beast: Animals, Pain, and Humanity in the Victorian Mind* (Johns Hopkins University Press, 1980). Serious consideration of animals' moral claims on humans was introduced by Australian philosopher Peter Singer in his review essay, "Animal Liberation," in *The New York Review of Books*, 5 April

1973; the response to the article stimulated Singer to expand his arguments in *Animal Liberation* (Avon Books, 1975). See also Jim Mason and Peter Singer, *Animal Factories* (Crown Publishers, 1980), and *In Defense of Animals* (Basil Blackwell, 1985), edited by Singer. The prominent philosopher of animal rights, Tom Regan, states his position in *The Case for Animal Rights* (University of California Press, 1983) and *The Struggle for Animal Rights* (International Society for Animal Rights, 1987). British philosopher Mary Midgley bases her more pragmatic animal welfare position on compassion in *Animals and Why They Matter* (University of Georgia Press, 1984). For a particularly informative book on federal and state legislation, see *Animals and Their Legal Rights: A Survey of American Laws from 1641 to 1990* (4th ed., 1990), from the Animal Welfare Institute, P.O. Box 3650, Washington, DC 20007; (202) 337-2332. James M. Jasper and Dorothy Nelkin present a sociological perspective in *The Animal Rights Crusade: The Growth of a Moral Protest* (The Free Press, 1992). The best source of independent commentary and analysis on the animal rights movement is the monthly magazine *The Animals' Agenda* (circulation 25,000), P.O. Box 345, Monroe, CT 06468; (203) 452-0446.

9. PROGRESSIVES

The progressive mainstream: The Farmers Alliance and the People's Party represented an intense effort to create a democratic culture in Lawrence Goodwyn's interpretation, *Democratic Promise: The Populist Moment in America* (Oxford University Press, 1976), abridged as *The Populist Moment: A Short History of the Agrarian Revolt in America* (Oxford University Press, 1978). A classic on populism and progressivism is Richard Hofstadter, *The Age of Reform: From Bryan to F.D.R.* (Random House, 1955). Alan Dawley rethinks the progressive tradition in *Struggles for Justice: Social Responsibility and the Liberal State* (Harvard University Press, 1991). For a history of American liberalism after World War II, see Mary Sperling McAuliffe, *Crisis on the Left: Cold War Politics and American Liberals, 1947–1954* (University of Massachusetts Press, 1978), and Richard H. Pells, *The Liberal Mind in a Conservative Age: American Intellectuals in the 1940s & 1950s* (Harper & Row, 1985). For a brief history of the Communist party and its splinters from 1919 to 1990, see Harvey Klehr and John Earl Haynes's *The American Communist Movement: Storming Heaven Itself* (Twayne, 1992).

How conservatives tipped the balance of power away from liberals is the subject of Thomas Byrne Edsall, *The New Politics of Inequality* (Norton, 1984); his recent book with Mary Edsall, *Chain Reaction: The Impact of Race, Rights and Taxes on American Politics* (Norton, 1991), continues the analysis. Robert Kuttner, *The Life of the Party: Democratic Prospects in*

1988 and Beyond (Viking Penguin, 1987), also follows the fate of the Democrats during the Reagan administration. For an incisive analysis of liberalism and conservatism from the 1960s to the 1990s, see E. J. Dionne, Jr., *Why Americans Hate Politics* (Simon & Schuster, 1991), which concludes with a plea for a new political center. For current commentary, see *The New Republic* (circulation 100,000), which has editors and writers ranging in politics from liberal to neoconservative; the neoliberal *Washington Monthly* (38,000); and *The American Prospect* (12,000), which seeks to revive liberalism in the New Deal tradition.

The New Left: The connections between the Old Left and the New Left that emerged in the late 1950s and early 1960s are illuminated in Maurice Isserman, *If I Had a Hammer . . . The Death of the Old Left and the Birth of the New Left* (Basic Books, 1987). A contemporary history of the New Left's leading organization is Kirkpatrick Sale, *SDS* (Random House, 1973; Vintage, 1974). James Miller reviews SDS from the vantage point of the 1980s in *"Democracy Is in the Streets": From Port Huron to the Siege of Chicago* (Simon & Schuster, 1987); sociologist Todd Gitlin, a former SDS leader, presents a wider perspective in *The Sixties: Years of Hope, Days of Rage* (Bantam, 1987). For contrary viewpoints by former leftists turned neoconservative, see Peter Collier and David Horowitz, *Destructive Generation: Second Thoughts About the Sixties* (Summit Books, 1989) and their edited collection, *Second Thoughts: Former Radicals Look Back at the Sixties* (Madison Books, 1989). Also from a neoconservative standpoint, see Harvey Klehr, *Far Left of Center: The American Radical Left Today* (Transaction Books, 1988). For current commentary, see such magazines as *Mother Jones* (circulation 165,000), *The Nation* (100,000), *The Progressive* (30,000), *Z Magazine* (15,000), and *In These Times* (24,000); and such quarterly journals as *Social Policy* (3,000), *Dissent* (10,000), and *Socialist Review* (7,000). *Utne Reader* (200,000) has been described as a "countercultural *Reader's Digest*" and bridge between the New Left and New Age. Efforts to rethink Marxist Left activism are being led by *CrossRoads* magazine (2,000), P.O. Box 2809, Oakland, CA 94609.

Community organizing: The history of community organizing is traced in Robert Fisher, *Let the People Decide: Neighborhood Organizing in America* (Twayne, 1984). Harry C. Boyte gives examples of citizen activism in a series of books expounding community organization as progressive populism: *The Backyard Revolution: Understanding the New Citizen Movement* (Temple University Press, 1980), *Community Is Possible: Repairing America's Roots* (Harper & Row, 1984), and *CommonWealth: A Return to Citizen Politics* (The Free Press, 1989). On the importance of Chicago, see *After Alinsky: Community Organizing in Illinois*, edited by Peg Knoepfle (Illinois Issues, Sangamon State University, 1990). The history and distinctive community education approach of the Highlander Center in Tennessee, begun in 1932 as the Highlander Folk School, is related in Myles Horton with Judith Kohl and Herbert Kohl, *The Long Haul: An Autobiography* (Doubleday, 1990); see also Frank Adams with Myles Horton, *Unearthing Seeds of Fire: The Idea of Highlander* (John F. Blair, 1975). Interviews with community leaders associated with Highlander are collected in *Refuse to Stand Silently By: An Oral History of Grass-Roots Social Activism in America, 1921–1964*, edited by Eliot Wigginton (Doubleday, 1992). Two books provide helpful manuals on community organizing: Si Kahn, *Organizing: A Guide for Grassroots Leaders* (McGraw-Hill, 1982), builds on the author's experience as an organizer and trainer in the South; the Midwest Academy's handbook is Kim Bobo, Jackie Kendall, and Steve Max, *Organizing for Social Change: A Manual for Activists in the 1990s* (Seven Locks Press, 1991).

Progressive public foundations: For a survey of progressive funders, see Alan Rabinowitz, *Social Change Philanthropy in America* (Quorum Books, 1990), and Teresa Odendahl, *Charity Begins at Home: Generosity and Self-Interest Among the Philanthropic Elite* (Basic Books, 1990), chapter 8. For the stories of philanthropists for the environment, peace, and social justice see *We Gave Away a Fortune* by Christopher Mogil and Ann Slepian with Peter Woodrow (New Society Publishers, 1992).

Directories: Three directories provide politically shaded overviews of personalities and organizations on the left. For a mildly celebratory, New Left Marxist viewpoint, see *The Encyclopedia of the American Left*, edited by Mari Jo Buhle, Paul Buhle, and Dan Georgakas (Garland Publishing, 1990). For a neoconservative slant, see *Biographical Dictionary of the American Left*, edited by Bernard K. Johnpoll and Harvey Klehr (Greenwood Press, 1986). From the radical right John Birch Society, a Communist conspiracy lurks behind every individual and organization profiled in *A Biographical Dictionary of the Left*, edited by Francis X. Gannon, 4 vols. (Western Islands, 1969–1973). For a directory and bibliography with minimal annotations, revised annually, see *Guide to the American Left*, available from Laird Wilcox, P.O. Box 2047, Olathe, KS 66061.

10. CONSERVATIVES

Conservatism and the Old Right: The best general introduction to conservatism as an ideology is Robert Nisbet, *Conservatism: Dream and Reality* (University of Minnesota Press, 1986). Russell Kirk, *The Conservative Mind: From Burke to Elliot*, 7th rev. ed. (1953; Henry Regnery, 1986), is an American classic. For an overview of the "respectable Right" see George H.

Nash, *The Conservative Intellectual Movement in America Since 1945* (Basic Books, 1976). The movement of the Right from fringe to mainstream has to be understood in relation to William F. Buckley and Barry Goldwater; see the interpretation of former *National Review* publisher William A. Rusher, *The Rise of the Right* (William Morrow, 1984). On Buckley, see John B. Judis, *William F. Buckley, Jr.: Patron Saint of the Conservatives* (Simon & Schuster, 1988). Buckley and Charles R. Kesler edited *Keeping the Tablets: Modern American Conservative Thought* (Harper and Row, 1989), updating Buckley's collection from 1970. Barry M. Goldwater (with Jack Casserly) discusses his career with typical candor in *Goldwater* (Doubleday, 1988). On the downfall of an American Conservative Union founder, see Robert Bauman's frank autobiography, *The Gentleman from Maryland: The Conscience of a Gay Conservative* (Arbor House, 1986). Buckley's *National Review* (circulation 150,000) remains the flagship monthly of traditional conservatives; *Human Events* (24,000) is a weekly newspaper edited by Thomas Winter.

The New Right: The demographic and sociological underpinnings of the new conservatism are analyzed by Kevin P. Phillips, *The Emerging Republican Majority* (Arlington House, 1969; Doubleday Anchor, 1970). The New Right from the Goldwater campaign of 1964 to the Reagan presidency is covered in such works as Richard A. Viguerie, *The New Right: We're Ready to Lead* (The Viguerie Company, 1980); Alan Crawford, *Thunder on the Right: The "New Right" and the Politics of Resentment* (Pantheon, 1980); *The New Right Papers*, edited by Robert W. Whitaker (St. Martin's Press, 1982); and John S. Saloma III, *Ominous Politics: The New Conservative Labyrinth* (Hill and Wang, 1984). The institutions of conservatism in the Reagan era are described in Sidney Blumenthal, *The Rise of the Counter-Establishment: From Conservative Ideology to Political Power* (Times Books, 1986). For an overview of contemporary currents and conflicts on the right, see Paul Gottfried and Thomas Fleming, *The Conservative Movement* (Twayne, 1988). *The American Spectator* (32,000), edited by R. Emmett Tyrrell, Jr., has the vitriolic edge of the New Right, but includes libertarians to neocons.

Paleoconservatives: The Rockford Institute publishes *Chronicles: A Magazine of Culture* (circulation, 12,000), edited by Thomas Fleming. Pat Buchanan's autobiography is *Right from the Beginning* (Little, Brown, 1988).

Neoconservatives: The classic critical discussion of the key ideas and personalities is Peter Steinfels, *The Neoconservatives: The Men Who Are Changing America's Politics* (Simon & Schuster, 1979). For the views of the original neocon, see Irving Kristol, *Two Cheers for Capitalism* (Basic Books,

1978), and *Reflections of a Neoconservative: Looking Back, Looking Ahead* (Basic Books, 1983). Neoconservative journals include *Commentary, The Public Interest,* and *The National Interest.*

Libertarians: The best overall introduction is Murray N. Rothbard's classic, *For a New Liberty: The Libertarian Manifesto,* rev. ed. (1973; Libertarian Review Foundation, 1978). Notwithstanding her intense emotional involvement, Barbara Branden succeeds in presenting a balanced view of Ayn Rand and her circle in *The Passion of Ayn Rand: A Biography* (Doubleday, 1986). Nobel Prize–winning economist Milton Friedman outlines libertarian economics in his classic *Capitalism and Freedom* (University of Chicago Press, 1962), and a libertarian social philosophy with Rose Friedman in *Free to Choose: A Personal Statement* (Harcourt Brace Jovanovich, 1980), based on their PBS TV lecture series. Political scientists William S. Maddox and Stuart A. Lilie redraw the political map to include space for libertarianism in *Beyond Liberal and Conservative: Reassessing the Political Spectrum* (Cato Institute, 1984). A Cato symposium connects Maddox and Lilie's analysis with the demographics of the younger generations in *Left, Right and Babyboom: America's New Politics* (Cato Institute, 1986).

The Religious Right: See Sara Diamond, *Spiritual Warfare: The Politics of the Christian Right* (South End Press, 1989), and an academic perspective by a British observer, Steve Bruce, *The Rise and Fall of the New Christian Right: Conservative Protestant Politics in America, 1978–1988* (Oxford University Press, 1989). Favorably inclined neoconservative viewpoints are presented in *Piety and Politics: Evangelicals and Fundamentalists Confront the World,* edited by Richard John Neuhaus and Michael Cromartie (Ethics and Public Policy Center, 1987). Neuhaus edits the magazine *First Things.*

The Radical Right: Nativism and its relation to the Right is traced in David H. Bennett, *The Party of Fear: From Nativist Movements to the New Right in American History* (University of North Carolina Press, 1988). The Far Right of the 1950s and its ancestors are considered in *The Radical Right,* edited by Daniel Bell (Doubleday, 1963); and Arnold Forster and Benjamin R. Epstein, *Danger on the Right* (Random House, 1964). For a recent update of the Birch Society's worldview, see William P. Hoar, *Architects of Conspiracy: An Intriguing History* (Western Islands, 1984). On the Liberty Lobby, see Frank P. Mintz, *The Liberty Lobby and the American Right: Race, Conspiracy and Culture* (Greenwood Press, 1985). Of the numerous books on the Klans, the best historical survey, extending from 1865 to 1987, is Wyn Craig Wade, *The Fiery Cross: The Ku Klux Klan in America* (Simon & Schuster, 1987). The new racist Right is described in John Coates, *Armed and Dangerous: The Rise of the Survivalist Right* (Hill and

Wang, 1987); Kevin Flynn and Gary Gerhardt, *The Silent Brotherhood: Inside America's Racist Underground* (Free Press, 1989); and James Ridgeway, *Blood in the Face: The KKK, Aryan Nations, Nazi Skinheads, and the Rise of a New White Culture* (Thunder's Mouth Press, 1990).

Guides and directories: For a brief guide to conservative organizations, with sections on campaigning and lobbying, see *The Intelligent Conservative's Reference Manual*, revised every four years or so, published by Human Events, 422 First Street, SE, Washington, DC 20003. Louis Filler's *Dictionary of American Conservatism* (Philosophical Library, 1986; Citadel Press, 1987) is a detailed if idiosyncratic reference. Gregory Wolfe, *Right Minds: A Sourcebook of American Conservative Thought* (Regnery Books, 1987), provides a bibliography, biographical sketches, and a listing of journals, publishers, and think tanks. For a directory and bibliography with minimal annotations, revised annually, see *Guide to the American Right*, available from Laird Wilcox, P.O. Box 2047, Olathe, KS 66061.

INDEX

The page numbers for organizational profiles are identified in boldface.

homosexuality, *see* gay and lesbian
rights
Hooks, Benjamin, 212–13
Horse Protection Act (1970), 303, 306
Horton, Myles, 19–20, 342
Hostetter, Doug, 122
Houser, George, 120, 121
Housing Act (1968), 212
Housing All Americans, 328
housing and homelessness, 288, 289,
291, 293, 321, 345, 347, 348, 349,
350
see also food, shelter, and
sustainable development
Howe, Julia Ward, 152
Hoyt, John, 306, 307
HRCF NET, 267
Huberty, Robert, 376
Hughan, Jessie Wallace, 130
Humane Methods of Slaughter Act
(1958), 302, 306
Humane Societies, 301
Humane Society International, 307
The Humane Society of the United
States (HSUS), 302, 303, **305–8**
human rights, 22, 113, 128, 159–96,
340
and age and ability, 269–85
animal rights and, 301–13
of children, 278–81
of the disabled, 281–85
of elders, 269–77
food, shelter, and sustainable
development, 287–300
international perspective on, 173–81
of workers, 181–88
see also civil rights and liberties;
gender and sexuality; race and
ethnicity
Human Rights Campaign Fund
(HRCF), 264, **266–67**
PAC, 266, 267
human rights organizations, 157–313
computer networks of, 32
Human Rights Watch (HRW), 168,
174–75, **178–80**
Humber, Robert Lee, 135
hunger, *see* food, shelter, and
sustainable development
The Hunger Project, 291, 299

Independent Sector, 328
Indian Removal Act (1830), 205

Indian Reorganization (Wheeler-
Howard) Act (IRA) (1934), 206
Indians, American, 127, 205–6, 321,
337, 358
Industrial Areas Foundation (IAF),
341, **342–45,** 351–52
Industrial Workers of the World, 181
Institute for Democratic Socialism,
332, 336
Institute for Food and Development
Policy, 291
Institute for Global Communications
(IGC), 32, 103–4, 184
Institute for Historical Review, 372
Institute for Policy Studies (IPS), 139
Institute for Social Justice, 345, 346
InterAction, 291
Interfaith Action for Economic Justice,
319, 339–40
Interfaith Center on Corporate
Responsibility (ICCR), 30
Interfaith Impact for Justice and
Peace, 288, 319, **339–40**
Interfaith Impact Foundation, 339
Intermediate-Range Nuclear Forces
(INF) Treaty (1987), 115, 140
International Covenant on Economic,
Social, and Cultural Rights, 287
International Fellowship of
Reconciliation (IFOR), 119, 120,
122
internationalism, 107–8, 112–13
International Labor Organization
(ILO), 182
International Lesbian and Gay
Association, 266
International Network of Engineers
and Scientists for Global
Responsibility (INESGR), 149
International Physicians for the
Prevention of Nuclear War
(IPPNW), 145, 146
International Planned Parenthood
Federation, 259
International Primate Protection
League, 303
International Rescue Committee,
371
International Shooter Development
Fund, 191
International Society for Animal
Rights, 303
Internet, 104

Mountain States Legal Foundation, 42, 90, 383
Moyer, Bill, 23
Muir, John, 38, 39, 40, 44, 45, 52
multiissue organizations, 315–90
  community, 340–54
multiissue organizations, conservative, 361–90
  legal, 382–86
  women and family, 386–90
multiissue organizations, progressive, 317–60
  national advocates, 321–40
  public foundations, 354–60
Muras, Belton, 303, 306
Muste, A. J., 120, 121, 131, 138
A. J. Muste Memorial Institute, 130, 133
Myers, Fred, 305, 306
Myers, Lonny, 254

Nader, Ralph, 15, 30, 80, 320, 330, 331, 382
Naess, Arne, 82
Nathanson, Bernard, 262
National Abortion Rights Action League (NARAL), 244, 245, **259–261**
  Foundation, 259, 261
  PAC, 259, 261
National Affordable Housing Act (1990), 350
National American Woman Suffrage Association (NAWSA), 26, 232, 233, 239
National Association for Humane and Environmental Education (NAHEE), 306, 307
National Association for Repeal of Abortion Laws (NARAL), 254, 256, 259
National Association for the Advancement of Colored People (NAACP), 26, 159, 167, 199, 200, 201, 202, 204, **209–15,** 216, 217, 223, 224–25, 354
  Legal Committee, 222–23
  Legal Defense and Educational Fund (LDF; "Inc. Fund"), 172, 210–11, 213, 214, **222–26,** 227, 229, 249, 250, 264, 279, 283, 304, 382
  Special Contributions Fund (SCF), 209, 214, 215

National Association of Arab Americans (NAAA), 208
National Association of Colored Women, 232
National Audubon Society, 13, 25, 39, **50–54,** 57, 63, 83, 97
National Civil Liberties Bureau (NCLB), 120, 163
National Coalition to Ban Handguns (NCBH), 195
National Committee for an Effective Congress (NCEC), 318, **326–27**
National Committee for a Sane Nuclear Policy (SANE), 133–34, 135, 137–39, 140
  see also SANE/FREEZE
National Committee to Preserve Social Security and Medicare, 271
National Community Funds (NCF), 355
National Congressional Club, 370
National Conservative Political Action Committee (NCPAC), 364, 370, 373
National Council of Churches, 265
National Council of La Raza (NCLR), 207
National Council of Senior Citizens (NCSC), 270, **274–76**
  Education and Research Center, 274
  Housing Management Corporation, 274, 275
  PAC, 274, 276
National Council on Independent Living (CIL), 283
National Council to Control Handguns (NCCH), 195
National Education Association, 390
National Endowment for Democracy, 371
National Endowment for the Arts, 267, 388
National Environmental Policy Act (1970), 41, 68
National Firearms Act (1934), 190, 192
National Firearms Museum Fund, 191
National Forest Management Act (1976), 58
National Gay and Lesbian Task Force (NGLTF), 264, **265–66**
  Policy Institute, 265
National Gay Rights Advocates (NGRA), 264
National Gay Task Force, 264, 265
National Humane Society, 305–6

NordNet/PeaceNet, 32
Norris-La Guardia (Anti-Injunction)
    Act (1932), 183
North Star Fund, 354, 357
Northwest Community Organization,
    343, 349
NOW Equity PAC, 251
NOW Legal Defense and Education
    Fund (NOW LDEF), 222, **249–
    250,** 382
NOW PAC, 251
Nuclear Non-Proliferation Treaty
    (1968), 114
nuclear weapons, *see* disarmament;
    peace and foreign policy
Nuclear Weapons Freeze Campaign,
    128, 359–60

Obledo, Mario, 227
Oceanic Society (OS), 70, 71, 72
O'Connor, John, 88, 89
Oglesby, Carl, 138
Older Americans Act (1965), 271
Old Left, 319, 332–33, 334
Olmsted, Mildred Scott, 124
Operation Rescue, 249, 255, 262
Organization for the Southwest
    Community, 343
Organize Training Center, 342
Osborn, Fairfield, 101
OUT: a Fund for Gay and Lesbian
    Liberation, 355
owls, 107, 108, 115–19
Oxfam America, **291–93**
Oxfam U.K. and Ireland, 292, 293
Oxford Committee for Famine Relief
    (Oxfam), 290–91

Pacheco, Alex, 310, 312
Pacifica Foundation, 131
Pacific Legal Foundation (PLF), 90,
    382, **383–84**
Pacific Peace Fund (PPF), 360
pacifism, 119–33, 318
paleoconservatives, 111, 365, 366, 367,
    371–72
Park, Maude Wood, 239
Parks, Rosa, 20, 200, 211, 212, 258
Paul, Alice, 233, 234
Pax World Fund, 30–31
peace and foreign policy, 107–8, 239–40,
    321, 324, 325, 358, 359, 360, 381
    establishment, 115–19

major arms control agreements, 114–
    115
organizations, 32, 105–56
see also peace movement
Peace Development Fund (PDF), 354,
    359–60
Peace Links, 145, 155
peace movement, 14, 22, 23, 30, 109–
    110, 263, 319, 354
    doves and, 107, 108, 119–33, 133–43
    and end of Cold War, 111–13
    hawks and, 107, 108, 110–11
    nuclear disarmament, 143–56
    owls and, 107, 108, 115–19
PeaceNet, 32, **103–4,** 126, 133, 141,
    143, 147, 156, 178, 184, 322
PeacePAC, **141–43**
Pearson, T. Gilbert, 51–52
Peck, Jim, 131
Pemberton, John, Jr., 167, 168
People for the American Way (PFAW),
    162, **171–73,** 389
    Action Fund, 171, 172
People for the Ethical Treatment of
    Animals (PETA), 304, 305, **310–
    312**
The People's Fund, 357
People's Resource of Southwest Ohio,
    357
Pesticides Act (1972), 68
Peterson, Russell W., 52–53
Pethick-Lawrence, Emmeline, 123
philanthropy, 25–26, 354–60
Phillips, Howard, 364, 370
Physicians for Social Responsibility
    (PSR), 104, 134, 144, **145–47,**
    152, 154, 155
Pickett, Clarence, 127, 137
Pillsbury, George, 151, 355
Pillsbury, Sally, 355
Pinchot, Gifford, 38, 40, 45
Pittman-Robertson Wildlife
    Restoration Act (1937), 62–63, 64
Planned Parenthood Federation of
    America, Inc. (PPFA), 15, 164,
    254, 255, **256–59,** 390
    Action Fund (PPAF), 256, 258
political action committees (PACs), 27,
    329
    see also specific organizations
Political Association of Spanish
    Speaking Organizations (PASSO),
    207

Strategic Arms Reduction Treaty (START) (1991), 115
Student Environmental Action Coalition (SEAC), 69, **89–90**
Student Nonviolent Coordinating Committee (SNCC), 201, 202, 211, 212, 236, 319
Student Peace Union, 134
Students for a Democratic Society (SDS), 138, 236, 319, 334, 351, 368
Sullivan Act (1911), 190, 192
Sutherland, Frederic, 95, 96
Superfund, 80, 88
Surface Mining Control and Reclamation Act (1977), 69
Swomley, John, 121
Szilard, Leo, 134, 142

Taft-Hartley (Labor Management Relations) Act (1947), 182, 183, 186, 187, 323
taxes, 325, 348
nonprofit organizations and, 26–28
Tax Reform Act (1969), 26
Tax Reform Act (1976), 64
Tax Reform Act (1986), 331
Tax Reform Research Group, Public Citizen, 331
A Territory Resource (ATR), 354, **358–59**
Terry, Randall, 255
third parties, 320–21
advocacy organizations vs., 28–29
Thomas, Norman, 121, 137, 163, 165, 166, 184, 323
Thoreau, Henry David, 37–38
Threshold Test Ban Treaty (1974), 114
Tijerina, Pete, 226–27
Tischler, Joyce, 304, 312, 313
Alice B. Toklas Memorial Democratic Club, 264
Townsend, Francis, 270
Toxic Substances Control Act (1976), 41
toxic waste, 351, 353
traditional conservatives, 365, 366–367
TRAFFIC, 102, 103
Train, Russell, 101
Trapp, Shel, 349–50
Triangle Institute, 266
Trilateral Commission, 116
Turnage, William A., 60

20/20 Vision, 104
Education Fund, 155
National Project, **155–56**

UNICEF, 290, 298
Child Survival Fund, 299
Unification Church, 370
Union for Democratic Action (UDA), 323
Union of Concerned Scientists (UCS), 13, 143, 144, **147–49,** 154, 155
unions, 14, 25, 29, 120, 181–82, 184, 270, 323, 324
see also labor issues, labor movement
United Auto Workers (UAW), 182, 242, 275
United Cerebral Palsy Association, 283–84
United Farm Workers, 207
United Labor Unions (ULU), 346
United Mine Workers (UMW), 181, 182
United Nations, 118, 124, 133, 134, 135, 136, 173–74, 182, 239–40, 279, 290
United Nations Association of the United States of America (UNA-USA), 116, **117–19**
United Nations Educational, Scientific, and Cultural Organization (UNESCO), 118
United Negro Improvement Association, 199
United States Committee for the U.N., 118
United Steelworkers, 275
United World Federalists (UWF), 133, 135
Universal Child Immunization Act (1986), 298
Universal Declaration of Human Rights, 287
U.S. Agency for International Development (USAID), 290, 291, 300
U.S. Committee for World Freedom, 111
UseNet, 104, 178
U.S. Taxpayers party, 364, 370
Ustinov, Peter, 136
Utility Action Network, 74

Vanguard Public Foundation, 354, 355, 357

Van Name, Willard, 52
Viguerie, Richard A., 362, 369–70,
    378–79
VISA, 50, 54, 62, 66, 68, 72, 92, 101,
    103, 173
Vision/Habitat, 296
Vocational Rehabilitation Act (1963),
    1973 amendments to, 282–83
Voting Rights Act (1965), 169, 212
    extensions of, 227–28, 240

Wagner (National Labor Relations) Act
    (1935), 182, 183
Wallace, Henry, 322, 323
Ward, Harry, 163, 165
War Resisters International (WRI),
    130, 133
War Resisters League (WRL), 104,
    119, **130–33,** 201
Washington Interreligious Staff
    Council (WISC), 339
Washington Legal Foundation (WLF),
    383, **384–86**
Waterman, Nan, 328
Water Pollution acts, 68
Water Quality Act (1965), 41
Watson, Paul, 76, 308–9, 310
Watt, James, 42, 49, 71
Wattleton, Faye, 15, 255, 257
Weiss, Cora, 139, 140
Weisskopf, Victor, 149
Welch, Robert, 372
welfare, 321, 345
Wertheimer, Fred, 328
Weyrich, Paul, 16, 362, 363, 364, 365,
    369, 370, 375, 377–78, 379, 380
Wheeler-Howard (Indian
    Reorganization) Act (IRA) (1934),
    206
White, Walter, 210, 211, 212
WIDNet, 284
Wilcox, Albert, 51
Wild and Scenic Rivers Act (1968), 40,
    41
Wilderness Act (1964), 40, 41, 58, 59,
    61
The Wilderness Fund, 61
The Wilderness Society, 39, 46, 55, 57,
    58–62, 63, 67, 81, 97
wildlife and land preservation
    organizations, 97–103
Wildmon, Don, 364, 386
Wiley, George, 345, 346

Wilkins, Roy, 167, 212, 213, 217
Willey, Zach, 91–92
Willke, John, 262
Wilson, Ann, 151
Wilson, Cynthia, 71
Wilson, Dagmar, 134
Wilson, Edward O., 102
Wilson, Margaret Bush, 213
Winpisinger, William, 139, 352
Wisconsin Community Fund, 357
Wise, Stephen, 130
Wise Use Movement, 43
Wolfe, Sidney, 330, 331
Wolke, Howie, 81, 82, 85
Women's Action for New Directions
    (WAND), **151–53,** 155
    Education Fund, 152, 153
    PAC, 152, 153
Women's Action for Nuclear
    Disarmament (WAND), 126, 144,
    145, 152
Women's Campaign Fund (WCF), 251,
    252
Women's Christian Temperance Union
    (WCTU), 232
Women's Equity Action League
    (WEAL), 236, 242, 248
Women's International League for
    Peace and Freedom (WILPF),
    104, 119, **123–26,** 155, 210
women's issues, women's movement,
    14, 16, 22, 23, 25, 29, 123, 125,
    128, 143, 150, 169, 202, 263, 301,
    303, 319, 340, 358, 386, 389
    contemporary, 235–37
    early, 231–34
    ERA and, 237–38
    legal organizations in, 248–51
    national advocates, 238–48
    see also reproductive rights
Women's Legal Defense Fund
    (WLDF), 248, **250–51**
women's organizations, 292
    conservative, 386–90
    PACs, 251–53
Women's Party for Survival (WPS),
    144, 152
Women's Peace and Justice Treaty of
    the Americas, 125
Women's Peace Party (WPP), 123
Women's Peace Society, 130
Women's Peace Union, 130
Women Strike for Peace, 124, 134

ABOUT THE AUTHOR

David Walls *has been an activist and student of social
movements for three decades. He received an under-
graduate degree in economics in 1964 from the University of California at Berkeley, where he was a member
of SLATE, the campus political party that inaugurated
the student movement of the 1960s. After graduation, he
worked for the Community Action Program of the Office
of Economic Opportunity in Washington, D.C. In 1966
he moved to eastern Kentucky to work as field coordinator and later executive director with the Appalachian
Volunteers, a community organizing project in the central Appalachian coalfields. Over the years he has been
active with numerous environmental, peace, human
rights, and multiissue organizations.*

*He received M.A. and Ph.D. degrees in sociology
from the University of Kentucky, where he taught in the
school of social work and helped establish and administer the Appalachian Center from 1974 through 1981.
At Sonoma State University since 1982, he is dean of
extended education and general manager of the SSU
Academic Foundation. He is co-editor of* Appalachia in
the Sixties.